KINETIC PSYCHO-DYNAMICS

KINETIC PSYCHO-DYNAMICS

PRENTICE-HALL, INC.

Margery Wilson

How to Set the Amazing Powers of Your Mind Into Motion

ENGLEWOOD CLIFFS, N. J.

KINETIC PSYCHO-DYNAMICS
by *Margery Wilson*

Library of Congress Catalog Card Number: 63-12305

Printed in the United States of America
51630-T

Prentice-Hall International, Inc.
(*London, Tokyo, Sydney, Paris*)
Prentice-Hall of Canada, Ltd.
Prentice-Hall de Mexico, S. A.

Other books by Margery Wilson

Charm

Your Personality and God

Make Up Your Mind

The Woman You Want to Be

The New Etiquette

How to Live Beyond Your Means

Believe In Yourself

I Found My Way

Double Your Energy and Live Without Fatigue

CONTENTS

The Amazing Mind of Man

A comforting fact, in the general unrest, is that growth and new power always come from the challenges of confusion and change. As man, down through time, has adjusted to cataclysmic change, he has learned to survive, to develop greater use of his body (even to make that body into the highly efficient machine it has become). His animal cunning has extended itself into genuine intelligence, which has developed ever finer points of awareness.

MAN'S HISTORY IS ONE OF SURVIVAL

Animal forms that made a completely happy adjustment to their environment have not changed in millions of years. Others that could not, or did not, adapt themselves to change from the outside disappeared from the face of the earth. But man, driven by the memory of experience (both bad and good), and imagination (the ability to look ahead and foresee the result of present actions and formulae), has never been perfectly happy with his condition. Therefore he has grown, and is growing, into still higher patterns and urges.

He now knows that he has access to the splendid, spectacular powers within himself—and that if he learns how they work, he can use them to improve himself and his position.

He has spent much time in learning how powers outside himself can be harnessed and guided into doing his bidding. He is just now, incredulously, finding that he has reached a turning point where he can manage, with surprising results, those forces of intelligence within himself—an area over which he has great control, almost sovereignty.

He Can Plan and Manage His Future

This book will guide him in taking control of himself and his life—not in egoistic orgy, but with the full support of scientific findings, the moral backing of philosophy, psychology, and (when rightly understood) religion.

I have used the name "kinetic psycho-dynamics," for it well describes the processes, the very mechanics, of Mind in its movements toward selection, decision, and creativity. These are the most important areas of application for man. His poor use of them has brought him a tangle of woe. His occasional mastery in these three areas, as demonstrated by some highly developed individuals, has shown him the solution to many of his difficulties, and given him a glimpse of a future worth all that he must put into it.

All Is Movement

At this point, it is well to make clear that man's progress is still in movement—hence "kinetic"—and that there is no final word, nothing static, in our findings. We simply state that man need not accept a helter-skelter experience as inevitable any longer. Up to now, his advances have come to him the hard way—through long, tedious, repetitive, painful lessons largely in the physical and material aspects of living. The realm of the *senses* has been his schoolroom.

A Step Beyond the Senses

Now, he is emerging into the realm of Mind and beginning to learn that it is in this wise that he is "created in the image and likeness of God." He is a long way from a truly great grasp of his inheritance. He is still swept along the path of the ingrained, almost automatic, reflexes of his animal past.

Man's Long, Long Past

Whether man has slowly developed from a one-cell organism in the slime of the young world, however many billions of years ago, or whether he sprang, a fully realized human being upon this planet (like Minerva from the brow of Zeus), is not our concern in this book, although the two versions of man's beginning could, conceivably, not be in conflict. Their greatest difference is the matter of time alone—and time is, to an extraordinary degree, a matter of concept. In both cases, man is the product of an initiating parent thought, force, pattern—how you will.

A Basic Cause

For many different reasons, the consensus among informed minds is that, of necessity, there is a basic pattern, an incalculable reservoir of possibilities, a force drawing (or urging) man onward, the name of which is usually "God." Even a decade ago, it was not acceptable in most scientific circles to mention that word—but today, many of these men are shaking their heads with awe and are saying, "There must be—there has to be." They understand now what Voltaire meant when he said, "If there were no God, it would be necessary to invent him."

But whatever one's religious convictions, it is important to relate man's history to his present in order that he may project intelligently his future. For he is now the sum of all his past experiences (plus his unfolding potential).

It is helpful for him to understand both the strengths and the weaknesses that he has accumulated and has brought with him in his brain, his nerves, his complicated, conditioned reflexes of mind, soul, and body. He must know the material with which he is dealing, else he cannot fashion a suitable vessel to sail the uncharted seas ahead of him.

Man Is Ready for the Next Step Upward

Man is weary of feeling helpless and suspects that if he only knew how, he could command a new way of life for himself and his kind. And, as always, the universe answers satisfactorily any real demand on it.

He is weary of going round and round like a squirrel on a wheel in a cage, continuing an unsatisfactory repetitive experience no matter how fast he runs. "History repeats itself" is an old maxim, and true only because man keeps running around on the wheel of "sense," refusing to break that imprisoning cycle by taking off into the realm of the vaster part of himself, Mind.

His Sometimes Misinforming Senses

In taking stock of himself, man can readily see the marked inferiority of his organs of sense as compared with his capacity for thought-command. His ear, for instance, isn't nearly as good as a dog's. A dog can hear a vibration so high and fast that man is totally unaware of it. People amuse themselves by buying a dog-whistle that emits this high tone just to watch the dog respond to it, although a person cannot hear it! But man's mind has invented a little box called a radio that picks up sounds otherwise nonexistent to his ear and enlarges them, thus enabling him to hear the sounds. Wherever he extends his mental command, he brings the universe under his dominion in spite of his inferior senses.

Man has learned to correct the misinformation his senses give him—such as the appearance that the sun moves around the earth (when the fact is that the earth moves around the sun), the appearance that a round table across the room looks oval (everytime he looks at it, he must correct the visual impression), and so forth. These are an oversimplification of the truth of inaccurate sensory reports that now penetrate man's entire physical self—reports that must be found, exposed, corrected and superseded by the power of man's mind.

New Thought Patterns Are Needed for New Powers

Einstein has done humanity an incalculable favor in contradicting our smug "inaccuracies" with the great truth of his theory of relativity. He blazed the trail for modern acceptance of the idea that all is kinetic (in motion). Einstein was *not* an atheist. Although he was not a Christian, he believed in many of the truths mentioned by Christ, such as, "I have many things to tell you, but ye could not bear them now." Einstein knew that humanity is not quite ready for some of the disturbing truths that had come to his meditative, reaching mind. Nevertheless, he was working on them at the time of his death.

"Greater Things Shall Ye Do"

But we must earn our understanding and our slowly developing skills in using our latent powers of Mind. The many failures that stand between us and mastery remind us of the millions of experiments of the Curies before they found radium. We must be willing to try and try again, knowing that the truth of our possible mastery over ourselves and our environment surely lies ahead. Come, and let us explore our own use of Mind that it may bless and expand our lives, our health, and happiness.

Psycho-dynamics, the power of the movement of Mind, is your key to a new breakthrough of human awareness.

•1•

You Are the Master of Your Fate

DESTINY DOES NOT CONTROL YOU—YOU CONTROL your destiny. So-called destiny is but the sum of all the causes of actions and reactions in your entire experience. These, you can begin now to choose—to regulate to some degree.

Although you may be called "the highest vertebrate," you are a *human* being with privileges and powers that accompany your achievement. But, unless you avail yourself of your privileges of conscious choice, you will remain in the great, practically automatic mass of animal compulsions, patterns, and limitations. This book invites you to experiment with your human potential of sovereignty —*to take control* of yourself and your life—and to build it on more satisfying lines. Your power of choice—the greatest gift of human intelligence—is the force you will use, the power of mind to which you have access.

Suppose we draw back to a very simple illustration. In your city there are many new buildings. One year, two years ago, they did not exist. How did they come to be? Some man stood looking at the vacant lot or corner and, inside his mind, he *saw* the building that is now there. Keeping this full vision before him at all times, he drew plans or had them drawn on paper. These paper plans were not the building; they were but a step in the process of its becoming a material creation. A large hole was dug for the cellar and the foundation. It did not resemble a building, it was but a step toward it. Then, the steel, or superstructure, was erected. Still, it was not a building. It was just the outline of one. Then the addition of roof, walls, floors, elevators, doors, windows, bathrooms, water supply, electric outlets, and furnishings down to decorations and keys turned it into a functioning building for the benefit of its intended occupants. Each step in its realization was preceded by a mental pattern. There is no other way for anything to come into being! Thought must and does guide matter into any form.

Alfred Adler, the great Viennese psychiatrist, called plan or pattern "the goal." He spoke of it as the only possible explanation of energy's movement into material (as well as unmaterial) forms. Because of this underlying law of all creativity, Adler believed (not at first, but later in his life) that the need for a goal was the force called "God."

For our purposes, we need to see that man must choose his goal, select the people, the materials, the "way of going" that will bring his plan to full expression. *This law is the basis of the functioning of all the aspects of human life*—not just the way a building comes into being.

ARE YOUR CHOICES CONSCIOUS OR UNCONSCIOUS?

We choose, either by direct selection, or by accepting (permitting) all the elements of our life and being. Too many of our choices are subconscious, belonging to the mass mind of established experience. It is time for man to accept the challenge of his inner potential and use his mind to shape the form in which he and his life, his world, shall unfold.

This thought is not new, nor peculiar to our time. Many individuals, down through time, have known the way that man was fashioned. They have tried to draw our attention to the leadership of Mind—but we have been too preoccupied with our material fascinations to listen.

But now, as we are learning through science that the higher understanding of material possibilities brings us into inevitable contact with the supporting reaches of Mind, we are beginning to wonder if these seeming opposites may not, after all, be the two ends of the same stick. This reasoning does not, however, simplify our problem of living with matter and Mind at our present point of development. It does give us a kind of consolation to see that behind the seeming conflict of substance and spirit there can be a basic oneness, a pristine harmony.

For with a supporting *oneness,* a rightness—or, if you prefer, a realm of accuracy stemming from a *single* law or concept—we have then a reason to respect law and order throughout ourselves and our universe. If there is a unity beneath all the seeming confusion, we have a stimulus to strive toward order, to believe in its possibility and its rightness. If there is a supporting basic order, we then have a right to expect its rewards and blessings in all the ways we approach it.

BASIC LAWS

No one knows the whole truth. We can only reason together with such knowledge as we have gained. Certainly we know the painful side of acting as though we believed there were no basic moral accuracy or rightness, with its laws of healing, mercy, and growth. Ignoring or breaking these laws, we bring confusion and agony upon ourselves and our kind. Groping toward respect for them, we find proof enough of their power to prompt us to delve more stubbornly into them.

The uses of Mind have proved to us that we must learn the laws of its action and reaction. Power without knowledge brings destruction. Without understanding we are as vulnerable as an infant crawling on the floor, sticking its finger into a light-socket. As a matter of fact, figuratively, that is what humanity has been doing.

There are still people who think that all law, morality, and regulation are devised by man to enslave his fellow man! Particularly do they blame religion (all of it) for "superimposing upon a happy, natural animal (man) the artificial taboos and regulations of an unnatural morality." It would be difficult to imagine a more ignorant and irresponsible statement!

There are no laws more demanding than the laws of nature. Those of heat, fire, water, electricity, light, atomic energy, etc. must be obeyed or the most dire results follow. All natural forces have their laws—and Mind is no exception, being the master of them all. When it is misused, all manner of confusion follows. So, let us get a wholesome respect for the power of Mind and approach it with awe, even reverence, and endless gratitude that it is open to us. We must recognize it as the basis of the entire universe, the medium in which we live immersed as though we were fish in the sea.

Mind is the common denominator of all; the final arbiter as well as the creative impulse itself. It is the law, as well as the machinery of the law, in action.

You are the only animal that is able to use Mind with no defined limits. You may use as much of it and reach as far as your concept and your confidence will permit. There has been too much superstition in the past to permit the human mentality to grasp its advantage. Fear and doubt take over—and even the great religions of the world have been tainted by this fear of "offending the gods." Many have advocated almost a grovelling humility or the desirability (and the virtue) of losing personal identity altogether. They did not see that there is just as much ego expression in choosing self-abnegation (as an ideal) as there could possibly be in lifting the self as high as possible in and with divine power—Mind.

SEEK SELF-MANAGEMENT

However, let us leave these points to others, and let us apply ourselves to the challenge of applying all the self-management we can achieve. No one knows the end result, but we can have justifiable faith that if we do well with the factors that now lie open to us, we shall climb higher in awareness to a place where we can, no doubt, enjoy the fruits of our victory and see a wider horizon.

Universal Duty

It is your duty, as well as mine, to take a personal step upward in evolution; otherwise, what is the purpose of living? All of us can contribute our experiments and our findings to the whole effect of mankind's progress and enjoy the higher freedoms it brings.

Be Wholehearted About It!

Dedicate yourself completely to this experiment of using your mind to manage your life in better ways. A half-hearted attempt, fired by a little curiosity, will bring very slim results. But, if you are willing to take a notch in your belt and resolutely face the necessary disciplines while we test some modern scientific dicta, supported by the "enlightened ones" down through time, you will be starting on a fascinating and a rewarding journey of self-discovery.

Here, as in all the facets of yourself, it is your own decision that counts. Make up your mind to have done with doubt, confusion, and any phase of discouragement. It will take a dogged determination to hold to the single path of self-management. There will be some points you will reach where it will take all your strength of purpose to adhere to the plan. But I think you will!

As you progress, you will find that, like the builder of the building described earlier in this chapter, much that you do is preparatory (i.e., making the hole for the foundation, the paper plans themselves, the steel structure, etc.) and will not create even a semblance of the desired end.

But, your rewards will begin immediately and gradually extend.

The First Steps

Do Not Fear to Find and Use Your Power of Choice

The ancient, superstitious Greeks believed that whenever man tried to rival the prerogatives of the gods, in any way, he only angered them and that they avenged themselves. This gave them a fine excuse for not asserting themselves or making the effort to be free of their binding past. Thus, their glorious culture, which is the source of our own in great part, was enjoyed by comparatively few people, while the masses were held in thrall by ignorance and superstition. The less fearful, more assertive Romans outnumbered and overcame them in battle.

In the end, however, the good values of the Greeks' gentle minds influenced Roman thinking and living, thus lifting Roman culture to the heights it reached (there are two sides of every coin). We will later elaborate on this fact, as it can throw light on some of our own dilemmas. For the moment the point is—*have done with superstitious fear* of all kinds, and with intelligent humility seek to examine the gift of choice that life has given you.

Be Patient with Yourself

One must make an investment of time and effort (or something) before one collects a dividend. All too many of us, in babyish fashion, are saying, "Give me first the reward, and then I will believe in your claims or principles." But that is not the way it works. One offers his effort first, and after it is put forth, the bountiful result appears. One plants before one reaps.

Do Not Imagine That Your Decision to Lay Hold of The Law of Choice Is Egotistical

One learns quickly that he does not *own* the processes of Mind—but that through the graciousness of the laws of life (made by the Creator) they are available to him. Christ expressed it, "I, of myself, can do nothing. The Father *within,* He doeth the works." Scientists or psychologists might use other terms, but all would be referring to the same thing—i.e., the process of mental energy pasing into outer form or expression. [Most of the opposition among these groups is a quarrel of terms, a matter of semantics. If each of them could overcome prejudice against certain words and symbols, harmony would come closer to us all. The average person, conditioned to the taboos and the symbols of his own group, practically closes his mind when he sees or hears those of other groups, even though they often mean very nearly the same thing!]

In the Hebrew *Ten Commandments,* Deity is referred to as "a jealous God." Therefore one must worship none other. On close, careful study, the wrath incurred by dividing one's allegiance may not be the anger known to humans, but instead the sure debacle of being untrue to any law that must be obeyed. It is not less truly scientific to say that God (law) is "jealous." It is a very understandable way of stating that His way (or the basic *way*) must be recognized and must be obeyed. Whether you see that way as the petulant demand of a humanly jealous Father, or as an inexorable law of the universe, you will get the same unhappy result from disobedience!

It is our intent to study these laws that you and I must obey in order to fashion our lives into the mold of a higher and ever higher pattern. We wish to "redeem" our erroneous or weakly fulfilled past and to share more of the power, peace, and bounty which is available to us. We believe that we are ready to evolve into being able to use greater power responsibly—and we mean to face up to it bravely.

We shall fail, at times—perhaps many times. And for such moments, we must decide *now* that we shall not give in to the temptation to think we are being punished for "presumption." We shall *know* that we simply aren't doing *something* in the right way.

Our universe is a responsible one. Our God is a God of *love* and we need not fear His wrath because we are trying to grasp and demonstrate more of the laws He has mercifully and generously put here for us. We shall be better Christians, or whatever we are, because we are striving to draw closer to the heart of Being, and to lay hold of our heritage.

The craven will always find an excuse for his weakness. *Progress is for the brave!* So, let us take "God and my right" for a motto, and ride forth into the world of experience. One is reminded of Omar Khayyam's verse:

> "Ah love! Could you and I conspire
> To grasp the sorry scheme of things
> entire—
> Would we not shatter it to bits
> And then, remould it, nearer to
> The heart's desire?"

We mean to do some remoulding! Anyone who has honestly applied himself has often achieved startling results. For *there are no blanks* in this teeming universe! Every extended hand receives something! For the simple reason that every pebble (thought) dropped into the pool of Mind starts ripples that extend through the entire realm of consciousness.

To Recapitulate

Since the purpose of this book is to help you as a person to muster yourself—i.e., your life—so that more good results follow your efforts, let us now become very personal. In fact, we shall veer between the personal and the general throughout these chapters.

1. Be willing to let go of the past—good or bad. Forget hurts. Forgive wrongs. Wipe out blames. You must walk clean and free into your future.
2. Be willing to accept the truth that ill luck and inharmony are unnatural to the advanced "human" man who has turned his face forward and upward. Man may be "born to trouble as surely as sparks fly upward," so long as he lives in the animal ambience, but he can set his sail toward his human authority.
3. Be patient with yourself. It takes a little time to change mental gears—and to find your way in the new ones.
4. Be willing to put forth considerable persistent effort in order to win the blessings of the state of harmony where "all things work together for good" and unbelievable gifts abound.

These are the four "musts" of becoming a dedicated person, who will become a more fortunate one. But do not be deceived. These four rquirements for beginning are deceptively simple. They are easy to read, easy to imagine, and extremely difficult to follow. But the prize is worth whatever it costs.

Our goal is self-mastery; and in that dominion lies a great deal of control of so-called destiny. In truth, your destiny is whatever the sum total of yourself has attracted from the responsive universe.

There is basic and supporting reason in all happenings. Nature is not basically temperamental and erratic. The formulae of chemistry will produce largely the same results every time certain component parts are put together. There may be a possible variable (Einstein was always pointing out this possibility) due to changing potencies, positions, in terms of unpredicted, infinitesimal amounts or qualities. But, fundamentally, your formulae are dependable.

Archimedes, one of the most penetrating minds our kind has produced, is reported to have said, "Give me a lever and a place to stand and I will move the earth." Though he was referring to an amazing law of physics, that same law interpenetrates the kinetics of Mind.

We, too, need a place to stand. Whirling through space though we may be, we nevertheless feel something solid beneath us, and we trust that the law of gravity will hold us firmly upon it.

Mentally, too, we need a stance, a point of view, even if it is only a hypothesis. But it would be better to have a basic principle, from the solidity of which we can act and have confidence in the outcome.

Your faith in your universe is your "place to stand." You can depend on its established (discovered) laws—and from that vantage point learn of others. In our time of changing values and shifting standards and goals, you can take your stand on the known laws of cause and effect. Supported thus, you can then learn to use them to your own ends. Knowing that further knowledge may displace and replace much that we consider immutable, we are still privileged to use as much as we know.

We may well marvel at the wonders we can bring about now. The future will unfold its progressive secrets, just as the wheel replaced the drag, the automobile replaced the horse, the airplane conquered space and time. (All of these widely differing ideas and efforts were bent on the same purpose—transportation.)

In our inward life—the life of the Mind—greater knowledge will supersede the techniques we have today. But let us use what we have—not with fear or prejudice—but, rather, with overwhelming gratitude.

Your lever, with which you can move your world, is your deeper thought process. Man will never get to the moon until he can first think it through. An old nurse, I had as a child back in Kentucky, used to say to me when I was shy about doing anything, "Honey, you ain't never gonna hit the moon if you doan throw at it!" I wonder if she knew, or felt, that we would someday do just that. Her faith was boundless.

WE DRAW THE LIMITS

How can I make it clear that it is you (no one and nothing else) who puts the brakes on great accomplishment for yourself? It is you who draws limits with your "logical" acceptance of just how far you can go.

You first think grandly—*and then you begin to pare it down.* You dilute and pollute a fresh, new concept with all the old dregs and drags of past failures. In the end it is your deeper conviction, your acceptances, your firm beliefs that move your life into largeness, or hold it to smallness. These processes shape, bind, or free you—and your life. Little by little, all branches of human knowledge are giving more credence and respect to this basic truth.

There is no crime or mistake in having a small life. In some ways, and for some people, it seems to be more comfortable than any other. But the fact remains that it is we who draw the limits. "The law of creativity doesn't care whether it makes a mountain or a mouse."

Just *why* are we so timid in accepting and using our power better? Because, in our long, long history, we have amassed a great bulk of *belief in defeat!* It is built into our mental reflexes. We have brought it with us from the jungle, where we were constantly confronted with the menace of being vanquished by another creature with sharper teeth and longer claws. We have shed many of the limitations and the fears of our precarious past, but the expectancy of doom lies in our very marrow. We have permitted pessimism to become the mark of the "intellectual." We have accepted the classic Greek estimate of the tragic end to all effort. Pindar, "the last aristocrat," the great Greek poet and philosopher, put into words five hundred years before Christ, the glory of the token fight, knowing defeat was certain.

Instead of throwing aside the imprisoning concept of pessimism, we have clung to it, probably because we think it makes us seem wise. With all our supposed enlightenment today, most of our books, plays, and operas depict the tragic end. Anything else is considered "shallow, unrealistic, unsophisticated, unworldly, provincial, unfashionable!" In a few years, these concepts will seem so ignorant, so decadent, that they will be mentioned only with some embarrassment.

Even today, good health and a measure of harmony and fulfillment are coming to be thought of as within the power of each person to achieve. One hears less and less of "Fate." We are giving our attention to the "how" of things.

WHY NOT TAKE COMMAND?

But we have really come a long way. The walls of imprisoning ignorance are beginning to crumble—there are many signs of it. In the seeming confusions around us, we can take heart in our ability to assert our own individual order, no matter what the outer chaos. Since everything is in movement, it is up to each of us to shift into a higher gear. We can *resolve* to speed our own personal evolution more rapidly. The slower, animalistic evolution I have called "the pain route."

Why not see how far you can leave the whip of painful experience by taking conscious control of yourself as far as possible? In this direction lies joy and reward.

There is no simple, straight road to well-being and good fortune. It is a matter of tuning yourself so that you pick up only the vibrations of melody, not discord. If this selectivity is possible for that little box you call a radio or a television which gives you (when it is working properly) the sound or picture you *choose*—why do you not use the same principle of *selection?*

And do not permit your less evolved ancestors of long ago to dictate your choices today, for you have inherited many of their habit patterns and automatic reflexes. *You must take a calculated risk in cutting that well-established umbilical cord and find your own values.*

You do not have to live a life of crossed wires, disappointments, pain, frustration, and slow attrition. Those belong to the faraway jungle. Step out of them as though they were a worn-out garment. The moving current of life offers you every component part of fulfillment and satisfaction; but you must put them together according to *your own acceptance, vision, and desire.*

In the vast pageantry of flowing life where do you stand? Never mind, for the moment, the hazards and the threats; you have a personal, an individual job to do. And if you do it well, most of the dangers cannot reach you—they will flow around you and disappear for the most part.

If you can be objective and analytical about yourself as we survey your status, you will see clearly your *obligation* to develop, to grow, in mental, physical, emotional, spiritual, and worldly stature.

Unhappiness and confusion always follow *when the avenues of personal individual growth are blocked or unused* for whatever reason. The Parable of the Talents states it bluntly. If we do not improve and increase the assets we have (are responsible for) they shrink and disappear—are "taken away." One may not, with impunity, remove himself from the law of growth.

What Have You Done With Your Assets?

You probably have an excellent mind. Have you used it well? For yourself? For others? Have you kept your musical ability? How long has it been since you wrote a lovely or an amusing couplet? Can you still touch the floor with your finger tips, bending forward? Can you tell a story well (without long digressions)? Can you delegate work—or must you fuss over every detail? How is your golf game? Your bridge? Is your medicine shelf getting fuller, or is your emphasis on fresh fruits and vegetables in the icebox? Is your chest still high? Are your lower ribs up out of your waist-line? Are you making new friends—deepening old friendships?

There is something you could do extremely well—or at least better. Are you doing it? Or, are you getting rusty—and dusty? You *cannot* resign. Life calls you to account! Your decisions are extremely important, for they color the whole human experience, to help or hinder. Why slide backward? Insist on going forward! You will be surprised at your results. But *you* must take the initiative.

Are You Willing to Pay the Price of Advance?

If you are not ready to work on your advancement, there is no point in reading this book. While there are a few short-cuts and some suggestions born of much experience, *I do not offer something for nothing.*

I must admit, however, that life gives us many multiplied advantages and bonuses as rewards for our upward efforts (not as pats on the back for being "good children," but rather as the inevitable result of exposing ourselves to her laws of bounty). Nature's generosity is, at some points, almost unbelievable!

Do You Make Excuses for Yourself?

How inventive the ego is in squirming away from taking responsibility for neglected advancement! Make this test. If you quickly shift the blame, in even one small way, to some other person, to some circumstance "over which you have no control," you are fooling only yourself! Your excuses may be "true," may be facts, *but they have no real power over you.* You can build a fortunate life anywhere.

Sometimes burdens make good ballast, holding your ship deeper in the water, protecting you from being tossed around in a gale. *Remember that everything has a use and can be turned to good.*

All excuses are clichés, worn threadbare by the repetitive failures of those, who for their own reasons, do not reach beyond the vegetable and animal experience of the race. Excuses do furnish some salve to their smarting egos, stinging from their own lack of wisdom.

The time-honored excuse, "I couldn't help it," should be stated as, *"I did not wish to help it."* And a wish was not the strongest sort of motivation. Even in the face of calamity, determined people, who will forego excuses, can find a better way of reacting, and a faster rebuilding.

When the human will sets itself toward wholesome, creative effort, the circumstances, no matter how dreary, are compelled to yield.

All of us have met handicapped people who would not take "no" for an answer to life. Some of these valiant souls have made brilliant lives for themselves, even from a wheelchair. (One of the best comedians in England convulses his audiences from a wheelchair.) These people have thrown off self-pity as though it were a dangerous disease—which it may well be called, for it eats away the concept of personal power, and holds the mind and emotions to the past; to the lack, the hurt. They know that one cannot be fortunate with the continued reactions of the "wounded animal." Wheelchair, handicaps, burdens, or no—one must heal himself and face life with the healthy spirit of wholeness. It is always an inner decision.

Look to the Future

Have done with excuses. They explain the past—and hold you there. Put your mind on explaining your future! You will find amazing strength flowing to you from the ends of the universe. Your difficulties will no longer imprison you. You may even learn to stand on them to reach higher!

The only thing that can hold you back is your own inner acceptance of defeat. And whenever you fail, if you will be searchingly honest with yourself, you will see that in spite of lip-service to success, you did not really expect to win. Wanting something and believing in it are two different things.

Why is it necessary to "believe" in whatever you want to have, do, or be? There is nothing mysterious about it, nothing essentially "religious." So-called belief is a focused mental pattern, a clear call on the universe to fulfill a definite outline. Belief is a projected demand. It draws to and around itself the appurtenances and forces that bring it into manifestation.

Belief is a blue print that the builders follow. Belief is a movement among the vibrations that activate creation at any point. Belief is a call to all that is like itself. And since the greatest single attribute of life is responsiveness, atoms fly together to answer and obey the pattern of belief.

It is a mistake to think of "belief" as only metaphysical, merely religious, or belonging exclusively to an immaterial realm. Belief is the gear that connects power to the wheels of your attainments—be they good or bad. It is about as material as the electric switch by which electricity reaches your lights and appliances in your house. Used adversely, it can also plunge your house into darkness.

Belief is the hub of all invention, commerce, and economics. Who would open a store or any other place of business, if he did not believe that people would come to patronize him? Who would step on the brake in his car, if he did not believe that it would stop the vehicle? Who would use soap in his bath, if he did not believe that it would help him to become clean?

Why do we try to make something ephemeral of *belief* in some areas and consider it as dependable as cement in other ways? Is it not clear that we must choose our beliefs, channel their force, discipline ourselves in their direction and thereby focus and order more of the events of our lives?

Why do we not "believe" that our thoughts have authority, when we see all around us dozens of times a day the evidence of their directing power, not only in our own lives, but also perhaps more sharply, in the lives of other people?

It was said of Christ that "He spoke as one having authority." Yet, he importuned the world to follow in his path and do "greater things." He spoke in parables that the people could understand, but his real message was of the latent powers to which the human race has access. His aim was to relieve mankind of its miseries of mind, body, and soul. These powers are neither miraculous nor mysterious, except as they are compared to the darkness of man's present state.

Higher Laws

When we finally come to know and use these powers which He described and demonstrated, we will know that they operate according to established laws, which were put here by a greater Power that evidently cares enough to place our liberation before us. It remains for us to recognize law and to educate ourselves and discipline ourselves so that we can learn how to approach and use it.

Any relief, any improvement, any advance along any line, in any way, is to be respected—and fitted into its proper place and used. We should waste no time looking down our noses at the accomplishments of anybody or any other group. Whatever helps mankind is of God. He speaks to us in many ways—and we should respect them all.

We cannot deny that up to now, man's advances have dawned

on him largely in the material sense—that is, man has been conscious of them largely through material benefits. He has little considered that back of all material advance, the mental, psychic, and spiritual factors either lead or go hand in hand. They do not follow. Nevertheless, since he seems capable of recognizing only material advance, thank God he has it to recognize! It is a step.

Who can say positively how much of man's supremacy actually stems from his opposable thumb, which goes back a long way in his evolution? With that thumb he could feel, judge, fashion, shape, create. He could make and use tools, refine and improve them. But only as ideas and the investigative urge lured him into experiments, did the advantage of his thumb serve him. Other animals, including the opossum, possess that great benefit, a kind of opposable thumb, that permits them to pick up and examine by touch and finer control any object they can lift. Yet, they do not as yet seem to have used it as the lever in areas of knowledge that have meant so much to man. It has not given them one skill at manipulation that man has enjoyed, and used to scientific advancement.

Just as man has made magnificent and extended use of his hands, he is also making magnificent and extended study and use of his Mind. And while we expect to show that he can use it, i.e., direct thought, to command a certain amount of his experience, we feel it necessary for him to approach this comparatively new area of power through a more skilled performance in some of the more familiar areas in which he is less than perfect. The latter will *lead* to the more advanced use of Mind.

Using his Mind, man must smooth his life here, as he finds it now, before he can go on to higher uses of his faculties. He cannot fumble through, say, human relationships, and claim superior power of Mind.

Therefore, a number of the chapters of this book propose to help him to minimize his confusions and difficulties—mental, physical, emotional, and material—*before encouraging him to express mental sovereignty.*

We propose to help him gain the many advantages and profits of a finely regulated instrument (the two sides of which are Mind and body) which will show him how to create for himself, no matter what "the world" is doing, a life of more accomplishment.

In one way, we have never been so involved with the rest of humanity—and in another way we have never been so dependent upon our individual selves.

•2•

The Fantastic Power of the Human Mind

IN THE PANORAMA OF MAN'S HISTORY THAT WE have seen—and from much that we can deduce—we see how man's Mind has improved his condition and widened his stage. Many diseases have been controlled, with other medical victories to come. The pathetic helplessness of early man before enemies, the hazards of weather, the challenges of constant hunger, drove him to multiply his strength with tools, to devise traps for animals many times stronger than he, and to develop the formidable tribe.

Through hundreds of thousands, perhaps millions, of years, he slowly developed sensitivities, awarenesses, reflexes, and techniques. He gradually extended his mastery over his world. He learned the force of a rock, a club; the usefulness of something that would float him over a body of water. He grew strong, agile, crafty.

He seemed to have many of the characteristics of other high animals, who, within their own spheres showed ingenuity in survival, too. Yet, most of these other creatures, through eons of time, did not improve or change their habits, while man sent his thoughts out into his world and envisioned first one advance and then another.

There can be no denying that the growth of his skill with tools and weapons had a dual effect. One, it perpetuated his animalism, simply refining the problems of attack and defense. Two, it exercised his mentality, polished his quickness of thought, developed the size of his brain, and sensitized the myriad cells ending in nerves.

NEW CHALLENGES

With each new accomplishment, man could envision still further reaches of supremacy. Unaware of exactly what he was doing, he built a system of recognition, awareness, imagination, and inventiveness that now can no longer be satisfied with mere material advance. He has become aware that he has a soul as well as a body, and that his soul has its sphere of action and being, expression and responsibility. He has become aware that his body is the tool and instrument of his soul—that his body is secondary in power to his soul.

Yet, he has needed his body's experience to find and know his soul, to use and know his mind. In his evolution, he has passed through one cataclysm after another. The transitional period he is presently experiencing is another type of slower cataclysm, and like all the others, requires a higher type of thinking to survive it. Now, just how does this apply to you—in your daily life?

If You Are Unhappy Today, You Need a Higher Type of Thinking

There is almost nothing that your Mind cannot transcend if you will put it to work. But be sure you do not simply mull around in the old limits, the old confusions and discord. *Your Mind must reach up and away from its tangles* and order a new list of reactions and blessings. The old angers, the old ego wounds, the old feelings of rejection, the old sense of expecting doom, of not being able to "rate," must be replaced.

In a way, the universe is not unlike a vast department store. In shopping (living) you make a selection, pay for it—and then if you find out it isn't suitable, you are very unhappy with it. You take it back, only to discover that somehow your case cannot be handled by the floorwalker, the sales person, or even by the department where such matters are usually resolved. What to do? Shall you flounce out never to return, angry, unattractive, bearing a scar of failure?

Wouldn't it be better to ask to see the manager? This may take some doing, but it is not impossible if one is persistent—and if one does not excite opposition by rudeness. You finally win your way to the manager and politely state your case, expecting him to use understanding and fairness. He not only accedes to your request but repays you for all your bother with some type of special consideration.

Learn to Take Your Problem to a Higher Authority—Within Yourself

Elevate your thinking above the routine crassness and see what shall be wrought! The higher you go, the easier your way becomes. It is so in every department of living—not just at the store. So often we fail because we are not striking high enough! Nor are we acting as our highest selves.

By shifting your mental gears from low to high you do not refute the laws and patterns of the low gear—you simply change your whole demand on the laws of locomotion and begin to make use of all the extra benefits of that level.

It is you who must choose the level of your demand. The universal laws will respond to you in whatever way you approach them. *You* set the sail. *You* turn the dial. *You* press the throttle.

Mind Is Unlimited

As man has learned to increase his use of Mind, his life has become infinitely easier. Invention has lifted the common man from the status of pack-animal to a worker who drives to his factory in an automobile. It has given him a bit of leisure in which to learn to think about his possibilities and to try to understand himself. As he realizes (even dimly) what he could be and have, he grows restive, dissatisfied with his lot, which is both good and bad, depending on the way he reacts and the conclusions he has about it.

"Divine discontent" drives a man to improve. But, if he does not elevate his inner life, his outward advantages simply provide a more pleasant background for his grossness. Even that, though, has its values.

In a general way, material advance has provided stimulus to thought, the exercise of which means inward growth of all kinds, however slow! For it is the richness of Mind (in its eternal, basic aspects) that offers man salvation from his lower states and puts him on the path to spiritual progress. He cannot *use* his heritage until he understands it.

There is nothing that Mind cannot do. Realize that the same mind that invented the simple wheel, that discovered the use of fire, has been able to produce (some thousands of years later) such complicated concepts as the hydrogen bomb, the guided missile, the space satellite. And what it has discovered up to this time is only the beginning. There are far more complex things to come.

The great difference between the human mind and that of the animal is that man's mind can understand the subtleties of its own process.

Man is coming to understand that low-grade mentation keeps the whole organism in low-grade atmospheres and muddy results. He is beginning to see that limiting himself to a three-dimensional thought pattern has imprisoned him for thousands of years. He is ready to accept the moral responsibilities of his next step in power, i.e., a fuller use of the kinetic psycho-dynamics that are open to him. In fact, he is beginning to suspect that Mind itself may be the power of action and manifestation, as well as being the power that activates it!

For it is his *Mind* that has conceived all the extraordinary things he has so far found in his universe. It is his *Mind* that utilized kerosene, steam, gasoline, electricity, and atomic power! Smaller and smaller grow the vessels that convey the great forces he is finding. Does it seem unreasonable to suppose that one day he will look at some tiny atomic transistor and decide, "*I* created the early huge, noisy, violent engines of power. *I* have refined and reduced them. *I* found the way to carry great power in this small container. Perhaps my mind, being back of all these things, is the power, itself. Maybe I don't need any of this. Do I dare think that I shall one day simply use my commanding mind to draw to myself what I want or need, without the use of cumbersome processes?"

Of course, such matters are in the far future, but it takes man a good many thousands of years to get around to an advancement, so he may as well start thinking of some far reach for his possible power. It has been said that the Atlanteans (inhabitants of the "Lost Continent," Atlantis) had progressed to the power of creating whatever they needed by the direct use of their minds.

The story is that at the time of the deluge, which sank their continent, some of them escaped into India, where even today, the fakirs pretend to make material things appear out of the ether. They were said to have lost their genuine power through the corruption of their hard-won virtues. True or not, it is certainly evident that if people with that power never lived, they most certainly *shall live* as man continues to explore his heritage of the divine gift of Mind.

Used well or ill, Mind is man's guiding force—and is the key to all that he has or will be or do.

Much that was good on man's animal plane—such as skill in killing both for food and defense—now lies across his path of mental and spiritual advancement. Tangled motivations, nullifying each other, create a psychic confusion that makes many modern men desperately unhappy. Life, on the old basis, doesn't seem worth living.

Yet, when a man inwardly decides to live more morally, he meets his own animal pressures and the threats of a world still engrossed in violence. He feels helpless again, for new reasons. What does it matter if he thinks in a high, fine way—in a world that is strenuously engrossed in finding the fastest way to expunge him?

It requires all man's courage and passionate idealism to stay on a lifted path. He *must not falter* and fall back. For as Kahlil Gibran puts it, we fail for those ahead of us and clutter the path of those struggling behind us. These are not his words, but his thought. When we fall back in our growth, it creates a block and a burden for all. What each of us does is extremely *important* to the whole!

THE NEXT STEP UP

When we really wake up to the power of our own mental processes, we will have a whole race of people ready for the next marvelous breakthrough of intelligence. Remember, *"It doth not yet appear what ye shall be."*

There are many apologists for the animal-man. There are occasional books and articles which wryly point out that trying to be otherwise is too much trouble. I think I saw a title the other day, *The Advantages of Failure.* The author's chief point, I was told, was that the failure has a great deal of appreciative companionship, and this is supposed to please him! Actually, failure is only a delaying action, puts off the day we can climb out of the "pain route." For all of us shall succeed one day. I just want us to suffer less, and for a shorter time, by *consciously* evolving into higher states, instead of taking the long, weary way of the past.

Suppose Mr. Edison had said, "Electricity for light, power, and home use is so new that it will make people feel strained and unnatural. So, I think I'll put it under a barrel and let them keep on using kerosene and candles." Instead, he gave us his findings and set the world several thousand years ahead in evolutionary progress. We owe him a great deal, not only for the concrete things he gave us, but for *opening our minds* to new ways and higher forces.

There is small comfort in the old fuzzy, fusty way of living. Great forces demand great vigilance and accuracy. This seems to be the hard part of it for most of us. At the core of anything is the truth about it—the best way to apply it, the direct way to its results.

The best way then becomes the law of progress. If our scientists find a better fuel, they discard the old ones and use it. If one chemical is found to clean better than another, it is employed in soaps and cleaners.

Let us be willing to improve, to become *accurate* in more and more ways. Rally your own powers of excellence. Our fumbling, bumbling inaccuracies, no matter how sweetly "charming," bring us too many fumbling, bumbling results—and they can be painful!

Suppose William Tell had not been an accurate marksman with a bow and arrow. He would have killed his son. In today's world of science and higher mathematics, would you want your son to work on a team of scientists who had graduated with an average of seventy-six? No, my friends, seventy-six *isn't passing* in our world. It never was really satisfactory. It must have been made a passing grade by our enemies, who would like to see us less than accurate in every way! But, today, it is dangerous in the extreme. Not only must a rocket's calculations be 100 per cent correct, there must be a team whose members check one another, and still others to check them! For the slightest miscalculation can throw the projectile out of its course, going at 17,500 miles an hour!

In the faster world of tomorrow it is going to be more and more unwise to cheat, lie, dissemble, or otherwise mar or blur the truth. For inaccuracies of all kinds will constitute varying degrees of hazards!

Crime appears to be on the rise now, only because the sharpened wits of amoral people, not grounded in disciplinary training of any kind, make it appear easy to take what one wants—from money to life, itself—no matter to whom it belongs. This heightened imagination, even without moral standards, is, nevertheless, the fruit of the progress which is general! The crying need is not to want less, but for more moral training based on respect for accuracies.

As all students learn respect for their higher mathematical principles, for their chemical formulae, for the results of applied force in jet propulsion, and thus learn the complete dependability of cause and effect, they will begin to see that moral principles (laws) are the demands of the interaction of people and events in an advanced civilization. With increased speeds one must get to the truth quickly, or perhaps perish in the pile-up of instantaneous inaccuracy. There is going to be less and less time for fuzzy thinking and all grades of untruth on any level. It simply won't be safe! Crime, which is always based on warped judgment, will tend to disappear.

Thus, very high material progress leads directly into moral accuracies of all kinds. Morality is seen, then, to be a requirement of the laws of moving, progressing life, itself, rather than an invention of man to make his society more comfortable. Man must advance from the jungle code of ethics—or be plowed under.

There will be (as we see now) an orgy of unmorality as man prostitutes his advanced thinking machine to wrong or completely selfish ends or tries to cling to the pleasures of a lower state at the same time he is intellectually climbing out of it. This is the phase we are in today. This is the sea of confusion through which each person must learn to steer his bark to safety. Some of the techniques he can use are given in this book.

Why Does Not Man Progress Faster?

Science, education, religion, and the individual ask this question. And the inescapable answer is that *he has not believed in his right to progress!* The past holds him in an iron grip. He is just now beginning to loosen its stranglehold upon him. Yet, he is still prey to some of the fears that beset neolithic and even more ancient men. *He believes in doom.*

Over and over through the ages, man has seen life begin, grow up to some level of maturity, and then be snuffed out by an enemy from within or without. What good were thoughts, dreams, visions, better ways of doing things? A stronger creature could come and take a man's gains, his mate, his children, and companions. Then he watched, as a slave, perhaps, the new conqueror go down before a newer one in the course of time. Bitterness at the injustice ravaged his thoughts. But railing did no good. Then *conscience and laws* began to make life a little better. Law heralded the development of *man as a human* from the animal beginnings.

Law, the Great Civilizer

Even the greatest of conquerors could not hold his people long in subjection without their feeling that they lived under the advantages of some kind of structure of regulating, fair, protecting law. And since law itself is born of fair, even kindly, consideration of others, it is the first glimpse of civilization, wherever found.

Almost 2,000 years before Christ, the great Babylonian king, Hammurabi, ruled in a stern but kindly way. Many of his laws, inscribed on a very tall stone (discovered in our time) admonish his people to be obedient and to recognize that he is like a "good father" to whom they can bring their troubles and their disputes and gain justice. Even this tyrant of unquestioned power used this kind of propaganda to satisfy the growing sense of fairness and humanness in his people. Without the rules and taboos of tribal life no body of people could function as a unit.

Laws Give Privileges— They Are Not Just for the Unruly

Someone said lately, "Just look at those red traffic lights, think of the thousands of police, and the great log of lawsuits backed up on our court calendars! Men must still be barbarians to need so much regulation."

And the answer to that commentary is that however slowly we come, finding it hard to leave the jungle ways of force, we still respect, accept, actually seek law. This acceptance shows us that conscience is deep within us (and not an invention of religion) even though it unfolds itself at a snail's pace. But we must understand conscience if we are to live comfortably in our changing world.

Conscience is awareness of the rightness of law of all kinds. It is the constant measurer, noting the gap between the ideal and the performance. In some ways, both of these meanings are abused.

The modern effort to eliminate conscience, and therefore, guilt, is a cheap attempt to rub out a million years of struggle to evolve. But, it will be found that, as always, there is no way to abolish this important gain of awareness in man's inward sense of justice. It can only be twisted and maimed.

Conscience does not exist merely as a punisher. It is a help. We should value it highly. It is inextricably bound up with man's further and finer sensibilities—the unfolding of his diviner pattern. The smartings of conscience are something of which to be proud. Their poignancy indicates the distance a man has come from the jungle.

Law, conscience, guilt, are the first steps of humanness. They are in each man's bone and marrow. What he does with them and about them is the measure of his character. He *must* deal with them. They came here with him!

You must make your peace with your sense of law and conscience before you can start on the road of raising your life to a more fortunate, brighter level. For we do not want your progress to be blunted or weighed down by an unresolved burden inherited from the past, remote or near. You are going to use your sense of law and conscience as steppingstones upward. Instead of a drag, they will be, for you, a lift!

We must get these primary, basic factors aligned correctly and use them for foundational support. They have been whips over our heads, making cowards of us long enough! Before you lay this book down as finished, you will have learned how to resolve the painful part of conscience and will know how to make of it an asset of progress—which is its chief function.

For our purposes, it is imperative to come to grips with this subject. Otherwise you will expect, and even unconsciously demand, punishment to equal your guilts, and because of this inward drama, you will expect the worst—defeat.

It is easy to understand how man collected this mass of belief in doom. It is harder to shake it off and step up into the directing, responsible humanness. It helps to realize that it is *we* who cling to the past.

There are no backward looks in all of nature. If a person sincerely allies himself with the ever-creating, ever-renewing, process of flowing life, he will find his feet free of the hampering past. We will discuss, in detail, the techniques he can use. Anyone, who has seriously dedicated himself to these purposes, can testify to the remarkable results he has gained.

DOES "GOD" CARE WHAT A MAN DOES?

Apparently, the parent Mind knew that man would need much help—and set about providing it in terms of many laws the earnest seeker can invoke. There must surely have been a *caring,* somewhere, somehow, that provided the law of movement that washes out the past, making all things new. The tenderest, most fatherly love could not have provided for us more mercifully. It parallels forgiveness and healing on all planes of living. Law, in this light, is both impersonal and personal.

But one must be honest with the law. One may not play fast and loose with it. It works only *one way*—that is when we turn to it, in all sincerity, and honestly displace the wrong with a right. But this we *can* do—thank God!

And as the picture in a kaleidoscope rearranges itself into a new pattern when one of its pieces is dislodged, our own entire life and being is altered when we dislodge the debris of past errors, and face the future cleanly unafraid.

A New Day, a New Way

Every moment is a fresh beginning. Shake off the dark, half-hidden, old belief that the wrongs of millions of years ago must still bring doom. Let the sun of faith in the salutary processes of life dry out all the damp, gloomy corners in the "memory" of failure. Shake off the cave—and the caveman!

Shape your life with your mind, that part of you which is made "in the image and likeness of God." It is your privilege to clear your path of inherited or personal clutter. How much of it must *you* deal with?

Most people do not use a hundredth part of their mind's capacity, largely because they underestimate their mental powers. Some are actually afraid that they will "overdo it." What a shameful waste! We are, only now, beginning to realize in this country that we have not put the minds of our young people to work full time. Fortunately, we are remedying the situation by demanding *more* of them rather than less.

The mind does not tire, does not wear out with use. (This subject is well covered in my book, *Double Your Energy and Live Without Fatigue,* Prentice-Hall, Inc.). Never worry about putting your brain to work too much, or about overtaxing it. Actually, the more you use your mind the keener it becomes. This point is the subject of much scientific experiment and conjecture. It has never been decided whether the brain energizes the body more than the body energizes the brain.

The great thinkers of the world are noteworthy because they use their minds at many times the pace of the average man. That is why they *are* great. Einstein could have remained a telegraph clerk all his life and never contributed his truths to the human race. But he decided early that he was going to use all the mental power that he could command—in a constructive way. The result was that this humble clerk shook the very foundations of the world we live in.

Decide now to put your mind to work at top speed. You may not discover new theories of the universe (on the other hand, you may), but you will accomplish a great deal more than you ever imagined possible. Don't let your brain get rusty. Senility can begin in childhood! At any age! Keep your mind going. Keep it running with ideas, thoughts and problems. Remember—Mind is a principle and is, therefore, inexhaustible!

•3•

Where Are You—and Where Do You Want to Go?

THE QUESTION THIS CHAPTER ASKS IS DOUBLE-edged. Where are you on the evolutionary trek—and where do you want to go in lifted awareness? The other side of the matter is: where are you in satisfaction and accomplishment—and where would you like to be? Closer study reveals that there isn't as much difference between these areas as might appear at first glance. It is my aim to close the gap between them as much as possible.

Worldly success, fine as it is and needed as it is by most of us, does not, of itself, guarantee satisfaction. That is why I strive in this book to place the advance you will gain from it on a solid foundation of knowledge and true orientation in our careening world. If you know something of how you have arrived at the point where you now find yourself; if you are brave enough to face the truth about yourself, you will set about strengthening your underpinnings, finding out the processes that have been used (and perhaps abused) in your development, and learn to select only those which have value.

It is possible to have worldly success and a well-rounded life and personality. This is my desire for you. Perhaps Sir Winston Churchill is a good example of a thoroughly involved (and evolved) personality at the top of the scale of completeness. His success has been panoramic, extending from marriage to literature, statesmanship to oil painting, as a friend of kings and of soldiers.

One of Churchill's "secrets" of a long, useful life was the awareness that a change of occupation is a "rest," that the mind itself does not suffer fatigue, but only boredom, which gives a thorough feeling of exhaustion. When he felt himself slowing down, say, at writing, he would turn to painting, or bricklaying, or he would go make a speech somewhere, or call on a friend. But no matter what he did, his concentration was complete until the task was finished.

Here, we come to a very vital point. Even the most evolved human being finds it necessary to change his focus of attention frequently, or he slows down and mistakenly thinks his mind is tired. But the real truth is that *sustained mentation* is comparatively new to the human being. In animals and in primitive types of men we find a very brief attention span.

YOU NEED A GOOD ATTENTION SPAN

Today, watching students in schools and colleges, one notes that the best grades do not always go to those with the most brilliant minds, but to those who have disciplined their attention span to stay with a study until it is mastered!

There are many brilliant "failures" in the world. They are men and women whose speed of perception was rapid, whose clarity of thought was phenomenal, but whose parents or teachers had never trained them to stay at it, so, in the tests of thoroughness, they fell by the wayside. How sad that evolution's brightest products sometimes are ineffectual because the animal past, in undisciplined attention span, has been allowed to remain unchallenged!

There is a general tendency for parents to think that a child must be *born* with a good attention span, as though it were something like blue eyes or long fingers. Therefore, they let many brilliant children go to waste, because they gave themselves the excuse that a certain child is naturally flighty and difficult to pin down. Often, the more "flighty" a child is, the brighter is his mind. Certainly it is more work to train his sustained thinking, but consider the gains!

Can You Stick with It?

How long can you apply yourself to a given task without getting bored and thinking you are tired? The longer you can make your span, the further you will put yourself on the road of human evolution. Let me suggest that the next time you think you are mentally "fagged," you get up, gather the whole family and all go to the zoo! Stroll from species to species and note that animals all have one thing in common—a very short attention span. When you get home, take a long walk alone and resolve to shake off this stubbornly clinging animal characteristic.

Once you start gathering data on this subject, you will become aware of men who are "killing themselves" by working overtime at the office to give their families more money and position. At a factory assembly line you will find men, who do the same job all day long, and who, at night, are dying of boredom—sometimes literally. In both cases, that of the executive and the factory worker, the problem is attention span. It has nothing to do with real fatigue and less to do with tiring their minds. An understanding of the real root of the trouble might save their lives. A vacation is only a palliative. It resolves nothing.

The superman of the future must be able to work longer than eight hours. He should be able to apply himself indefinitely. And once he gives up his simian drama of playing at fatigue, he will find himself unharmed by continued application. No longer will he permit himself to function on an inferior, vegetable-animal plane. For he is a *man, a human being, whose mind is ruler.*

In our school programs we practically encourage a short attention span by providing many and swift changes for the children. We are doing them a disservice, offering nothing to help them in this most human of advances. Not so with the Russians. Their children are in school many hours a day and must earn their change of pace and their play. A policy halfway between the two countries might be better.

But why leave such an important matter to the schools? The home should provide some training for the human attention span.

I have often dreamed of having a school where one subject a day would be studied. In my own experience, just as I got deeply immersed in a subject a bell would clang and off I would be herded to take up another theme. And just when I was deep in that, the bell would clang again! My dream of a special type of school took shape when I was tutoring my stepson who was about to fail in history. We had a week in which to work! We rose early and kept at our study all day and all evening. Of course, much humor and various ways of pounding the facts home were employed. He passed his examination and later said that history was the one thing he knew "for sure."

Kinetic psycho-dynamics, the power of the movement of Mind, will best be utilized by the person who has trained himself to stay with a subject—and who knows the difference between fatigue and boredom.

Make This Simple Test

How long can you hold one thought in your mind to the exclusion of all else? Do not be discouraged if you find you can scarcely hold it one minute at first. *Your mind will quickly respond to training along this line.* The benefits are many. You will be astonished at the values that will come to you as you extend your ability to hold to one thought! This is often the only difference between a man of force and a man of weak personality.

Set aside a few minutes every day or night, or both, to exercise your mind in this way. Do not think it childish, or unrewarding. It is the *cornerstone* in the building of your future of glorious self-management. Without it, you can do little. With it, you can do everything. For this reason, we will discuss this point a number of times.

It is patent that if your mind is to be your catapult into a better state of being, your mind must be one that is trained, disciplined, capable of the exactitudes that spring only from excellent controls. Your mind must be as powerful, smooth, and responsive as the finest motor which delivers its force almost silently, silkily, and at the slightest touch or call upon it.

The results of exercising your mind will please you so greatly that they will be worth your while, keenly worth your effort. There are few pleasures to equal the feeling that one is using his mind well. There is an interpenetrating joy when there is effective functioning throughout one's entirety—and with it goes the sense of pride in accomplishment.

No matter what your goal, you are on your way to it with a disciplined mind. And when the clutter, loose ends, and digressions of the "animal" mind are brushed aside, your path is clear for the most swift and flowing advancement.

Interesting, isn't it, that a *"practical"* training in mentation has the result of lifting the mind to its *diviner* areas of operation and command? There are those who try to set up a conflict between these two aspects of the mind. But experience will show that one is an extension of the other. This is good news to the practical person—and a warning to the ones who think they can just sail off into Elysian fields without cleaning up the debris left at home.

TAKE A GOOD LOOK AT YOURSELF

And now let us concern ourselves with you, personally. Stand before a mental mirror and take your measure, as it were.

Look at yourself "in the round," as sculptors say. Scan your overall effect, and you probably will have to admit that you have done rather well. Oh, you've had setbacks, one or two humiliations, and you bear a few scars. But a close observation shows you how the signs of battles well fought add up to a look that might be called *distingué.* You've met the world and so far, you've had the last say. You've survived! That means you have gained strengths, some wisdom, some saving graces. And probably much more!

But, still, there are some dreams unrealized, some depths unplumbed, some unexpressed urges that are beginning to stir somewhere within you. For life constantly reaches, however slowly it may move.

The future *you,* for eons folded and closed, unknown, is beginning to open!

Your full design is a bit indistinct, but what we can see is as accurate, balanced, and beautiful as nature has ever produced. This movement is in the depths of you. You may not know that you are a giant beginning to wake from a long, long sleep. You may be unaware of your vast potential.

You *do know* there is a certain unrest in you that is difficult to ignore. What you *can be* pushes insistently against the smugness of what you *are*. It is more than mere ambition. You may or may not be interested in worldly gain, but you can't help wanting to climb as far as you can in awareness, just for the fine view from up there, if nothing more!

Time to Move Upward

There are few thrills equal to knowing that one has grown taller in spirit, higher in knowledge, larger in concept, in obedience to the urges of life itself. It is time for mankind to move upward into the *familiar* use of some of his latent powers. It is time for him to shift into a higher gear that will give him more propulsion for less effort (more mileage for less gasoline). It is time for each man to prove this possibility to himself. It is time for you to begin.

If you and I could sit quietly while you turned your thoughts to the best way you could progress as an individual, both of us would probably be examining the possibility of your becoming the sort of person who almost automatically receives more of the good things of life. We call such a person "fortunate," yet his living in that rosier ambience has little to do with "chance," as we commonly think of it.

In the higher levels of human and spiritual mentation, we are dealing with definite laws where that which is fitting flows together more satisfactorily and more often than on lower levels. The details of living assume harmonious and profitable results. One *rises* out of the lower, confused states where too much goes amiss, where most people actually expect things to go wrong.

We cannot expect perfection—at least not now—but we can certainly build our consciousness of increasing good to the point where our lives are smoother, richer, happier.

If you, for instance, did not have to spend so much time and energy fighting chaos and things that go wrong, both large and small, you could apply yourself, almost exclusively, to your talents; to real growth. You would not have to digress so much. This is my wish for you.

Some people rise in life by herculean effort, by sheer storming the gates of Heaven. They batter with their bare hands, as it were, and break resistance to their wishes by sheer force. But the cost is too great. They know intuitively that such bombardment is not the best way—and, in the end, they lose confidence in their own attainments. They may have believed in the whimsies of "luck" rather than in becoming grounded in the "field of the fortunate."

Where Are You Going?

It is self-evident that if you wish to travel somewhere you must buy a ticket. But first you will have chosen your destination. It is surprising that many people will buy high-powered, expensive cars, with no concrete idea of where they expect all that power to take them. They wish to arrive somewhere but do not choose a destination.

You must have a plan, though you change it later on. There must be a beginning point. You must draw back, choose a target, a goal, and take aim. The mechanics of "beginning" are told with stark simplicity in Genesis, the first book of the Bible. The mechanics of any beginning are equally simple:

1. There must be goal—and directive.
2. There must be simple and complete faith in the process. Otherwise, one would not be speaking with the so-necessary authority.
3. There must be complete acceptance of one's *right* to use the law.

Before you decide that this is too much for you, let me assure you that you are constantly using the law of creativity. It is *always operating* in response to your directive. But what are you telling it to do? What off-the-beam dissonances are your inner acceptances asking for?

It is not a new thing I am asking you to do. I simply point to the fact that you can make far better use of your access to creative laws. The universe is *always* responding to you according to your composite demand, which, I hasten to add, is partially unconscious. Also, bear in mind that your acceptances, your doubts, and your fears are as definite a part of your demand as are your more direct requests. One finally comes to understand that the quality of his expectation is the exact replica of the result he will achieve. And this will be true of him no matter where or what he is.

So, *choose your goal.* Have several of them, and think toward them—never away from them. Just as an understanding of air travel cuts down the time of getting from one place to another, so advanced knowledge of the uses of Mind brings you faster to your chosen objectives. Just as in electrodynamics, a charge of power leaps from one cycle to another, the very desire to lift your thoughts and life into higher channels brings contact with the atmosphere you seek. The sustaining material follows. The response of Mind is not less swift than that of electricity—*when* the way is cleared, and the contacts are clean and true. You are not dealing with a stubborn, unyielding factor, but are in touch with the most dynamic, plastic, facile force imaginable.

Let Others Alone

Do not clutter up your mind with comparisons. Shakespeare was indeed correct when he labeled them "odious." It is a waste of time to explain your own shortcomings in terms of someone else's lack along any line. Have done with blames!

Many people believe that if they were in a different environment, or had a different mother, father, brother, husband or child, they would be far better in every way. This is simply not true! The truth is that if *they* were different, their environment would be, or seem, different in over-all effect—or lack of it.

The odd reaction to a first resolve to lift one's life, is to demand that others change! This childish performance is putting the cart before the horse. Work on *yourself* only! You have only one problem—yourself. You have only one enemy—yourself. And when *you* change your inner pattern of demand, the outside world will change in relation to you.

You Are "In Charge"

Many of us who want to improve, to raise our status, are passionately devoted to the premise that we are the victims of all that is around us. We live, then, in a prison—and someone else holds the key! This idea is contrary to the very purpose of existing at all; to progress as individuals.

If a person is truly imprisoned, put upon by violence or otherwise unhappily situated, he can still occupy himself so constructively that he will make a gain of the whole unfortunate matter. No one can put a person who knows the law of inner freedom where he cannot improve himself. For instance:

1. He can learn self-control.
2. He can improve his memory by exercising it by the hour in recalling people and events and numbers.
3. He can learn a foreign language.
4. He can learn how to use real meditation for constructive purposes.
5. He can determine to be a good influence on everybody who comes near him.
6. He can improve his posture and his muscle tone by exercising, if only by tensing and relaxing.
7. He can build up the belief that the time will come when he will be as free of physical fetters as he is of mental ones.
8. He can acquaint himself with the law that says he has the power of choice to construct a fine thing, wherever he is, no matter how crude his tools, or how mediocre the material at hand.

Life is always becoming something—and as long as he has life, man must become something better.

Say "Yes" to Life

To gain freedom from the imprisonment of our own level of consciousness, it behooves us to *agree* at every possible point; to have a positive reaction. It is amazing how many arguments and resistances arise in our minds and emotions. If one could keep a check for one day on the number of times he has *agreed* and the number of times he has *resisted,* he would have some idea of how much dangerous and numbing negativity he carries with him.

This is not to say that the yes man is a strong vessel. Agreeableness and "yessing" are two entirely different matters. For "yes" and "no" are not always based on pure intellectual considerations. They can be based on our false, ego-protecting criticisms, or on our laziness, or on our envy.

Study the causes of your likes and dislikes and you will have a key to clearing your path for progress. You will understand why you have gone ahead in some areas and retrogressed, perhaps, in others.

A dislike is a definite opposition. And every opposition invites that which is like itself. The result is conflict. A dislike is one of the major blocks in your upward climb. You must build up your inward content of agreement before you can benefit from the flow of agreement into your life. For this reason it is excellent training to *call everything good* (almost everything is good for something).

While you are thinking that the "good" approach is impractical, impossible, or certainly very difficult, let me tell you a true story. I have a friend, a wealthy woman, no longer young. She had had several warnings of a heart attack, to which she paid little or no attention. Then one day she fell at her ranch and broke her leg. She called me to tell me of her sad plight and I interrupted her. I said, "It's the best thing that ever happened to you!" She was aghast. She replied, "I don't see how you can say that. I know you believe in calling everything good, but what's good about this? I'm missing dozens of wonderful parties and trips."

I answered, "Never mind about them, now. You will be immobilized for several weeks. Your vital organs—particularly your heart—will have a rest, which they need. As you quiet down, certain disarranged values will assume their proper place. You will have a chance to do some excellent mental and emotional housekeeping. Your nerves will get a wonderful new lease on life when you stop whipping them with restlessness and chafing.

"Just shift into a gear of *trusting life.* Listen and learn what God has to teach you in every experience. *Declare* it good, whether it seems to be or not. Write lovely, long letters. Listen to great music. Catch up on reading. Improve your own voice by reading aloud with careful modulation and enunciation. Improve your posture."

"Improve my posture! Lying in bed! Or sitting in a wheel chair?"

"Certainly," I said. "You can come out of this seeming calamity with a firm, shapely body—or you can clump and spread until you look like a bundle of laundry. You can do dynamic, deep breathing and tensing and relaxing. You can diet. Also, practice being appreciative and gracious (though she is really one of the world's most gracious people). Your heart will have a chance. You'll shed several years in appearance and well-being. Darling, it's good, good, *good.*"

She replied, "You remind me of the story of the old lady who always had a good word for everybody. Once when she was defending a wrongdoer in her usual valiant fashion, her hearer was vexed and said, 'Oh, you'd have something good to say about the devil.' 'Well,' the old lady replied, 'I don't know anyone who attends to his own business so well.' "

The fact is that my friend benefited in a number of ways from her enforced immobility. It is now six or seven years since she broke her leg and, as far as I know, her heart is still behaving itself, and she looks prettier than ever! She could have let her accident give her a sour expression and simply added a calamity item to her thinking and conversation. But she avoided all that, and made of it an asset.

There are many stories I could tell you of the dramatic benefits of calling everything "good," no matter what. It is on our problems, often, that we whet the sharpness of life's advances in many ways. I include this point here because I want you to resolve that you are going to have a fruitful, satisfactory life based on your inner *decision,* no matter what outward conditions are presented to you. You will use no excuses, whatever. Like a real thoroughbred, you will shoulder your blames yourself! And deal with them!

Though you will learn many techniques as you proceed, you are now ready to focus on your higher moves to accomplishment within and without.

Check Over Your Achievements in Your Personal Life

Ask yourself these questions:

1. Do I have good health? Do I take good care of my body?
2. Do I have a loving family? Or a reasonable facsimile?
3. Do I have good friends? How many people really wish me well?
4. Am I well-adjusted emotionally? In what areas am I immature?
5. Am I a respected member of my community? Do I work for the civic good?
6. What have I achieved in my career? Could I get another job if I should leave my present one? Do I have good prospects for the future?
7. Am I in the right career? Do I enjoy my work?
8. Do I get along with co-workers? With my employers? Those under me?
9. Am I satisfied with my income? Is there anything I can do about it?
10. Would I like to travel more?

Where Do You Stand as a Homemaker?

Ask yourself:

1. Have I achieved a happy home—with or without a husband or wife?
2. Have I helped the members of my household to better self-expression?
3. Have I created an atmosphere of peace, harmony, and growth for my family and myself?
4. Are my children healthy in body and mind? Can I help them more?
5. Am I satisfied with my role in life? In what ways can I inspirit it?
6. Am I a good organizer? Do I achieve cooperation?

What Do You Want Personally?

Ask yourself:

1. Do I want to increase my income—by 25%, 50%, 100%—in the next five years?
2. Do I want to change to another job? Somewhere else? Where I am?

3. Do I want to go into business for myself? Have I the capacity for it?
4. Do I want a new house? A new apartment?
5. Do I want a large family?
6. Do I want more friends? More community activities?
7. Do I want more interesting pastimes? More companionship?
8. Do I want more education? Should I not always be studying something?

Make a check-list and be specific in your answers. Do not say, "I don't know. I'm not sure." Give your directions a clear outline—even though you may change them later. Be sure you date your objectives—for a few weeks, months, or years from now, you will want to compare your plans and your attainments to see how you have progressed.

Aim High

Remember, there is always room at the top. As you rise in awareness, you draw to yourself the forces that support and aid you. Remember that the higher you go, the easier your path is. And probably the strongest rung on the ladder is the one of service to others. People who merely seek their own advantage at every turn have very hard won gains—and these they must guard in constant and often ugly ways. Whereas, if you have gone out of your way to bring advantage to others, rolled their logs, found the right people for them, smoothed their path, you have the strength of their gratitude behind you—and even lacking that, you have invoked the laws of enrichment by your very contributions of caring beyond yourself.

In my own life, I have met a little ingratitude, some envy, and so forth, but I must also testify to the fact that most of my pleasure and profit comes from those people and institutions that I have befriended without hope of reward.

Set your sights high—but extend love and friendship wherever possible.

•4•

The One Essential Key to Harnessing Your Mind-Power

REPEAT TO YOURSELF THAT YOU MUST TAKE UP your authoritative position in your use of Mind—or remain in, or revert to, the mass-decisions of the vegetable-animal consciousness.

To support you in assuming your *human* role of decider and controller, you must keep before you the evidence you can gather through personal success with it. There is much more of it than you may realize.

If you did not make thousands of decisions each day, you would be inactive indeed. There are some thinkers(?) who would have us believe that all our so-called independent thought is simply the end result of foregoing compulsions which we do not in the least control as individuals. Of course, we are the result of all that has gone before, but to subscribe to the theory that it has all been mechanistic and predetermined, nullifies the role of education, or indeed, any kind of effort, even life itself.

Despair is born of this dull acceptance of futility, which often stems from simply a bad liver, or an ego-shattering failure with love or finance. We are indeed the most vulnerable of beings—for which we should be thankful. Without a high degree of sensibility and sensitivity, we would not now be ready to realize our potential sovereignty.

The key, then, is to draw sustenance from every source. Let every experience be grist for your mill. Prove your way. Be watchful, and see how you may bend many moments to your ends (if they be worthy) by a clear concept of finally good effects. Do not try to protect your habitual prejudices and opinions.

KEEP ALL DOORS OPEN

Expose your mind to new ideas. You need not agree with them. If they do not fit into your higher level of thinking, they will simply flow away. One of the great laws you may use is that of how *matters and things that belong together will flow together, if you let them.*

You do not need the many stiff, ugly resistances that you, in the past, may have considered "protective." If you make your own psyche a healthy, vital one, the untoward, the unfitting, will not find lodging within it.

A small but telling story comes to mind. At the Huntington Hotel in Pasadena, California, there used to be a huge, beautiful area to the left of the business desks, covered by a large, lovely, oriental rug. Every afternoon the resident hostess would preside at a well-appointed tea table, at the far end of the room where the guests could come for a time of pleasantry, relaxation, and a cup of sociable tea. There was no charge.

When I was discussing this with the owner, I said, "But, aren't you imposed upon in this matter? Don't people who don't belong here take advantage of this situation and gather here for tea?"

He smiled and replied, "Do you see the edge of that rug? Well, there seems to be an invisible barrier at that point. People who don't belong here do sometimes decide to bring a friend or so, and start to cross that floor to the tea table. Before they have taken half a dozen steps, their brashness begins to crumble. They hesitate, then stop. Then, they suddenly think of an excuse to turn and escape. I have watched this so many times that it has become a kind of interesting puzzle to me, one I mean to unravel when I get the time."

The fitness of things is one of the great laws of happiness, harmony, and success in all areas! The older I get, the more I depend upon this law of natural attraction; the less I seek to defend myself or my position. There is a wonderful release, a fine sense of freedom, in eliminating another type of strain. To be sure, nothing is 100 per cent perfect, and a few untoward things drift to me, but they are very few, and constantly becoming fewer. I have learned not to be unduly upset when something disagreeable or unfitting does get through to me.

Let Your Mind Take in Everything

Don't put a fence around your mind. Give it free rein to soak up many new and different thoughts. This is one of the splendid aspects of your mind. There is no chance of overburdening it, unless you have built up a false drama of this kind. Overcrowding Mind simply cannot happen. You will probably sift through much that is worthless, but you may also catch a gem of a great idea hidden in some seemingly insignificant matter.

Listen to everybody. Let every person who touches your life teach you something. Mentally brush aside people's faults and search, instead, for worthiness. They, too, have come a long way and have fascinating values for you, if you will relax your notions of self-interest, laziness, and hurry—and listen.

A friend of mine who is vital, sparkling, and always seems to know what is going on, once said to me, "I talk to everybody. I always engage a taxi-driver in conversation. They know all about politics. My husband wonders how I can always predict an election—and he won't believe me when I say I get much that I know from these taxi drivers!" Another friend, a teacher of political science in a Los Angeles high school, smiled when I told him about this and said, "I drive a cab at night. Perhaps she has been listening to me!"

So, in even casual encounters with other human beings give and take ideas. You will be astonished at the amount of sound thinking going on in our world—in surprising places. You will be astonished by the growing wisdom of many young people and by the sweetness of most of the oldsters.

You will learn much about humanity by talking with so-called "ordinary" people. You will learn that their minds are much more advanced than you had, perhaps, thought. You will learn that their taste in music is extraordinarily good. You will find amateur botanists, spouters of poetry, travelers from afar, people living with their memories, others convinced they can lead the world to salvation. But oddly enough, all of them are contributing something fine to the reaching, burgeoning, collective soul of our world. People are wonderful! There is not one of them who is not a valuable human being.

Open your mind—and learn to choose without condemnation of the rest all that is worthwhile. Let the other parts of your impressions flow on through your relaxed, receptive mind. It is as though you were mining. You would waste no time criticizing or condemning the ore that contained the precious metal for which you are searching. You wouldn't let disgust or hate clutter up your mind. You would simply ignore it, and focus on the values you found.

If your mind is either closed or too filled with the symbols and cant of the groups with which you identify yourself, you limit your ability to draw on universal power, Mind. It is good to select certain groups for which you may qualify and in which you may move—but be sure you do not allow *their* limitations to stultify your larger significance as a guest of the universal god on this large planet. You are here to *grow.*

One must decide on an attitude toward the entirety of humanity in order to place oneself in the deep and rich flow of universal substance from the very heart of *being.* A person must open up to a larger scope if he is to embody largeness in his life. Mind is an all-embracing principle that no person or group owns. It is open to all.

The movement of the power of Mind is an outward one that has no limits. So send your mind soaring. Do not think and live in a narrow, insular way. Your life and the pleasure and profit it brings you will be exactly the same size as that of your view of the universe!

The Human Family

Now we begin to understand that our own advance cannot be secure unless we share our advantages with all mankind and regard everyone on this earth as our human family.

Fritz Kreisler was a sublime example of a *human* being who

understood his responsibility to the whole. He never owned a home. For he said he did not want one as long as any other human creature was homeless. He was passionately devoted to his favorite charity, the Salvation Army, because he was convinced that group did more direct good than any other. Periodically, he gave a great benefit at the Metropolitan Opera House in New York at which he raised hundreds of thousands of dollars for the "Army" in admissions and donations.

Here we see how his intense humanity grew exactly beside his genius. And it is so with all great, truly successful people—their hearts are in consonance with their clear vision of man's potential dignity and importance. One remembers that the first Commandment after the recognition of God, is "Thou shalt love thy neighbour as thyself."

It is important to know that any urging to make you loving, peaceful, and harmonious is not to make you good, but to make you wise, healthy, and prosperous. The profit that is stolen from (or tricked from) others will never bring health and a happy train of events. True, there are gangsters, dictators, and an occasional business tycoon who seem to refute that statement—but they are exceptions and not the rule, and usually their end is disastrous. *We will do well to build our personalities, our persons, and our lives into the fabric of upward reaching life* if we want peace of body, mind, and affairs. And then even the holders of brute power will respect us and seek us for their profit!

Gather the Light and the Energies of This New Day

"Let your light so shine," says the Bible. That doesn't mean in any smug, goody-goody sense. It means ally yourself with the forces that bring light to every soul.

Just recently, on a street in Los Angeles, two men had engaged in a battle of angry words and blows. I instinctively got between them and just kept saying, 'Gentlemen, gentlemen! Come on, bring peace to the world!" They separated. I cannot honestly say they parted in love—but they did part, and went their separate ways. A voice had called them "gentlemen." I hope it rings in their memories forever.

Some years ago in New York I was on a bus when a man, obviously befuddled by drugs or drink or both, provoked the anger of two well-dressed girls. In a muttering fashion he kept on insulting and abusing the girls for no reason. Finally, one of them sprang at him and grasped him by the coat front and shouted her demand that he stop. The scene promised to be a very ugly one.

I rose, and touching the girl gently, I said, "Why don't you just ignore the man? He is scarcely responsible. It is beneath you." In her rage she shook off my hand and turned to me with, "Don't you try to sweet-talk me! I know my rights."

I said, "Yes, my dear, you know your rights—but do you know your privileges? You have the privilege of being a lady."

Her companion joined me in the argument. The angry one continued to sputter, but she gradually ran down and sat down. At the next stop several men surrounded the man who was annoying the girls, and wafted him off the bus.

When I got off, I caught the angry girl's eye, smiled and made that sign with thumb and forefinger that means, "Fine, perfect!" She smiled and waved a little.

What does it solve to ignore discord? It may not solve anything, but it certainly does not add to the world's difficulties—and it does add to one's self-discipline. It is another small step upward. It is a little more light on the path of everyone involved, even the passing spectators.

When we do not waste time and energy on anger and lower themes we have a clearer path for pleasure and progress. We can then put our focus on the real issues. Is it not true that a clever lawyer, examining a witness in court, tries to confuse and anger the witness? He knows that an angry person is likely to do and say unbecoming things that will militate against him with the jury. He also knows that anger impairs the memory, and affects the voice detrimentally.

Anger is probably the most persistent of our animal reflexes.

Watch any species of reptiles, four-footed animals, fish, or birds and you will soon see a display of irritation and swift anger, especially in the protection of the creature's very special rights, such as his accustomed place, mate, or food. Even in the lower animals, ego is often the root of quick anger. *For man to continue expressing this archaic, jungle reaction is retrogressive in the extreme.*

Don't Let Your Capacities Wither

It is assumed by many scientists that man once had a tail. It is said that we shed this appendage (if we ever had it) ages ago because we have no further use for it. Certain glands in the body are said to be larger (sometimes smaller) than formerly because they are more or less needed than in ancient times. Man is slowly shedding the fur that used to be heavier on his body because he now wears clothes. It has been suggested that if people do not walk more they will gradually lose the use of their legs.

You may recall in H. G. Wells's book, *The War of The Worlds,* the earth is invaded by Martians who are only brains—soft oyster-like creatures living in metal saucers with legs and many-fingered metal feelers run by machinery inside the contraption. The implication is that the Martians had lived so long using only their minds that the metal-legged saucer was the result. All of these creatures were born in the mind of H. G. Wells. Nevertheless, he was a great student of anthropology and history of all sorts. He "imagined" these Martians from the knowledge he had as something not only possible but probable.

In any case, we should, with forethought born of known laws of physical changes, train ourselves in the best uses of our capacities, lest we lose them! An unused muscle will disappear eventually. An unused talent will vanish. A pattern of reaction repeated billions of times will strengthen and perpetuate itself. All follow the same law. Energy and substance tend toward activity. Inaction is death.

That part of us which we constantly use will develop. By this token it becomes important to select those characteristics we wish to perpetuate and exercise them all we possibly can. It is equally important to discard those we no longer need. And it is even more important to loosen the grip of ancient habits that are detrimental to us in our modern life—habits which blunt our progress.

Move Forward

Throw the light of knowledge of past, present, and future upon yourself. See yourself as a creature in movement, however slow, and move toward that which is higher, more agreeable, healthier, more conducive to longevity.

Aligning yourself with the forward forces of life draws into your periphery of action those salutary results that are called "fortunate." There are more reasons for this expectancy of good. Holding to a decision of betterment can be likened to carving a groove in which your concept of fine choices moves out from you and through which returning good flows to you. In the pulsing movement of life that which is sent out can be likened to a seed that is planted. Life moves through the seed with the drama of fulfillment and the harvest is the result. The harvest is the return flow of the planted "expectancy"—the seed. It can also be likened to an investment which is profitable and pays back a large return.

Since you draw that which you send out (which is exactly like your bases of acceptance within yourself) you can recognize the fact that you thus have the power to attract the good you desire. Your choices (man's) down through the eons of human development have you locked in the patterns of the animal past *until* you look up—"look unto the hills (higher vision) from which cometh your help."

By continually demanding, expecting, planning for, and articulating only that which is good, the old needs, fears, defenses, treachery and their accompanying tragic ends are displaced. You will have burst the bonds of that old squirrel cage of man's defeat and come out into the bright light of man's next step in self-awareness.

The Brighter Your Light, the Farther It Will Shine

Compassion, pity, and the desire to help will speed our world into a swifter evolution out of the "pain route." Does *your* light shine across a room to a timid newcomer? Do you ever have the time or the impulse to take an aging or ill person home with his or her packages? When you're calling on a friend in a hospital, do you ever take a moment or two to speak to some other patient who is frightened and lonely?

If your answer is "no" to these questions and a hundred like them, then, I must say it, *you're only half alive!* If your light is a bright one, it is *meant* to shine in many dark places. If it isn't bright—why isn't it? If you just beam it on your own affairs, your own family or immediate circle, it is bound to grow dimmer.

Each of us can heal vast amounts of the world's hurt. Civilization depends on its "fortunate" ones, the knowing ones, to brighten and lift the others. How greatly they bless you! Not just a beggar's mouthed blessing, but the sort that comes from the heart that is so grateful for attention and help. People in their own struggles are often as moved by your caring as they are by your gifts. And who can say with certainty that the gratitude of these people doesn't have protective strength as it reaches you?

I am convinced that gratitude has a magic all its own.

When the light of loving gratitude returns to you, don't forget that it can shine into *your* dark places. And who is completely without them? None of us has, as yet, found perfection. The ancient civilization of China developed the interesting custom of putting in the center of a beautiful garden a gnarled and twisted old bough, a stump, or a broken piece of statuary or jar. Thus, the carefully arranged beauty of the blossoms and the plants was thrown into sharp contrast with imperfection. *Also, there was a deep, philosophic point, too.* Perfection must accept the broken to show that pity and understanding of frailties are not lost in all the excellence. Yet—and here is still the finer point—perfection must accept the perfection that once existed in the broken thing. And it is to this delicate appreciation that the true Oriental pays his respect. How civilized!

Is it not this understanding of values, no longer apparent to the eye, that supports our compassion for the wrongdoer; prompts us to steady the weak; and gives us such great respect for the doctor who works to cure disease? Is not this the basis of the respect and good manners we give to our aged and to the female, not only as the bearer of life, but as the weaker vessel? Hold an infant in your arms, and feel the joy of its promise!

These are some of the points that make us know how far we have come. When we are too shocked by our lack of development in some areas, we can take comfort in these delicate themes that prove we are slowly moving away from the jungle.

Let me suggest that you give more time to these tenderer themes. The pleasure of investing yourself in other lives will become the nucleus of a greater joy that will be yours. It could not be otherwise.

Then, if and when sorrow and loss come to you, they are mitigated, softened—and you are miraculously comforted. For your entire self is already in line with the ameliorating grace from the heart of *being* that shields you in so very many ways. One may not escape *all* the untoward things of life, but one can have miraculous protection from most of them—and from the harshness of the ones that seem unavoidable. Somehow you are shielded!

·5·

How to Create an Atmosphere in Which Mind-Power Will Flourish

THERE MAY BE TIMES WHEN YOU WILL HAVE TO pursue your path alone. And you must be equal to it. You will be able to go ahead more swiftly and more comfortably if you are in a sympathetic environment. It will help to have the cooperation of those immediately around you.

START WITH YOUR FAMILY

If you have a family, it would be generally beneficial if you all worked together on pulling ahead of the vegetable-animal reactions and toward the human and divine expressions. You can give children an inspiring memory of parents who thought they had vast possibilities and invited them on some experiments in that direction of their development.

Children adore a family project, especially if the basic premise is flattering to them. One should be careful not to press too hard for perfection, lest the children feel that it is all too much for them. Nevertheless, all civilized reactions should be noted and rewarded in some way. Sooner or later one of them will say, "I don't expect anything for this. I'm doing it because I like to do it." And you may be surprised to find some of their responses an inspiration to you.

There will also be jokes, fumbles, and much comedy to enjoy

unless a sense of competition and/or self-consciousness develops. I remember one mother saying to a lazy, teenage son, "Don't expect your little brother and sister to wait on you all the time. You are getting too selfish. It would develop your soul if you got up and did for others." To which the lazy one replied, "Well, just see all the good I'm doing, letting them develop their souls at my expense."

Good Manners Can Be Construed as a Step Away from the Jungle

The disciplines of seating the ladies, wearing a jacket to the table and making pleasant talk, tactfully veering away from anything embarrassingly personal or critical are all good training for life. On the other hand, each member of the family might be required to face criticism from the others—learn to "take it" as it were—in good spirits. These disciplines would call for a reward. The reward system might drive home the law that nature's return to us is extremely generous. In fact, obeying her laws is a direct way to great profit. I see nothing wrong with rewards, if they are handled intelligently and if the whole matter doesn't degenerate into a kind of grab bag theory.

But one must crawl before one walks—and all tries are good ones, regardless of the outcome. They are steps on the stairs of progress in awareness. Properly handled, a family project of constructive criticism could be the perfect cure for self-consciousness for the members of all ages. If someone's ego gets too much of a bruising, then set that one up as monitor for a couple of weeks, where he, himself, is immune to comment and criticism. After a rest of that period, plus some responsibility, anyone will be ready for further action in the game.

Watching children striving to get their "human" feet under them should give you all the faith and courage you will ever need. The blessing to them—and to you—will live always. And don't get discouraged if there is much backsliding. Rome wasn't built in a day. And after several million years of human effort, you can spare a few more days! Patience, love, compassion; these will flourish.

Seek a close relationship with your wife (husband) and watch family solidarity bloom! Now you are seeking to be the creator of the atmosphere you need to gain more control of your mind-power. For no matter how many scientific tomes you may read by professors, who have many letters after their names, you still must bow before those disciplines which will bring your personal controls into focus. And you need all the help you can get.

Free Your Mind from Usual Bickerings

Try to make your home a place where the short-circuit of petty quarrels does not drain away your mind-power. A certain amount of opposition here and there is something against which you can whet your diplomacy, practice your charm, and learn some healthful truths. But see to it that this emotional gymnasium of home life does not take on a tinge of tension and ugliness.

It is your responsibility to keep all discussions on a polite and amusing keel and the laughter must not be at someone else's expense. Use laughter as a flag flying over the attractive home. Laughter is like the gong that calls us back to our seats in a theatre to enjoy the next act. But let it carry the overtones of sheer good humor, rather than the drop of lemon of sharp satire. Some satire is clever and acceptable, but when it is clumsy—and it usually is—it does too much hurt, even though the person who is the butt of it may smile valiantly.

Cut jokes out of papers and magazines. Send them to friends, hand them to members of the family or—better yet—ask your wife, husband, guest, or a child to read them at the table. Create the atmosphere of pleasure and laughter at your dinner table. The matter of eating should suggest that we need other types of nourishment as well. The table is a good place to give and get it. Approval; compliment; notice of a job well done; comment on an attractive appearance, a delicious flavor, some good news—all make excellent table talk. Never discuss bad news or indulge in criticism at the table. The immediate effect on digestion is deadly. The effect on your whole life is to lower its tone broadly and subtly.

In trying to correct a habit of bickering, be sure to take your full share of responsibility for it. Go out of your way to soothe, smooth and change *patiently* the atmosphere of petty, habitual resistance into an agreeable one. It takes some doing, but it will be the most profitable triumph of your life. It will give you a sense of inner success, a feeling of power on which your ego can feed. Who can feel triumphant in an atmosphere of quarreling?

FIND FRIENDS WITH A GOOD, HEALTHY OUTLOOK ON LIFE

It is not helpful to be around people who insist on long recitals of the tragedies of their lives *unless* you feel that you are strong enough to help them. Resisting them and criticizing them are not good for you. While you are trapped, listening to a long tale of woe, it will pay you to put your thoughts on some attractive aspect of the person before you. It is quite possible that the narrator has been telling this same story for years, forever seeking a listener. As soon as possible ask this person about some talent, some fine experience, perhaps a trip that was taken, and try to get the subject changed. Be as persistent as the other person and you will win—for in the end the agreeable is far more powerful than the disagreeable.

Naturally, *you* will not go about the world reciting woes, either audibly or silently, for you are too intelligent to key your life to debacle, inaccuracy, or hurts. Even the best doctors and nurses are those who, besides their actual skills with the human body, know also how to plant the seeds of powerful resurgence of hope and strength in the mind. They are recognizing more and more the interplay of mind and matter. I have heard a number of doctors say, "The patient who recovers fastest is the one who *expects* to get well."

Turn your gloomy friends into bright ones, if you have the time and patience. But is this *realistic?* Shouldn't we be very upset about the wrongs of the world? No! You should be very upset about doing all you can to help the world, but it is not helpful to go about wringing your hands and clucking your tongue, unless you mean to contribute something toward the solution of the woes you deplore.

The mental atmosphere, in which you live, not only keys your life up or down, but also helps or hinders the entirety. You should be vigilant about the type of matters you register habitually.

And here is an important point. You must find a way to meet the problem of other people's negativity. The best way is to develop so much strength, yourself, that your very presence lifts and brightens every atmosphere you meet. All of us know one or several people who are a delight to meet. When you see such a person coming you know that you are going to be stimulated, interested, pleased, and amused. It is very profitable in many ways to be this type of person and to seek this kind of company.

Keep Your Relations with Others Harmonious

Most quarrels begin because someone denies us our share of ego-nourishment. Each of us forgets that every other person is just as hungry for self- and other approval as we could possibly be. The sharp retort is a refusal to be understanding and generous.

Ill-nature (quarreling) is the most strongly animalistic habit that man has brought with him from the jungle. We must clean up these leftover attributes before we can emerge into a place where we can lay hold of our full human advantages. I know a number of people, who are talented, hard-working, self-sacrificing, and religious, whose lives are a series of shambles *because they are trying to lead advanced lives with some of the drawbacks of the animal past* (quick temper, largely). Time after time, I have seen their careers burgeon and then sink. There was a hole in the armor. In building a salutary atmosphere, in which to grow toward human mind supremacy, we must shed these quick irritations.

One may not bring an animal to share the power of the gods! We must evolve out of our animal past in every possible way before we *earn* higher power and the knowledge of how to use it.

KEEP YOUR MIND MOBILE, RESPONSIVE

I'm sure we have mental and spiritual "muscles" that, on their own planes, are the counterpart of physical muscles. They require exercise to be kept functioning easily, quickly, and well. Just as you are wise to keep your physical reflexes swift and alert, it is more than rewarding to keep your mental responses well trained.

For instance, when you hear of some untoward thing, such as an accident, have you trained your mind to think immediately of helpfulness or do you mull over the horror of it? The human race has for thousands of years trained itself in the latter! That is one of its stumbling blocks. You are privileged to step up and away from this barbaric practice.

Unless you are actively doing something about a situation, such as an accident, draw to one side and pray. Pour the mental conviction of the matter's being righted, as far as possible, into the scene. Mentally comfort those who are hurt or distraught. The effect of your orderly and helpful thinking is often instantly effective. It is bound to help somewhere along the line. And it helps *you* to bring orderly thoughts into chaos.

Let Your Mind Soar

Many people are turning their minds toward their mental possibilities. Some of them are shy about admitting it, but will disclose that they read science-fiction "all the time." They switched from old-fashioned murder mysteries.

They turn quite casually to a conversation about a man's *willing* himself to leave New York and be in London in an hour. They've read about him—and sure enough (in the story) there the man is in London in exactly one hour, able to cope with the drama afoot there, and winning all before him!

And without batting an eye they will relate that he had to pass through two sets of locked doors to get where he was going. But to him it was very simple. The man in question was an ordinary man—that is, a regular human being—who had applied himself to learning how to transport his body through space and through any barrier.

The interesting part to me is that neither the reader, nor the man in the story, saw anything too extraordinary about it. There was no religious involvement. There was no trickery. The man in the story simply *knew how* to do it. He had know-how, not magic. He used laws of magnetic calculation, understood the required rate of vibration to sustain any of his moves, etc.

Even if all this is the sheerest fabrication today—it presages an eventuality that will assuredly come to pass. For "what man can think, man can do."

Today such things make interesting talk around the fire, when the logs burn low and inhibitions thin out. One can always stop and smile anyway—a great defense when one's common sense (for which Einstein had not the slightest respect) wants to assert itself.

I wonder what people around what tribal fires, long ago, talked of flying through the air like a great bird. The weaver of such tales, perhaps with a lyre's accompaniment, held old and young fascinated. They tried not to believe the words of his song, but somewhere down inside they *knew,* just the same, that some day man would fly. They didn't know *how.* They just knew he would. Their minds told them so.

Today, we have much better reasons for believing that man will one day go where he pleases *without* an airplane. We are not yet prepared to explain it in its entirety, but down inside we *know* it is so.

As our knowledge of new forces continues to grow, we will discover that power must be directed by intelligence in every field. And the day the idea dawns in some man's creative brain that intelligence *is power,* we will be on our way to a whole series of wonders.

It is in the area of our personal lives that we receive the most immediate benefit from the lifted use of our minds. This is true in all the ways of our going, our small and large conveniences, the working out of our efforts, our thoughts and feelings, our wish to excel, acquire, create. These are the matters over which we can exert control, gain strength, and extend our influence. It is here that we stand or fall as successful human beings; as happy people.

My own astonishment grows as I see the working out for good of most of the matters upon which I have tried to shed a higher thinking. When I have met them on their own plane of discord, I have sustained bruises of one kind or another. But when I have refused the discord and kept my thinking to the harmonious core of possibilities; have forced my thoughts upward—most of the time the matter has resolved itself at least comfortably, often splendidly. There is a certain percentage of what the British call near-misses, but I have learned to dismiss the near-misses quickly, giving them as little importance as possible.

YOU CAN SET THE TONE OF YOUR LIFE

The Bible says very plainly, "Prepare the vessel—and the spirit will descend." This is to say that when we come prepared with appropriate controls, facility in self-management, unselfish ideals, we may enter the realm of our divine potentials. *When* are we going to do something about it?

Apparently the universe, having functioned for eons of time, is in no hurry. Obviously it is up to man to promote himself by qualifying. We are certainly not going to be allowed to pass into the next grade until we know the lessons of the one we may be in.

You are the creator of the atmosphere, the tone, of your life. Take the responsibility. Clean up the old, outworn, unprofitable dams and fetters that bind you to a lower level of being.

Bring matters of interest into your daily living. Study. Take courses that inspire you and stretch your mind. Enjoy hikes and such sports as are available to you. Read, write, express yourself in every way. Learn public speaking, dancing, plumbing, gardening. Study foreign trade. Learn a language. Get into the atmosphere of important things—and high, personal skills. Attend lectures. Listen to famous men and women. Keep up with your local and national governments. Keep in touch with your mayor, your senator, your representative.

Cultivate an atmosphere of caring about your world. But don't grumble and stew about it. Don't believe those who say the world is worse. It isn't. It's better, much better. And you are going to make it better still. You are going to help yourself *and* humanity upward into another groove of action and realization where higher mind-power will bring more freedom and joy, more accomplishment through creativity.

·6·

A Simple Way to Make Better Use of Your Mind-Power

YOU NEED EXTRA TIME TO DISCIPLINE AND ORDER your thinking. In a sense, to step ahead in awareness of your possibilities is to be "born again" into the new world. You must arrange your days so as to have the time for meditating and for orienting yourself.

Start from where you are and move into the glories ahead! Add fifteen minutes to your present active day. Either get up fifteen minutes earlier in the morning or go to bed fifteen minutes later at night. Or you might cut fifteen minutes off your lunch hour. Or, take time right after lunch, depending on your day. *Then use that time for stretching your potential.*

EXPAND YOUR POWERS

When John Glenn was orbiting the earth for the third time, a commentator said that the only limits of man's future are defined by his imagination—or lack of it. Certain words fire the imagination: extended . . . vast . . . more . . . glorious . . . infinity. These are the words that will lead you into your own new powers. Think of these words and others like them. Write them down and add to them every day. Write a list of words on the left side of a sheet of paper, and on the other side write words that the list on the left brings to your mind, as follows:

Extended	Growing
More	Additional
Vast	Spacious
Glorious	God-like
Endless	Infinity

As your mind opens, so will your life. You must channel this insurging, energetic concept of growth and extension. *Make actual use of it* in some project that *adds* to your skills in some way. You will be astonished that very soon you will be expressing and receiving *more* in a number of ways.

Make a channel for extended action as well as concept. Do *something* that moves you even an inch toward some desired objective. Read two or three pages of a book on your subject or subjects; or a book you thought you did not have time to read. Take up a hobby, such as music, sculpture, painting, photography, or a language. Write to an old friend. Do some charity work. Call on a neighbor with the idea of giving him some value, such as appreciation or encouragement. All these are excellent investment thoughts. You will be investing in your own spiritual growth while you benefit someone else.

Learn to Separate "Investment" Thoughts from Profitless Ones

Waste no time on thoughts that add nothing to you or to somebody else. Reject, or turn from, thoughts that tear down anything or anybody, for, in the end, they will tear you down. How could it be otherwise? If you are entertaining certain ideas, though you may think they are *for* somebody else, they are *inside you.* Whatever is inside you is coloring every aspect of *you.* Your body, your affairs, your happiness, success, and beauty of self or surroundings are definitely influenced by *all* the ideas that you allow to lodge in your brain. We should be careful of our thoughts of others. The Orientals state it, "The outer world, of which you are aware, is but an extension of *yourself.*"

You have access to endless mind-power. Why insult it with petty use of it! Think largely, grandly! Do not think that speeds of 17,000 miles an hour are just for the astronauts. Remember that they are but blazing trails that you and I will follow shortly. We will go even faster than that!

Learn to switch your mind to constructive thinking quickly. Test yourself. See if you cannot shorten the time it takes you to calm a growing resentment; to forgive; to evaporate rising anger; to maintain a balance of feeling.

Soon it will be considered archaic to remember grudges; to hold onto ignoble thoughts. It never was sensible, but now it is becoming completely out of tune with the swiftness that is demanded of us in our new environment. We must learn to dissolve ill feeling in split seconds!

The Uses of New Knowledge and New Power Put Man in New Conditions

We must change, adjust, expand, and discard old, useless, harmful ways. The more quickly we adjust to the new conditions, demands and challenges, the sooner we will emerge into a higher state.

The opening of man's mind toward new physical horizons will open it also to his own inner possibilities. The scientist is today more willing than the layman to admit that man has untold, undiscovered potentials.

A fascinating area of awareness lies in the fact that in speeding around our globe in a little over one hour, one passes through a series of days! Some of them are tomorrows *not yet come into being at the starting point* and from this nonexistent day, one speeds back into the measured time! Flying East at such terriffic speeds, one reaches a day that has not yet come to the West. One flies out of it in circling the globe and passes back in to the day that comes before it.

Unless one becomes accustomed to thinking in these terms, he will find it hard to orient himself in his new world. Such thinking opens up staggering calculations. Time and space take on new meanings. One can conceive that, eventually, speeds will be so great that one will simply *be* where he wishes to be and will scarcely be aware of the process of going there. One's choice or decision to do or be or go somewhere, or to have some particular thing or experience, will seem to bring it instantly to pass.

Man must recognize his potential power and seek to grow into its use. He should remind himself that his future progress will be much swifter than his advancements in the past, for he is now moving *consciously.*

Look at Yourself Now and See a Person Who Is Due to Unfold Greatly

It will not be too long before *you* will be darting about the world and arriving wherever you want to be in a matter of minutes! You will heat your house and swimming pool with cosmic rays, and light your house and cook with them.

You will run your automobile and your private helicopter with atomic power in a tiny, ornamental tube about the size of a lipstick. You will have conquered most of your body's weaknesses and diseases. And your swiftly moving world will put new demands on your personality. It will demand new mental patterns and new physical and mental reflexes.

Speed demands consideration and courtesy. Selfishness and immoral getting for oneself has always brought destruction, but the law moved in our older, slow world so gradually that we doubted the process. Speed brings the facts sharply into focus. Good manners will become universal because they are intensely practical.

Civilized attitudes will permit the spirit of man to flower. There will be no time for the stumbling, fumbling, spilling, sprawling awkwardness of poor manners or out-dated, ill-timed selfishness. Laws will be respected, for they will spell life or death quickly. Beauty of living, thinking and being will be the order of the times.

Survival will demand that you make excellent choices and make them quickly. You will train yourself to do so. You will develop techniques of disposing of unwanted mental material. You will acquire skills in using your mind to *good* effect.

WOULD YOU INCREASE YOUR PLEASURE IN LIVING? THEN BECOME AN ARTIST IN IT!

Will conscious advance make you artificial? No indeed! Does it spoil the color green for you to know that it is made of blue and yellow? Does it spoil music for you to know that it is composed of exactly counted measures and that that is the name of them! Does it spoil an exotic, delicious dish of curried turkey or lamb when you know the recipe for it? Or when you know the enticing condiments that should go with it?

On the contrary, the more you know of the ways that must be traveled to arrive at a splendid achievement of any kind, the more pleasure it gives you. At a concert look about you for the people who have brought the score with them and watch their faces as they follow it page by page. Rapt, enchanted, sensitized to every note of bass or strings or woodwinds, or percussion, the symphony comes alive for them! No bliss exceeds ours whenever we can identify the intenseness of our own knowledge and appreciation with some great theme in any branch of art.

We are not born knowing any of these things. We are born with *potentials.* It is up to us to educate, train, refine, direct, discipline, coordinate our forces, our awareness, our confidence, and our skills. For these are the tools of bringing higher and higher victories to human experience on this planet. If we do not train ourselves and our children we are doing both a sorrowful disservice! We are putting off the time when they and we will rise more surely out of the "pain-route" of slow animal evolution.

This thing of being natural can be a trap that turns into a vise (also a vice) when we fall into it or permit our children to do so. As I wrote in my very first book, *Charm,* many years ago, "Being natural is whatever is easiest to us through habit." See that it becomes natural for you to be poised, healthy, happy, successful in serving the world and your own immediate circle.

See that it becomes natural for you to think extremely quickly; to speed up your reactions several hundred per cent. Settle on certain salutary patterns of reaction and imbed them in your consciousness.

Trade Some of Your Old Reactions in for New Ones

Completely eliminate from your life:

1. Jealousy—for it is born of lack of self-confidence.
2. Irritability—for it ties you to your animal past.
3. Self-seeking—for the self is better served by good manners and kindness.

These three detriments are very much like the ropes that tie a balloon to the ground. Cut them and you will soar up to a place where you will see larger vistas, more distant horizons.

I can almost feel your thinking that some people with all these faults and more (especially the self-seeking), are great big successes. Yes, some of them flourish as the green bay tree, mentioned in the Bible. But there comes a time when the accumulated errors bring disaster to the entire structure built by selfishness. When one is in harmony with mind-power and its way of working, there is no need of selfishness. Too much self sometimes shorts one's wires to any sort of power.

The fifteen minutes set apart for self-training will yield wonderful results. Do not think it is too short a time to matter. One has to start somewhere. As you achieve satisfying victories over old, weakening, limiting habits, the joy you will feel will richly repay you for the necessary effort. And material rewards will not be far behind.

To your great delight, you will find that your mastery in other quarters manifests itself as you master those old, leftover animal reactions. Gradually, you will learn how to substitute higher mentation for the lower thoughts that continue to present themselves until they are vanquished.

It should always be borne in mind that one type of thought will objectify and materialize as well as another. The process of working *idea into matter* is always going on. You do not control the process. You do control the quality of thought that is put into the established process. Therefore, you do control the result.

•7•

Act As Though You *Are*—And You Will Be!

HUNTERS PLACE A WOODEN DUCK IN THE WATER among the rushes, to attract live ducks within range of their guns. They know that *like attracts like.* This is a law of all phases of life.

If a man owns a painting it is easier to sell him another. His familiarity with the first one creates a susceptibility toward further acquisition. In the matter of languages, people flock together who speak a common tongue. Every church spire testifies to the faith that draws together people who mutually agree on tenets of a religion. The Bible says, "To him that hath shall be given." The kernel of the truth of this law is found in every area of life.

THE GREATEST LURE TO GOOD FORTUNE IS HAVING SOME OF IT

You must create about yourself the atmosphere of being fortunate if you want to attract more good fortune. Ancient wisdom gives us two striking sayings that bear out this truth, "*Act as though I am, and I will be*" and "*As the inner, so the outer.*"

During the stock market crash of '29, a certain rich man lost all he had—everything. This man came to me wringing his hands, saying his life was over, and that he intended to kill himself as his two partners had done. I had difficulty dissuading him. His despair was pitiful.

I kept up a stream of encouraging talk. He was incapable of

listening, so filled with misery was his mind. But out of the torrent of my talk, finally, several words found lodging: "New beginning" . . . "value of experience" . . . "Why must everybody know that you are down and out?" . . . "Why don't you start something as though you preferred it to dealing in stocks and bonds?" . . . "Why advertise a temporary failure? Put up a brave front and go ahead." . . . "You're a clever man—you'll make good. Don't breathe a word about your losses."

This man (we will call him Charles Logan, though that is not his name) instead of getting a tenement room, took a suite at the old Ritz Hotel in New York on a year's lease. He was driving a Rolls Royce and arrived at the hotel with a chauffeur-valet, a secretary, and his handsome personal equipment.

The hotel, hard hit by the staggering losses everywhere, welcomed this man who was seemingly untouched by the crash. They bowed low in the presence of this elegant, serene patron of their best services, who was addicted to the most expensive of everything and ordered caviar by the pound.

When, after three or four months, the manager had the temerity to ask for payment, Mr. Logan replied that he had a year's lease and had taken his quarters that way because he knew that his assets would be tied up in the international banking crisis for about that length of time, but if the hotel annoyed him again with any such picayune demands, he would settle and move at once. Nothing more was said! The hotel had many empty rooms.

Mr. Logan looked around for a business opportunity. One of the big radio concerns was in the hands of a receiver. It was about to be liquidated for about two cents on the dollar. Logan's reputation as a maker of huge sales contracts helped him make a fantastic deal with the controllers of the radio manufacturing firm.

At first they were naturally suspicious, but in the end they appointed him vice-president in charge of development and sales (which means he was, under the circumstances, in complete control). The deciding factor was that while he wanted a very handsome salary, he did not wish to collect any of it until the company was making a profit. In the meanwhile, he wanted large amounts of stock, with the continuing privilege of buying it.

Logan soon had the company on a paying basis. He advertised spectacularly, frightening the other holders almost to death. He conducted the business as though it were booming skyward. Unusual publicity, contests, sales rewards, and all manner of special stimulations had the whole world thinking that this company was certainly sound and in a very fortunate position. Slowly it became so!

Occasionally, the manager of the Ritz would smile at Logan wistfully from the hotel office door. But Logan regarded him with expressionless face and went up in the elevator as though he hadn't seen anyone, his mind on more important matters. Thus things stood for more than a year, a year of activity, tension, vision, and unbelievable courage.

Meanwhile, prices were slashed to meet the lowered purchasing power of the public and more and more buyers were lured to the radio put out by Logan's company. Some of the best strokes of business went into the physical appearance of the cabinets. Logan went to Tennessee to buy special woods, imported others from South America. His products were beautiful.

Whenever he was balked by the men above him in power, he took his troubles to court and was granted further and further powers to protect the stockholders who had stood to lose everything before he came along.

His success was phenomenal. Once, I said to him privately, "Weren't you afraid to make some of your magnificent gestures and plunge into debt so far?" "No," he replied, "it takes money (or something that looks like it) to make money."

Then he scowled at me. "You're a fine one to question me so closely. You're the one who pumped me full of the courage to do this. What you said was true. And I learned something else—if what you are trying to do is good, thoroughly good and beneficial to a number of people, you have all that weight on your side.

"Sometimes, when I began to wonder if I was right, I would remember all the widows who held that losing stock and it again seemed very much worth another big bid for business. Yes, I've made a lot of money now, and I'm convinced that you can't make big money unless you are serving a lot of people."

One day Mr. Logan sent his secretary down to pay his hotel bill. The poor girl nearly fainted when she saw that the total on all the papers handed her was thirty-five thousand dollars! Many elaborate dinners for clients were listed, many cases of the finest wines, many pounds of caviar—and the amazing thing is he had never been pressed for it!

Logan's manner, his appearance, his associates, all inspired a confidence that was well justified by his vision and ability. It wasn't the first fortune he had made, but this one he kept and it grew and grew. He is a fabulously rich man today, considered very "fortunate" by everyone who knows him.

And that man had once held a revolver against his temple! But he changed his mental pattern. He refused to accept the world's estimate of the time and place of a man's defeat. He used *the appearance of good fortune* to attract more of it. He did not nibble cautiously at that idea. Once he was convinced, he went all out. There were no chinks in his armor of faith.

Logan's past experience in successful selling gave him assurance. He knew what he was doing. It is doubtful that without his successful past he could have carried that corporation to success. But faith in his own ability supported the law of "like attracts like."

WATCH WHAT YOU SAY

One's speech must be cleansed of all words unlike the desired end. Too many people are desperately working in one direction while their tongues are wagging in an opposite way. *Make your speech conform to your purpose.*

Your words are like molds that give form to flowing life. What you *say* tends to become true. Words are congealed thoughts, conviction, sharp mental patterns. For this reason they are creative. Mind moves over the formless and creates form. Words have authority. They accomplish that unto which they are sent. They initiate action.

Speak only of life in the way that you wish to accept it. Turn the light of this divine creativity into every small part of yourself and your life and see what God hath wrought. Words are the tools and the material of life's structure. *They are the forms that bespeak sanity out of chaos.*

If you were building a house of bricks, you would not stack them haphazardly and expect the building to stand and serve your ends. But people speak in careless, unlovely, destructive ways and then seem surprised that good fortune eludes them. In cruder, simpler terms, if you want to catch rainwater, you must provide a bucket!

If you were making a gelatine pudding and poured the mixture into a mold shaped like a serpent, have you a right to complain that you wanted it star-shaped? Your words carry you and your intent. Look to them!

Your thought images are also like seeds that every day sink into the productive soil of life, there to produce after their kind and return to you multiplied. So select carefully your words. *They are the nucleus of your tomorrows.* Even though this is a discipline that seems at this moment also impossible of accomplishment, know that a little practice every day will soon bring you skill and more ease. The French say it well, "*Usage rend maître.*" (Practice gives mastery—or the master.)

Wrong words are stones in your path. The right words are added power. No sensible person will work against his own best interests. Certainly profanity and curses are the worst possible use of words. In damning other things and other people, even lightly, one eventually damns himself. It could not be otherwise.

If there is no law of dependable meaning and sequence of action at work in your universe, then it is simply a large pot of alphabet soup being stirred by energy with no aim. Man must make the effort to understand the *law* operating from causation that he sets in motion toward the effect that inevitably follows. *Our Creator has honored us with access to the law of causation through the use of words. We are supposed to use them with human responsibility.*

PUT YOUR THOUGHTS IN ACTION

Take your mind off ill-luck and put it on the action you desire. And hold to this salutary pattern in the face of much evidence to the contrary.

Another friend of mine used this dictum, "Act as though I *am;* and I will be" in another way. He was a young man of a moderately rich family. He was well born, well educated, but he was miserable because he could not find his particular niche in life. The Second World War interrupted his dilemma. But several years later he was back at home, facing the same old issue again. His mother, a charming, highly sensitive woman, did her best to help her son. But it seemed impossible to get to the problem deep within him.

She and I were discussing this impasse one day, and guided by some flash of intuition I said to her, "It is possible that your son deeply desires a career he thinks you wouldn't approve of. Has he ever mentioned any interest in acting?"

"No," she replied, "he has never mentioned that. In fact, I don't recall his ever showing a preference for any type of career since he was a little boy."

"What did he think he wanted to do then?" I pressed.

"Oh, it wasn't anything he spoke of very much. But he did say several times at different ages when we would be traveling in Europe, 'Wouldn't it be nice to find just one restaurant that is run the way the patrons would like?' It amused me, because he never even made a sandwich in his life so far as I knew, though he certainly has had the opportunity to know good food about the world. But he hasn't mentioned it for years."

I said no more at the time, leaving her to ponder the matter. But I felt that we had a clue. Time passed. Her son was very restless. She took several opportunities to plant the thought in his mind that there was nothing of which she deeply disapproved. She let him know gently that in her mind nothing was *déclassé* if it was done well. Then she waited.

Presently, one evening, it all came out. He told her he was going into the restaurant business! She was surprised, yet she was glad he had made up his mind to something. But she feared his inexperience and dreaded a failure for him almost more than any loss of money he might suffer.

She suggested as tactfully as possible that he defer his opening a restaurant until he should have gone to school somewhere to learn about such things. She was willing to stand by him in the whole program if he would only go at it sensibly, learn where to put his feet, and not go off without preparation.

"But, Mother," he protested, "that is just what I don't want to do. I don't want to learn how to run a place as other people run theirs. I want to go into this business because I want to do it in just the opposite way at a number of points. I don't care how they run theirs. I *know* already how I want to run mine. I've been thinking about it for years and years. This is not as much 'all of a sudden' as you may think. I have hundreds of mental notes. Anyway, I imagine a restaurant is something like a ship. She has to find herself as all the parts learn how to work together. And each one is an individual."

She told me later, "Here was a young man, willing to risk his patrimony in a business venture that was to be fashioned along lines that pleased him!" Finally, she caught his vision. Naturally cautious, she had a job quelling her sense of insecurity—but conquer it she did.

"It probably sounds utterly mad," she said, "but I haven't a shadow of a doubt about it any more. We who believe in the working out of a mental picture must stand behind our own tenets. And I do it wholeheartedly—without reservation. His own vision is so perfect, so sound. He is so sure. I know he and his partner, a most capable young man, will make it successful."

On a shoestring, a different and highly appealing restaurant appeared in Pasadena, bearing a most peculiar name, "The Stuffed Shirt"—and the menus were in that shape! Here was no modest try to get started with a hamburger stand. It was a simple, quietly tasteful appeal to genuine, globe-trotting gourmets. The prices were not exorbitant, but reasonably substantial. The food was superb.

After a few difficulties, the new sensation in restaurants built up a loyal clientele. In the nature of things, expansion loomed. Presently there was another restaurant at El Monte. And down on the coast near Del Mar there is now another.

"Act as though I am, and I will be" is a quotation from ancient Eastern religious lore. It has puzzled many people down through time. Now we understand it, when we know of people like the young restaurateur, finally seeing the pictured desires of many years come to materialization. How many times over how many years had he visualized his restaurant? Apparently, no matter what else he was doing this envisioned restaurant lay in the back of his mind.

It did not suddenly come into being, though that might appear to be the case. But he had acted it out, over and over. He honestly wanted to serve people as he thought they should be served. And his vision became actuality.

You Can Begin Now

What is it *you* want to achieve? Start acting as though it existed.

1. Take on the manner of people in that *métier*.
2. Begin to use the words, the expressions, of these people.
3. Gather the appurtenances of this field of action.
4. Collect books on the subject.
5. Write to other people who are interested in your subject.
6. Join a club devoted to that interest, if you can find one.
7. Take trips, if you can, to meet people sympathetic to your cause.
8. If you cannot travel, then read and attend lectures that will keep you steeped in the atmosphere you desire.

BE CAREFUL OF YOUR POWER

A peculiar fact is that though man may not recognize or respect his authority in the realm of constant creativity, the law of cause and effect *does* act upon his continuous decrees. He is triggering *something,* some result, every instant of his life. And a dangerous power it is, for the discord that activates much of his thinking is just as creative as the happiest and sunniest of his thoughts and feelings. Thus man perpetuates his miseries. He rationalizes them. He explains them in terms of the mistakes of others or their sins against him—or he may even believe that God has sent him pain for some obscure reason.

The truth is that without God's processes of mercy and amelioration man would have destroyed himself long ago by his ignorant and willful breaking of salutary laws! We do not suffer completely for our sins, for God's merciful laws are always trying to knit together the broken edges of a wound in flesh or tree bark. The urges of growth are always seeking to overcome weaknesses. Experience, even the painful sort, seems to be seeking our good in that we learn and extend, extend and learn, by the trials and errors of our way of going.

All thoughts reproduce. Since our bad thoughts and acceptances are just as productive as our good ones, it seems the height of folly not to concentrate on forming the right ones, the ones that will get us to our desired goal in the shortest span of time, and with the least effort and pain. Isn't it strange that man does not pay more attention to the quality of his thoughts and emotions, for they are *forming a nucleus* which will draw to itself its own general kind and thus influence every area of his life?

One need not understand the mystics and the sages in order to know by experience that he most certainly *can* choose the atmospheres of his mind. He can think what he decides to think. He can devote himself to the pleasures and satisfactions of higher themes.

Every man can decide to set a nucleus of value in his mind and, therefore, in his life. For a nucleus will grow. That is its nature. It will expand, gather, grow, extend, produce after its kind, and return home with multiplied blessings "'til there shall be no room to contain them." This was the promise for tithing, the giving of a tenth. Surely you can give more than a tenth of yourself, your mentation, your time and effort to the creation of good. And if you do, you will be searching for a place to contain your blessings.

The Natural State of Man Is "Fortunate"

God never willed for man to exist in a state of emergency or disaster. Man is "far from home" when he is in misery and want, that is, suffering ill luck.

Consider the story of the Prodigal Son. His wrong thought patterns brought him to want and disgrace. And as he lay among the swine, so low had he sunk, he began to feel that he would like to reverse his position. *This story is remarkable in that it follows the exact steps that must be taken to change any unhappy pattern:*

1. He "came to himself." He remembered who he was, the son of a loving, generous father.
2. Then he said, "I must rise—"
3. "—and go to my father."

We know how splendidly he was received.

God means man to have a garment of fine linen, as the father, joyous over his son's return, gave to the Prodigal. That Biblical father, you will remember, put a ring of gold on his son's finger and killed the fatted calf to celebrate the home-coming. All the giving, loving, generous lavishness was the outcome of the "three magic moves." These moves, 1-2-3, take a man into the atmosphere of his intrinsic worth, his true heritage, his father's house.

In gambling, at Las Vegas or elsewhere, huge winnings are occasionally made and the winner is considered lucky. But the good luck of such isolated, unpredictable gains is as nothing in comparison to those a man may enjoy when he is truly in his *fortunate, native element,* where "All that I have is thine." Not just at the turn of a wheel or the chance number on a board or a die, but at all times good fortune pours into his mind, heart, body, affairs, and through him to others! This is a winning worth seeking.

So choose the nucleus you want to see multiplied. Place the lure that will draw more of its kind. What do you really want? Place a nucleus where the law can and will act upon it.

Suppose you want a trip. Then saturate your mind with ways

and means of travel. Choose your baggage. Select your clothes. Even though, for a while, your trip will be an armchair one, get ready in all the ways that reach your mind. Thoughts are things. Mentally board a plane or a ship. Go aboard physically if you can get on a ship in the future. Hang up your clothes in your stateroom mentally. Be assigned a place at table in the ship's dining hall. Stand aft and watch the wake of the ship in the water. You may as well make it moonlit, too, for a wave sparkling in the softly bright reflections of lunar light is truly lovely.

See yourself finding the objects or facts for which you wish to search. Is it the diggings in Ischia that fascinate you? Visit them mentally. Read about them and marvel over the evidence of a lost past being unearthed there.

Is it the art of Florence that makes you yearn for Italy? Look at photographic reproductions of these masterpieces. Steep yourself in all the details for just as surely as you are now reading these words, one day you will find yourself looking at the originals!

Your desire, your clearly chiseled mental picture, is your nucleus. And about it will gather the material appurtenances. It will all be logical and reasonable; so logical that you may question yourself, wondering if it wouldn't have happened anyway, whether you had done all the planning and thinking, or not. For the law works logically, not erratically!

Do you want to be happy? Then project your nucleus of satisfaction by *being happy now!* "Oh," you may say, "but I can't be happy until I have achieved some goals." I must reply that you have the cart before the horse. You must be happy *now* in order to attract the happiness you desire! That is the way the law works.

How can you be happy now? *You decide, as a sovereign being, to be happy—now.* It is something like showing a shopkeeper a sample of silk you want to match. If you show him a sagging, shoddy, faded, limp, colorless sample, he will give you exactly what you show him.

You provide the nucleus. You have always provided the nucleus; and you will always provide the nucleus around which the happenings, the gifts, the tenor of your life have gathered. It could not be otherwise.

If you are happy now just because you decide that you *can be what you like,* it will be something like placing a decoy on a lake to attract ducks. You may not get immediate results, but one day other ducks *will* settle in your waters—and there you are!

Actually, you do not really need lures and decoys; these just appeal to our present understanding—or lack of it.

Your Faith Will Grow

What you really need is a nucleus of faith, which will grow to magnificent proportions. If your faith is pale and weak, then pray with that suppliant of long ago, who cried, "Lord, I believe, help Thou my unbelief!"

There is tremendous pathos in the situation of humanity's wanting to believe in the incredible good luck of its dawning idea of its sovereignty, but being unable to do so because of the beclouding mist of fear and superstition.

Even the smallest bit of faith can grow until it blesses your whole life. Just as a bulbous plant produces dozens of tiny bulbs, your ideas bear the equivalent of offspring, that, following the laws of their being, develop, flower, seed, and produce other rhizomes. Life always multiplies its expressions. ". . . Prove me now herewith, saith the Lord of hosts, if I will not open you the windows of heaven, and pour you out a blessing that there shall not be room enough to receive it." (Malachi 3-10.)

Everything in the natural world increases. Adding this law to the study of nuclei, Einstein in his later years veered toward the opinion that the earth and other planets increase in size as time goes on, and that probably the known universe increases as well. (This was opposed to the theory of friction and attrition held by many scientists.)

Growth, reach, aspiration are instincts deep in all living matter and creatures. Consider the uncanny intelligence in a vine searching for something to entwine that it may reach still farther!

Expect that from your nucleus of faith you will achieve both understanding and material gain. For the entire drama of it takes place inside yourself. Life acts upon itself, moves upon its own ideas, brings to fruition the patterns of its own creation. You are supported by this interpenetrating law that operates for you at all times and brings you great good fortune.

"Act as though you are, and you will be!" This is a deep law of life.

•8•

How You Can Become More "Fortunate"

There is a recognizable aura around the fortunate person. It shows itself in a number of ways. I remember hearing Douglas Fairbanks, Sr., say that failure and success had definite odors! He said poverty and sadness could be detected by the nostrils of sensitive people. He added that animals could tell a person's mood or state by the odor emanating from him.

Whether or not there is a detectable scent, there are certainly vibratory emanations that go out from us to others all the time. When we sometimes read these vibrations we are not always aware of the process and we are likely to say, "I *feel* that so-and-so is not himself today. He has problems. He needs help." Or, "I somehow *sense* that John is on the upgrade. He has an atmosphere of well-being." *One way or another, one must create the atmosphere of being fortunate, if he is to enjoy it.*

IF YOU WISH TO JOIN THE GROWING BAND OF FORTUNATE PEOPLE FOLLOW THESE RULES

1. *Decide* that you will pay whatever price and make whatever effort is needed.
2. *Decide* that you will focus on *ideas* of good fortune; that you will never again think of ill luck as either normal or inevitable, as somehow a part of your particular fate.
3. *Decide* that even if there were such a thing as "inexorable *fate*," the

laws of divine individuality give you power to overcome it. Know that when all outer influences have spent all their ammunition, there is still the power within you to *choose* what you will do about it and to create your world from within.

4. *Decide* that you are not a victim of anything! No matter what your problems or how confused your way, or how heavy your load, the laws of *life* rush to your aid when you consciously believe in them and invoke them. They work best when you recognize them and, in a sense, command them. (Why should this human attitude be regarded as too bold? Its critics prove themselves to be afraid of power, and therefore still neolithic.)

5. *Take note*

    a. That the accident prone people have most of the accidents.
    b. That the good fortune prone people are the ones who seem to get most of the plums. Sometimes they have been born into such an atmosphere. But more often, the fortunate person has chosen to build up the *habit* of getting the edge on whatever he is doing.

6. *Decide* that for two weeks, at least, you will not notice and will not make any comment on *any* type of ill luck—your own, or that of anyone else. But you *will* take definite note, even write down, if possible, every small item that is a satisfying, comfortable, convenient or happy occurrence. You need not announce that you are making this experiment. It will probably be better if you keep it to yourself. However, there is no law broken if you and someone dear to you decide to make it together.

   Brush the scare headlines quickly out of your mind. Unless you are going to help personally, don't mull over the disaster in the news. No. This is not selfish! For you are building up a wonderful kind of strength and its orderly sanity will help heal the confusions that touch you and some of those that afflict the world.

7. *Decide* to give yourself better "breaks." Learn to snatch extra minutes during the day for a little study, meditation or work. How about learning just one phrase of Spanish or French? I know a business woman who painted her house in fifteen-minute and half-hour stretches of time. She kept her brushes in a solution that prevented their drying. There was a carpenter's apron (bless them!) and a pair of gloves (35¢) lying beside the paint-bucket. Thus, she was always ready.

   You might use five minutes early in the morning to write a charming short letter to bind or develop or serve a friendship. One every day would amount to 365 in a year. Imagine the power in that! Do you now have 365 people wishing you well? And the good wishes will be doubled because you are wishing them well! This is no small matter!

You might use an extra five minutes for meditation or prayer. We should often take cognizance of the fact that the wonderful laws of *accruing benefit* were put here for us by our Heavenly Father. It keeps us in line with truth and law to realize that the power we use is but *loaned* to us, as it were. It is *correct* to appreciate its force and availability, but wrong to imagine that we can use it in arrogant or cavalier fashion.

We Can Remind Ourselves Several Times a Day That We Must Be Grateful and Responsible in the Use of Our Vast Privileges

But vast they are and it remains for us to learn the laws and disciplines of their best uses. I suggest a return to saying grace at the table before we eat. The old-fashioned expression was "returning thanks" which, while quaint, says it well. At my house I often find my guests visibly moved when I ask them to indulge me in saying it. They often express their pleasure. So many people are yearning for a return to civilized manners in our daily recognition of our *source* that one need not feel strange or apologetic when one wants to say grace. Do so! *Gratitude is one of the strongest steps toward good fortune.* Remember that in a theatre, if you do not applaud the entertainment given you, you will not receive more, i.e., an encore. By the same token, appreciation anywhere is quite likely to attract or create more of the blessing enjoyed.

8. *Praise your good fortune.* Like applause to a singer or water to a plant, recognition and praise of the many wonders of your life tend to multiply them. But if you say when some disappointment or inconvenience comes along, "Just my luck," *you are claiming for your very own that which you do not want.*

9. *Call everything good.* If you are caught in the rain without an umbrella with your best clothes on, ignore the bad features of it and say smil-

ingly, "It's just what we need for our gardens and crops. This is worth millions of dollars to us."

And if you take cold and have to stay at home for a couple of days, do not say, "What rotten luck. How unfortunate!" Say, instead, "I'll get caught up on my letters. I'm being protected from something much worse. My heart and vital organs are getting a rest. I'll try some of those horizontal exercises I've been hearing about. I'll listen to those new records. I'll listen to my wife and my children. We'll read something fine aloud together, even if they do have to sit across the room from me, lest they catch one of my germs. The treatment for this cold will cleanse my body of other and all impurities and that will be a fine blessing. I don't care how crazy it sounds. I'm going to call the whole thing good." Thus you set up another vortex, a nucleus for other "good."

It is cocky and conceited to be upset when your little earthly routine is disrupted for a couple of days, a couple of minutes, or a couple of years. What makes you think it is all perfect and mustn't be changed? There is a mind within you that knows everything and its choices are far wiser than yours. Take the benefit of everything that comes your way. Declare it! Enjoy the *good* aspects of every occurrence. You will find them, if you look deeply into the matter.

When you find a good parking place, praise your luck. Don't say, "Well, it's about time I had a break." Such remarks articulate your belief in your usual bad luck. There's a far difference between praising your good fortune and noting it as unusual in a cynical fashion! It is surprising how dependable the *expectancy* of convenience and help is, when it is needed.

You will be tested and tried in the matter. As you praise your good fortune and it begins to grow, you become aware that you are dealing with a genuine force about which we know all too little. Everything will not go your way. But, if you remain true to the principle of gathering the impressions of fine solutions and ignoring the so-called frustrations, the latter become fewer and fewer.

I did not say it was easy to discipline your mind into making only salutary notations. It requires a great deal of strength—but the strength, too, grows as we call upon it, exercise it.

If you still feel that this path is unrealistic, and that we should meet disasters on their own terms, then I am afraid you are going to remain on the common path of modern man, the "pain route."

Show me a man who believes in disaster and I will show you that he is killing himself.

People have died of their hates. Of course *"hate"* was not the word the doctors put on the death certificate. That word ended in –osis, or –itis, which was simply the identifiable consequence that could be measured in a test tube.

I know a young lawyer in New York who, in dealing with man's shadier activities and weaknesses, has come to have no respect for the human race. He is suspicious, believes almost no one, and constantly makes cynical remarks. While he is well off financially, he has a failure's point of view! He has sinus trouble, indigestion, and is tired all the time. He is ruining his personal life by bringing his ugly, unflattering attitude into every conversation.

Certainly, human beings are weak and many of them still manifest treachery brought along from the trickery and selfishness of the jungle. But that does not alter the fact that they have divinity and high potential folded in the deeper parts of them.

Life is like a skyscraper. At what floor do you get off to transact your life's business! If you prefer the cellars of the world, poor darling, you have a long, painful way ahead of you.

Even if yours is a respectable life "of quiet desperation," as Thoreau once said of all humanity, you must shed the animalistic belief in confusion and set about cultivating the patterns in which things come out well!

It is truly important to your body, your mind, and to the way your life will unfold itself before you, that you weed out all gratuitous condemnation—all sweeping, derogatory opinions.

10. *Decide to think well of the human race.* You need not like people's faults. You are not required to trust your treasure to unworthy, irresponsible ones. But you *must,* for our purposes, see that each man has divine potential and, especially with your thoughts, help him bring it forth.

    You can bless people you pass in the street, who are obviously troubled. You can free them momentarily from the weight of sadness,

> poor posture, poor taste in clothes, or whatever they are manifesting. Take a split second to see them (with your mind's eye) lifted out of their wrongs into the rights. It is highly probable that the person you are thus blessing will turn and look at you—and you just may exchange smiles.

A man once said to me, "But I don't like people enough to do that."

I said to him, "Then like yourself enough to do so. For if you walk around with your mind in the gutter of other people's unfortunate status, you will soon or late land in the gutter yourself."

Whatever you think becomes you, no matter to whom it may be directed. Besides that, you have a duty to your fellow man to lift him as and where you can. You can do it in split seconds. You cannot help having *some* picture of other people. And it is healthier for you to have a good one.

This is a subtle area that is difficult for most people. Jealousies of others, who may get ahead of us, make it easy for us to think the other fellow down. There may be a temptation to trip him up if you can. But just as there are laws in a football game as to how and where you may attack an opponent, there are laws of the moral conduct of business and social life.

Failing to observe these laws will net a temporary gain sometimes, but the snide evil of the matter sinks into your subconscious mind, to multiply there, to grow, and bubble to the surface of your life in ways so subtle that it sometimes takes a psychoanalyst years to uncover it.

Why build these hazards for yourself! How can one believe in good fortune, *knowing* that he has taken every advantage of unfair tactics! Why not take every *good* advantage? What is *true* must be true for every other man, as well as yourself.

You are building your life toward higher themes; into areas where one expends less effort and gets better results. You cannot operate on two planes at once. Leave the cheap, snide tricks, impulses, and habits of the half-developed man and walk freely, knowingly, onto the plateau of a risen man. Take a step up!

Good luck is a stream. You may not have the great flowing blessing of good fortune for yourself alone. Once you feel you are in its stream, you will feel constrained to loose it out to others. You want every living person to be healed of his confusions, to let go of his terrified, drowning man's hold on the exigencies of the low logic of selfishness.

11. *Decide to have and express more of life every day.* This means that you must believe in and *do* extra things at every turn. Give an extra smile, an extra compliment. Make an extra telephone call to comfort or help or amuse someone—or to find out something for yourself. Brush your clothes more perfectly. Put a flower on a tray of food. If you are a man, give extra courtesy to your callers this day. See women to the door of your office, or call a gentlemanly conferee to do so. All such extras lift one into finer dimensions.

Good fortune is simply a name for the extras of life. And as the ancient mystics have always said, "One must *be* that which he wishes to *have.*" Put an extra shine on the silver, the door knob, or your shoes. Make your hair tidier, smarter, glossier, more lively. Brush it an extra instant. Give extra effort to your job. Don't be a clock watcher.

Think up ways to give more at every turn. It is truly astonishing how much time most of us spend trying to give less and less, while we hope for more and more! It doesn't make sense. The only place we should give less should be in cutting down the time we spend in dissatisfaction, fatigue, disaster talk, and grumbling. Make your extras those of value, appreciation, fun, and beauty. Oh, how it pays and pays! Then, as your momentum gathers and propels you forward without so much conscious effort and fuel, you begin to enjoy your harvest.

You must put yourself in line with that which you desire. If you wanted a sun bath, you would understand quite clearly that you must place yourself where the sun can pour over you. This is a good metaphor, for the sun shines on the just and the unjust, on everything and everybody its rays reach. Just so with all natural forces. They operate for anyone who operates them.

Put yourself in line with returning profit by investing yourself in the extras of self-extension. I've heard men say, "I've put myself out for everybody all my life and I've decided to quit. For people just pile things on a person who is willing to help."

Usually, the speaker has made two mistakes in his supposed "giving." He has expected gratitude, which he may not have received. He has developed a third arm that constantly pats himself on the back for being a "good guy" and he has begun to bore people with the stories of his generosities.

The laws of mind are exact. If you give yourself joyously to the *extras* you decide on, without immediate thought of return, but just because you wish to express your power to do so, you enter the "field of power." And there the returns are far greater than the little tit-for-tat return on the lower plane.

Entering the "field of power," you attract, absorb, and become alive to other kinds of power with all their generous benefactions. These returns may appear to the casual observer to be a matter of chance, "luck." But if one values consciously the opportunity to express life for its own sake, one will reap the harvest.

·9·

Intuition—the Mind-Power You Must Recognize

THE HARD-HEADED BUSINESSMAN SOMETIMES DERIDES intuition. Yet, when he is on a vacation and talking in a softer mood, he may surprise you by saying that many of his best deals were made on "hunches." When you ask him to define a hunch, he will flounder a bit and then say it is probably intuition.

Ask for a definition of a hunch from a dozen different philosophers, teachers, thinkers, and get a dozen different answers. However, their differences are largely a matter of semantics. Since most scientists, in the past, have zealously fought any but empirical findings, they have largely ignored the field of intuition. But in recent years we have been greatly occupied with our interest in man, himself, and especially his mind. It was inevitable that we have come upon the need for knowledge of different levels of awareness.

One finds highly developed intuition in surprising places. We have mentioned the business man's "hunches." And it is easy to see that he may have earned his sensitivity in certain areas by years of application and prolonged attention, much as a pianist earns his extraordinary facility and memory of long, long piano works through the untold hours of practice.

There is also the child's intuition, which apparently springs from an untrammeled mind and sees beyond the presented facts to the truth of a matter or person.

One cannot ignore the extraordinary intuition of the unlettered natives in places like Haiti. Having spent a summer there, I came away deeply impressed by the strange *knowing* of these people. My maid, who slept on the floor across the open door (by her own preference), would often tell me when someone was coming, what gift would be brought, and sometimes news that would arrive. She was not set apart from the others as a seeress. Most of the natives had, more or less, the same ability.

It is possible that living for many years where communication and transportation are difficult, these people have sensitized the parts of their mental functions that have to do with coming events. Their knowing seems to concern itself with trivia, seldom a matter of great moment. Yet there it is as a phenomenon, which is proved at its own level. One wonders if they could not employ it more importantly. Their minds are almost innocent of any education, as we know it, although they are highly intelligent. The possibility looms that since their minds have not been occupied otherwise, they have focused on this area of awareness without physical communication or material aid in any way.

For instance, on a trip to the beach they will know which road someone else took an hour before. They are great observers and always notice tracks. However, they have been known to give directions even blindfolded and many times there is absolutely no material support for their knowing.

Going on a picnic in Haiti is a novel experience. One just goes, without packing a lunch or any other preparation. I was greatly surprised when we all just piled in a car and started out for a day at the beach. "But what will we eat?" I asked.

My daughter smiled and said, "You will see." We donned our bathing suits, fins, and snorkels, and enjoyed the waters for several hours, then came out to dry off. We were hungry and thirsty.

On the beach stood a porteress, carrying on her head a vast amount of coconuts. With her machete she whacked off tops of coconuts in the crude shape of spoons and handed one to each of us. The coconut milk was cool and delicious and then the meat was eaten with the spoon. She was paid and left.

Then, silently, there appeared the banana woman and after that the oyster boy. Haitian oysters are tiny, about the size of your thumbnail, and grow along the exposed roots of shore trees in the water. The boy milks them off the tree roots with a downward stroke. Then he squats before each person and opens the oysters and serves them with the juice of *citron* (lemon). They are delicious! The boy carefully counts the shells and is paid according to the number of them.

Soon a fishing boat circled toward the shore, apparently waiting to be hailed. With shouts and pantomime a deal was made for some fish, strings of them having been held up for inspection. Then suddenly there was a man in clean, white shirt and trousers, squatting beside a hot, small fire, readied for the fish. Who this man was and where he came from no one seemed to know.

There is breadfruit and with mangoes for dessert, we had dined regally! Nothing ever tasted so good. Perhaps hunger, sea air, and sea salt had something to do with it, but we felt that we had truly feasted.

But how did these people know exactly where we were going to be since we didn't know ourselves? We might easily have gone to another beach far away. And what does one do when a maid leaves a note pinned on a summer evening dress, "I didn't do the ironing you told me to do because you need this dress." And of course, events transpired that required the dress she had prepared!

It is doubtful that the Haitians properly appreciate their own gift of knowing. Building upon it, they might become very advanced indeed. But they do not bother with it; they just use it and enjoy it in their simple way. They aren't even interested in the fact that it is evidence of the response of *Mind* to their manner of trusting and expecting its development. To them it is perfectly natural.

I felt very privileged to have witnessed this development at first hand. There are those who try to make a connection between this knowing and the practice of their Vodun religion—but, after considerable study, I felt that the religion hurt rather than helped this type of mentation. It is probably the chief reason why they don't do more with it.

The white man can, however, take a lesson from this development. It lets him see that independent knowing can and does exist; that it is not always a matter of coincidence and shrewd observation, though these may play some part. He would do well to study it, to experiment with it himself, to try, at least, to make it a part of his own equipment. For the time has come when all of mankind will grow toward the dawning light of Mind.

WE DO NOT TRUST OUR OWN INTUITION

Since some children, uneducated natives, and highly educated businessmen have demonstrated independent *knowing,* we are safe in assuming that this ability is based on some common factor possessed by every cognizant creature.

Who has not, himself, experienced strong inner promptings either for or against some proposed action? All of us can remember having strong feelings against some individual at the time of meeting. Then circumstances forced us to approve of this person. But later events proved that our first impression was right—for us.

Often, my mother used to speak of her "inner voices." She would say, "If I would only listen to my voices! But I push them aside, turn a deaf ear, because I am not strong enough to go against the tide and pressures of circumstances. I'm always wrong when I fail to obey my inner promptings." I can certainly say the same thing.

Another very successful man once told me, "Sometimes my inner urgings are so strong they seem actually physical. It is as though something were pushing me with two hands, so powerful is the idea that I must or must not do a certain thing. When I go against it, I am always wrong."

When I was a child, a lovely young woman in our neighborhood was planning to marry a certain attractive young man. Her family and friends had pushed her into the engagement, although she was not wholehearted about it. Her minister, the family doctor, who was like a special adviser, and all the mature wise heads around, approved and encouraged the marriage.

Finally, the young girl's inner promptings became so strong that she ran away the day before the wedding was to take place, leaving the whole town horrified and gasping. A few days later, government agents came looking for the young man on bigamy charges.

One instantly thinks, "Why was not intuition prompting the wise people of the town and her parents and friends?" The answer is that it probably *was* busily active, but their attention was completely focused on the suitability, the charm and prospects of the young man, as well as the feeling that they mustn't split hairs when one of the young women was about to become married. They may even have argued with their inner message saying, "Well, there's something wrong with everybody, even with me and thee."

Intuition Is Working All the Time We Are Not Always Listening

Let us not discredit this wonderful faculty of the Mind within us, by thinking that it is acting for our pleasure and protection only at *unpredictable* times. It is we who are unpredictable. We are sometimes willing to listen. At other times we do not *want* to hear a prompting that is opposite to our cherished notion of something or somebody. We do not even listen when a loving friend tries to tell us we are mistaken. It just isn't a welcome message. We resist it with all the mechanism of the ego.

Intuition is our direct wire to headquarters. It cuts across the usual channels of communication, rendering way stations unnecessary. It is not based on obvious facts, but on basic truth, and, as such, it has no need of a carrier. There is an *"isness"* about the truth that requires no support. One must still the noise of the outer world with its evidence and its reasons and say quietly, "Nevertheless, I *know* the truth about this issue because truth is interpenetrating. A lie has the limits of its immediate function and needs support." Truth is like water, sunshine, electricity—it seeps in everywhere! And if we are *willing* to register it, we may. It is denied to no one.

Can you still the clamor of wishful thinking, of ego, and hear truth? It is an ability much to be desired. It is part of maturing to the point of taking the next steps in awareness. Intuition puts us in touch with unsullied, pristine fact.

Why do we not use intuition to help bring great truth to the world? The answer is that we do! Many a researcher will tell you that while his approach to his experiments is based on logic, as a rule, he reaches a point where he simply *knows* (or believes so strongly that it feels like knowing) that his breakthrough in his subject lies in pursuing a certain course. Usually he is right. Sometimes he is wrong, for intuition naturally depends on its own laws. The factors that bring it through to a human mind are not always favorably in juxtaposition.

THERE ARE SUBTLETIES IN INTUITION THAT SHOULD BE UNDERSTOOD

Intuition can be the reward of much preparation, which gives one high sensitivity. That same preparation, bludgeoned into a habit, can blunt intuition.

The secret seems to lie in our sensitivity, in our belief in it, whetted to a sharp edge of credulity. We must keep reminding ourselves that intuition is a function of mind, a type of behavior, the *way* a certain level of our intelligence acts under certain circumstances. Apparently it is open to all people of all ages.

Benjamin Franklin considered intuition as the "extraordinary powers of deduction." Whereas, Voltaire thought it the "climax of both inductive and deductive reasoning." Whether one thinks usually from the individual to the universal, inductively (considered masculine), or from the universal to the particular (feminine), one arrives at a point of view exactly similar to the other. The two lines merge at a point of acceptance.

The use of intuition in daily life does not demand that a person follow his leadings no matter what the cost! That would be tantamount to telling the truth all the time tactlessly and foolishly, which would only cause hurt and bring chaos. One is supposed to register his opinions with the aid of clear intuition.

One must use mature judgment in revealing his knowledge. Sometimes one must weigh values and decide that the virtues of the individual being judged far outweigh his faults—and that his virtues are needed in the place where he will function. Intuition may well tell all the others involved that a certain man possesses the type of talent and strength that they need. If it also tells them of his weaknesses, they may be able to help him overcome them. Knowledge of another person is not always just a yardstick of judgment, but a human weighing of values.

Intuition should tell us of the good more than the bad. We can train ourselves in this lifted use of intuition. It can tell us of our advantages; lead us into making the better choices and let us know where our best opportunities lie. We abuse our talent for direct leading when we use it only when it warns against disaster.

Warnings

In any conversation about intuition, everyone present can remember a time when he felt a sharp urge to get in touch with the family, only to learn that there had been a death at home that morning. Or the time that Aunt Katie dreamed that there was a fire and two weeks later the church burned down in the village. In any family, there are a dozen or more such stories.

Real warnings of real dangers are registered by many people—and should be heeded. Studies have been made by various teams here and there in the world. And the consensus is that beyond doubt, some factor of intelligence beyond the normal was active in the matter. The way of the story is not nearly as important as the fact that it came about at all. Whether a dream was involved, or a vision, or the very strong inner urges we have mentioned, the manner of warning was the most unimportant part of it.

With each individual the inner knowing had to get through to the conscious mind in a way that would be recognized and accepted. It is conceivable that the inner mind would, under these circumstances, be highly inventive in order to be effective.

Does Man "Invent" a Source?

It should be mentioned here that while the thought of protective warning *might* be coming from somebody else, it is not necessarily so. There is a faculty of knowing within each of us that can become aware of an urgency of some kind—and seek extraordinary ways of getting through to the limited conscious mind. A thought of loving protection could be dramatized right within a person's own mental processes as coming from someone the person knew cared about his welfare.

He might not be able to accept the possibility that the message came from himself, for he knows little or nothing about this area within himself. So he is likely to *invent* the presence of another entity, since he cannot give credence to his own extended power of mind! The leading comes through in a way he *can* accept; in terms of a voice, perhaps of a loved one, a dream of someone's coming to warn him, or some other invention. *It is a strange fact that the human being will accept any fabulous, unusual explanation of the higher use of Mind except his own access to it.* At this, he balks!

This is not to say that protective influences, laws, and entities do not exist. I am sure they do. But the fact still remains that the subject has no less contact with the sea of his own mind than with any other mind that can reach him.

The subject has just as many areas and facets and functions in his entire make-up as any other person does. It remains for the subject to recognize his own completeness as a child of the universe and seek to develop the wonderful uses of extended self that are open to him.

The Marvel of Man's Own Potential Should Be Recognized

Just as all our modern inventions and discoveries lay about us, unknown and unused for thousands or millions of years, man has within his own complex being strata of awareness that he has not recognized because he will not. For some reason, he thinks so little of himself that he is uncomfortable claiming anything beyond the most ordinary, limiting equipment!

Using my own intuition, I can comprehend the splendid powers that are the natural gifts of the human being. And when we have mastered the ones that are just now coming to our attention and consider them as something more than old wives' tales, we shall stand high enough to see farther and farther vistas.

Man explains his powers away. He speaks of coincidence to explain a fine, intuitive working out of a problem. He will accept "guardian angels" before he will believe that he himself is in direct touch with the sea of Mind that produced him. I have no quarrel with guardian angels. I think they are a delightful and charming idea; and I, personally, do not see why they should not exist. But I'm sure also that one of their chief functions is to help me get a personal hold on the power they use! I do not agree that one obliterates the other. We have a very shallow habit of throwing out all of an old belief if someone comes up with an explanation of the "how" of some function.

When our great mathematicians have worked out the calculations of outer space—each having the advantage of the others' efforts down through time—there is a great hue and cry that God has been explained away and that sensible people are therefore going to be atheists! How absurd! How narrow and blind! The more the exact laws and designs of the universe come to our recognition, the more we should respect the parent Mind from which it all springs.

Today we seem to be on the verge of discovering the very (chemical) secret of life itself. Even when we have found it, *if* we do, we will have but discovered a process set in motion by the Parent-Mind or God. Instead of abolishing God, it proves His existence to us. To understand the grandeur of our universe is to marvel at the wonder of it all and to be deeply grateful to the Creator!

By sharpening our own wits through the disciplines of close attention and persistent experiment, we are simply becoming more and more aware of the wonders of our world, put here, *available to us,* by the "Prime Mover," "Nature," or God. The word you use does not change the fact!

Intuition is but one of the refinements of mankind's growing gift of awareness. Through extended use of this valuable ability, we receive the many benefits of higher knowing. We also open our minds to further reaches.

By recognizing the peculiar availability of the All-Mind we should become more cognizant of the magnificent generosity shown to us by Nature. Instead of seeing in it a coldly impersonal process, one should instead see the evidence of the most exquisite kind of caring.

Would an uncaring machine process have instigated, for instance, the laws of healing, of knitting flesh together in a wound, of persistently trying to close tree bark over a cut in the trunk? This process demonstrates "forgiveness" on the physical plane. It is an established basic urge to make all right again; to restore wholeness. Without this help from the Parent-Mind, the animal man would have long since wrecked the world—and himself. But with healing (forgiveness), he can restore himself and continue his expanding (however slow) awareness of the riches of the universe.

The counterpart of the physical processes will be found to be identical on all the planes of his being. Erasures and corrections are made in the human brain itself; not only on paper! And truth continues to supplant erroneous beliefs, wherever it is recognized.

HOW CAN YOU IMPROVE YOUR USE OF INTUITION?

You can learn more about your own inutitive powers by keeping a check on yourself. For a period of a month keep a written record of your strongest motivations. Carry a small notebook with a pen or pencil attached and write down immediately, or as soon as possible, your impressions and thoughts or chance opinions that seem noteworthy. Record also what you do about them.

Then watch carefully for the gentler, quieter leadings. Write these down, too, in your notebook. Listen for your still, small voices. Write down all these urgings, whether or not you act upon them.

At the end of a month, evaluate your notes. Check your intuitive urgings for tone, quality, and especially for exactness. See if they were reliable. Only a careful check will reveal their worth, will sort out merely vagrant thoughts from the real messages of your inner knowing.

Do Not Confuse Wishful Thinking With Intuition

Try to separate intuitive thinking from the daily tangle of negative or egoistic thoughts, those little dramas of self-excuse or aggrandizement that insidiously intrude themselves.

Do not use intuition as an excuse for doing wild things or making irrational decisions. That is not intuition; it is just impulsiveness.

When you permit your emotions to dictate decisions on the spot, that is impulsiveness. When your mind does it, that is intuition.

Just thinking *about* something is not necessarily intuitive thinking. Pondering a point does not imply deep thinking. It might be just indecision. You can become sensitive to the difference in the month of watchfulness. Intuitional thinking is coming from the deep wellspring of truth, while much of our outer thinking is colored by the pressures and tangles of the outer world.

Most successful people are highly intuitive, though everyone can improve his use of inner knowing and lift his life several notches. One should always reach further and further, thus evolving consciously and faster. If you make a more sensitive instrument of yourself, you attract the melodies of life.

Have you ever had the experience of intuitively deciding to do a certain thing; then, after thinking it over, you change your mind; and later, you discover that you *should* have followed your intuition in the first place? This is common with all of us. It happens because *we do not trust our intuition.* But, why don't we? I think that we would all follow our inner knowing more often and strengthen our grasp of it if we organized our ideas about it. Let us restate some of them.

1. Intuition is a "tap-in" to the All-Mind, or universal truth. It is *always* available, *always* functioning. It is not just a sometime matter.
2. It is a matter of *awareness* and thus, can be cultivated.
3. You (and your mind) are created by the All-Mind, God, and this Mind flows into you at the level of your awareness of It and your faith in It. No mystery, miracle or other entity is necessary to your contact.
4. You extend your use of intuition by learning to separate inner leadings from surface thoughts, or emotional impulse.
5. You can earn by attention and disciplines a more highly sensitized intuition. By speaking the truth, abjuring exaggeration, the slightest misrepresentation, or low thinking of any kind, you clear your own path to *truth.*

Bear in mind that *all* advance is the bringing through into consciousness of more pure intelligence. In this way we are not confined always to the reports of the senses, but reach far beyond them. Yet, we can prove ourselves superior to the senses only by using them well! And by the skill and strength we gain by disciplining the senses, we rise to a higher cycle of understanding.

While it is definitely true that man on earth has come thus far by employing his senses, there is more for him. One does not wish to develop a contempt for the senses, but neither does one wish to be imprisoned in or by them.

This decision is before mankind today. This is the point he has reached. His future depends on the way he turns *now.*

·10·

The Mysterious Energies of the Subconscious Mind

Every one of us has two minds. At least, there are available to us two functions of Mind that can be separately described—the conscious and the unconscious. A trained use of both is the only way to benefit from the privileges they hold for us.

An oversimplified diagram would show that the conscious mind (or its function) is located in the frontal brain lobes, while the subconscious appears to be located largely in the back lobes of the brain. Dr. José Delgado, a Yale researcher, has done brilliant work in locating the brain areas that control definite acts or offices, such as speech, locomotion, etc. His work has been largely with monkeys.

On one occasion I had the privilege of donning proper garments and going into the laboratory with these animals. They had names which they knew, engaging personalities, and apparently a sense of humor at times. They could be very mischievous.

They also apparently had recognized that the doctor was drawing them into something of great importance and each was proud of his relationship with the doctor. They seemed to know the difference between the head man and the assistants. They vied with one another for his attention. So, far from being in pain or unhappy, they were a joyous lot and came to be somewhat obedient, although not dependably so. Work with them was very rewarding and revealing.

Location of specific brain areas was accomplished largely by electric impulses using elaborate equipment. Humanity has gained much knowledge from this research. Gradually we are learning the hows and whys of our access to sovereign mentation.

The frontal lobes of the brain may be, in part, likened to the front office of a place of business. Here one states his errand, is identified, and listed. His information is filed away. It is an area of recognition, of conscious noting. Directions, patterns, orders are sent back from this area.

The rear lobes seem to hold sway over the processes that operate unconsciously in sequences, some of which were set up millions of years ago. Here is where the functions of the body are directed, the heart is kept beating, the digestive process is animated. The rear lobes are like a vast switchboard for alerting messages, muscular reflexes, coordinated movement, habit reactions.

This mind, having function, but not volition, must accept and deal with whatever material is sent into it by the conscious mind. I have likened it to a great stomach that does the best it can with the conglomerate food and drink it receives and from which it selectively tries to meet the needs of the entire body. Its ingenuity in this area knows no bounds.

Its chemistry, generally operating in known and habitual ways, can, under changes or excessive stress, alter its admixtures. It can even demand of the glands a change of substances under certain conditions! The inescapable conclusion is that, though it may not have original volition, it does exercise some independent intelligence in carrying out the calls on itself.

There are those scientists who cling to the rapidly fading notion that nothing can change the sequence of chemical reactions, except another chemical. Even though that may be true, one must make a careful study of how and why the triggering impulse, or chemical, is introduced into the usual sequence.

The slower change is the one that concerns most of us in our daily lives. It is the challenge of our consciously giving the unconscious mind good materials on which to work—i.e., good thoughts, higher feelings—that will give it the opportunity to give back into our bodies and lives a better, higher result.

WE CAN USE THE UNCONSCIOUS MIND TO RAISE AND STRENGTHEN OUR ENTIRE ORGANISM

There are people who give their subconscious area of function important problems to solve, ask of it intricate answers, demand of it health, wisdom, and social success. Most people do not realize the tremendous power that the subconscious mind can wield. Those who do recognize it and use this power have a great advantage.

Edison was said to have used his subconscious faculties constantly. When he was weary or had reached an impasse in searching for a certain solution, he would lie down and appear to be napping. Perhaps he would drift off into a short sleep. But he would first request his subconscious mind to provide him with the answer to his problem. Apparently, he *believed* that the mind within knew all the answers to all the riddles of all the worlds. He usually got his answer!

Belief in the Response of the Subconscious Mind Is the Key to It

If you do not believe that you have direct access to the contents and the powers of the unconscious process, your demand on it will be weak and ill defined and will bring an equally weak result. But if you can convince yourself that this vast sea of mind lies available to you, contact appears to be made.

You must assume the authoritative position, however. If you were an executive writing out instructions to your various departments, you would not add, "Do this if you really are working for us—but do it only if you feel so inclined, and only if you chance to get this note, and only if you aren't too busy doing other things, and only if you are truly in a position to do so, and only if you truly want to, etc., etc."

Yet, this wishy-washy, tentative use of his mind is the way the average person approaches his inner source of extended power. A more positive attitude would bring dependable results.

Your Subconscious Mind Works Even While You Sleep

The subconscious mind is never at rest. Therefore, if you are bothered particularly by some problem that you cannot easily solve, think about it for a while before you go to bed. Then cast it out of your conscious mind, feeling that it is where it belongs in that sea of intelligence we call the subconscious. Now, go to sleep. Your unconscious mind will take hold of it and work on it while you are sleeping. In the morning, you may not have the full answer to it, but you will have a new approach to the problem you never thought of before.

During the day give yourself time to relax and think of possible solutions.

Do not permit yourself to think of failure. Give your whole attention to building up the acceptance of success. Cultivate the *feeling* that you are on the right track. With your thoughts, your emotions, and your expectations focused on a proper solution from the richness of the subconscious mind, you will certainly find your solution.

Like a High-Powered Car

In some ways, dealing with Mind is like driving a high-powered car. It is, in that frame of reference, necessary to assume authority in order to establish firm guidance, or, if you prefer, to establish the channel by which the subconscious can supply you with your solution.

In other ways, the relation appears to be one of supplier and suppliant. It is in this imagined relation that all too many people turn to superstitious ways to "placate the gods" or to "make the signs come right." It has been so difficult, down through the ages, for man to *believe* that he has direct access to the powers in the universe. He wrongly feels he has to please some reluctant, evil guardian of his good before he can receive it!

Here it is that the memory of his eons of helplessness and inevitable loss and failure prompt man to form the wrong mental picture and blunt his acceptance of his good, even when he is intellectually convinced of the truth of its availability to him. Remember those front and rear lobes of the brain!

Man may try to believe that he has only to reach with unerring grasp into the sea of subconscious power to achieve his own desires, thus using the intellectual part of his brain. But he will not get results that please him until, through firmest thought and repeated stroke, he can furnish a sharply chiseled form for the new manifestation.

The other and best way is to have arrived at such an interpenetrating faith in the availability of Mind as set up by nature (God) that he can turn his problem over to it in a perfectly relaxed attitude, feeling sure of the response he will get.

Remember, Your Subconscious Mind Is a Part of You!

Your subconscious is not a foreign place, alien to your natural self. It is yours as much as your eyes, or your elbows. Learn through meditation how to get into it and use it. When you are relaxing, permit your deep desires, old ambitions, and lovely dreams to float to the surface again.

Let your mind wander. Be uninhibited in your thinking. Examine ideas in your mind that you may not think of at any other time of day. Let them stretch and beguile your mind. Your subconscious thoughts will come to the surface and you will learn much of value from them. They will probably entertain you. They will also give you confidence, feed your aspiration, and make a higher way so familiar to you that it will soon become actual.

Do Not Feel That You Must Work Rapidly in These Areas

If it has taken millions of years to bring you to this point of awareness, you certainly need not be in a hurry now. Trying to force something through can blunt the whole matter. You cannot force ideas. Let them float gently as they rise to the surface of your thinking. They will flower in beauty and value.

Remember that the subconscious processes are natural. You do not have to entreat them. Just obey their laws—and "see what God hath wrought." You cannot grow a vegetable. You can only plant the seed. The process of plant growth—*already established*—receives the seed and acts upon it. The subconscious mind receives the seed of your thought, hope, or aspiration and immediately sets about developing it into a fruitful product of some kind.

Turn to Your Religion to Make Your Grip Firmer

Remember Christ said, "I, of Myself, can do nothing. It is the Father within. He doeth the works." The divine source is present in all the wonderful areas and processes which I have already cited. The "Father within" is in them all and it is that *Presence* that gives authority to all the wonders *He* has wrought. It is not weakness, but strength, that recognizes the truth of that statement. Neither is it weakness to recognize your kinship with the Father.

The swift response and mobility of subconscious processes let us know that the force in them is dependable, rooted in *Mind* which is *God.* No matter how you approach them, you get some kind of response. Whatever you plant in the soil of the subconscious bears fruit.

Let Your Subconscious Help You

The general tenor of our subconscious results becomes the general tenor of our lives. One may set out to get better results, being sure that his whole life will profit thereby. There is no area of living that does not depend on this great supporting sea of mind for its actions, reactions, inspirations, and fabrication.

To complete the picture of the frontal lobes of the brain being the counterpart of a "front office," it follows that the rear lobes are the "factory" where parts are assembled into a whole, where dies are chosen, where fabrication takes place, where habits are like an assembly line, repeating and repeating their established theme.

Cast off the patterns that hold you back. Be patient with yourself. Be willing to take some time to untangle the snarls that enmesh your feet at this time. Work with your subconscious mind in getting straightened out and ready for other steps ahead.

Your subconscious mind will both help you make a decision and help you carry it out. Look over your ambitions again. What was it that you wanted to do, but have put out of your mind? Give yourself the task of freeing those thoughts from the grip of your conscious doubts and fears. Take time enough to pull each thread away. Those threads form the rope that holds you back. Make of it instead a rope to draw you forward.

Tie your rope of aspiration ahead of you, not behind you. Free yourself from the inhibitions of the conscious mind—all that illogical logic of *why* you can't do this or that! Your full talents will probably come forth to fulfill your dream. Your conscious mind probably holds captive some part of your power. Only you can release it by employing the power of the subconscious.

It may seem odd, at first glance, to explain the subconscious as holding both the entire past of man and the power by which he can *free* himself from stultifying habits and paralyzing patterns.

One's concept of a sea of universal Mind must stretch to contain each man's particular life. Otherwise, we would seem to be dealing with simply a vast generality. Here, we think dually—just as we do when we look at the oval table and *know* it must be round.

Man is both the general and the particular. He has the qualities of both the infinite and the finite. Looking at his small, physical self, he seems hemmed in by the sheer limitations of measurements. Then, the other side of him that touches the infinite, looms as a pathway of the mind into the largeness of conceivable space *and* Mind (which may prove, in the end, to be the same thing). However, at this point of our development, we are very fortunate indeed to have such a concept at all. We now need the benefits of our present awareness.

Thus, we seek to employ the privileges and bonuses we now can touch. And they are many.

•11•

How to Use Mind-Power to Solve Personal Problems

THIS CHAPTER IS MEANT FOR YOU, SEPARATELY, privately, alone, apart from everyone else in the world. If you seek a solution to some difficult, intimate situation that concerns just yourself, it is quite likely that you will find your solution in these pages. But first, we must know your strengths and weaknesses.

ESTIMATE YOURSELF

Write down your assets. There is nothing like seeing, in black and white, a list of your accomplishments and resources. Do not exaggerate; but do not be too modest. Look in the mirror and make a detailed list of your physical attributes that could be counted as assets.

If you carry yourself well, put it down. If you make a good entrance, put that down, too. Do you answer your mail promptly, graciously? No one can have a successful business or social life without the virtue of writing quickly many short, but gracious, notes. The most important people I know are the ones who write the most enchanting notes.

Put on your list every virtue you possess. Do you move well? How is your voice? Can you arrange flowers effectively? Can you welcome people warmly or see them off with charm when they are leaving? Do children like you?

"Ah," you may say, "my problem is deeper, more serious than any of these things you mention." Perhaps. But let me say that negative answers to these and kindred questions can add up to the very serious problem of a sagging life.

In any case, as you may already have divined, my own conviction is deep that we need but to sweep out of our paths the debris of our accumulated negations. The chief reason we have personal problems is that our way is cluttered with small lacks. It is the "little foxes that spoil the vine." Of course it may be more dramatic and, therefore, more interesting to deal with some tragic, involved problem. But even if you have one of those, you can handle it better if you clear the path of debris.

Trivia Cause Trouble

As a matter of fact, most of the difficulties of life and most of the keys to progress are rooted in details. I often think of an aged music master, who lived in New York many years ago. His wit and wisdom were famous among his friends. His name was Rienzi and he was a dynamo of talent and verbiage. He hated a certain woman we shall call Lisa. One day I arrived at his studio in time for all his fine-edged fury. I tried to put in a good word for her, but he would not have it. He advanced on me, shaking a trembling finger at me and yelled, "Lisa can make a fool of herself in fourteen different languages! Yes, I know she is educated! But she is like a glass of good wine with a drop of kerosene in it—you can't drink it! ! ! "

Lisa's "drop of kerosene" was two-fold. She talked all the time and she was always late. Either of these was enough to set off a rage in Rienzi.

Why did Lisa talk all the time? For the same reason that anyone else talks incessantly. She was trying to compensate for other lacks, for a lifelong sense of inferiority. She had to try to prove something; try to sell herself as an intelligent, well-informed person. No one had ever taken her aside and said, "Calm down, dear. It isn't necessary to have an opinion on every subject that comes along. Don't pick up every glove that is thrown in your arena! Be too fastidious to expose your views of everything. Let people woo your opinions."

Lisa had been a leader of a certain international group. She had served her years and then someone else was elected. She knew this had to happen, but she still bore it as an ego wound. She could not take a back seat, or even a secondary one. She had to explain this away by talking, talking, talking. She still wanted that audience—and she was going to get it even if every one else never could say a word. At a dinner table, a hostess could not even find a moment when she could inquire about her other guests' preferences of drink or food. The talk flowed on and on. It was spectacular. Most of it was interesting, in a way. But it was timed badly and all added up to egotism and poor taste. Few hostesses cared to risk it a second time. And Lisa couldn't understand why she was avoided when she was such a fascinating woman with such a fund of good stories!

Constant Talk Is the Cry of a Wounded Ego

Men advertise their inner hunger for attention in this way quite often, although not quite as much as women do. Both men and women can let the talking habit grow on them. They just use everybody for an audience.

Probably the most deadly aspect of too much talking is that with it there grows the urge to be always right. The constant talker is unhappy if someone differs with him, or challenges any of his facts. Since it wasn't a conversation to start with, it may turn into a duel of words with the innocent bystanders the worst losers of all in it.

For some reason it is worse for a man than for a woman to talk all the time, probably because women are historically and otherwise at something of a disadvantage. There is no good and lasting reason for a man to be a loser. When he insists on the middle of the floor *all* the time it is because he is deeply insecure and is under some kind of compulsion to win every point. He is "selling something" *all* the time.

The successful person of either sex has a controlled tongue. He is mannerly enough to want to hear other views and is skilled at drawing them out. His thoughts are controlled enough to allow him to judge the moment and allocate the proper amount of verbiage to it. Only experience can give one that feeling for the moment.

Often the person who talks all the time is filled with chagrin when he remembers how he held the floor instead of getting others to speak. But as far as I know, these twinges of conscience do not deter him from grabbing the spotlight at the next opportunity.

Protection Against the Temptation to Talk Too Much

1. Train yourself to be genuinely interested in other people's experiences. This virtue has to be learned, for the natural animal instinct of man is to be focused on himself. The civilized man can always be silent when good taste and politeness dictate that he yield the floor.
2. On the other hand, the civilized man is ready to talk when he should do so. Train yourself to be articulate. The art of speech will teach you when you should be listening instead of speaking.
3. Train yourself away from self-consciousness. You may think you are shy. But in truth, the self-conscious person is quite close to the aggressive, animalistic man in that his mind is on himself! By training yourself to concentrate on other people and their issues and points of view, your mind stays free of those dreadful confusions we call self-consciousness.

One can practice keeping the mind off the self in conversation by seizing every opportunity to talk with strangers. Practice drawing them out. Talk just enough about yourself and your business and your town or family to stir their tongues to tell you of theirs. Never forget that a virtuoso practices.

Do not give an opinion unless you are asked for one. Then, clearly, objectively, and calmly state yours without hemming and hawing. If your manner is gentle and casual, there will be less pricking of irritation in those who disagree with you.

Are You Too Self-Conscious?

Self-consciousness is not unique. Many people, who are prominent and successful, still suffer from it. But what it costs them to carry it! It would be much more sensible to set about conquering it or, at least, minimizing it. And anyone can accomplish his release by training his mind to stay where he puts it. He will naturally focus his mind on something or somebody besides himself. Self-consciousness is no respecter of persons. It can attack kings and commoners alike. No one is immune—nor does it necessarily stay cured. Like some undulant fevers, it may return.

Usually one is self-conscious in some ways and not in others. Certain people or situations can bring that clammy desire to turn and run, while in the presence of certain others, there is great pleasure, warmth, and the desire to show and share.

But when one is more self-conscious than he should be, it is possible that he is getting crusty, too retiring. Such a person gradually develops certain physical difficulties, usually in the digestive tract. He does not like to explain this, so he begins to avoid people altogether, or, as much as possible.

If he is situated where he cannot indulge his desire to get away, he may become seriously ill. The body is very accommodating—or, perhaps a better word is obedient. It does what you tell it to do; not on a superficial level, but on the direction of your inner convictions.

So, use your mind-power to visualize yourself as comfortable with people, comfortable when speaking, accepting honors, being received as a representative of some important commission.

Why not resolve that you will never again, as long as you live, permit the discomfort of self-consciousness to overtake your mind? Just one such resolution does little but start the idea going. But if you will repeat it every day, several times a day, it begins to build into an inner command that will be obeyed. Once you begin to take command, other avenues of strategy against the enemy are seen to be available.

Yes, you can also decide to live with it. But this means that you will live without the freedoms and advantages and comforts of its absence. People carry certain handicaps, certain physical deficiencies and certain fears and bravely build a life in spite of them. *But it probably takes less effort, intelligence, and stamina to get rid of self-consciousness than it does to live with it.*

Besides, any time you can vanquish an inner enemy, you have climbed that much higher in inner strength and can apply that added strength to other matters that will net you genuine rewards.

You have taken an important step in your evolution when you *decide* to overcome your personal handicaps and save your talents for getting along with other people.

Face Yourself Squarely

Use mind-power to make a wise choice of those matters you will correct and to give you the moral strength to live with the difficulties you cannot correct.

If you are going to decide to live *with* a fault then you must mentally grasp it and pull the venom out of its fangs. For you must not settle for a continued suffering. Take measures to keep your feelings from being hurt in the matter.

If there is something you have heretofore hidden, lest you be shamed by it, pull it out in the open. For down in your own soul it can rankle until it damages your body and finally your mind. It can warp your whole personality. Far better to put up with the temporary embarrassment of revelation than to try to live with the fear of it or the point of inharmony it creates within yourself.

Even here, one is supposed to use a modicum of intelligence. Judge and weigh the matter. If a public declaration is going to injure your standing or your ability to make a living for your family, then you should find other techniques of release. Intelligence can be turned on every problem.

Inwardly you can rout the enemy by deciding to build something worthy in its place; to substitute one habit for another; to correct mistakes by going at things properly. And, as you go, take comfort in the salutary laws that a loving Father has placed here for you.

All progress depends on this resolve for correction and betterment. Without it we should simply stand still or slide backward. When you decide to go forward and upward, you have aligned yourself with the basic purpose of existence and you will be surprised by the many aids you will find extended to you—once you prove that you mean what you say. One must speak with authority before the natural forces pay much attention. This seems to be the big secret!

Whatever lack is yours that embarrasses you, set about eradicating it. If you don't make friends readily, for instance, study the art of friendship. Don't imagine that any potential friend is going to force an entry into your life. Each must be won on the merits of your intelligent effort.

Cultivate the smooth, lighter point of view. No matter how tensely our world may be poised on the brink of war, there are ways in which we can bring relief to ourselves and others with a lighter touch here and there.

Get that solemn, tragic look off your face. It drains and empties you of personal force. Fill your personal batteries with the electricity of confidence. Decide that whatever life requires of you, you will behave as the thoroughbred you are—a child of the living God. With such decision, you will discover that you have an astounding amount of inner resource and that it will benefit, not only yourself, but others.

Just Starting Toward Correcting Our Faults Puts Us in Line With the Forces of Right Action!

Why do we keep repeating and repeating our ownership of an old fault? Wouldn't it be more intelligent to set about eliminating it! Are you one who says, "I've always been awkward at entering a room where there are other people," or "I've always had the bad habit of forgetting appointments," or "I've never been any good at arithmetic. I have to get my ten-year-old son to figure out how much roofing or paint or wall-paper I may need for a certain area," or "I'm a poor correspondent. I hate to write letters," or "Yes, I know I have poor posture. I've had it all my life"?

Imagine so-called "intelligent" people living in this slipshod way! Then we wonder *why* the matters of our closer, personal interest fail and fall between the fingers of our grasping hands. Having invoked slipshod ways of going, should we be too surprised that other matters fall into the ditch we ourselves have dug?

List your virtues to keep your self-confidence afloat. Now make a list of, say, three weak spots in your makeup or performance that would be beneficial to correct. It matters not whether they be grave or slight. The important thing is that you take command of yourself and run yourself and your life in a higher gear.

Sometimes the small thing takes on stupendous importance. Suppose on a long motor trip in the summer, your windshield becomes darkened by bugs and other debris. As long as you can see out of one little space, you do not bother to stop and clean it up. Presently, a rainstorm comes. You turn on your windshield wipers, but the wiper blade in front of you smears bugs over the little space that had been clear. At that moment a truck comes around a curve. You don't see the curve or the truck. So failure to clean the windshield may cost you your life or other people their lives. We have no right to be slipshod "as long as it hurts no one but ourselves," for who can tell when it will suddenly concern other people!

I hope you're not one who says, "What I do affects no one but myself. It is nobody's business." I'm sure you are too intelligent to delude yourself in such a blind way. You wouldn't be reading this book if your mind were imprisoned with such notions. Every thought you think, every smallest act, adds weight to the constructive or the destructive aspects of the movement, the kinetics, of life.

I have often bought remnants or rejected items at the outlet store of a huge silk mill. A fault, a little knotting of a thread, or a spreading of one, can run undetected until the end of the weaving. The silk is thrown on sale at, perhaps, a tenth of its value. It is not a total loss, as you see, but it is downgraded from the top classification. It will not be used by a famous designer for an important gown or room. It is second- or third-rate.

Our Little Faults Downgrade Us from Life's Larger Satisfactions

It isn't a bad idea to get some teenager (they're so very frank) to tell us what our small personal faults may be. That is, if life doesn't seem to be bringing us the rewards we think we should have —if we lack appreciation. It's possible that we have picked up mannerisms that are unattractive. Have you ever had someone stand while you are speaking and constantly mutter, "Um huh, Um huh, Um huh, Um huh"? This person has no idea he is doing that, yet after awhile you find yourself very annoyed by it. Set some rules in your mind and check yourself against them. A well-bred, mature person—

1. *Keeps his hands off his face and head,* and relatively still, unless making a descriptive gesture to aid conversation or direction.
2. *Does not interrupt a speaker until he has finished his thoughts.* Neither does he keep on dribbling phrases, so that one can't tell when *he* has finished.

After some thought, it really seems that these two points, if they are well tended, would keep any personality on a much higher level than one might suppose. These suggestions are fathoms deeper than they appear, for they connote so much more than is in them at first glance.

Find Ways to Become Superior to Hurry

In bustling about, a person is simply not at his best. He looks jerky. His voice becomes tense and at least a tone higher, with no overtones of appreciation and warmth. He may accomplish his errand—but at what a cost!

If one's life is full of pressures, one can continually find more and more ways to eliminate worry and flurry points. About keys, for instance—put duplicate sets where you can always get them. Arrange dozens of the details of your life more conveniently. Anticipate your needs and have them at your fingers' ends. It is seldom the big things of life that trip us up. Oh, we attend to those matters diligently, forgetting that the small matters like tiny threads can weave a rope to hang us. Couldn't you improve the care of your clothes, your laundry, and dry cleaning necessities, for instance? You are the only one who can arrange that.

I have read somewhere that when our forefathers were shaping the Declaration of Independence, they took many hours in wording, rewording, rewriting, arguing and criticizing each other's contributions. Their coachmen grew weary waiting as the hours dragged on. Each of the signers was a man of highly individualistic mind and there seemed to be no end to each one's desire to have some phrase extended or clipped to his liking. Finally, a few bees buzzed into the room (one wonders if a small boy had been paid by a coachman to put them in). Somebody was stung. It was hastily agreed that the Declaration was in excellent shape. All hurriedly signed it and escaped the bees. (?)

THE RESPONSIVE UNIVERSE

The nature of *your* universe is that it contains everything of which man can possibly conceive. It holds many forces of which he has not, as yet, become aware. But, however and whenever he asks anything of it, according to its laws, it responds to him. He begins to understand the words, "Before they call, I will answer."

The deeper meaning of these words could be that the universe holds all that man wants and needs, but he must claim it according to its established laws. *He must put himself on the plane of that for which he asks. He must fulfill the conditions by which the satisfaction of his desires and needs come to him.*

Beginning with the invention of the first wheel, man has extended his powers by extending his mind. The *idea* of the wheel had always been in the potential of his environment, waiting to be discovered in his mind.

Now jet power may supersede that great boon of the wheel. The *idea* of various mechanical devices brought convenience and immeasurable help. The *idea* of flying was recognized in man's mind first. The concept of mathematics as a recording and an ordering science and as an aid to further projections of power of all kinds waited millions of years for man's mind to receive it.

Already an automobile has been invented that has no wheels and travels on water as well as on land. It is propelled by gusts of air that force it above the ground or water. It has no particular acceptance at the moment, but it is an advanced phenomenon that will, no doubt, find its place in usefulness in the near future.

Lying next to man's satisfaction in his findings is that accumulation of memory of fear and failure. Back in that retentive, habit-patterned mind lies the sting of much ignorance and error, resulting in a smarting ego and the burden of guilt and fear. He must find a place to lay that burden. He must have relief from that weight if he is to rise.

If you have had your special problem for a long time, you probably think you have some very special disadvantage. But this is not true! No matter what hand pulls the throttle of a boat whistle, the same sound comes out! Your universe will react to you favorably if you will put yourself in the flow of its active laws.

Too many people just sit down under the conclusion that they are especially cursed in some way. But this belief is the rankest superstition. No matter how long you have carried your particular problem, the solution lies available to you in your *mind-power.* And, if you keep digging for it, you will find it. Do not take "No" for an answer. If you fail a dozen times, either personally or in business, just keep on starting again. Sooner or later, you will come upon your answer. *It is there.*

Never Permit Yourself to Become Bitter, Cynical or Disillusioned

Don't display the reactions of the failure. Bitterness and cynicism advertise the misfit. If you will eschew the gestures and sounds of the failure, the rest of the picture will dissolve into its native nothingness.

Always present a gallant, erect, vital picture of yourself to the world. Bravery always gets citations—eventually. But we do not wish to turn to the right way just for the rewards, important though they may be.

Our success will be more penetrating in all the avenues of our lives if we stand on *principle* because it *is* principle. The rewards will be taken care of—more than we would dare plan—by the generous, amazing, always flowing laws of *life.*

But for whatever reason you approach it, life responds. It does not ask your reasons. If you want to be different, *begin to be different.*

Do not accept your problem as unsolvable. Go to the different people it may touch and tell them of your new picture of it and yourself. They will cooperate.

BETTER YOURSELF IN BUSINESS, TOO

Realize that these ideas are not just ephemeral. They work in the marts of business, but they must follow the laws of business, which is often the reflection of one's personal status. Domestic harmony often carries over into business. Follow through on every plane on which you need to succeed.

Brought down into the world of material exchange with a practical thud, theories no longer serve. Obvious, immediate facts are the chief concern. Competition in the markets of the world grows keener and keener. Yet many people with seemingly less to recommend them than the next person get the appointment, make the sale, win the prize. How do they do it?

One hears the bitter remark, "It's not how much you know, but *whom* you know that matters!" Occasionally it does help to know someone who can say a good word for you, but more often than not it works in reverse. An employer may think, "Well, he can't have so much on the ball if he has to ask someone to push him." And all too often the job given a friend or the son of a friend is one which buries initiative, talent, and advancement. A man often gets lost in these friendly, nondescript jobs. He never gets a chance to prove his hard hitting ability. And finally the security of his tidy little graveyard of dreams engulfs his ambition, even his pride —and there he stays.

Another American Dream

It is far better to strike out on one's own and make another American dream come true. One may have to take several detours in order to learn every aspect of certain businesses or careers. This is time well spent, not wasted. How often do you hear someone say, "I wasted all those first years trying this and that." But that time of trial and error was not wasted. A man must know what he doesn't want as well as what he does desire before he can make dependable choices.

Henry Ford once said that a man shouldn't try to make a fortune until he was forty years old. He said that it took forty years to learn how to succeed and hold that success. Early successes, he thought, could leak away through inexperienced judgment. A man needs a few failures to sharpen his wits. Then, thoroughly prepared, not only with knowledge but with firm character and experience, he can then make a fortune in from five to ten years—and keep it.

Turn Failure into Success

Some of our most brilliant businessmen started with nothing and could not even find jobs when they came out of World War II. One such young man got himself a cart and from it sold, on the street, fresh fried fish. He quickly had a loyal clientele, for he had a talent for preparing fish. Soon he needed larger quarters, so he rented an abandoned streetcar and made it, with his own hands, into a quick order seafood restaurant. The crowds grew.

I forgot to tell you that our young man had learned to cook fish on fishing trips—and really excelled at it. He also had made a study of the produce of the sea. There was little he didn't know about it—and the markets for it. He had a fine background for his efforts.

Finally he took a partner and they opened a small seafood restaurant farther downtown. It was a fine success. But he and his partner began to disagree. So they separated and each of them opened his own place. Together they had made money enough for each of them to go on alone—with spectacular results.

Another Success

Before the Ritz Hotel was torn down in New York, I was there in the lounge one day and was reaching into a beautiful lacquered bowl, for the most delicious popcorn I had ever eaten. Each kernel was huge, salted, and buttered—and tender as could be. I finally found out after much difficulty the address of the man who had supplied it. His place was downtown in the financial district in a tiny hidden street, only two blocks long. He had a corner of a small room for his machine. He worked entirely alone.

I began to use great tins of this popcorn as gifts for families at Christmas time. His business grew and grew. He moved frequently, always farther uptown and into larger and larger quarters. For several years I followed the man-with-the-popcorn. Finally I found him in a tall, fine building. He owned the building and occupied one entire floor himself!

What was his secret? He had the best popcorn in the world! He used the best ingredients. He filled orders promptly. He was dependable. His clients relied on him. He worked like a beaver! And lastly, as he began to succeed, he did not begin cutting down on quality as so many manufacturers do. He still works on a definite margin of profit and gives all he possibly can. He tries to see how *much* he can give, instead of how little! Everyone trusts him and likes him. He is a happy man.

Some of this man's lazier friends say, "Yes, Frank has been very, very lucky." I leave the answer to that up to you! But I must say, if Frank has been lucky, he certainly has *made* his luck.

Let's analyze Frank's success

1. He spent several months searching for the finest corn. He went to South America and found it.
2. He took a risk in contracting for enough of it to get it at a good price. But he was fair, even generous, to all the people who had to handle it along the way. He did not try to "chisel" anywhere. So all along the line, people wished him well. It paid in many ways.
3. He worked many extra hours. He attended even to small orders, just as to the large ones—making friends by emergency service at times. In other words, people felt he had their good at heart.
4. He never rested on his laurels. He sought constant improvement, even invented improvements for the processing and packaging of his goods, and added several other party tidbit packages.

Yet, there was a nameless ingredient in Frank's success that might be termed "personality." It was a *genuine caring* about the other person. He thought the best was none too good for his friends and he regarded everyone as his aggregate friend.

When people would talk of the bitter struggle for survival and the duplicity of human nature, Frank would slip away, and go do somebody a favor! He loved people! He loved life! And life and people loved him back! Because of this real interest, he never counted the hours he worked!

Going Back to School Could Help You

Good manners and education are proving to be a solid asset in the business world today. Haven't you noticed that for some years now, many of the most attractive advertisements carry some historic story and picture? The copy writer then relates that incident to the product he is selling. But without a knowledge of literature, history, and biography, the copy writer would be bereft of ideas.

If you want to be "lucky" in business, really digest a good liberal arts course. Perhaps you got one in college, but did you digest it? It is not too late, at any age, to go back to school and thoroughly assimilate such a course. There is much to be gained from the mistakes, as well as the virtues, of many historic and literary figures. Mythology has given us many of our art themes. The personalities, virtues, and weaknesses of the ancient gods and goddesses give a seasoning outlook on life in general. The flow of history shows us what trifles have sometimes bent that stream—and gives us wisdom for the future.

A man is not ready for contact with the world, either socially or in business, until he has informed and educated himself. There are a few exceptions, but their success often turns to ashes since their money will not buy them the recognition they desire. Today, more than ever before, education is necessary to success.

A FOREIGN LANGUAGE IS AN ASSET

With the world shrinking in size because of our speed of communication, the man with an extra language may be right in line for a fine apointment, which, if he proves adequate to it, may be the first of a number of excellent opportunities. Would it be "luck" that brought such a man an opportunity to sell, let us say, tobacco to Germany and bring back some fine German products? I have a young friend whose mastery of Spanish got him a rewarding position in Peru, where he has been a briliant success.

IMPROVE YOUR SKILLS

Evening classes in higher mathematics helped another young friend to a post in a science project. Courses in general science helped another youngster into electronic work where he is distinguishing himself already. He found he needed classes in English and public speaking since he was so often called upon to explain his experiments and findings to large classes and, later, to examiners. And so it goes—all personal skills make good fortune more likely.

Night school has provided the opportunity for many a run-of-the-mill worker to gain that extra value that sent him to the top of his chosen field. The government needs talented people with the mental energy to prepare themselves and the patriotism to stay with it to the end.

A course in Chinese art and its history gained an appointment in a Philadelphia museum for a young woman friend of mine. From there she obtained a post as curator of a famous private collection. She was sent to Germany to buy some pieces from another private collection. There she met her future husband, a diplomat whose career furnished her with an exciting social life among international diplomats.

People Who Want Something for Nothing Usually End With Nothing

There must be an equivalent in inner faith and outer skills in order to attract and to hold success. The few exceptions do not disprove the rule under which most of us operate. Willingness to prepare oneself and to work hard are the soundest foundation for any type of accomplishment.

Willingness is the important word in preparation. Just ploughing through studies grimly may gain a high grade eventually, but the full effect is felt in the result only when one is willing, even enthusiastic, about preparing oneself. Joy in the task is like lubrication to a motor. It seems to smooth over difficulties, melt opposition, and cause all the component parts to work together splendidly.

Many people work hard and are disappointed with results. They have, without doubt, left out some of the other important demands, such as willingness and enthusiasm. Just to drive oneself along joylessly is better than nothing—but only a little better.

A young person said to me recently, "Well, it seems to me that life asks a great deal. Not only must one work like a beaver, but one must *like* it." A great deal, or not, that is the way it is. Take it or leave it.

Dull attitudes eventually shape dull results, whereas the brightness of enthusiasm will carry all before it, eventually. One must be able, in the face of disappointments, to believe in the principle of rightness and brightness and to continue persistently in that full faith. Mr. Micawber of Dickens's creation spent much of his life saying, "Something's bound to turn up." And surely enough, it did. Then came the family chant, "Fortune has, at last, changed in our favor. Fortune has, at last, changed in our favor."

•12•

How to Use Mind-Power to Solve Family Problems

Get to know your family—but really *know them.* It is astonishing how many families spend all their lives together and never actually get to know one another.

Do the same thing you did with yourself. Count up the assets of each member of your family—and count up their faults. Be honest. Give them credit where it is due. Blame them if they are wrong. Keep this list private, but keep it where you can refer to it and perhaps change it from time to time.

Actually this advice is not just for family heads, it is for each member. What is sauce for the goose is sauce for the gander. Getting the list together could be engrossing, even amusing.

Why not make a family project with all members making a list of the virtues and faults of all the other members? This would be something like the "truth sessions" we used to have when I was growing up. Each of us told exactly what we liked and what we didn't like about each other. Though we had promised not to cry when our faults were under discussion, I remember having a hard time choking back the sobs a number of times.

Still, when I was told that it was better to have these irritating matters out in the open instead of rankling behind a veil of silence, I could see that our family would profit as a unit by an honest evaluation of our lives together. In a spirit of love and cooperation and general helpfulness, each of us tried to overcome those faults that were uncomfortable for the others.

When this truth session was first suggested to my mother she was very much against the idea. "Somebody will get his feelings hurt and they may never heal," she said. But later she said that we could do it because we really loved one another and would seek only to help through our criticism.

IT IS IMPORTANT TO ENJOY EACH OTHER

Home is a place for fun. It is also a place for satisfaction, recognition, compliments, and occasional extravagance for a luxury that lets everybody know how much you really value the tenor of your family life. Even if you cannot agree with each member of your family, you can give the amount of attention that says more loudly than words *"you are important to me."* Actually those words and the true meaning of them have often saved a marriage; saved a teenager from falling in with criminals; have even tided the servants over the ravages of some personal shock.

These are the magic words in any intimate relationship, whether it be at home, with friends, or in business. And our families, friends, and business associates *should* be important to us. When people think of you they should always say to themselves inwardly, "There is one person who understands and appreciates me."

Within the walls of your house, it is possible for *you* to see that there is love, protection, loyalty, and support. Not just the support that costs money, but the kind that gives backing to opinions, attitudes, and points of view. You should never let an atmosphere of division and tension arise in your house. Always say, "At *our* house"; never, *"my"* house. Just the other day I heard a man say, "Now, when I decorated my house the last time, I used that African theme." The wife stood by, looking dutifully appreciative, but also a bit wistful. Why couldn't he have said "our house"? And perhaps, even, "when we decorated it"? What did he prove by saying "my" house? He proved that he was fearful of his authority; that he was a little boy who was not going to give up his place to slide down the park slide to any little girl. In other words, he was still very immature emotionally, not a man to trust with a business because he would be likely to do other childish things. And so it is that we brand ourselves by the pressures of our poor, little, screaming egos.

TURNING MIND-POWER ON THE RUNNING OF YOUR FAMILY AFFAIRS SOLVES THEM WELL

There is no problem without a solution; no question without an answer.

Periodically, the family comes in for some downgrading analysis by the press, our comedians, and the cynical harbingers of general doom. Nevertheless, it is difficult to rear birdlings without a nest; difficult to live unto oneself; and impossible to find happiness that is not shared. The family is still the finest place for comfort, satisfactions, amusement—and for soul growth.

Whatever the members of our family are, it is we who have made them so! It remains for each of us to do some genuine soul searching to determine whether we are doing all we should do to make them ideal.

Never mind what someone else is not doing. Ask yourself if *you* have left a number of matters untended. It will do no good to shout to others what *they* should do, if your own family job isn't done. Nevertheless, if you have a family problem (and who hasn't?) find out the facts about it. Find out *who* is responsible. It is entirely possible for you to suppose one person to be at fault when, in truth, it is somebody else who is remiss.

Much hard feeling can result from scolding an innocent victim of a chain of circumstances. A very clever father I know never scolds anybody. In times of crisis, he calls a family meeting and says not a word of criticism; only, "Now what can *we* do about this?" The strong feeling of family unity that results usually brings out any appropriate criticism from the age group of the guilty one. The youngesters keep each other in line, leaving the parents in the position of being there to help and love; not to punish.

Punishment Is Necessary at Times

Direct disobedience, petty dishonesty or being unreliable in ways that cause others distress and inconvenience—these should be punished severely. Carelessness, forgetfulness, and untidiness should be handled on a different basis: that of training, with rewards for good performances "like trained seals," until the children grow up enough to be embarrassed by being rewarded with some kind of "fish" for every good deed. You know you've won when they say, "But, I don't want anything for that." But, since they have to get their money in some way, that might be a good time to outline the jobs they do as contributions to the family, and the others they do for pay.

There Must Be a Schedule

The household schedule shouldn't be one that is so strict that the members of the family feel they are living in a police barracks. But it should be stiff enough to give some sort of *form* to a day. If everyone is allowed to go his own way in *all* matters, confusion will reign. While there must be a great deal of freedom of movement, there should be one or two points—occasions—where custom will be established and adhered to.

The dinner hour could well be the chief one. And number two might be the time of retiring. If people are going to run in and out of the house at outlandish hours every night, there will be neither routine nor respect through which to gain family solidarity. For teenagers, there should be definite hours agreed on with no deviations except for once a year celebrations—and these should be chaperoned.

The Family Conference

What your young people are allowed to do and what they are not permitted to do should be a matter of family conference with an eye to the good of the whole. The family conference we have been describing is an excellent place to establish a set of boundaries. If they are seriously and mutually established, there will not be the stresses of irregularity that would arise were they lacking.

When you call a conference, don't let it sound as though they were going to court to be put on trial. Let it be known that each person will have his say; that every voice will be heard. Also, connect the conference with some privilege or pleasant occasion, or special dinner so that there is a bit of festivity in the connotation. Do not permit it ever to sink into a grim affair.

TRUTH WILL OUT

It is just possible that the family problem is *you.* Take your own medicine and follow the loving suggestions of the rest of the group as to how you can best eliminate the trouble spots. Be impersonal, no matter who is being discussed—yourself or some one else.

NO RECRIMINATIONS

Never say, "I told you so," or "How many times do I have to tell you?" or "Just as I thought!" or "You'll never get anywhere with that attitude." The obvious answer will be, "But I don't want to get anywhere. I just want to be let alone!" Be careful not to close the door of the conference by assaults on others' egos.

Talk with the Wrongdoer

After the conference, try to help the persons who have been proved to be at fault. If a son is under fire, go to him privately, sit down and have a warm, intimate, sympathetic talk. Be more frank than you have ever been before. Don't be angered if he doesn't show appreciation at once. He doesn't know, for the moment, how to respond to you without letting down some barriers that may be important to him. He has to feel his way. Be patient. Let him know what you expect of him.

Teach Him to Apologize

If, in your home life, apologies come easily and perhaps often in gracious, even light terms, your children will not find it so hard to ask forgiveness in important matters.

But if they have grown up in a tight-lipped atmosphere where apologies were considered tantamount to surrender, they will never be able to make a clean breast of an error or a rudeness.

Teach your children that thoroughbreds apologize because they can so richly afford it. Only cheap, little, inexperienced, half-baked people find it hard to use the graciousness of apology. It is not a sacrifice of dignity to say, "I was wrong. I'm sorry." It raises the person in the estimation of every mature mind within hearing.

Best of all, apology dissolves a resistance in the soul of the person doing it, and thus maintains a healthful flowing of salutary forces. All little knotty points of resistance tend to reflect in the body sooner or later. We should make every effort to keep our psyche as *clean* and *free* as possible. It is interesting that nearly all points of good manners have a spiritual (and often physical) connotation.

Explain to Your Child That His Mind-Power Can Guide His Acts

Tell the erring one to call upon the Mind within him to help him in making decisions before he acts impulsively and, perhaps, wrongly. Tell him not to hesitate to lean on the judgment and considerateness deep in his own mind when he needs to do so. Tell him there is a *Mind* within him that knows everything and that he can draw upon it. He has just as much of it as all the "right" people.

Tell him not to think of himself as a black sheep or a moral or spiritual cripple. *Mind*—intelligence—is innate, intrinsic, and, like the sun, available to everybody who will walk out in it. It has no favorites. *Those who seem to be favorites are simply those who have presented less resistance to the good forces. They are the people who expect the right to work for them.*

Tell him not to expect miracles as he works with his faults, but to be willing to build slowly and well within himself. Tell him he will not be nagged or teased if he will make a sincere effort to right himself. Above all let him know that you love him.

Love Is the Great Healer

In your son's presence relate some generous or brave act from way back in his childhood to stir again those manly impulses that may have been overlaid with the impact of his present poor examples among his friends. And, speaking of his friends, let your love extend to them.

Ask him if he would like to bring them to meet his mother. Even if he accepts, he will worry about the contrast between them and his own dear mother. And even if they come, he will be more sharply aware of the gulf between their moral and other points of view and yours. But if he knows *you* are willing to accept him and his friends, *he will bestir his own good judgment,* which may have been lying fallow.

Bring him small gifts, little conveniences for his desk, such as paper, rubber bands, stickers, etc. Not all at once, but day by day, to show your interest in the details of his life. This is a far better way to show it than merely asking questions, which sound as though you were prying. Sometimes it is necessary to do both. But do try not to look disapproving. Let him know you have faith in both his ultimate judgment and certainly his good taste.

Try Using Suggestion Rather Than Direct Assault on His Judgment

Paint a picture of your child's future in comfortable, acceptable terms. Retell some anecdote in which he came out well, showing him that the right approach to other problems would bring about equally happy results. Show him that somewhere along the line he has *already used mind-power* to solve a problem or to gain an end. Thus, you are not asking him to take up a strange innovation.

Explain to him that everything that happens to him is a result of his own ideas or ideas he has accepted from others; that everything is the direct result of logical procedures, inherent in what he does. These of necessity will work for him—in the way he directs—*if* he will furnish the salutary pattern.

Show him that he has made the bed he is presently lying in—and having made that, he can make something else. Explain to him the forgiving laws inherent in nature. And that this means his own mistakes will be washed out, replaced by better sequences of events, if he follows the laws governing such matters. Explain that these laws are *friendly laws,* not punishing ones and that they will work *for* him if he will arrange it that way.

Go over his strong points appreciatively. Show him where a kindness or a wise act somewhere along the line has brought approval and compliments to him. Remind him of his good appearance.

The End of This Interview Is of Overwhelming Importance

See that the talk ends pleasantly, even if your child has made angry contributions to it. Just say, "Oh, you'll get over feeling that way. You're smart enough to guide your emotions and decide how you want things to turn out."

Do not let him feel that you think you have moved him around to suit yourself or that you have won some contest, because you have right on your side. This will only make him feel more belligerent. If you are sure your good suggestions have at least landed, then change the subject.

Suggest he take a ride with you down to the office where you'd like to show him something or ask him something. (This last one is a winner.) Ask him to watch the game on television with you—or better, take him to the game being played. Give him two tickets for some attractive event, whether athletic, cultural, or social, such as a dance. Take him to lunch at your businessmen's club or haunt. Do something *together*—bowl, fish, play pool, or a good card game.

Ask him if he'd like to have a dance at home some weekend. Turn the rugs back and let the youngsters have a fling. Join in. It isn't unlikely that youngsters get off on the wrong ways largely because there isn't enough family fun together. Too many young people have come to regard home as a place to get money one way or another; get scoldings; get preachings; do dull, or outright unpleasant things.

MAKE HOME A PLEASANT PLACE, WHERE YOU SHARE, AND CARE, WHAT HAPPENS THERE

Don't come home and retire into your paper, television program, old slippers, and silence. At least not for more than twenty minutes. And you would be far better off lying down with the door shut for that twenty minutes. Get in a horizontal position when you want to rest. Don't try to rest sitting up. This merely means that you crumple, and cause yourself a possible injury.

Then, once up on your feet, *join the family* for a time. More than anything else, this being *with* your wife (husband) and children knits the family circle. Have something pleasant to say to each of them. *Don't be afraid of extravagant compliments.* People go all their lives (some of them) hungering for some extravagantly foolish approval. It helps all of us to know that *somebody* sees us through rosy glasses that minimize our faults and magnify our good points.

My own father used to ask me to go for walks with him and usually he talked to me while we strolled in woods, parks, or on city streets. He fed into my mind seeds of confidence and courage.

He had noticed some phrase of mine in a letter that he thought was especially good. He had observed some attitude of mine, if only a fleeting moment, that he thought I could extend to my profit. He laughed attentively at my jokes. He said I was very witty.

He noted that I seemed to be studying people when I was listening to them and said, "You have naturally, a very analytical mind." Under this type of encouragement my natural *curiosity* did turn into the channel of analysis! It might have remained curiosity without his shrewd suggestion.

My parents encouraged us to express ourselves at the table if there were no guests. (Otherwise, children should be seen and not heard.) Alone with the family, my sister and I were required to debate briefly any given subject. We were supposed to defend our point of view (the one given us, of course) without recourse to sarcasm or hurtful personal remarks. But if one of us did get our feelings hurt, we had to face it down and not return in kind. If we cried, we had to leave the table and eat in the kitchen. "The table is for mature people."

Both father and mother spent a great deal of time with us. We sang together with or without an accompaniment. In fact, when either of us would begin to cry about anything, father would start lustily singing "Onward Christian Soldiers, Marching As To War." It is an inspiring song, as you know. And it always suggested to us that we should be soldiers and keep our chins up, as well as being forgivingly Christian. Besides that, we thought it was amusing that father would start singing in the middle of a family crisis and we would laughingly join in, while we were wiping our eyes and getting our faces back to normal.

Make Living at Your House Important in Little Ways

My father never came to the table without wearing a coat. In hot weather (and it gets very hot in Kentucky, Tennessee, and Virginia) he wore a thin alpaca coat or a thin white linen. He had been brought up to believe that the family's gathering at the table was an important function of living and he did not think it should ever be slighted. He thought if people meant to grab and dash, wearing any old thing, that they should not do so in the dining room, but elsewhere.

I'm glad he never saw a roomful of teenagers eating untidily off television trays while they sprawl in rude, unhealthful postures, gradually absorbing a completely irreverent attitude toward parents, law, and God, Himself. What can you expect of young people being formed in that mold!

Far from being a stiff, serious, dull affair, a meal at our house was often hilarious; but always within the bounds of, at least, a loose structure of good manners and good taste.

A Vine Will Grow the Way It Is Trained

About the silliest idea ever foisted off on the American public is the notion that children are going to develop all by themselves, permissively and without training, into the finest kind of ladies and gentlemen. Well, we have at least one generation of that kind of thing! It costs the taxpayer a great deal to try to pick up the pieces of that debacle—probably more than foreign aid.

If permissiveness made children happy, I would be a little less against it. But they are not happy. People are pleased only when they feel they are expressing the best of themselves to some degree.

If your sons and their friends see the man of the house seating the ladies at table *always,* not just sometimes, they will develop a more wholesome attitude toward women, in general, and the mothers and sisters of their group, especially. A man loses a portion of his innate manhood when he ceases, or never learned, to respect women.

Of course, since today's women are quite likely to do the cooking and the serving, it is a little harder for the men to be gallant at table. Nevertheless, it can be managed at the beginning of the meal—even if mother does have to get up and get things later. If she plans with this very thing in mind, she can reduce getting up to a minimum.

"Why bother?" you may say. Well, you can't go about shouting, "I respect women. And I'm for some form in behavior, whether I act that way or not." Oh, no, children and neighbors go by what you *do*. If you give your home life some form and beauty, they must respect it!

Have you ever noticed that grownups will actually brag about the demands of their parents back home? But have you ever heard them bragging about the permissiveness? No! And you never will! Because no one is proud of it. You can, at least, give your children something to brag about.

Having a crowded, modest home is no excuse. Even on a hay ride and picnic, the amenities of gallantry and respect can be observed *while* you are having a hilarious good time! Solemnity and stiffness are no part of gracious living! "Informality is the greatest test of breeding," so thought Lady Mendl, who never invited anyone the second time if he thought informality meant that one could open one's collar and loll about. Yet, she was famous for her amusing parties and people vied for invitations to them.

One's manners should be no different riding in the front of a truck than they are at a gorgeous house. At a beach, mountain cabin, lake resort, or backyard picnic, manners are quite the same. Gentlemen are gallant, act in good taste, are properly clothed, and contribute to the fun with merry conversation. Ladies, except for the appropriate costume for the moment, look and act the same no matter what they are doing. They never fall apart; never shriek with laughter.

Teach your children that they can have more fun without breaking social rules than they can by flouting them and bringing out ugliness and awkwardness and embarrassment. Make your house a place where people like to come; where the children like to be. Family problems have a way of dissolving in such a place.

·13·

How to Use Mind-Power to Solve Career Problems

TO GO AHEAD DENOTES ACTION. TO GO AHEAD REquires new mental pictures. To go ahead is to break with the past. The latter point is, perhaps, the most important. Going *ahead* means leaving the present, moving up, changing for the better.

While one should always be progressing in the inner and the outer life, the ambitious person would do well to understand thoroughly that he cannot move ahead and at the same time hold on to old faults. Therefore he must focus *all* his forces on the forward movement. He must not stubbornly say, "They must take me as I am—or else!" This attitude has killed more careers (and marriages!) than any other.

CHANGE—AND FOR THE BETTER

If one makes changes, improvements, in those parts of himself and his life that he does now control, he will find that he has created the image of improvement in his own mind, and in the minds of others.

If his employers, or associates, notice that his posture, or voice, or disposition is better than it was, they will, quite unconsciously, suppose that he is due for other kinds of improvement.

Decide How You Want to Change

What do you really want from your career? Have you achieved the position and the income you ultimately want? Can you go further? Answer the following questions privately:

1. What is your real goal?
2. Can you achieve it where you are working now?
3. Could you go further immediately?
4. What does your present field hold for you in the future?
5. Should you get out of this field and get into another?
6. What are the possibilities for getting another job?

It will behoove you to make a decision on your career now. Decide which way your career should take you. *Now* is the time. The decision is probably long overdue!

Change—or Stay

It sometimes happens that the new field is found right where one is. It could be a different angle on your present occupation, a different action or service in the same business. Changing does not always mean a complete uprooting and a moving to another location or city, although it might.

Ask yourself if the *change* needs to be in *you,* rather than in the place or activity. It is entirely possible that if *you* showed a different spirit—a concentration of more detailed interest in the work in which you are now engaged—that advancement and reward could be had right there.

What Would Constitute Your Improvement in Your Job?

Would your employer be more interested in you if you came in a little earlier and stayed a little later? Would it not enhance your standing if you had some good ideas for more business: some short-cuts in buying, or the paper work, or in some creative fashion? Can you think of any way to make your employer's day easier, less harassing? (This might create a new office with your name on the door.)

Do You Need More Education?

Wouldn't it help you, and your employer, if you knew more of the technical background of what you are doing? Even though your post may not be an executive one, wouldn't you feel more solidly helpful if you know the details that confront the inner workings of the business?

Howard Hughes built his empire on knowledge of what he was doing. He has always gone to the base of every enterprise and knows from personal experience every angle, every move, every effort of every man in his vast activities. He invented many of the improvements that have been enjoyed, not only by his own firms, but by all kindred ones.

How Is Your English?

Many a man knows his business but does not possess the flawless speech that alone carries conviction, dignity, and persuasion. Even though you may have gone through school and college with high grades in English, you must not assume that you have a graceful and convincing facility with words. "It takes many drops of water to wear away a stone."

Only constant practice gives one facility with words. As you will meet repetition of this thought often in all my writings, you will come to know how deeply I believe in the efficacy of words, well-chosen and spoken in the best tone of voice.

How Do You Sound?

Is your speech a fine representation of the company for which you work? Is your speech a good representation of your own excellent qualities? Your speech, almost more than your body, is really your show window, where the wares of your usefulness, your character, your level of culture are immediately displayed.

Is your speech the bearer of sympathetic understanding, *awareness* of the other person? Some "perfect" speakers seem only in need of an audience, an effect you must avoid with all the energy of your mind.

Never seem to be listening to your own speech! How often do you hear a *glib* talker sound as though he were reciting a piece and enjoying the sound of his own voice! The *good* speaker is using his skills to carry ideas straight to your mind and heart. He has learned his techniques, polishes them occasionally, but otherwise becomes almost unaware of them.

Mind-power is nowhere better shown than in the best uses of words and voice. For instance, the finest, most remembered orators turn out to be the men and women with excellent minds, highly disciplined lives, and extended talents. If you recall the most effective speeches you have ever heard, it is more than likely that the speakers are among the people who have and have had the greatest influence on the greatest number of human beings.

BE OBJECTIVE ABOUT YOURSELF

Oversensitiveness has no place in the reactions of a man who wants to get ahead. The ambitious person would do well to seek criticism instead of resisting and hating it. As a proverb says, "Faithful the wounds of a friend." The person who tries to give you helpful criticism is risking the loss of your friendship. His (or her) unselfishness in the matter should be valued beyond rubies and diamonds!

Oversensitiveness is the mark of the immature person. Suppose our leaders should react to criticism as the average person does! They would crack under the strain. Think of the insults that are heaped upon nearly all public figures. They must endure the caricatures, the honest and dishonest evaluations of themselves, and not permit any of these impacts to disturb the steady forward flow of their self-esteem and their efforts in their responsible posts.

Suppose the late Eleanor Roosevelt had burst into tears at every derogatory attack? She would have been a nervous wreck instead of having weathered it all and won the respect of her enemies and the love of her friends.

The emotionally mature person knows that he should improve every day. He knows he cannot rest on his laurels. He must be constructively active every day. He must keep his blade shining, his mind at top efficiency, his body hard, compact, and responsive. This is not too much to demand of himself. *It is only when he has done the best he can and has won his way at some points* that he is able to see the value of criticism.

Just to say that one realizes the value of friendly criticism is merely a movement in the frontal lobes of the brain, an intellectual conclusion. The *real conviction* must fall into the subconscious, involuntary brain processes located usually in the rear lobes before one is free of the animalistic urge to strike back as though one had been attacked.

This is an important point in a man's progress. When an animal's position is challenged in any way, he prepares to fight. This reaction was imbedded in his make-up by millions of years of repetitive experience and his response is predicated on that mass of experience. But man no longer has use for this outmoded reaction. While it may have protected him in his earlier phases, now it is a detriment to him and must be thrown aside as a worn-out garment.

Man's mind has brought him into a higher set of demands and responsibilities that are not to be found in the animal status. Now he must understand that he must leave no stone unturned to bring himself to top, personal power. He must understand that *petty revenges* are closely akin to the strike-back of the reptile and that he must rise above this state if he is to claim the other strengths and privileges of his humanness. In other words if he wants a larger life, a larger job with larger pay, he must become a larger person.

This does not mean that he is not to defend himself when necessary. It does mean that he must not weaken and confuse his mind and soul with wasteful, cheap, low emotions; for they tend to keep him base and small.

Outmoded Defense

One can easily trace the history of the wrong picture of *ego,* which is distorted by the phenomenon of unnecessary self-defense, triggered by an honest criticism, perhaps. There was once a time when this type of defense was needed. But, to repeat, that time is past. Yet, when fighting off attack, the animalistic man won, he was quite likely to roar or bellow his supremacy. Thus, his world was taught to beware of him, to fear him, and to treat him with the proper respect.

This was fine as long as he stayed on his two feet and in fighting trim. But let him falter and none would come to his aid. The dislike that his impingement on the egos of his environment had brought against him was, in the end, his undoing.

Certainly a modern man seeking advancement in his career must be more than careful of the egos around him. Yet he must waste no time in the animalistic phase of ego himself. For it shrivels his forces, his inspiration, and personality almost more than anything else. His worst enemy could do little more to him than he does to himself in this destructive mire of ego.

When he has disciplined his emotional reactions toward criticism, then, and only then, is he executive material, capable of leading, judging, and planning the efforts of other men. Only then can he remain calm, see clearly, retain his forces intact for the creative leadership demanded of him by a higher post.

The words, "the *you* attitude," are indeed cliches. Even so, each of us can number on the fingers of one hand the friends we have who are disciplined enough to have a firm grip on this attitude. *Many of us know of its rewards and benefits* and because of them we try to unself and to place the other person first. We develop a surface sort of politeness which bears the appearance of "the *you* attitude." But just below that surface the rampant ego is pulling at the reins to grab for itself the center of the stage, the credit, the fair or unfair advantage. What can be done?

GETTING AHEAD IN A CAREER DEPENDS ON THE EXTRA VALUE ONE GIVES

What is your extra value? Here are a few extra values that will get results:

1. *Do you know more of your subject than anyone else?* (If not, why not?)
2. *Are you willing to travel to discover advantages?* Invest? Study?
3. *How is your disposition?* Is it beguilingly pleasant? Or do you lose

your temper and use abusive language when you are displeased? (Yes, I know that some people with tempers have won. But have you?)

4. *Do you have faith in your future?* Or do you think that promotions go to people who "buy" their way or are related to the employer? (If you think that it isn't *what* you know, but *whom* you know that helps you, you are heading for failure, for you will have dwarfed the force of your own personality. Cynical points of view *appear* to be justified at times. But in the end, capacity wins.)
5. *Are you in a good state of health?* (If not, why not?) Some accidents and even physical handicaps have been overcome by other virtues. Even though all of us knew that Franklin D. Roosevelt was a paralytic, few of us were acutely aware of his handicap, even when looking directly at him! It was the fact that he made little of his condition that caused others to follow his cue. His inner resolves and drives gave him great physical and psychic magnetism which even his enemies recognized. *So do not use your body as an excuse.* It isn't a good one, other than temporarily.
6. *Do you think of yourself as an unusually fortunate person?* (Or do you tell the world over and over the misfortunes of your life?) Both friends and employers gravitate toward the person who is fortunate. *Probably this is the most effective point in the book.*

If you think matters are going to work out well for you, you build a nucleus of forces that draws to itself solutions that are convenient, timely, and harmonious. If you go around thinking and talking about how much goes wrong for you, you are extending this false pattern into the future.

I say "false" because that is exactly what it is. Every American, certainly; and probably every human being has countless blessings and advantages, myriads of conveniences and comforts which he shares with others, but which he had no part in contriving.

If you will put your mind on being aware of your gains instead of your losses, you cannot help attracting more. For, as we keep repeating, you are a sovereign being and your word is eventually your law. What you say becomes true for you.

Repeat and Repeat

No matter how dark matters seem to be, keep calling the situation "good," even though for the time being it sounds nonsensical to you. Certainly you will never find the *good* if you don't claim it, articulate it, repeat it, become acutely aware of it, plant it like a seed in the soil of life's flow of events—and *expect* it to come.

Certainly, to people trying to bring order to their own disordered lives, emotions, and businesses, you will become distasteful if you insist on presenting yourself as unfortunate! That is just what they want to avoid, to shun! Why, in the name of common sense, will people persist in picturing themselves as victims!

It isn't that one's friends are unsympathetic. They will gladly listen once or twice and do what they can—but they do not want to be subjected to the "germs" of things going wrong, disaster. They get all they want of this in the newspapers, which seem to give them a neatly vicarious knowledge of life's dissonance. But they want it no closer than the printed word, which they can put aside at will, and which makes them feel so fortunate because they are not a part of it.

However this explanation may strike you, there is no avoiding the truth that if you let a reputation for ill luck (fostered by yourself) become attached to you, you are building your own toboggan to nonentity.

MIND-POWER IMPROVES WITH AGE. THUS NO MAN SHOULD FEAR RETIREMENT

Our laws and customs in the matter of retirement may be somewhat faulty, when one considers our extended life expectancy. But the individual can still build his life on his own energy and ability. I used to think that the retirement age should be extended. But, since giving the matter more study and observation, I perceive that early retirement gives many a man the opportunity to create for himself another career, one that may fulfill his hopes and dreams more fully. Many a man over 65 finds his greatest satisfactions and larger earnings after that age.

The man of 65, healthy and able, often resents being "put out to pasture" at the peak of his powers. But instead of poisoning his mind (and body) with rebellion against the so-called "ingratitude" of his employers and criticism of their unwisdom in not recognizing that he has not slowed down in his usefulness at all, he would be far better off using his full energy in planning a *new life* for himself.

A Second Career

I know several men and women who have grown rich dealing in real estate after their retirement. One woman used her original savings to make a down payment on a three-unit place, where she lived in one apartment and rented the other two. The rentals covered the payments on the place and left a generous margin. By saving this margin and adding to her current earnings through part-time work as a designer, she soon made a down payment on another property. On she went until she has now built an estate to enjoy as long as she lives, which will be left a substantial bequest to her daughter when she dies. The last time I saw her she looked younger than ever. She was chic, happy, and full of energy.

Another woman I know has spent her time complaining, criticizing, resenting her plight. She spends her money on spas, seeking cures for her many aches and pains. She will tell you all about them at the drop of a hat.

One should begin at 35, 45 at the latest, to prepare for a career after retirement! It is difficult to find a new way suddenly. But every living person knows he is going to be older next year and the next year. Instead of dreading or fearing that steadily approaching age of 65, he should be eager for it, whetted, *ready* for the new thing.

He should be *projecting* plans into the future. Never say, "But, how do we know what the future holds? I don't want my plans to go awry. I don't want to be disappointed." I constantly repeat, "to project yourself into the future is to lengthen and strengthen your life." You may change your plans—but have them you must! In any case, working *with* the laws of becoming, having skills, polishing expectations, gathering data and packing one's mental bags for another journey into experience after 65 will keep you healthier, your step firmer, your eye brighter, your laughter merrier.

I know two men who warded off arthritis in their hands by taking up piano and organ playing when they were over 70. I know two others who learned to play the guitar and the accordion and augment their income by playing for groups and parties.

As a matter of fact, I know several young men who learned to play musical instruments and used their skills to help themselves through college. One of them was a pre-med student in Seattle, and the other was "Buddy" Rogers, later to become the husband of Mary Pickford. When he was a college boy, "Buddy" wanted to travel. So he, with a friend, started out on a cattle boat. They had almost no money and would have had a difficult time, if they hadn't been able to play their horns. Fortunately, music is a universal language, so they could get an audience here and there and a little money. In telling me about it years later, "Buddy" said, "It was a good thing I had my horn along!" All of us should have a "horn" of some kind.

A college girl I knew gained quite a reputation for fortune telling and became much in demand for parties. She was able to pay for most of her college costs in this way. Another became a part time cateress. Others sang, gave readings and some of them sewed to provide extra income. One became a part-time assistant to a florist and created beautiful floral arrangements.

One can serve in some way the needs, appetites or amusements of others and call that the extra value that will become substantial to his life, his popularity, and his bank account. (A millionaire I know is a first-rate amateur magician.)

It Is Important to Have a Growing Bank Account

No temptations or dilemmas should keep one's savings a void. Put your extra money, no matter how small the amount, *away.* Buy United States Savings Bonds, on sale at most post offices as well as banks. *Buy a "Baby" Bond each week or each month.* The cost for one is $18.75. In ten years one receives for it $25, a tidy and sure way to have some small, but solid, stones in one's foundation. If one is poor, the $25 is a real bonanza. And if one is affluent, it becomes a pleasant extra, a possible gift to help educate some deserving young person, or to help some older person's dream come true. You work for your money. Why not make your money work for you?

However convenient money on hand may be, its greatest boon is that described in *I Remember Mama,* which told of the psychological effect of an inner peace and dignity—the natural result of having something to fall back on, the feeling of calm assurance because of some manner of support.

An inner feeling of worth is favorable to increased mind-power. At least it should be! But, if one spends too much time congratulating himself about anything, his emanations curve in upon himself and he makes no impact upon the world. His smugness may even be irritating. But if he lets his growing financial support simply smooth his brow and calm his hands so that he can have even *more attention for others,* his Savings Bonds will have served their best purpose.

Get Ready Now

Having decided what career you would prefer, get ready for it. Perhaps you feel trapped where you are because of benefits and the possibility of a pension after a certain amount of time has been spent there.

Instead of feeling trapped, take on the extra work or study that will bring you into career number two. You think you can't? That is nonsense. Break with the limited energy patterns that bind most people to small accomplishment! Do not listen to the people who "sympathize" with you because of your burdens. They weaken you and reduce you to an animal state where your very life will be in jeopardy through brevity and the acceptance of a number of lower indignities! Tell them to run along!

Extended mind-power will enable you to have two careers at once without harm to your mind or body. But it will do this *only* if you will break with the accepted notions of fatigue. At least you can *prepare* for the second one.

If your present income does not cover both expenses *and* savings, then take on a secondary job one or two nights a week. Bookkeeping, baby-sitting, housework, or, at the other extreme, helping a scientist with the hundreds of small tests he must carefully record and index. Even at $1.50 an hour, two evenings of four hours each will give you 12 extra dollars—and these can be saved. That is $48 a month, or

$576 a year. In two or three years, you could have enough for: *a trip through Europe, a down payment on a piece of property, a year or two of college.*

Do not buy perishable things with your savings! Do not buy a car, furs, fashionable, expensive clothes, or anything that is going to wear out. Buy silver, jewelry, travel, education, real estate, bonds, furniture, paintings, art objects (if they are well chosen).

If you must have a car, then buy it out of current expense money, not out of your extra earnings. If a car is a necessity, then don't buy it with luxury money. That is confusing the entire issue. Buy a used car and go to night school to learn how to take care of it. Every male and many females should study mechanics, simple electrical wiring and connections, and elementary plumbing. *In the course of a long life, this knowledge will be worth anywhere from five to twenty-five thousand dollars.*

Profitable Buying

I know several couples who saved enough in two years for a fast trip to Europe simply by changing their way of buying food supplies. By going a couple of miles out of their way, they found unbelievable reductions in current prices; and by buying in bulk they cut their total cost of food almost in half.

Do not accept the current, popular notions of status buying. Be original, imaginative, creative. Plan ahead. You might get another family or two to share your bulk buying savings.

Even perishable fruits and vegetables can be bought in bulk if provision is made for distributing, preserving, or storing them. A little forethought solves the problem. By turning your refrigerator up to the coldest point possible, everything in it will freeze, giving you time to deal with its contents. Discover the convenience and the boon of having supplies on hand by buying a second refrigerator and connecting it in a spare room. It is not absolutely necessary to have hundreds of dollars invested in this type of equipment.

Perhaps I should care more about what the neighbors think. But somehow it doesn't seem half as important to me to have a new car, the latest freezer, or television set as it does to get the same service and have money enough left for the matters that are important to me, such as entertaining my friends, buying books, and travelling (all grist for anybody's second career).

Many extras we may have thought beyond our incomes can be had if we sit down and sort out our expenses independently. (Never mind the usual way!) Many a time I've decided to give a party rather than buy a new suit. Many a time I've sent flowers to a friend instead of buying my dinner. Most of us can skip a dinner occasionally with a great benefit! A partial fast rests the digestive system and clears the brain. I don't believe in overdoing the idea, but it just is not necessary to keep one's body stuffed at completely regular intervals. It is often more important to feed our minds and souls with the beauty of nature, with a poem, or a song, or a generosity. It pays to break into the routine of physical tyranny once in a while.

At whatever point we can put Mind in the ascendancy, we should do so. For it is by constantly recognizing that Mind can set up new patterns that we keep the door of possible advancement open.

What has all this to do with your career? More than you may think!

SEEK YOUR DREAM

If you firmly believe that nothing can permanently hinder you from attaining your goal in life, neither age, calamity, nor time can keep it from you. You will one day live to see your dream come true.

Your only real enemies are hopelessness and despair. And if you will permit yourself to see, to become convinced, that by breaking out of certain compulsive routines of community and group thinking, you can *find a way to do what you want to do,* you will, at that very moment, have started on your way.

Let us go back to the idea of your keeping the job you have while you begin to work on another one. I have tried to convince you that you can find the energy for this double activity without hurt to yourself, if you will not fall into the pit of thinking you are overtaxing yourself.

The virtues in such a procedure would be that you would be making a living *while* you were experimenting with your other talents. You might even try out several paths of endeavor. And, of course, there is always the possibility that you might like to break away entirely from your present occupation and throw all your energies into a new direction.

To make a complete change, sacrificing seniority and the privileges of retirement benefits, requires much thought. There are few circumstances that warrant such a great risk. But should you be the exception where such a move would be for the best, it is still prudent for you to move cautiously.

Never Air Your Disapproval or Distaste for Your Present Occupation

Undisciplined expression of pettiness, resentment, and kindred weakening reactions would militate against your getting any help whatever from your present employers. Whereas, if you stated that you simply felt you must widen your scope and felt grateful for the long support you have had where you are, it is quite possible that they might help you make a new connection, or give you a better job where you are.

Gossip, complaints, and sly feuds never add anything to a man's stature. See that you do not gather them around your name. *Gratitude, respect, and loyalty put a man in the executive class faster than anything else.* You want to present yourself to the field of employers as a mature, controlled, responsible, and therefore valuable, employee. Anything else is sheer, childish nonsense.

Suppose you want to go into business for yourself. If you have refused to make petty enemies where you are, every man in this organization may be the means of some advantage to you in your new business. At least you will not have shut doors in your own face. It is never good sense to burn your bridges.

See to it that you leave a good taste in the mouths of your employers. Whatever petty satisfaction there may be in "telling someone off" before you go out and slam the door, is the pleasure of little souls and has no place in the record of a man who is building a fine life or a great career. If you desire largeness of scope, of opportunity, of action, then do not brand yourself a petty, little man with a small animal's temper and reactions.

Show your controlled, analytical, lifted, executive mind, by understanding any criticism of yourself, any seeming injustice to yourself as something that your own personality would have attracted wherever you would have been at the level of your present development. It is likely to be partly true anyway. Even if you do not deserve it, your best interests are served by behaving and speaking as a superior man. Keep an attitude of calm understanding and your mind can then function at its highest and best.

Don't move away leaving behind enemies who may arise to destroy you later. Speak only about the best of each man you have dealt with. This is not hypocritical. It is a high and just judgment. Why should you record another's faults, when it is much more truthful and much more profitable to record his virtues?

You Take Yourself Along

Using mind-power to adjust your life to a new gear, you see how useful the better parts of your past are. The life you have drawn around yourself where you are is about the same life you would have attracted somewhere else. For you are the center, the nucleus, the focal point of your own life. And don't forget that when you move to a new job or even a business of your own you are going to take yourself along.

If you want your new life to be really new, then you, yourself, must be new.

Add as much elevation as you can muster to all the departments of your thinking, your reactions, your entire outlook. Move up and don't bring any of the debris along with you. Remember that all other men are capable of the same growth that you are making. They are or will be changing for the better. See them as potentially fine people and they will, soon or late, become that to you.

The man of extended mind-power does not foolishly drag the heavy burden of other men's lower reactions. He focuses on their higher, better ones, thus bringing them more into manifestation. Without the clutter and cross currents of the trivia of discord, he steps easily ahead. He can travel without friction because he is unencumbered by unnecessary weights and tangles.

His steps are clean, sure, strong, swift. Others marvel that all goes so smoothly for him. The wiser among them may well ponder, "Is his life so smooth that nothing untoward happens to him, or is it that he picks his way unerringly through the disorder of this planet? Perhaps he recognizes only the higher way of each soul he encounters. How strong he must be!"

He never takes "no" for an answer. He may politely accept a temporary rejection of himself or his ideas, but like water, he simply flows into other channels. The only finality he knows is his own feeling for expansion, for growth, for the flowering of plans and patterns of worth. Nothing in so-called experience can alter this inner knowledge of the sureness of the process of life's becoming—constantly, ceaselessly, moving ahead creatively.

He feels himself to be part of that surging life force that moves outward into form and substance. Therefore, if he works with the laws of that force, he can reasonably expect results of growth.

He feels that by obeying the laws of career growth he becomes master of them. He knows that decisions are made in the executive office of his mind and he intends to keep that initiating, sustaining, authoritative place in clean, smooth working order.

Enlightened minds for several thousand years have known that inner order must precede outward authority—that is, if it is to be permanent. Plato has given us this thought, well expressed in the *Dialogues:*

"Then, tell me, O Critias, how will a man choose a ruler who will rule over him? Will he not choose a man who has first established *order in himself,* knowing that any decision that springs from anger or pride or vanity can be multiplied a thousandfold in its effects upon the citizens?"

How Will You Sell Your Talents?

Now that we have discussed some ideas that may help to break up your habit patterns into more useful ones, what do you consider your extras to be? Since, in order to have more, you must give more and be more, how do you propose to qualify for more?

Let us suppose that you have readied yourself, or have naturally some salable ability, how will you use *mind-power* to sell yourself? It is elementary that you will go to an area where your talent can be used. How now will you gain the ear of someone in a position to employ you, join your plans, invest with you or buy your ideas?

There's an amusing story about a young man who applied for a position as office boy. He found a long line of hopefuls ahead of him. After a few moments in which he decided that he didn't have a ghost of a chance, he had a sudden inspiration. He darted across the street to a telegraph office and sent this message back to the firm he hoped would engage him. "The tall, redheaded boy at the end of the line is your best bet. He'll make a crackerjack office boy." Needless to say, he got the job.

Originality, inventiveness, and humor are cherished by most employers.

•14•

How to Use Mind-Power to Conquer Fear

FEAR OF THE UNKNOWN IS AS DEEP IN MAN AS HIS marrow! All of us are afraid of the things we do not understand. That is why we try so hard to reject the unfamiliar and to cling to old ways, whether or not they be good. This type of fear, as well as most of the others, can be cured by the techniques of mind-power. Ask yourself: why am I afraid?

TAKE YOUR FEARS APART

Analyze your fearful reactions to people and places and situations —and get at the cause. You can gain the knowledge that will alleviate your fear. Learn the sources of your fears and you can learn the solutions.

1. **Are you afraid of audiences?**	Then you are too self-conscious.
2. **Are you afraid of rejection?**	Then you do not have enough self-respect.
3. **Are you afraid of some strong, dominating personality?**	Then build up your self-confidence.
4. **Are you afraid of failure?**	Then learn the elements of success.
5. **Are you afraid of ill-health?**	Then learn the rudiments of health and practice them faithfully.
6. **Are you afraid of punishment?**	Then learn forgiveness.

These are the major fears that plague us all. And each of them can be conquered by the best uses of Mind. If you try to live with them, they will cost you too much in time, tensions, and loss of standing in your world. Fears are expensive.

Some Fears Serve a Purpose

Fear of accidents would cause one to be careful. In that frame of reference, fear can be constructive. Fear of financial loss would make one careful in his business dealings. But if these protective fears become exaggerated to the point where they might be called neurotic, it is time to loosen their hold upon you.

If fear of loss is going to make you miserly, if fear of audiences is going to prompt you to become a recluse, if fear of punishment is going to give you a crushing feeling of guilt, then you must get rid of the lot!

Too often a man is considered stingy and selfish and his wife is in tears over his lack of generosity when the poor husband is simply being tortured by *fear.* Fear of the future, of not being able, perhaps, to tide over a bad time, can make anyone unresponsive, even to another's urgent need. Then such a person gets the reputation of being very cold and indifferent.

Fear is such an insidious enemy of human happiness and well-being that every one should analyze himself closely quite often to see if he is permitting it to close in upon him in any area.

The Best Weapon Against Fear Is Mind-Power

Take the self-conscious person who thinks he cannot get to his feet and make a talk without getting into panic, his heart beating wildly, his thoughts frozen, so that no words come to his tongue. Whether or not he has any ambitions to be a public speaker of any kind, he should certainly be able to make a good toast at a birthday party or a wedding reception. He should begin his assault on this type of fear *alone.*

In the privacy of his bedroom or bathroom, he should practice a memorized speech before the mirror, gestures and all. He cannot help laughing at himself, and this, in itself, will relax some of his tensions. He may be surprised that the walls do not fall in upon him. And finding that he is neither injured nor killed by this type of speaking, he will gain courage to memorize other short talks. There isn't much to be gained by torturing himself in public at this point.

All by himself, he can gain a certain facility in making gracious remarks. The only way to learn to talk is to *talk.* The only way to learn to sing is to *sing.* So *talk, if you are one of the victims of this fear.* One day you will become so fired with a desire to come out either for or against some issue under discussion that you will spring to your feet and express yourself with fluency and fire. You will discover that you have *decided* that you are able to say whatever you wish to say. You have won in that area! You have also learned that when you have fear on the run, many abilities that were latent within you can find outward expression. Fear no longer paralyzes your mind and mouth. You are free! Since you have freed yourself of one kind of fear, you will find it easier to conquer other types.

Gradually you will assert yourself in all areas as a man free of fear. One of the greatest thrills on earth comes of knowing yourself to be in control of fears. You have been in a prison and now you are released. The wide world awaits with its beauties, satisfactions, explorations, and inventions.

Fear of Rejection

Fear of rejection often has its roots in childhood, when a baby brother or sister comes along to "break your nose" and you seem to be put aside for the newcomer. Such childish tragedies could be alleviated somewhat if the expectant mother would condition her existing children to the new one by taking them into her confidence and asking their help. If she could say, "I'm going to be compelled to give *our* little new baby almost all my time. I just don't know how I'm going to do that and be with you older children as much as I would like for a while. Perhaps you can help me. If you take over some of my work, that will make time for me to be with you." Some such explanation and request works in the majority of cases. Thus, much fear of rejection could be stopped before it started.

But if you have reached adulthood with this type of fear, you must handle it in truly mature fashion. You can tell yourself truthfully that you wouldn't notice so-called "rejection" at all, if you were emotionally mature throughout your being. But if there are areas within you that hurt, that feel inferior, that have learned to look for slights, you will read them where none exists!

Try saying, "I'm entitled to my shortcomings. Everybody seems to have a few. I don't notice others going around with a hangdog look or a fear of being rejected, so why should I?" Then, you will be starting the race of life with your toe on the line with everybody else.

The best cure of the feeling of rejection is public service of some kind. In it you can find an excellent welcome somewhere along the line. You develop a feeling of being rich enough to be on the *giving* side. You begin to learn to give without hope of reward—a mature point of view.

Therefore, if you suffer from this type of inferiority feeling, go at once and offer your services to a children's or a veterans' hospital. Give gratuitously some hours of tutoring, either privately or at a school. A school which is overcrowded will welcome you to help the laggards in their grades. Club, church work, or public welfare of some sort in your town will furnish you with a proper opportunity to serve.

In both fear of audiences and fear of rejection, one's thoughts should be trained away from the self *after* proper appreciation of one's good points has been settled. This is a very important point. For taking the mind off a suffering self that is low in one's own estimation does little good other than temporarily. One must inevitably come back to this grovelling self. Again it pays to count up your virtues!

Fear of a Dominating Personality

It is a common experience to fear parents, an employer, someone whose excellence surpasses yours, or just someone who is above you through seniority. This type of fear is one that almost all of us must deal with and it behooves us to get it settled once and for all.

1. Accept, with dignity, the fact that on the ladder of life lots of people will be on a higher rung. No reason to fear them. There's nothing you

can do about them, except to adjust to them, find ways to harmonize with them.

2. Realize that those above you in authority or age have needs like your own. Seek to satisfy one or more of *their needs.* Don't always be so fascinated by your own wants. This attitude is one of the really big secrets of a successful life. Jack Paar has an amusing confession of how he conquered a fear of appearing before an important person or persons. He said, "I just close my eyes and visualize them all as sitting out there in long, red flannel underwear. They look so silly, I can't be afraid of them any more."

3. Be proud of your important people. Shield their faults and extol their virtues. This will psychologically put you on their level and you will not feel the uncomfortable aspects of the difference between them and you. Wishing people well is one way to lose fear of them. If you are "on their side," you are not so conscious of a yawning gulf between you.

There is a modern tendency to debunk our heroes, to tear down our ideals, and to decry all virtue as "imaginary." For the sake of your own mental health, it behooves you to glory in the talents of those people of any nation who are leading us into our human ascendencies—up away from animalism. Any one who has *earned* a position of leadership in any area deserves our admiration. Oddly enough, in our own times of grief, loss, or peril, the awareness of the heroism latent in us gives us the solid footing that keeps us from losing our grip.

Let the light from those minds that are somewhat beyond you at the moment shine like a beacon to guide you in your own upward climb. Make room for their faults and draw strength from their splendid qualities.

Beware lest your fear of dominating people flow over into a hate or resistance to all regulating law. This can set up a most uncomfortable conflict. Realize that a certain amount of domination is protective. School yourself to be grateful that you are guarded by loving parents, traffic laws, police protection, the laws of Nature—and God.

Change your fear into appreciation, admiration, and love. It takes some doing but it is richly worth the trouble. Any time that you substitute a constructive viewpoint for a destructive one, you are the gainer in more ways than one.

It is only natural that as teenagers reach adulthood they feel annoyance at the guidance and restraint of authority. As rapidly as possible, they seek to be on their own. Their rudeness to their elders is normally but a temporary fever that passes as their disease of inferiority is cured by real maturity. This rebellion should be anticipated by long training in respect and in ease of verbal expression that gives them some pride in their standards of conduct. Then, as the pressures of ego dictate the trying out of their own wings, neither they nor their parents will be so uncomfortable. The teenagers should have been schooled in restraint. The parents should school themselves in a gradual letting go of the reins. Anticipation and preparation are the only known ways to obtain any form of harmonious protection.

The ego does not like to be dominated. Yet, for an individual's own good, he must learn restraint and respect. Otherwise, we shall revert to the jungle, which we are trying so hard to leave! Admiration, love, and appreciation of all the protection we receive from established authority will actually give us more freedom than we realize. However, that is another subject.

Oddly enough, if you conduct yourself with dignity, with wit, charm, grace, and good sense, the dominating personality near you will begin to lean on you! This is the natural, the comfortable way to make such transference.

Fear of Failure

Of all our acquired fears, fear of failure probably has the longest roots. As man, long ago, learned to think consciously, he could imagine desirable things beyond his capacity to achieve. His first crude attempts to fashion an object that he could see clearly in his mind were, no doubt, a disappointment to him. He was clumsy. The difference between his ideal and his performance began to worry him.

He could envision much that he could not accomplish. Yet he was constrained to try. In some things he succeeded. In more things he failed, or succeeded only partially. He felt *good,* satisfied, happy and proud when he succeeded. When he failed, he felt *inferior,* ashamed, wrong. He was embarrassed before his tribe. He lost the confidence of his women. To fall short became a dreadful thing. A feeling of blame grew within him. *This feeling (as we have said) came to bear the name of "conscience."*

When conscience had sorted out his acts and labelled some bad and some good, he had to admit that the fault behind the bad was due to some deficiency of his. The stigma of the deficiency came finally to be called *guilt.*

With thought projection, which allowed him to perceive a result before it happened, he could envision the way a series of acts would end. This drew upon him the responsibility of assuring himself and his kind a "good" result. He had then to judge his acts. This is a process of conscience. It is *deep in man's nature,* enmeshed in the steps of his growth.

Guilt is equally imbedded in man's primitive processes and originally had nothing to do with laws, taboos, superstitions, or religion, being older than all of them. All these matters grew out of his latent capacity for clumsiness and inaccuracy. Guilt was a logical step following conscience.

Man, the Novice

In the realm of his inner life—ideas—man is always the novice, the amateur. He is forever dealing with some new matter. Herein is the secret of his progress. His evolution depends on this fact. Yet, because of it, he is forever awkward, prone to error, maladroit. (This is a logical process and is not inherently evil in itself.) As soon as he becomes skilled in one set of motions, he gives himself the task of new ones.

Being able to envision more than he can perform, man is always falling short. He perceives, at once, the fault within himself and bears its discomfort. So aboriginal, so basic, is it in his nature that it has been mistakenly called "original sin" in the sense of ineradicable stigma. All his life, man struggles with the resulting feeling of inadequacy. While the reason for it is basic, it is still possible to alter it, since it is a process, of which the elements can be changed.

In order to assuage the constant pain of these twin companions, conscience and guilt, he has devised various protections. The first is to try to tear down the challenge of them by attacking religion (while the real cause is much farther back in his evolution). The second is to deify bestiality. Neither works for the evolved man.

The burden of civilization is the burden of guilt. And how each man resolves it is the story of his character.

Man's acceptance of his own weakness and his sense of inadequacy are stronger obstacles to man's progress than anything else. In his nightmares he imagines he is still a failure and Nemesis stalks him. And he has been prone to *find excuses outside himself* instead of uprooting the weeds of inferiority in his own makeup. This tendency has held him back for incalculable years.

He has invented vicious gods—and devils—as an explanation of his difficulties. How can he progress when some evil power wishes him harm? What can he do against the cunning and the constant temptations of his adversary? Thousands of years ago he kept fires burning all night and beat tom-toms to keep away evil spirits. Later, he placated these evil, angry gods with human and then animal sacrifices. The fortunes of war were decided by beings other than himself—gods of his imaginings—so he made himself believe. Many are his inventions to avoid taking personal responsibility for himself and his life.

The influence of the stars and planets, the prophesying of medicine men and witches, unbelievable superstitions that birds' flights or the casting of animals' entrails foretold his fate—nothing was too fantastic to believe—if it would remove responsibility from him! Somebody or something else must be to blame, no matter what was wrong. This desire, or need, to fasten blame elsewhere is deep in the primitive nature of man. His low opinion of himself has caused him to castigate himself for eons of time. But to explain it all as beyond his control.

No doubt as soon as aboriginal men could communicate by some sort of language, they discovered that each man carried this inner stigma of inferiority. Each felt *he was so very much less than he could imagine!* Some of them decided to accept this position with humility born of accepted inferiority. Others decided to resist the feeling and sought, by force and skills, to justify a higher opinion of themselves. But anyone who thought he was above this general, humble status was summarily dealt with. He had too much of that embarrassing element known today as "ego"—and around that word there grew a kind of stigma, as thought it weren't quite nice not to grovel with the rest.

To be assertive at all, one had to be vociferously so in order to pass the dam of disapproval. One was compelled to be a rebel (and still is) in order to defy the dead level of defeat of the individual. In ancient times it was feared that a man who claimed any power or place for himself would be struck down by the jealous and angry gods. And to this day it is socially unacceptable not to talk one's self down politely. The price man has paid for this absurd tribute to fear of assertion is a long delay in finding his inner power! Too often he has left it to the criminally assertive to get the glory.

However, when a man snatched leadership and power, the masses followed him in a glow of admiration! He was their alter ego. He had the daring, the courage, the vision to do what they could not bring themselves to do. They followed him as jackals follow a lion, to share his kill.

Thus was born the worship of material success—for loot was the mark of the winning aggressor. There has not been much change in this situation. Other people frown on assertion unless it is big enough to be admired. Then they follow along with the rest of the adoring crowd, as a rule.

Let us examine the phenomenon of the ego—rampant or crushed. A male wanted to seem admirable in the eyes of a female. For reasons of lack of training, courage and discipline, he could not *be,* or produce, as some other male could. This must be explained—explained away. It really wasn't his fault, he said. Fate, to begin with, was against him. The gods were vicious, angry. The cold froze his produce. The rainstorms blew it away, or it was stolen from him. And if some such story couldn't be made to hold water, he took refuge in illness. And, though he often saw men who had been maimed in battle or crippled by disease find some way to express a talent or give some type of service, he still made the excuse that the forces of life were against him. It saved his smarting ego to feel that he was the victim of overwhelming opposition or ill luck.

Too Great a Challenge?

The idea that man struggles against odds too great for him is as old as the first excuse of that kind told by some remote ancestor to some woman. Handed down to each succeeding generation, it has bred a desperate kind of courage in many men—the courage of the cornered rat who doesn't expect to win, but does intend to give his enemy a bad time for as long as he can! Troubadours have sung of such courage. Women have wept over their valiant men who gave their all—and went down.

One can imagine tales of these token fights told around tribal campfires in a young world. And who shall say that they were not fine, worth commemorating? But, unfortunately, the drama of this courage was built into the nature of man and we find the Greeks of five hundred years before Christ accepting a *philosophy of defeat!*

They were neither the first nor the last to accept it. The weaknesses in the Greek character that caused the nation to break up into warring factions and laid them open to invasion were the real reasons for their defeat. But they chose to believe that defeat is the lot of man! *The taint of this philosophy has come down to us.*

Man is just beginning to suspect, faintly, that while defeat may often be his lot, it is not necessary, inevitable, or inescapable. In the meantime, he takes strange refuge in its questionable comforts to the ego and has built what may be termed the *defeated hero pattern* which is one of the great dams to his progress.

As the general figure in his own drama of living, each man is, *per se,* his own hero. Through his inherited and acquired thought patterns, he is put upon in every conceivable way in the story he is enacting. Man, with his newly found powers of inner imaging, found himself to be his nearest and most convenient image. Thus, he became his own playwright and *observed himself* playing the part he had written for himself!

Books on psychology usually begin with the idea that the human mind is subject-object. It is its own subject and its own object. Man is not likely to agree to a premise he has not already accepted for himself, or one he cannot fit into his accustomed patterns with the least amount of trouble. He has tried to function under the assumption that he has chosen well and that what he has is already the best. This is the deception he practices upon his quiveringly uncertain, basic ego.

But since age finally overtakes a man in any case, all that he can do, he says, is simply to make a token fight. He cannot win.

The defeated-hero pattern is a plateau whereon man has wandered, lo, these many ages. As we have stated, modern man is still struggling with the residue of it in the rich heritage of Greek art, literature, and philosophy. Much of our culture comes to us directly from ancient Greece, but also this tragic-hero theme against which we throw our enlightened energies with little effect, because we really like—and use—the excuses it furnishes us.

No matter what a man does, he ends in the position of defeat—horizontal. We dignify this final collapse called death. We lay out the remains, making them look as well as possible in as beautiful a place as we can afford, make a show of respect and grief, build a monument (if there is money enough), and keep it laden with flowers. Thus, we make of this final defeat a great drama, the crowning enactment of the defeated-hero—this end of the vegetable-animal life of a man.

Death, the Last Enemy

Man, at this time, knows no other end but death and will not listen to the possibility of any other, although the Bible clearly states that *death is the last enemy to be overcome.* One need not belong to any particular faith or church to realize that an idea penetrates the brain of man very, very slowly. People talked of flying for thousands of years before the Wright brothers decided to try it. Man must begin to talk of his further progress so that in another eon he can have further victories.

Amazing wonders lie ahead for this remarkable creature called *man.* Having, for eons, lived life in a vegetable-animal consciousness, it is not surprising that he cannot accept with credulity any step beyond his present bondage to sense and limitation.

He has been mobile and self-conscious perhaps, but still fulfilling only the vegetable-animal cycle of seed, embryo, growth, maturity, productivity, aging, and death. He still, for all his brain development, retains some of the urgencies of the past. He stalks his prey and eats his kill. Then, one day, prone or supine, he dies—the sure end to all his finest reaches, his visions, and imaginings of his higher self.

Each of us will die following this same pattern. But we can begin to exercise supremacy by lengthening our lives almost unbelievably. Recently, the papers carried a picture of a woman, aged 103, who was recovering satisfactorily from an appendectomy! Step by step we can envision a distant future where man will be independent of many things which seem inevitable to him today.

However, let us get back to our immediate problems. Glancing ahead does give us a different view of them and places them in a proper perspective of importance.

Fear of Ill Health

Fear of being struck down by illness can make us more attentive to caring properly for ourselves. But it doesn't seem ever to stop there. It draws continually more attention to itself until, in some cases, it is exaggerated to the point we call hypochondria; then to a pathological dread. By the very law of Mind, the more we fear ill health, the more surely we attract it. Remember Job's "the thing I greatly feared had come upon me." The process of "becoming" works upon the idea given it, no matter what it is!

If you have this fear, then face it squarely. It does no good in dealing with any fear to say simply, "Now that's foolish. I'm going to stop that." Admit your fear, then set to work to take it apart and substitute within yourself patterns and acceptances of good health. You can begin in this way:

1. Go to a doctor—or enter a clinic for a complete check-up. It is best to *know* your condition. If the doctor, or doctors, tell you there is nothing to worry about—believe them and try to put your mind on other things. If you are told you have a certain malady or irregular functioning, obey their injunctions and do as you are told. There are marvelous

advances in medicine today—and there just might be a "specific" for your difficulty.

2. Never disobey the considered opinions of medical men. How foolish to say, when you are flouting instructions, "Oh, if my doctor knew what I was eating today, he'd be so upset!" It isn't your doctor you are upsetting, it is your own best program for recovery. *Stay* on a diet, if one has been prescribed for you. Half measures never work. It isn't cute, feminine, or amusing (if you are a man) to be half on and half off a diet. It only makes you look silly and lightheaded.

3. Change your mental picture of yourself. Hold up, daily in meditation, and constantly, if you can, the figure of yourself as having perfect health, fine strength, and an overflowing joy that comes from feeling good. This practice is using the mind-power within you to bear on your health.

4. Stop talking about ill health—your own or anyone's else. Speak only of well-being, even though you may be hospitalized with some malady or surgery! No matter what has happened to you, *there is still the job of healing to do,* and you only delay and confuse your powers of recovery when you keep the ill picture before you. Ask other people frankly to please not talk sickness to you. Explain that you are trying to get rid of it and you do not wish to mull over its atmosphere. Ask them to tell you something beautiful, funny, or encouraging; or something that is exciting good news about anything or anybody.

Do not rush on past this advice because you may have heard it before. Ask yourself quite seriously if you do not spend more time thinking about illness than you should spend. Men and women who read good advice every day keep right on in their destructive habits of speech and thought. Be warned! You can build your health any time you get ready to start. Why not start now? There are many kinds of fears and they have fascinating names, ending in "phobia." But there is no fear that can take over your mind unless you permit it to do so.

INVOLUNTARY FEARS

We have spoken of the involuntary reflexes of the body. Sometimes these are involved in a fear of high places, or a fear of being closed in, fear of the dark, fear of elevators, etc. I once had a fear of the dark, which began back in my childhood. It was dissipated when a friend identified it for me as a fear of failure! Strange how a fear will seek to perpetuate itself and transfer itself from one thing to another until it has nowhere else to go—or until its unhappy possessor takes strong, direct measures to uproot it!

My fear began by my being frightened by a bear and transferred the fear of bears to any furry animal. Then when my liking for fur coats became stronger than my fear, it transferred itself to a fear of falling. It was an easy step from falling to failing. But when the path of this devious route became clear to me, I turned the full light of my genuine faith in life upon it—and it was quickly gone. I use a great deal of light these days, but only because J. Edgar Hoover thinks our houses should be lighted at all times. I no longer have a definite fear of the dark.

You can use the processes of mind-power to give you the assurance of supremacy over involuntary fears. Sometimes our fears take the form of gripping dreads. We may fear to lose a loved one. This would naturally be difficult for anyone to handle. You must not live with a dread. You must face up to it, and by building up your *faith* in the rightness of the underlying pattern in all life. Become willing to accept whatever outcome is inevitable. We cannot hold our loved ones forever. But, seeing that our universe is, at base, wise and kindly, we can, and must, *trust life*. We must commit our loved ones to *its* care and be comforted by knowing that they could not be in better hands. Dread, fear, resentment, rebelliousness, these emotions can only wreck your health. Substitute *faith* for them.

The late D. W. Griffith, the great motion picture director, once told me that as a young person he was the victim of many types of fear. But he became ashamed of having them. So one day he looked at himself in the mirror, and said, "Now, look here. This has gone far enough. What *are* you so afraid of? You're afraid you may fail and have to go back home? You're afraid your relatives will all die, and then you won't have a home? You're afraid you're going to run out of money? You're afraid a truck will run over you and there won't be money to bury you?"

Then he told himself that he was just going to face each of those disasters and see exactly where they took him. He visualized himself penniless and thumbing a ride right to Kentucky. He mentally experienced the whole thing and he found it wasn't as dreadful as he had thought. Everyone was kind, the trip was beautiful, and in fact, he had a very good time!

Then he unrolled in his mind the story of all his relatives dying and leaving him alone. He realized for the first time that in the nature of things this eventuality was certain to come about. He decided to face the situation with the proper dignity. After his first engulfing sadness, his sorrow was assuaged by the love each of them showed in leaving him personal belongings—there wasn't much else. In grief, love takes on a shining importance—and he was comforted. This was a page of life turning before him and since it was his experience, he must face up to it.

As for the fear of running out of money, he learned that some of our richest men are prey to that fear, and he laughed. At last he had something in common with rich men! He took a long breath and stuck out his chest.

But there was that last fear—of being run over by a truck and there not being money enough to bury him. He was a Mason. One day he was asked to go to the funeral of a brother Mason, a man whom he did not even know.

At this funeral, old gentlemen went through Masonic burial rites, which to his poetic mind were quite beautiful: the symbols of brotherly love, of hoping to know the deceased somewhere else, the evergreen twig dropped in the casket to denote that their interest and love for their brother Mason would never die. "They didn't even know this man—and they were absolutely sincere about this sentiment!" Griffith recalled. "I sat and listened. Then I thought—there is kindly and even sentimental provision for such as I, in any eventuality. And even were I not a Mason, I am a man and in this great country, human life is held sacred enough to honor the dead in some dignified fashion, whether he has money, or no. It gave me great comfort."

One by one, Griffith's fears left him. He felt the companionship of *life,* people, the way his country looked after its own—and through his renewed faith in God. This man, one of our great creators and intellectuals, cured himself of morbid fears.

If you have a morbid fear, face it out. Get to the end of the thing and find out that there is always some ameliorating factor that enters somewhere along the line. Sometimes when we turn and face a thing, it slinks away, like all bullies. Turn on your fears. Follow them. Face them down. As you take control of your own thoughts and guide them well, you invite the salutary processes of the whole structure of mind-power to help you fashion your life.

Fear of Punishment

While our courts and punitive systems have largely to do with mature people, we must face the fact that the whole procedure that makes them necessary proves our immaturity. Just so, *fear of punishment* is operating in the infantile areas of our makeup.

It is childish to disobey a known law that our peers and legislative bodies have deemed was for our best good. It is equally babyish to fear the consequences. A reasonable amount of emotional maturity would dictate that we refurbish our respect for law—all law. It also calls for us to walk up and take our punishment, if it is just and due.

In our family, while we were small, we were not punished if we told the truth about some infraction of parental law. But after, say, the age of seven or eight, we were supposed to tell the truth *and* be willing to accept the consequences. If we did not and were not, the punishment was doubledl!

My mother said that it was beneath our dignity to lie and squirm away from punishment—that it was common, second-rate, and not worthy of us at all. My mother said aristocrats walked up and took whatever was coming to them. "What's the good of blue blood, if it can't stand fire," she would say—and lay on the switch. We didn't feel very aristocratic across her knee with our panties down, but we did try to reconstruct the picture of *her* expectations and live up to them. And we later admitted to each other that there was a strange satisfaction in walking up, owning up, and paying up. One felt clean and free of the thing.

Fears lose their grip when they are faced down.

·15·

How to Use Mind-Power to Achieve Physical and Mental Well-Being

THE AREA OF PHYSICAL AND MENTAL WELL-BEING is one that each of us can largely control if we put our minds to it. For the body is beautifully responsive to its day-to-day treatment. Knowledge grows in its chemistries, its timing, its rate of metabolism, its interactions.

More people are reaching old age looking healthy, young and happy. One is constantly astonished to hear of the great age of someone who looks far, far younger; is still strong; has fine resilience and almost unbelievable energy. Many people are living more active lives in their eighties than they did in their sixties! There seems to be a general feeling that one should not retire at any age. And today the last people to leave a dance, at say, one or two in the morning are likely to be oldsters who wanted to have that last dance together.

What has happened to the old-fashioned notions that at 40 or 50 one must settle for the ill health that will surely catch up with him by that time? The enemies of the body are being conquered by doctors, chemists, philosophers, and ministers of the mind. (The Bible speaks of death as the last enemy to be overcome.)

Romance, once the province of the young, today lives on and on. Lately, I was present at a party celebrating the hundredth month of marriage of a couple well along in life, whose romance had flowered in their maturity. These friends of mine, the Fred Jungquists of Los Angeles, entertained about 75 guests at dinner in their spacious house, and their happiness was contagious.

These people are keeping the thoughtful, appreciative devotions alive that express and prolong life. Not for them the dry, dull, take-it-for-granted attitude that kills romance and people, too! Incidentally, these two love to dance—and one sees them at all the parties. They have a kind of agelessness. They do take excellent care of themselves, using all the known helps sensibly, and they have certainly gotten results.

And there was the romantic marriage of the no-longer-young, but still glamourous Blanchie Bagnall, who, when she married Chester Bagnall moved their whole wedding party to Madrid! Pictures of this fashionable and beautiful ceremony appeared internationally.

LET'S CONSIDER THE BODY AS AN INSTRUMENT OF EXPRESSION

Your body talks with every move and every posture. Attitudes and positions convey thoughts. Every sculptor decides what he wants his figures to "say." There are two requirements for a fine body: erectness and mobility.

At first glance, these two points seem to contradict one another. But after watching a person who is master of his body, it is apparent that one is the complement of the other. A straight spine says, as though in words, "I have self-respect." A high chest might as well have a sign across it, "I am healthy and am a 'treasure chest' of vitality and interests." But this is only a beginning. If one is stiff, keeping straight, rigid and his chest high, there is small interest for the beholder.

Besides being straight, *one must be mobile,* thus giving the appearance of having room in one's mind for the interests of others, their concerns, and welfare. When one looks completely unyielding, the world flows on by, either discouraged or disinterested.

A gently mobile body that bends toward a newcomer ever so slightly; that receives the impact of a new idea with a visible movement of reception, gives the impression of a person who is eager, one who will fit into any worthy cause, and is open to conviction. In other words, a mobile body belongs to someone who is somewhat unselfed, worldly wise in the finer sense, and willing to listen to the other side of the story—in short, a civilized, well-adjusted person. A diplomat learns to listen with his body.

Oddly enough my Virginia grandmother, an elderly woman who knew nothing whatever about acting or actors, drummed into me the polite, physical responses that are acceptable in good society. Not because they are special or snobbish in any way—but because they carry the message of polite interest to other people.

She strewed cushions about the room, moved chairs here and there, and made me walk among them without stumbling or bumping into them. "My child," she would say, "you must learn to keep your body balanced at all times. You must be too fastidious to lunge, lope, or bump about. Since life is likely to be somewhat disorderly, you must keep your movements organized, and learn to manage yourself with poise and grace in the midst of confusion. This law is for men as well as women."

You cannot order the world—but you can order yourself. And when you have mastered control of your body, you will be amazed at what life will wash up on your shores as a consequence. It is as though *life* itself had said, "Well done, thou good and faithful servant. Thou hast been faithful over a few things, I will make thee ruler over many."

Start with what you have—*yourself.* Put it in good condition. Your body, your mind, and soul have been entrusted to you as a holy charge. It is up to you to develop them toward perfection as far as you can go, then care for them and keep them in excellent condition. Anyone can learn to keep his body fit.

Holding your body and moving it as though it were fit actually helps to make it so! So generous are Nature's "laws of correspondence" that when graceful movement is made a habit, the muscles become more resilient, and coordination improves.

Extend the idea of coordination and you will be astonished to see how interpenetrating it is. For instance, if one has trained his body to good coordination, the mental discipline involved will extend to other areas of living. You will find it easier to fit in more duties; easier to handle difficult people or situations. At first glance there seems to be little connection, but if you study it, you will see that ideas flow from one area to another. Any *good* you accomplish in one department of yourself will flow over into other needs, and your whole self and life will be blessed.

If you do *one* thing right, a vortex is set up to make other rightness more attainable. You will have turned your face toward correctness, the fullness of which is God. Though your success in your primary effort may be small, it nevertheless has turned you *toward the ideal. You have readied yourself to achieve many extra values.* Don't forget that the *ideal* holds accuracy, truth, perfect functioning, beauty, energy, fresh ideas—and the urge to embrace and express them. You have "touched the hem of His garment" when you do *anything* in the way it should be done. Never consider it unimportant to do some small thing well. It might give the last push to a whole train of fine happenings for you.

Smoothness of movement is not only soothing to the person who has it. To the beholder, who may be harassed and edgy, it can bring a strong suggestion of peace and restful harmony. If the beholder happens to be an employer, and the one who has smoothness of movement is seeking employment, it is entirely possible that the harmony of movement will win the place.

People who are able to dominate their bodies usually succeed in life, usually win the higher places, usually overcome most illnesses, usually make comebacks when they go down temporarily. They have resilience. They have the habit of well-being. They have put themselves in line with the forces and ideas that "accomplish that unto which they are sent."

Make Your Body Obey You

To be sure, many of your body's functions are unconscious (seemingly), involuntary, acting upon a natural pattern which corresponds to those in animals and even in vegetables. These insure a certain length of life, barring violence. They guarantee the propagation of the species. They provide hunger for the maintenance of the body and sleep for its repair. Nevertheless, man can, if he will, train his body to further actions and habits, in harmony with the natural pattern. The past becomes a ladder upon which he can climb higher in personal awareness. His inner universe is as rich and vast as his outer one.

The Three Most Important Steps

In attaining and preserving three basic requirements of well-being, we will find that we really are in control of the situation. They are:

1. Cleanliness—not only of the surface of the body, but of the tissues, and of the mind in daily thinking.
2. Nourishment—not only for the tissues, but for the nerves and blood and for the mind and soul.
3. Tone and quality of flesh—through cleanliness, nourishment, and the right movement to keep muscles resilient and responsive; full of life and eagerness to keep mind and body firm.

The big word to remember in achieving anything is movement—exercise. Practice makes perfect. A muscle must be taught, just as any skill must be learned. It is movement that takes the wastes of the body to the organs of elimination. It is movement that brings in the fresh materials from sun and air and food and water for the body's refreshment and rebuilding. Your body renews itself by change.

So stretch many times a day. Tense and relax whenever you think of it. Do not give dead cells and refuse matter a chance to lodge in your joints. Do not permit them to slow down and lodge in your brain, thus cutting down your imagination, your willingness to think dynamically. Often people think the world is against them when it is only that the refuse of the body is moving too slowly! Nothing is really against us except our own poor use of the matter at hand!

Life, as it flows to us, is pure power. Why not take more of it by preparing your body to need it and demand it by being ready for it. As you expand your lungs, they will demand more air, thus giving you more life-giving oxygen. As you cleanse your tissues through pure foods, great quantities of water and exercise, your flesh becomes firm and demands more of the goodness of natural materials and practices.

As you train your body to healthful actions and habits, your mind and soul are blessed also. A clean, refreshed bloodstream flowing to and through your brain gives you a mental reach you cannot have when poisons are there. Your muscles, your thoughts, your energy, and understanding are all increased by a clean, rich bloodstream.

Drink More Water and Fruit Juice

On rising, drink a glass of water—with lemon juice in it if you like. In mid-morning drink water or fruit juice or a mixture of them. In mid-afternoon drink water or fruit juice or a mixture of them. On retiring, eat fruit, drink fruit juice and/or water.

Vegetable juices may be substituted by those who have formed a liking for them. Both vegetable and fruit juices have their place in a truly healthful and cleansing regimen. Use apples more. Eat them as fresh fruit. Use them in salads. Fry them lightly to serve with meats. Use them in desserts. But use more apples.

Eat More Vegetables

Eat more rhubarb. The old-timers always thought of rhubarb (the first vegetable to come up in the spring) as a spring tonic, a cleanser. It serves the same purpose at any time. It makes a delicious beginning for breakfast and a fine dessert at any meal.

Eat more squash. The ones with heavy rinds may be cut into pieces and baked with no further preparation. With a bit of margarine and salt they are delicious. No pans to wash! All yellow vegetables are rich in vitamin values.

Eat more greens. Spinach, collards, mustard, dandelion, any kind! Mix them for good flavor and cook them with a hamhock, or ham essence, or bacon dripping (or olive oil) put in just before serving. For excellent goodness, add some chopped onions and lemon juice or vinegar. This hot salad is considered a delicacy in many foreign countries. It is coming to be popular in our own country. Served with a poached or a sliced hard-boiled egg on each serving, it is very substantial.

Americans are discovering lentils. At our house we make a very large vessel of lentil soup. Beginning with four or five large onions, add lentils (a pound) that have been soaked in water for a few hours, a bunch of celery, five or six large carrots, a half pound of China peas, a large can of tomatoes (or six large fresh ones), a large pod of garlic, a tablespoon of oregano, a fresh green pepper, and any other vegetables you care to add. Add meat stock or several bouillon cubes, salt to taste; add pepper, red and black, to taste—and you will have a most nourishing, thick soup that a crowd of skiers or swimmers will devour quickly. For the family we usually have a pot of soup on the back of the stove. It makes lunches very simple and nourishing.

Eat More Sea Food

At least twice a week make a dinner of fish. Mackerel is delicious served with lemon and almond sauce or lemon and peanut sauce. Remember that the expensive seafoods have no more of the sea's goodness in them than the lowest priced ones! However, crab, lobster, and shrimp in season can be delightful. But for the run-of-the-mill fish dinner use the kind that is plentiful at the moment and therefore cheap.

With fish, serve corn and/or cornbread and tomatoes, stewed, baked, or raw. Oysters and clams, in season, can be delicious either raw with a sharp sauce, strong with horse-radish, or made into wonderful stews or soups. Fish, baked with thinly sliced onions, thyme and in a well-seasoned white sauce can be delicious.

The sea existed before the land, we are told, and, therefore, in its depths are all the elements of life. The people of those nations who depend on the sea for the greater part of their food are hardy, long-lived, and intelligent.

People who live inland can today enjoy seafood because freezing at the site of the catch brings fresh fish to tables anywhere. The trace minerals are all found in fish together with other values for which there are, as yet, no names. Since so many of our farms and commercial fields are poor in natural minerals due to constant forcing of production, a plentiful supply of seafood assures you of getting a healthful balance of these needed elements. Cultivate a taste for it. My father used to tell a story of a man who lost a huge contract for heavy machinery because he didn't like oysters. The buyer from a foreign land was entertaining his American friends and he served oysters. The manufacturer who thought he had his goods sold, turned down the oysters because he thought he disliked them. The host was displeased and opened up negotiations with another company whose president had a more cosmopolitan appetite!

With the world's growing smaller, it does not pay to be unable to eat any edible and good food—even snails and rattlesnake meat.

Do More Walking

Learn to think beyond the boundaries of your own environment. Americans ride everywhere. Europeans, the English, and most Orientals walk whenever possible. Therefore an American will make more friends, if, when getting about the world, he will take a great interest in walking. It is not luck that makes the cosmopolitan man popular, sought, beloved. It is his honest interest in the interests of his hosts, wherever he finds himself.

We Americans say we are too tired to walk. The European walks to refresh and rest himself! Swinging along at a lively gait (no ambling, please) he uses a different set of muscles and the brisk action calls for more oxygen and a faster flowing blood stream. Hence he is rested after about a 15-minute jaunt! Or he can swing along for hours—*after he hardens himself*—and think nothing of carrying a knapsack for a seven-mile pull up a mountain and seven miles back down. I know, for I have done it many a time!

The secret is gradual conditioning. Do *not* start out walking more than a mile. Slowly increase your distance. Progressing gradually, one can train his body miraculously. Driven too rapidly, it may rebel and much trouble can ensue.

Walk, dance, stand on your head, jump rope—do any kind of exercise if you want to develop that sparkle and stamina that will win the prizes of attention and good will that will cause you to be called "lucky." You will feel so good that you will be supple, your laughter will come easily, your interest will flow out to others.

You will sleep like a top, awake refreshed, and think nothing of working at some beloved task many extra hours. This task may bring you fame and fortune. Anyway, it will fetch a deep satisfaction. Then, as this type of satisfaction settles in your soul, you will make people *feel* that it is pleasant to be with you. And if you don't think that is "fortunate," do try it and see!

Dance! Alone or With a Partner

Put on some lovely waltz records—pull down the shades if you are afraid the neighbors will think you've gone a bit daft—and create your own dance to the wonderful rhythms. Bend, twirl, sway to beautiful melodies and their lovely, limpid grace will find the way into your entire body and seep into other areas of your life.

Dance! Iinvite a dozen or more people in for a buffet dinner, then push back the rugs and have a dance. People who haven't danced in years will enjoy a waltz or an old-fashioned two-step. Give a prize for the best couple, the worst couple. Make it fun to come to your house. It won't be luck that extends your popularity.

Take the Pledge Never to Lounge Again!

If you can't sit up, then *go to bed!* Sitting bent like a pretzel with your vital organs squashed up together is shortening your life by ten years! There is no law that compels you to sit up in any position whatever. It is absolutely permissible to excuse yourself, go somewhere and lie down in a horizontal position until you feel like getting up again! But *don't lounge.*

It is rude to lounge. It says to the beholder, "You're not interesting or exciting enough to bring me to a full sitting position—but I'll give you this fractional, folded up version of my concern." It's so much effort to try to make contact with a lounger that most people give it up and go away. In time, the lounger finds himself alone! The teenager, who is allowed to fold up like a praying mantis and read, while visitors are in the house or while grown-ups enter and leave the room, should sue his parents for neglect of his welfare and the shaping of his body and character!

In acting, the position of interest is alert posture bending slightly forward. One is thus going *toward* something or somebody—in thought, at least. My mother and grandmother trained me not even to lean back in a chair. I was supposed to be interested in the person before me and therefore not lolling backward while I looked casually and wearily at the world. To this day, I almost never lean back. I have learned to sit "on balance" and it is far more restful than leaning back at an angle that throws the throat muscles down and the dowager's hump at the base of the neck out a bit more in the back. *Using no muscles, but sitting perfectly balanced, I am not tired.* People who rush for those pretzel chairs are always talking about how tired they are! Not only does that ridiculous posture not rest them, it makes them more tired! And they will be more tired next year than they are this year!

A straight spine is the number one help for general well-being and for personal effectiveness. The vital organs have room to function and to draw their needs from the system unobstructed by the close encroachment of something being pushed against them.

Leaning back says, "I am not in the action. I am out of things." The leaners-back slowly separate themselves from the flow of *life* around them and soon are mere spectators. Watch it! You will have some interesting surprises. Be careful of leaning back yourself. You *invite* inaction, separation, disinterest!

Leaning forward says, "I am eager for life—a part of it— and I am interested in it and *you.*" As steel flies to a magnet, the actions of *life* will be drawn to you when you look as though you are ready for the next thing or person. Sit forward in your chair, sit straightly, and see what *life* will bring you! The leaners may criticize you; may say that your look of energy tires them out. Pay no attention to such sour grapes. Even the criticizers won't leave you out! You impress yourself not only upon the minds, but also the memories of others. You enjoy life more when you are eager.

Your posture is not only your best but your *only* advertisement.

It tells the world what you think of yourself and of it. It tells *you* what you think of yourself and of life, which is often more important. The constant suggestion of worth bears fruit for you in all the departments of yourself.

Good posture creates a channel through which interest flows from you and back to you. The good fortune that ensues cannot be termed "luck." It is a natural, almost a fixed result. Suppose you have an orange grove. You must irrigate it and spray it, which you do well and thoroughly. You reap a fine crop. The juicy, succulent oranges have drawn from the earth the moisture that you channeled to the roots of the trees by carefully planned and maintained irrigation ditches. Was it "luck" that took the water to the trees? No. It was intelligent use of natural laws. You dug, or had someone dig the ditches. You provided the water. And gravity and absorption did the rest. The crop was the result of *law.* If you channel the "waters of life" to your own roots, a fine crop will result.

A LONG, HAPPY, AND USEFUL LIFE

Most of us believe that the pattern of our longevity is built into (or by) our genes from the moment of conception and that we cannot change it. This is a moot question. There is more than one school of thought on this subject. We do inherit tendencies and certain materials, impulses, and their attendant strengths.

Here is where environment becomes an important factor. By providing the environment favorable for our own development, we can extend, expand, and lengthen the span of our lives. We can certainly make our lives more comfortable, fruitful, and useful.

You are born, of course, with some kind of a pattern. But it is certainly open to change, since you are neither a vegetable nor only an animal. You have a deciding mind, a choosing process, through which you can improve your situation, whatever it may be.

The Bible says, "Who, by taking thought, can add one cubit to his stature?" But it also states, "As a man thinketh in his heart, so is he." Just "taking thought" can be a passing, surface thing. But, when that thought drops down into "the heart" (the *feeling* nature), then it becomes the adjusted pattern of our very being. If you demand health of and for your body you will gradually achieve it. *You* decide what kind of a body you will have. Work at it diligently and patiently.

The Amount and Kind of Food and the Way You Eat It Is Extremely Important

In test after test with laboratory rats, various teams of scientists have discovered that a diet of less food adds to length of life and health. Two groups of rats were fed the same food. Group 1 was allowed to eat constantly as much as they wanted. Group 2 ate the same food but in limited amounts and at stated times.

Group 1 became overweight, developed tumors, ulcers, cancers, swollen joints, respiratory difficulties and died after only half their normal life span.

Group 2 stayed healthy—no tumors, no swollen joints, lots of energy, and their life span was extended to almost twice the normal length!

These same tests are being made with human beings, but it will be many years before results are fully known. However, even after a few years, the difference in health is apparent.

Most people are overfed and undercontrolled, our scientists believe. Extravagant appetites, they say, are simply emotional outlets for some inner pressures. Such appetites are called compulsive eating, similar to compulsive drinking.

A limited diet, well digested, gives more value than a mountain of partially assimilated food. It has been suggested that if one chews his food well to gain from it all possible values, he would actually need very little of it. That would not be entirely true of proteins, for they are not digested by saliva, but by the stomach acids. However, it spares the stomach a great deal to break meat up as much as possible. It stands to reason that smaller bits would be more quickly handled. All animals who swallow huge chunks of meat have a short life span, we are told. So, however one looks at it, one benefits by thorough mastication of all foods.

Prolong the Pleasure of Good Food and Drink

If food is good, the pleasure is prolonged by dealing with it in the mouth. It is certainly more flattering to a hostess to savor her food as long as possible, than to gobble it up as though it were feeding time at a zoo.

Have you ever watched helplessly while someone tossed down a glass of fine wine or a liqueur, while the horrified host looks on? A Frenchman will fondle and sip a single glass of wine all afternoon at a sidewalk cafe in Paris. And after dinner, his tiny glass of excellent liqueur will be enjoyed by small sips. He will even delight in the beautiful color of it as he holds it between himself and the light and turns it.

Non-Fat Milk Is a Help to Many People

Some time ago only those people under doctor's orders drank skimmed milk. Today, many others have discovered that once used to it, they prefer it for its fresher, lighter flavor. Some people add several spoons of dried skimmed milk to the non-fat liquid thus enriching it in flavor, milk sugar, proteins and valuable minerals without the cholesterol-ridden fat. Skimmed milk is cheaper—save money and health by using it.

Watch the Tidbits

Eat dried fruits instead of candy. Reach for a dried apricot when you want a tidbit in mid-morning or mid-afternoon. Apricots are especially valuable. A fig, a date, even a dried apple satisfies the desire for a sweet with no harmful after-effect. On the contrary, one receives definite benefits.

Cottage Cheese is very valuable. Mix it with yogurt and curry for a delicious dip. Use yogurt wherever you used to use sour cream. If the mixture is too acid for your taste, add some natural sugar or honey—or your favorite sugar substitute—and all will be well.

At the bridge table, pass small squares of cheese instead of candy, and thin, whole-wheat crackers instead of cakes. At the most fashionable clubs, cheese and peanuts are provided as refreshments.

Slivers of carrot, celery, or turnip in crushed ice may be served at any time. Rolled water cress sandwiches, using wheat bread, are always good. On small round crackers, put a round of sliced apple, on top of which place a small round of thin cheese, and in the center of that put a slice of stuffed olive. There you have a wholesome and a fine-tasting hors d'oeuvre. Sliced apple and anchovies are an excellent combination. Apple tidbits must be made just before eating or the apple will darken. Soaking the pieces in a weak vinegar solution helps to retard the process, but the best way is to make them fresh.

Baron du Budai's Meat Loaf

One popular and delightful host, Baron du Budai used to cook dinner himself for as many as a dozen guests. His *pièce de résistance* was a meat loaf, which he claimed with a twinkly smile would lengthen life and make one very strong. Gradually I coaxed the recipe and the method from him.

It seems that in most *cordon bleu* cooking one always begins with an onion—minced and sautéed. In this case, begin with two large onions, minced and sautéed. Into about two pounds of ground sirloin work sage, garlic, thyme, oregano, and salt. Work into it also the sautéed onions, a pound of cooked soybeans, and a can of mushroom soup (the thick kind) or, if you prefer, the same amount of fresh mushrooms. Add also finely chopped green pepper.

Put the mixture into a loaf pan and bake about 45 minutes, more if you like it better done, basting it occasionally with well-peppered tomato juice. The baron told me confidentially that he sometimes added a small box of cornflakes or Grapenuts to the mixture.

With this meat loaf the baron used to serve triangles of cabbage with scorched butter (or margarine) into which a small amount of curry was sprinkled. You could serve also tiny, boiled potatoes with a sauce of minced chives in yogurt. The baron always served fruit as dessert. There was no salad, for we had the equivalent of it as "finger food" on arrival.

Beware the Deep-Fried Things!

Chicken fried in a little soy, peanut, or corn oil—only a little—will taste just as good as though it had been immersed in lard for 45 minutes. After browning, cut the fire as low as possible, cover the chicken tightly and let it finish cooking in its own moisture for perhaps an hour.

More Baked Dishes

Baked lamb chops are an interesting departure. Baked beans we know are favorites of most men. They also like baked apples. Baked sweet potatoes bring a light of appreciation to the eye. Baked rice and rice pudding are a joy. Have you tried baked carrot? Baking brings out their sweetness. Baked onions are a treat. Make up your own one-casserole meals.

If you live alone, you can buy one of those potato bakers for the top of the stove—and use it for other things, too. There's always a way to do anything we really want to do.

Simple—But Good

If you have a large family to feed, there are economies one may employ without sacrificing quality or flavor. The most inexpensive "fillers" for hungry members of the family are beans, potatoes, rice, corn, carrots. Don't forget to include potassium—found largely in green produce—in your daily diet.

Imagination or the excellent recipes in most daily papers or women's magazines will show how all foods may be made to be attractive and delicious. A freezer gives one the opportunity to buy meats and other produce when they are on sale so that one has them later when those same items are priced above the budget. With the variety of foods available, we should be able to supply our bodies with the finest of first-class nourishment, with small residue of unfriendly material—and all the needed values.

Good Sleep Is as Important as Good Food

Get plenty of sleep. If you have heavy mental problems, have early dinner after some rousing physical exercise. Then be quiet toward bedtime, read something unexciting, eat a bit of fruit, and you will probably drift off into very sound slumber.

While you are asleep, your subconscious functions will be working on the strongest impression you have given them. It behooves one before bedtime to put aside all resentments, hates, emotional disturbances of any kind and give the inward self a pattern of calm kindness, full acceptance, and a feeling of doing well while reaching for something better. Thus, you will be served by those areas of awareness that work while you sleep.

HOW REMARKABLE IS NATURE TO HAVE GIVEN US SO MANY BLESSINGS!

With our growing understanding, even our young people are coming to value the part a fine body plays in a successful life. We may not all have great beauty, but all of us can have the attractiveness of disciplined, supple, graceful bodies that exude a magnetism of well-being, joy, humor, and helpfulness. Then people will be drawn to us, include us, seek us for pleasure or assistance—and life will widen and deepen and stretch out gloriously before us.

With the splendid energies of a finely functioning, straight, and vital body, a man has more worth for the world that will recognize him and employ his force. He will go the extra mile, carry the additional burden, make the extra call, write the extra letter, dance the extra dance, help the timid beginner, cheer the sad one about to pass him, push an extra load—all because he has found the source of unlimited energy. Then people will say, "If I had his luck, I'd do fine things, too." The speaker may never discover that the truth is the exact reverse. The fortunate one *does* fine things—and therefore *draws* his fine result. In this sense he commands his life!

Mental Well-Being Is Supported by Good Health

Chemistry plays a large part in today's treatment of mentally disturbed people. Certain of the "mood drugs" can calm a patient so that he may receive the other types of care that will help build him back to normalcy. Does all this not suggest to us that we should look to the daily intake of salutary chemicals in the right diet so that we do not develop deficiencies and therefore encourage poor mentation?

Isn't it true that people in poor health are likely to suffer from personality problems? The body affects the mind and the mind is helped or hindered by the body.

Thoughts and Emotions Alter the Body's Chemistry

Yet the power of mind over the body is truly extraordinary. Even though chemistry may be the final, deciding factor in the body, emotions and thoughts bring about both swift and slow chemical changes.

If a person is in danger, an alert, based on sight, touch, or intuition, is sent, in a split second, to the brain, which, in turn, sends the command for quick, muscular movement. These reflexes are fast because they have been ingrained by millions of years of the techniques of survival. They call on the body's resources and keep action at an unbelievably high pitch until the danger is over. Then, as most of us know, we are quite likely to feel entirely spent. We sometimes collapse.

How wonderful that we have these protective mechanisms. But we should keep them for real emergencies and not continually live under stresses. Take command of your emotions and your thoughts in full knowledge of what they do to your body! Build your health by daily exercise of your power of choice as to how you will react to life's challenges, your personal relationships and all emotional stimuli. Cultivate the *habit* of salutary reactions.

A Help for Pain

Even pain can be alleviated to a great extent by mind-power. You do not feel pain when you are asleep. This means that your mind is so completely relaxed that you are not aware of your body. If, while you are awake, you can approximate this type of detached relaxation (and you can) your pain will be lessened. Doctors will tell you confidentially that when a Christian Scientist comes for surgery or other help they are sure the patient will get well very quickly, be less trouble than others; and that their fine example will help other patients. The reason is that their minds are trained to concentrate always on the good outcome. I am not a Scientist, but I have the deepest respect for all people who are advancing the human race by the best uses of mind-power. Practically all religions are focusing today on this point of view.

St. Paul wrote, nearly 2000 years ago, "Whatsoever things are true, whatsoever things are honest, whatsoever things are just, whatsoever things are pure, whatsoever things are lovely, whatsoever things are of good report; if there be any virtue, and if there be any praise, think on these things."

This same St. Paul with a penetrating knowledge of man's potential sovereignty through the All-Mind within him also wrote: "Who shall change our vile (ill) body, that it may be fashioned like unto His glorious body (the ideal) according to the working *whereby he is able to subdue all things unto himself*."

One begins to see a parallel pattern in the thinking of modern medical scientists (even the chemists) and that of the ancient seer St. Paul. Approaching the problem from two opposite poles, they meet on the pure truth in the middle!

Great minds down through all the ages have foreseen the victory of man's human and divine intelligence. Do not be afraid to try to use your own, and see to what extent you can control the health of mind and body. Use all the fine helps on the physical plane that are here for your benefit, knowing the while that your mind is the supreme commander.

•16•

How to Use Mind-Power to Live in Today's Complex World

WHEN JOHN GLENN WAS ORBITING THE EARTH for the third time, a commentator was saying, "The only limits of man's future are defined by his imagination or lack of it." A voice from Canada expressed it in these words, "John Glenn and his rocket are speeding into history for the benefit of all mankind."

Whatever the result of any particular thrust into space, we know that man will conquer it—and anything else on which he puts his wonderful mind. How far we have come—how gloriously, tediously, unbelievably far!

Our earth is said, by some scientists, to be about 2,000,000,000 years old! Our sun is much younger, practically a baby. It has existed only about 5,000,000,000 years. Many stars and galaxies are still younger, only about 10,000 million years old. So say the men who read the fossils and sift the sands (literally) of time. They tell us that life appeared on this whirling planet about 1,000,000,000 years ago. All these calculations are constantly being revised.

YOU HAVE COME A LONG WAY— AND HAVE FARTHER TO GO

For our purposes, try to forget the time it has taken to arrive at today and think only of learning all you can of the basic properties you share with all created things. Get into the story of your progress and you will be entertained beyond words; amazed by your own extraordinary forces, your tenacity, and your courage, born of experiment and imagination. When you become aware of what you have accomplished, your present problems seem dwarfed by comparison!

We repeat the popular saying that never have we faced such hazards as today. That is simply not true. We have never faced anything *but* hazards and we have developed into the human race because we faced them well—and won!

Beginnings

Take an interest in the fact that it seems that types of life existed in water before there was dry land. The Bible story in Genesis that "waters covered the face of the earth" is accepted as true. And in that water tiny living organisms appeared. Sex, as we know it, was nonexistent. Neither sex nor death, those twins of evolution, had yet come into being. Death, they tell us, is a fairly modern innovation—that living cells, barring violence, *could* last interminably. No one knows how long water-life was alone on the earth. Fossils, however, show that 300 million years ago there were fish in the water, which possessed hearts and internal organs similar to modern fish, animals, and man.

It is believed that as the waters receded, vegetation developed rapidly on land—first, the ugly little "naked plant," a single stalk, unadorned, which became, finally, the tall, magnificent fern trees which still survive. Perhaps a hundred million years later, there appeared the ginkgo tree. It is considered to be not less than ten million years old but it is probably much older.

Alone among its contemporaries, it still exists, as the hardiest tree we know. That is why it is planted along the sidewalks in cities where it survives conditions that would kill any other growing thing. (New York abounds with ginkgoes.) It is referred to, in science, as a "living fossil." These trees appeared before the age of the larger reptiles. (It is surprising that these monstrous creatures reached our modern consciousness only as dragons in fairy tales *until* their bones were found.) It is accepted that the tremendous trees, the sequoias (redwoods), existed at the same time as the dinosaurs.

The dramatic lesson for us in the history of our world is one of infinite patience, dogged persistence, and a sense of long, long dignity in our struggle toward the light of knowledge. Apparently, we never gave up trying!

Persistence Is the Deepest Urge of Nature

The trail that growing intelligence has left tells a story of sheer, clinging, scheming survival through tenacity of purpose. One can only conclude that some urge moves through all nature and man. Its slow relentlessness is very near incredible to our modern impatience. This ceaseless reach and growth of all life gives it a dignity that never accepts defeat.

Life continually builds. It does not recognize demolition. It climbs over destruction and debris to create other new forms of beauty. Neither fire, flood, nor fury of wind has the final say. Life creeps across devastation and begins anew. Man continues to try to fathom the secret.

We, today, are called upon to make swift adjustments to the continuous findings of science. Things are changing so rapidly that in the fields of chemistry, computing, and nuclear developments, whatever you are looking at is already in the process of being outmoded!

The Secret of Life

We have now the exciting discovery of DNA, which may hold the very secret of life itself, and is known to control the type patterns of all living organisms, thus causing the difference in men, mice, cabbages and kings. DNA is a chemical molecule with a spiral shape, highly suggestive of a roll of microfilm on which each individual's form and "itinerary" is imprinted.

The rapidity of our progress in the microcosm (the world of small things) rests almost wholly on the progress that has been made in electronics and new powers of magnification. Each branch of learning climbs on the other. Each new discovery serves all its brothers. And in the unravelling of the mysteries of DNA, it may be found that all the elements of nature work, synthesized, toward the goal of Life.

The swift changes in the world tend to give the thoughtless person a sense of rootlessness, of insecurity. This either saddens him, as he looks behind him and interprets change as chaos, or he thinks that since everything is shifting, perhaps his old restraints and moralities are as old-fashioned as the horse and buggy. He may consider that all the bars are down, once-accepted virtues no longer have meaning—and he may start on an orgy of sensuousness and disrespect for all law.

The thoughtful man, whose mind likes to think behind and beyond the seeming, is quite likely to take vast satisfaction in seeing that the only changes are in the way we shall go—that the goal itself is untouched.

How are you going to react to the discovery of the germ of life itself? If your mind is a penetrating one, you are not going to think that God has been removed from his throne as Creator, just because someone has uncovered His method.

Religion is not shattered by our finding the secrets of DNA or any other marvellous processes.

Who or What Instituted These Wonders?

Man's mind, being a reflection of the All-Mind, is capable of glories beyond even his present imagining! We have only scratched the surface of possible discoveries of powers, formulae, processes, and materials.

Do not discard your church. Realize the firm base on which your church rests. Even some of its practices, rites, and claims that may have always seemed useless to you, may, in the light of what we know, take on truer value.

We have a long way to go before we can do without the benefits of aid from those approaches to the all-knowing Mind—and if we should arrive at such independence, we would realize that all of it is a gift from the Parent-Source. Do not be shallow enough to throw over eternal values. On the contrary, encourage the religious organizations (all of them) as the greatest servants of burgeoning Mind.

A World of Challenge

The stronger we get as individuals the closer we are to the Parent-Mind. Use the grand prerogatives that science and your own intuition tell you belong to you. There is no chain reaction of inevitability that cannot be altered. Do not fall into the trap of thinking discovered patterns are unchangeable. By bombarding genes with sufficiently powerful rays, mutations occur. At first, this seems disconcerting to say the least. But, it is also good news. Man can harness this process to heal his body, improve agriculture, and raise his standards in many ways.

A whole world of challenge lies before man in finding out exactly what (and how much of it) alters any existing pattern. It is not beyond the realm of the possible that continuous bombardment of thoughts on some unsatisfactory pattern can change it for the better. Many people already believe in this procedure and cite many instances to support their faith.

There is no doubt that we shall find more and more evidence of man's sovereignty in all the aspects of his manifold nature. It is not completely bright to have immovable reservations about anything that spells advance. Slowly, slowly, these things come to our lives.

Remember that in the field of aviation the ancients believed that man would one day fly. It is mentioned in Sanskrit! Da Vinci left drawings of a possible airplane. Little by little, ideas gain attention.

Let us take the benefits given us by innovation, in the meanwhile not being too disturbed in the basic visions, reactions, and goals of our own lives. *By clinging to the eternal values* of our own religious philosophies we shall have quieter nerves and thus more stamina to meet the kaleidoscopic life presented to us.

People Have Always Feared Change

New things have always been somewhat disturbing, yet most change has been for the better. The die-hards are always predicting disaster in the face of any invention. They have always been sure, as each major invention arrived, that the end of the world was at hand!

The steam engine threw thousands of sailors and oarsmen out of work. Power-run machines throw millions of handworkers into unemployment. Mechanization brought panic in many areas to many people. The automobile was considered an evil by some lazy minds that did not wish to adjust to it. And today, automation is taking work from millions of workers. What will these people do?

The Advantage of Having More Than One Skill

I frequently assert that the man with more than one way to make a living is in a stronger position in our changing world than the man who "has all his eggs in one basket." There is just no way to tell when change with a capital "C" will strike. Your secondary hobby or business may loom important when you least expect it. (A wise investor tries to have a varied holding in stocks and bonds. If one goes down, another may hold.)

It would also be more than prudent to have a part of your attention go toward some activity that has to do with the basic needs of people, i.e., food, housing, and clothing.

Education Is the Watchword of Our New, Careening World

Invest in yourself! Learn whatever you need to know. And don't be ashamed to do so at any age. The world is drawing close together, so learn languages. They are often the basis for a career—the deciding factor in fresh opportunity. Your new world needs you at your learned best! Don't be ashamed to go slowly, if need be. Always be studying something. You will be adding to your worth.

Among the people whose lives have touched mine—and there are many thousands of them—the ones who have served their world wholeheartedly are the ones who have gone forward most surely and rapidly.

This old world needs *you;* needs *your* help. Perhaps you will be serving yourself best by giving without too much thought of reward all the help you can possibly give wherever you can reach, either at home or in the undeveloped areas of the world.

Awareness is light on any given subject. "Oh, I see," is the popular way of expressing a dawning understanding. You *are* what you know. You cannot operate beyond your knowledge. Perhaps man's present focus on the study of himself is the best clue to his readiness for another step forward and up.

You Stand to Profit by Man's History

You hold the result of man's complete history—his slow accumulation of intelligence—and you now stand to profit by it all. It will be necessary to understand more of how you gathered your present reflexes, tendencies, intuition, attention span, and direct knowledge.

Your unconscious reflexes, your unvolitional physical and emotional responses are largely those gathered as protective ones by eons of experience in survival. Some of these responses are no longer serviceable; in fact, they may be a menace to progress. So the time has come to select and discard some of them.

There is no denying that man misuses much that he has learned; prostitutes it to shallow expediences; and protects his efforts with special cruelties. Actually, this misuse is to be expected, *for man has had to use the utmost cunning to survive as a species* and more to survive as an individual among his own kind. The same type of aggression and defense necessary to escape alien enmity had to be employed against his brothers who wanted what he had gained.

We tend to think of Attila the Hun, called "The Scourge of God," as a barbarian of the far past. But is not every aggressor a spiritual brother of Attila? The questions arise: Has man come very far from the jungles? Do we not today fear the attack of an enemy? Isn't the hydrogen bomb a threat to all mankind?

Such thoughts tend to throw us into a disgust for some of man's "advances." For we do not consider material accomplishment in the field of destructive discoveries as advances. It is the same jungle man, we say, enacting his drama of killing and theft against a modern background instead of an ancient one.

But it is not the same man! True, he seems, on the surface, to be doing the same things he did millions of years ago—killing for his own ends as do other beasts. But he is caught in a web of necessity, dealing with men whose development is far behind his in many areas. Ask any individual and he will tell you he hates war and yearns for a world where kindness and constructive occupations engage all our energies. But unevenly advanced groups mistrust one another. Even as recent a patriot as Theodore Roosevelt advised his countrymen to, "Speak softly and carry a big stick." But at least he said, *"Speak softly."* Here is a small, but undeniable clue that man knows there are other means to resolve his fears, suspicion and mistrust.

What Man Can Conceive, He Eventually Becomes

It seems clear that we cannot emerge from jungle tactics until there are no more jungle people. Therefore, any individual who wants a safer world for himself and his children will sensibly set about trying to even up the world's fund of knowledge. With knowledge, people will gain their own material advance. As usual, man is going ahead walking backward. We are trying to help the world by money and food, which, while pleasant, are so very temporary. *What the world needs is education—knowledge!* True, it is difficult to teach a starving man. But aid to him should not stop with food and tools. It must reach his mind.

Where do you stand in all this uneven welter? Your opinion of your present world is the foundation for your expectancy of the future. How are you going to have a sunny belief in a flow of *good* to yourself from a world still functioning in the treacheries, the violences, and the self-interest you see all about you? Well, there is a way.

You must learn to see beyond the surface—and be able to estimate the gathering force of upward trends. The apothecary's scale is a good simile. The side filled with humanity's wrongs may be dominant now, but we must not ignore the other side. We must observe that it is not empty. Bit by difficult bit, a mass of good effects is gathering.

Man is questioning the virtue and validity of his animal experience.

Although he is still enmeshed in it, he is examining his status as never before. Still driven by ancient compulsions, he is very uncomfortable being pulled backward and forward at the same time. Something has to give!

As he studies and understands himself, he perceives that more and more light beams ahead. The promise of the future is like a great shaft of light from a far-off lighthouse, showing him the way to safety.

A Dishonest Man Is Living Still in the Jungle

The growth of man's moral nature lags, perhaps by a million years. The concept of being a human man, however, presses at the door of his consciousness. The call upward may be faint and weak within, but it is there, nevertheless. He is still operating as an animal seeking its own advantages, and paying no attention to those urges which H. G. Wells has described as being "the weaker, wider claims of the common good." How much evolving this jungle man has before him—and most of it is painful!

The Necessary Gods

As evolving man has occasionally noted that *he must obey the inner voices of justice to all creatures,* he has set up various gods to oversee the matter. As mercy, tenderness, kindness and unselfishness have shown that they lead to health and happiness and a contented community of families, man has assumed that these are the qualities of the powers above him.

As he has come to believe that these powers seek his good, and not his ill, he has been willing to worship in faith instead of in fear. Not knowing the road ahead, but sensing that it is there and that he must travel, he has accepted rules of behavior—rules which his mind can accept as right, but which his body and instinctive reflexes often do not yet fit.

In revulsion to complete absorption in sense, animal craft and self-interest, many men have banded together in various "religious" groups and denied the earthly, physical man completely. The pendulum swings always in extremes. While one can understand the revulsions that prompted these denials, and accept the ideals they promulgate, one must, if one is to help groping man, encourage him to express ideally the threefold aspects of his being—physical, mental, and spiritual. They are inextricably intertwined.

At several times in known history, civilization has stood in disorganized confusion, ripe for a leader with higher and newer vision. And usually it has fallen prey to an impudent, assertive aggressor. And again, the wheels of government—and unfortunately the intellectual and spiritual life that went with it—ground around once more in the same old tracks of the past cunning, self-seeking, vicious aggression.

The outward arrangements of government do not correct bestiality and the urge to attack and overcome, or to wrest by force what one wants. For within a state, warring factions will rise, one against the other; we have "civil" wars as well as wars of aggression. Feuds develop within a community in the best of democratic societies.

The War Is in the Soul of Man

We may say, "When education is general, the world will have peace." This is not true unless the education brings man to the inner decision to be gentle. We may say, "When raw materials are available to all nations, there will be peace," but prosperity has never yet brought peace, regardless of its pretty face.

In the future, new power will be based on the skill and understanding of the scientist. Then, and only then, will intelligence take the lead. Many of our past kings could neither read nor write. Pursuits of the mind were left to men with weak bodies, who were incapacitated for anything but "book work" and records. But this is true no longer. In our time, the finest athlete may well be the valedictorian of the class—and future victory over enemies may well lie in a test tube!

In more ways than these, we face a world where the mind and the spirit will be supreme. That day is not far off. The bully, who bangs and shouts and threatens, whether he be head of a corner gang of teen-agers or the head of a great state, will soon or late meet the fate of all bullies—defeat. Strange, isn't it, that a populace that doesn't mind a bit of bluff and brutality in personal life, is secretly disgusted with evidences of it in a leader?

Straws in the Wind Indicate a Better World To Be

This tendency of almost everybody is another straw in the wind that tells us that standards are changing, slowly perhaps, but changing for the better—the while we *look* as though we were in the same old animal grooves. We are not quite ready to step from the old ways, but the pressures for that move are building up.

You Hold the Future in Your Hands

Think of yourself as a developing entity, who is at home in a moving world! Thus, you will be thinking of yourself as *"kinetic,"* sharing in the great and ever-moving power of Mind.

You hold in your own hands the reins of your own future. It matters not if (at the moment) you stand in line to collect your salary and live in a community of houses that are all alike. On the other hand, you may be the ruler of a country. Whoever you are, you are an amazing product of eons of time and billions of experiments. At this point in your development, it is yours to say what manner of creature you decide to be.

You have emerged from the dark struggles of the past into the white light of self-determination. The way is not clearly defined. Your role is almost frightening with heavy responsibility. Yet all you need do is reach out your hand. Search for the way. You shall find it.

You have to try over and over again, and for that you will need faith. Faith in the supporting Parent-Mind from which all derives, and faith in your own mastery of kinetic psycho-dynamics.

Walk ahead confidently. The mind-power of the universe walks with you. *For you are mankind,* so lately aware of your kinship, your sonship to that Parent-All, so newly knowing that your *humanness* leads you straight to God!

KP-D PSYCHIC ENERGY ANALYZER CHART

Score 1 to 5 for each step, marking the degree (1, 2, 3, 4, or 5) of your kinetic psycho-dynamic energy in the space provided at the end of the sentence. The headings on the left are the main divisions and the check lists on the right are your sub-divisions. The perfect score for each sub-division is 25. You must have a score of at least 20 for each division before graduating yourself to the next rung of the ladder which leads you to your destiny. A total for the entire chart of 100 is great! If you pass each group of five questions and do it correctly you will have to have a grand total of at least 80.

TOTALS		START		CHECK HERE NOW	CHECK HERE LATER
____	Control	____	*I have wiped resentments out of my mind	____	____
			*I am patient with myself	____	____
			*I have accepted the fact that I can be fortunate	____	____
			*I look forward, not backward	____	____
			*I am willing to put forth effort	____	____
			*I daily increase my use of mind-power	____	____
			________**________		
____	Channelling	____	*I expose my mind to the world around me	____	____
			*I pay attention to every thought that comes along	____	____
			*I take one idea at a time	____	____
			*I sift out my thoughts	____	____
			*I think before I act	____	____
			*I have no desire to "get even" with anyone	____	____
			________**________		

TOTALS		START		CHECK HERE NOW	LATER
____	Utilization	____	*I can influence and persuade people	____	____
			*I use my subconscious mind to better effect	____	____
			*I can see each task to the end	____	____
			*I am putting my personal life in order	____	____
			*I am meeting my professional goals	____	____
			________**________		
____	Fruition	____	*I have achieved a sense of well-being	____	____
			*I have adjusted to new phenomena	____	____
			*I have broadened my life with at least one new cultural interest	____	____
			*I have self-confidence in everything I do	____	____
____			*I look forward with joy to each new day	____	____
____	Grand total		________**________		

Index

Index

Hindu and Muslim Mysticism

Hindu and Muslim Mysticism

R. C. ZAEHNER

SCHOCKEN BOOKS · NEW YORK

First SCHOCKEN PAPERBACK edition 1969

This edition published by arrangement with The Athlone Press

Library of Congress Catalog Card No. 74-83675

Manufactured in the United States of America

For Nicholas

The Louis H. Jordan Bequest

The will of the Rev. Louis H. Jordan provided that the greater part of his estate should be paid over to the School of Oriental and African Studies to be employed for the furtherance of studies in Comparative Religion, to which his life had been devoted. Part of the funds which thus became available was to be used for the endowment of a Louis H. Jordan Lectureship in Comparative Religion. The lecturer is required to deliver a course of six or eight lectures for subsequent publication. The first series of lectures was delivered in 1951.

PREFACE

This volume consists of eight lectures delivered (in a slightly abridged form) in May 1959 at the School of Oriental and African Studies in the University of London, when I had the honour of being invited by the Director and the Academic Board of the School to give the fifth series of Lectures under the Louis H. Jordan Bequest.

I chose the subject of *Hindu and Muslim Mysticism* because it seemed to me that, voluminous as the literature on mysticism is, much of it starts from the quite unproven premiss that mysticism is a more or less uniform phenomenon appearing in all the great religious traditions. So far from this being the case, certain varieties of mystical experience are attested not only in different mystical traditions but also in the same religion. I chose the Hindu and Muslim varieties for three reasons: first because I am better equipped to deal with these two than with any other, secondly because in Hindu mysticism the types are most easily and clearly distinguished, and thirdly because so little has been written on Muslim mysticism in English.

I have treated the two streams of mysticism separately, the first four lectures being devoted mainly to Hinduism and the last four to Islam. Constant reference from the one to the other, however, has been made throughout wherever such comparison seemed illuminating, as has surprisingly often proved to be the case.

I have not, of course, attempted to cover the whole field of either Hindu or Muslim mysticism since that would not have been possible in eight lectures, but I have attempted to trace the development of mystical thought within the formative period of both traditions. In the case of Hinduism I have concentrated on what seemed to me to be salient in the 'classical' Upaniṣads, the *Yogasūtras*, the Bhagavad-Gītā, and lastly on Rāmānuja's commentary on the latter. Similarly in Islam I have concentrated on what can be called the monistic revolution introduced into Muslim mysticism by Abū Yazīd of Bisṭām in the ninth century, on the restoration of the theistic balance by Junayd of Baghdād, on the re-affirmation of a pure monism in Ghazālī's later writings, and on the refutation of this by Ibn Ṭufayl in the name of sanity and by Najm al-Dīn Rāzī in the name of Islamic orthodoxy.

The book may be regarded as the vindication on a smaller scale and in a narrower field of the theory of mystical experience I evolved in my former book *Mysticism Sacred and Profane*. Particular stress has been laid on the theistic interpretation of the 'monistic' type of mystical experience in which the mystic claims identity with the 'One' because the opposite view of the absolute monists has, ever since the time of Deussen, received far more attention than it would appear to merit. Further I have attempted to show in some detail that the monism of Abū Yazīd, so far from being a natural or inevitable growth in Islam, is, on the contrary, a direct infiltration from an Indian source.

If this book has succeeded in introducing some small element of clarity into the study of mysticism, it will not have been written in vain.

In conclusion I would thank Dr. S. M. Stern of this college for the great trouble he took in checking through my Arabic versions. Any inaccuracies that may remain are, of course, entirely due to me. I would also thank Mr. John Caute also of this college for his great kindness in helping me with the always tedious business of checking the index references.

All Souls College
Oxford
28 June 1959

R. C. Z.

CONTENTS

LIST OF ABBREVIATIONS

BG	Bhagavad-Gītā
KS	Al-Ghazālī, *Kīmiyā-yi Sa'ādat*, Tehran, 1319 A.H. (solar)
Qushayrī	Al-Qushayrī, *Risāla*, Cairo, 1948
R	Rāmānuja
Ṣabrī	Al-Ghazālī, *Al-Jawāhir al Ghawālī*, ed. M. Ṣabrī, Cairo, 1934/1353
Sahlajī	*Shaṭaḥāt al-Ṣūfiyya*, Pt. I, containing the *Al-Nūr min Kalimāt Abī Ṭayfūr*, a collection of the sayings of Abū Yazīd by Sahlajī, ed. A. Badawī, Cairo, 1949
Sarrāj	Abū Naṣr al-Sarrāj, *Kitāb al-Luma' fi'l-Taṣawwuf*, ed. R. A. Nicholson, Leyden–London, 1914
[Upaniṣads]	
*Br*Up	*Bṛhadāraṇyaka*
*Ch*Up	*Chāndogya*
*Śvet*Up	*Śvetāśvatara*
*Taitt*Up	*Taittirīya*
YS	Patañjali, *Yogasūtras*

Hindu and Muslim Mysticism

I

Two Trends

'BEFORE entering on our exposition, we must form an adequate idea of that which renders it so peculiarly difficult to penetrate to the essential nature of any Indian subject. The knowledge of these difficulties will either facilitate the progress of our work, or serve as an apology for any shortcomings of ours. For the reader must always bear in mind that the Hindus entirely differ from us in every respect, many a subject appearing intricate and obscure which would be perfectly clear if there were more connexion between us. The barriers which separate Muslims and Hindus rest on different causes.

'First, they differ from us in everything which other nations have in common. And here we first mention the language, although the difference of language also exists between other nations. If you want to conquer this difficulty (i.e. to learn Sanskrit), you will not find it easy, because the language is of an enormous range, both in words and inflections, something like the Arabic, calling one and the same thing by various names, both original and derived, and using one and the same word for a variety of subjects, which, in order to be properly understood, must be distinguished from each other by various qualifying epithets.'[1]

So does Bīrūnī open his great work on India: and like him I must plead that 'the knowledge of these difficulties . . . will serve as an apology for any shortcomings of ours'; and shortcomings there are bound to be, for I can lay no claim to specialist qualifications in either Sanskrit or Arabic. Like Bīrūnī, my original point of departure was Iran, and though no Iranian, I may make some

[1] *Al-Beruni's India*, tr. E. C. Sachau, London, 1888, i, 17.

claim to be, or at least to have been, an *iranisant*; and, like him, I see both Arabic and Sanskrit through Iranian spectacles. For one schooled in the austere discipline of Pahlavī, the utter denudation of whose grammatical forms could not fail to attract a sluggish mind, the complexities of both Arabic and Sanskrit are not readily digested. Yet, ill-equipped though I may be, it seemed to me that in a set of lectures devoted to the comparison of religions, I could scarcely do better than to compare the mysticism of the Hindus with that of the Muslims, for whereas the comparison between the orthodoxies of religions of Semitic origin on the one hand and the orthodoxies or predominant trends in the Indian religions on the other are often forced or inapplicable, comparison between the mystical writings of quite divergent religions are at least comparisons between like and like.

It can be maintained that the strictly monotheistic religions do not naturally lend themselves to mysticism; and there is much to be said for this view. Christianity is the exception because it introduces into a monotheistic system an idea that is wholly foreign to it, namely, the Incarnation of God in the Person of Jesus Christ. Such an idea is as repulsive to the strict monotheism of Islam as it is to that of the Jews. Judaism, on its side, never developed a mystical tradition comparable to that of the other great religions because it held that union with a transcendental God who manifests himself in history could not be possible to a finite creature. 'Ecstasy there was,' writes Professor Scholem,[1]

> and this fundamental experience must have been a source of religious inspiration, but we find no trace of a mystical union between the soul and God. Throughout there remained an almost exaggerated consciousness of God's *otherness*, nor does the identity and individuality of the mystic become blurred even at the height of ecstatic passion. The Creator and His creature remain apart, and nowhere is an attempt made to bridge the gulf between them or to blur the distinction.

In Islam, too, we cannot help feeling that Ṣūfism is so radical a distortion of the orthodox doctrine as to constitute almost a separate

[1] G. G. Scholem, *Major Trends in Jewish Mysticism*, London, 1955, pp. 55–6.

religion. Neither the Torah nor the Qur'ān naturally lend themselves to a mystical interpretation: both emphasize overwhelmingly the complete otherness of God—*lam yakun la-hu kufuwan aḥad*, 'like unto Him hath there never been anyone'.[1]

The mystical approach does not come naturally to anyone schooled in a monotheistic creed. It is, on the other hand, the very stuff and substance of the religions that have grown up in India. This, too, was clearly understood by Bīrūnī who, after expatiating on the difficulties of the Sanskrit tongue, goes on to say:

> Secondly, they [the Hindus] totally differ from us in religion, as we believe in nothing in which they believe, and *vice versâ*. On the whole, there is very little disputing about theological topics among themselves; at the utmost, they fight with words, but they will never stake their soul or body or their property on religious controversy.[2]

This is perfectly true, for the mystic is by nature tolerant, seeing, as he does, truth in all religions which, for him, appear as the outward manifestations only of a single and essentially inexpressible truth. This, at least, is true of one type of mysticism; it is much less true of the specifically theistic kind, as we shall see in the sequel.

Nietzsche said somewhere of France that it is '*die Hauptschule der Geschmack*': so we might say of India that it is '*die Hauptschule der Mystik*', it is the high school of mysticism. It is this for two reasons: first, in Indian religions theological thinking is mystical through and through. Secondly Hinduism is bound by no dogmas, as Islam is, and the mystic is thereby quite uninhibited in expressing any view he pleases. In Ṣūfism the reverse is true; for in Islam it was not safe to advocate views that ran directly counter to orthodoxy as officially interpreted, as the arraignment of Dhū'l-Nūn of Egypt[3] and of Abū'l-Ḥussayn al-Nūrī[4] and his companions before the Caliph and the subsequent execution of Ḥallāj[5] and of

[1] Qur'ān, 112. 4.

[2] *Al-Beruni's India*, i, 19.

[3] Qushayrī, p. 8.

[4] Ibid., p. 112: cf. A. J. Arberry, *Pages from the Kitāb al-Luma'*, London, 1947, p. 26.

[5] L. Massignon, *Al-Hallaj, Martyr mystique de l'Islam*, Paris, 1922, i, 291–330.

Suhrawardī al-Maqtūl[1] all too conclusively showed. Hence the earlier writers on Ṣūfism strove desperately to show that their teachings, however much they might seem to be at variance with official orthodoxy, were in fact merely a deepening and interiorization of the *Sunna* or outward law. Yet it is doubtful whether they convinced even themselves of this, for 'they discussed matters which, in the opinion of ordinary men, were sheer blasphemy (*kufr*) against God'.[2] The great Ghazālī, too, found himself in this predicament; and whereas he is ever-ready to condemn those Ṣūfīs who considered that Islamic law was no longer applicable to the 'perfect',[3] he nonetheless admits that some of the more extreme utterances of the Ṣūfīs 'appear to be rank infidelity'.[4] Furthermore it is not at all easy to tell what his real views are, for each and every time that he appears to be about to reveal his inmost thoughts, he checks himself with some such words as these: 'Beyond these truths there are further mysteries the penetration of which is not permissible.'[5] Shiblī, the companion and friend of the martyred Ḥallāj, it will be remembered, reproached the latter as he hung upon his cross not with having proclaimed a false doctrine but with having made public, against all expediency, a secret truth.[6] Thus, in assessing the testimony of the Ṣūfīs, we must always bear in mind the peculiar disadvantages under which they laboured and which prevented them from putting into plain words the actual nature of their experiences as they seemed to them at the time.

Among the Hindus there was no such restraint, and Hinduism is therefore likely to teach us, within its single tradition, more about the varieties of mysticism than we can glean from those manifestations of this phenomenon which, in the nature of the case, have to be interpreted against a given dogmatic theology. Whether or not

[1] R. A. Nicholson, *A Literary History of the Arabs*, 2nd ed., Cambridge, 1930, p. 275.

[2] Abū Ṭālib al-Makkī, *Qūt al-Qulūb*, Cairo, 1932, iii, 114.

[3] Ghazālī, *Fayṣal al-Tafriqa bayn al-Islām wa'l-Zandaqa*, *apud* Ṣabrī, p. 94.

[4] *KS*., ii, 745.

[5] Ṣabrī, p. 123.

[6] See Massignon, op. cit., pp. 320–1.

'mysticism is essentially one and the same',[1] as Professor Arberry maintains, whatever the mystical experience may be, it is certainly very variously interpreted and nowhere more so than in the Hindu tradition itself. Moreover, even a nodding acquaintance with that tradition will convince us that, whatever the nature of mysticism may be, it is scarcely 'a constant and unvarying phenomenon of the universal yearning of the human spirit for personal communion with God'.[2]

I have said that Indian religious thinking is mystical through and through, and it is therefore time to consider what we mean by mysticism. Elsewhere I have described it as 'the realization of a union or a unity with or in [or of] something that is enormously, if not infinitely, greater than the empirical self'.[3] This definition seems to be wide enough to cover what appear to me to be the three distinct types of mysticism I have discussed elsewhere.[4] However, let us consider for a moment some of the definitions put forward by the Ṣūfīs themselves.

Mā al-taṣawwuf?—'What is mysticism?' is the question they are continually asking each other. Their definitions vary greatly, but it will suffice to quote only a few. Some describe an attitude to life, others a state of soul, yet others a relationship to God. Among the first we may quote the following: The Ṣūfī 'possesses nothing and is possessed by nothing'; 'Ṣūfism has three fundamental characteristics, it embraces poverty, it is disinterestedly generous, it eschews meddling and gives up the [individual] will.' Or again, 'Ṣūfism means an empty hand and a good heart.' Ṣūfism here means a way of life, in this case a way of denudation, asceticism, and poverty. Asceticism, however, is never an end in itself, it is merely a means, and in all mystical disciplines it is essential. What, however, is the goal?

Let us quote a few more of these aphorisms. 'The Ṣūfī,' says Nakhshabī, 'is soiled by nothing, and all things are made pure by

[1] A. J. Arberry, *Sufism, An Account of the Mystics of Islam*, London, 1950, p. 11.
[2] Ibid.
[3] R. C. Zaehner, *At Sundry Times*, London, 1958, p. 171.
[4] In my *Mysticism, Sacred and Profane*, Oxford, 1957, esp. pp. 168, 184, 198.

him,' and Ṣūfism is 'the purity of nearness [to God] following on the defilement of estrangement'. In this second definition two quite distinct ideas are brought together—purity of heart and nearness to God. The one, it is implied, is a stepping-stone to the other. Ruwaym, however, sees in purity itself the essence of Ṣūfism without, in this particular case, relating it to God. This is probably fortuitous, but should be noted, for, as we shall see, the suppression of all 'impurities', which is even more characteristic of Indian mysticism than of Ṣūfism, does not necessarily bring the mystic nearer to God, for neither in Buddhism nor in the Sāṁkhya system is there any God whom one may approach.

Ṣūfism too means separating oneself off from all created things. It is 'to be exempted from the contemplation of the world of becoming'. But it is more than this: it is, according to Junayd, the father of 'orthodox' Ṣūfism, 'to be in God's company without attachment', or 'to sit in the presence of God without care'. The Ṣūfīs, says Dhū'l-Nūn, 'prefer God over all things as God prefers them over all things'. More typical of much Ṣūfī thought, however, is this: 'Ṣūfism means that God should cause you to die to yourself and live in him.'[1]

Ṣūfism therefore means giving up the world, self-discipline, separating oneself from all created things, denial of self and turning to God. How does all this tally with Hindu mysticism?

Ṣūfism, as we have seen, is a type of mysticism which is to a large extent conditioned by a monotheistic creed. Hindu mysticism, on the other hand, develops along its own lines irrespective of creed or dogma. In his admirable little book on Hindu mysticism Surendranath Dasgupta has distinguished five different types of mysticism: the sacrificial, the Upaniṣadic, the Yogic, the Buddhistic, and that of *bhakti*. The first, which is of historical interest only, can be discounted in our study, but we shall have to consider Dasgupta's other four types a little more closely. To all of them the ascetic discipline, which means turning one's back on this world, is common. But apart from this what is there in common between them?

The purpose of all Indian mysticism is *mokṣa*, 'release' or 'libera-

[1] All these quotations are from Qushayrī, pp. 126–7.

tion', and this means release from our human, conditioned state. Indian religion in its early stages is not so much concerned with God as with immortality, and by immortality is understood not what Muslims mean by *abad*, often translated as 'post-eternity', or an endless prolongation of existence in time, but a condition in which time itself is transcended. This, indeed, is the lowest common denominator of every form of mysticism, and where there is no trace of it, there there would seem to be no 'mystical' experience. *Mokṣa* means release from time and space and causality, it does not mean union or communion with God. It corresponds to the 'purity' of heart of the Ṣūfīs, but does not carry with it the additional implication of nearness to God. That it came to do so and the manner of its coming to do so will form part of the subject-matter of these lectures.

The Yogic, Buddhistic, and *bhakti* forms of mysticism are genuine enough categories, though the almost total silence of the Pālī canon on the nature of Nirvāṇa makes it difficult to classify the Buddhistic experience except in purely negative terms. The mysticism of the Upaniṣads, however, falls under no single head, as Dasgupta himself is the first to concede. All he maintains is that, given the fact that the Upaniṣads are 'a depository of diverse currents of thought' and no 'systematic treatise',[1] there are certain outstanding ideas which can be taken as typical. Dasgupta sums up these leading ideas in what seems to be a perfectly fair and balanced manner.

The chief features of this Upanishad mysticism [he writes], are the earnest and sincere quest for this spiritual illumination, the rapturous delight and force that characterize the utterance of the sages when they speak of the realization of this ineffable experience, the ultimate and absolute truth and reality, and the immortality of all mortal things. Yet this quest is not the quest of the God of the theists. This highest reality is no individual person separate from us, or one whom we try to please, or whose laws and commands we obey, or to whose will we submit with reverence and devotion. It is, rather, a totality of partless, simple and undifferentiated experience which is the root of all our

[1] S. N Dasgupta, *A History of Indian Philosophy*, Cambridge, 1951, i, 42.

ordinary knowledge and experience and which is at once the ultimate essence of our self and the highest principle of the universe, the Brahman or the Atman.[1]

'A totality of partless, simple and undifferentiated experience': what does this mean? It means that man sees his deepest essence as being fundamentally identical with the common source of all things, and he can therefore say, 'I am this All'[2] or 'I am Brahman'.[3] This is usually called pantheism: the soul feels itself to be coterminous with all that is and therefore with God: man is God: *so'smy aham*, 'I am He'.[4] And again since He is All, I too am All. 'Whoso knows, "I am Brahman", becomes this All. Not even the gods have the power to prevent him becoming thus, for such a one becomes their own self.'[5] This absolute identity of the human soul with the godhead is attested in several passages in the Upaniṣads, and it is the very thesis of the *Māṇḍūkya*. It is also basic to Śaṅkara's *advaita* (non-dualism) and to Śāktism. It appears in Islam with Abū Yazīd of Bisṭām and, in its more pantheistic form, in Abū Sa'īd ibn Abī'l-Khayr whose mystical slogan was *hama ū'st*, 'All is He'. I shall try to show in another lecture that there is probably direct borrowing here from an Indian source.

'There is, however, another line of thought running through the different Upanishads in which Brahman appears as the supreme Lord from whom everything has proceeded and who is the source of all energy.'[6] Signs of such a strictly theistic concept of the Supreme Being are clearly visible in the *Iśā*, *Kena*, *Kaṭha*, and *Muṇḍaka* Upaniṣads, and are quite explicit in the *Śvetāśvatara*. This is the second strand in what Dasgupta calls Upanishadic mysticism. To us it appears obvious that there is a distinction between 'the All' and 'the Lord of All', but this distinction was plainly not thought of as ultimate by these early Indian sages, and Dasgupta is again quite right when he says:

[1] S. N. Dasgupta, *Hindu Mysticism*, Chicago/London, 1927, p. 42.
[2] Cf. *Kauṣītakī* Upaniṣad, 1.6.
[3] *Br*Up., 1.4.10.
[4] *Maitreya* Up., 3.1 ff.
[5] *Br*Up., 1.4.10.
[6] S. N. Dasgupta, *Hindu Mysticism*, p. 48.

The different phases of experience and belief which we find in the Upanishads . . . may all be regarded as stages of experience between which the minds of the sages oscillated in attempting the realization of a truth which was beyond speech, beyond thought and beyond all sense-perception. It was sometimes felt as the great over-lord, the controller, creator, ordainer, and master of all, sometimes as the blissful spiritual experience [itself], and sometimes as the simple unity in which all duality has vanished.[1]

Quite other than Upaniṣadic mysticism is the Yogic. This is expressed in the word equally dear to the *Yogasūtras* and to Śaṅkara—*viveka-jñāna*, 'knowledge of difference', that is, to know the difference between eternal being on the one hand and being as conditioned by time, space, and matter on the other, or, in the case of Śaṅkara, between eternal being (*brahman*) and illusory being (*māyā*). This corresponds exactly to Junayd's definition of *tawḥīd* (the affirmation of God's unity) as 'the isolation (*ifrād*) of eternity from origination'.[2] But it is on the subject of eternal being that the fundamental difference between the two schools of mysticism appears. For the Muslims, of course, God alone is eternal Being. There is and can be only one such Being. For the Yoga system, however, matters stand quite otherwise. Though the *Yogasūtras*, unlike the Sāṁkhya, allow for the existence of a god, they also allow for the existence of an infinite number of souls which are eternal and have their being outside space and time; and the goal of the Yoga system is not at all union with God but 'the isolation', as Junayd puts it, 'of the eternal from the originated'. But this isolation is not that of God in his essence, but of the human soul in its own eternal essence which is proper to it and not contingent on a first cause. Thus the whole point of the Yoga technique is to realize the eternity of the individual human soul outside space and time. Here again, Dasgupta, unlike many popular commentators who would have us believe that the *Yogasūtras* are really a Vedāntin textbook, sees the distinction clearly—for, indeed, it is self-evident—and brings it out with his usual lucidity. The Yogin, he says, 'steadily proceeds toward that

[1] Ibid., p. 55.

[2] Qushayrī, p. 3.

ultimate stage in which his mind will be disintegrated and his self will shine forth in its own light and he himself will be absolutely free in bondless, companionless loneliness of self-illumination'.[1] This is all very reminiscent of the *tajrīd al-tafrīd* ('the denudation of isolation') of the Ṣūfīs which we shall have occasion to deal with later.

Now it is interesting that both Patañjali in the *Yogasūtras* and Śaṅkara define true existential knowledge as *viveka-jñāna*, 'the science of difference'. For both there is an absolute distinction between the relative world of time and space and the absolute world in which time, space, matter, and causation have no meaning. The final goal is in each case the same, the 'companionless loneliness of self-illumination', the experience of one's own soul as a pure light, utterly independent, autarchic, deathless because beyond time, eternal, and alone. One of the aids to attaining to this vision of one's own true nature is, indeed, *īśvara-praṇidhāna*,[2] 'meditation on the Lord'; but this meditation on the Lord does not lead to union with him, but rather it enables the still bound soul to become what the Lord always is, an eternal monad wholly independent of matter. The final experience is always one of isolation. Thus we now have two quite distinct types of mysticism in the Indian tradition, the pantheistic or pan-en-henic, as I have elsewhere called it, which sees all as one and one as all, and the mysticism of total isolation, the separating of the eternal in man from the temporal. With this latter form of mysticism Śaṅkara's form of *advaita* would seem to be identical so far as the experience itself is concerned; for in each case the experience is one of totally undifferentiated oneness, which it is possible to interpret either as the isolation of your own essential being or, since this isolation is completely beyond space and time, as the identity of your own being with the ground of the universe, that is, Brahman. This, of course, is the position of Śaṅkara's type of Vedānta.

Dasgupta classes Buddhistic mysticism as a separate type, but the evidence of what the early Buddhists understood by Nirvāṇa is so slight that we can afford to by-pass it for the moment.

[1] S. N. Dasgupta, *Hindu Mysticism*, p. 80.

[2] *YS.*, 2.45.

Professor Arberry, as we have seen, has defined mysticism as a 'constant and unvarying phenomenon of the universal yearning of the human spirit for personal communion with God'. This may be largely true of Christian and Muslim mysticism, but not a trace of love or yearning for communion do we find either in Upaniṣadic or in Yogic mysticism. The yearning, if yearning there is, is all for *mokṣa*, 'release', from our wretched conditioned humanity into our true immortal state which is beyond space and time. It is a yearning for a changed condition, not for a Person. Even in the theistic *Śvetāśvatara* Upaniṣad God is still only the perfect exemplar, he is not the object of the mystic's passionate attachment: nor, indeed, could he be so since attachment of any kind is regarded as the greatest obstacle to liberation. The paradox of the theistic Yoga is that the contemplation of God in his perfection does not lead to any love of him or desire to unite with him, but rather spurs one on to emulate him in his total detachment from everything that is associated with coming-to-be and passing away, in his absolute independence, freedom, and isolation.

In all Indian mystical writing before the Bhagavad-Gītā as well as in Patañjali's *Yogasūtras* there is no trace of love for the deity. It is only in the Bhagavad-Gītā where God emerges as in some sense distinct from and superior to both the created universe and the human soul that an element of love creeps in. This is scarcely surprising, for if the soul is regarded as either being identical with Brahman or as so constituted as to be unable to commune with other souls, then its final fulfilment will not be an ecstasy of union but an 'en-stasy' of introverted narcissism.

In the Bhagavad-Gītā, however, we have the beginnings of *bhakti* mysticism, and this is more nearly comparable to Ṣūfism which, from its very beginnings, is essentially a mysticism of love. As I shall be devoting another lecture to the Gītā and Rāmānuja's commentary on it, there is little that need be said now. What I would, however, stress is that in the Hindu tradition the tendency is from monism to theism as the higher form of religious life, whereas in Ṣūfism the tendency is from theism, that is, a mysticism of love, towards what amounts to monism in that, in the states called *fanā* ('annihilation') and *infirād* ('isolation'), it is claimed that there is no consciousness of anything but God, man thereby realizing himself as God. This seems to be quite clearly what Ghazālī himself believed, at least in the *Mishkāt al-Anwār*.[1] This monistic conclusion which claims that at the height of his mystical experience man actually *is* God, is frequently challenged by the Ṣūfīs themselves, notably by Ibn Ṭufayl who offers a short refutation of it. Nowhere, however, is the case so clearly stated as by Rāmānuja in his commentary on the Gītā.

The respective rôles of personal effort and divine grace are as much the concern of Hindu as of Muslim mysticism, and the answers given in either case are largely conditioned by the theological background against which mystical experience is viewed and according to which it is explained. Thus for the orthodox Muslim—and the vast majority of the earlier Ṣūfīs would claim to be such—with their firm belief in predestination, it is frankly impossible to deny the divine initiative. For the Hindu, however, who is free to believe more or less what he likes and who enjoys the widest latitude in the interpretation of his own corpus of scripture, it is perfectly possible to hold that liberation can be obtained entirely by the mystic's own efforts. Indeed this must be so in the Sāṁkhya system as in Buddhism where there is no God on whose grace one could rely. Indeed even in the earlier chapters of the theistic Bhagavad-Gītā it is freely admitted that liberation can be achieved entirely by one's own efforts without the intervention of divine grace. The general Hindu view would seem to be that man's final end is liberation, and that this can be achieved either by his own efforts or by the intervention of the Supreme Being. The first method, which is that of the classical Sāṁkhya-Yoga, is regarded as being a severe discipline too difficult for the average man, whereas the second is open to all men and is therefore the surest as well as the easiest path to liberation.

What, however, are we to understand by liberation? All schools of Hindu mysticism agree that liberation means release from our own human condition, release from what the Sāṁkhya

[1] See below, pp. 164ff.

calls *prakṛti* and the Vedānta *māyā*, that is, the objective world on the one hand and our own mundane nature, conditioned by time and space, our emotions and mental processes on the other. Such a condition is very often referred to as the *paramā gatiḥ*, 'the ultimate goal'. The Sāṁkhya-Yoga is content to define this as *kaivalyam* which means the isolation of the individual soul in its eternal essence: and that this is a condition of complete bliss no Hindu would deny. What, however, is in question is whether this splendid isolation of the soul which, it is claimed, man can achieve by Yoga without any reference to an external divine agency, is identical with the *unio mystica* of the theistic mystics. The monist would claim that to speak of a *unio mystica* is merely to mis-state the case: reality is one, and if this is really so, then to speak of 'union with God' must be ultimately meaningless:

> For where there is duality, as it were, there one smells another; there one sees another; there one hears another; there one speaks to another; there one thinks of another; there one understands another. But where everything has become just one's own self, then whereby and whom would one smell? then whereby and whom would one see? then whereby and whom would one hear? then whereby and to whom would one speak? then whereby and of whom would one think? then whereby and whom would one understand? whereby would one understand him by whom one understands this All? Lo, whereby would one understand the understander?[1]

Thus what the *bhākta* sees as a love-duet between himself and God in which the self is finally united to God in an ecstasy of surrender, is really no more than an inexact representation for simple theistic minds of the ineffable ontological unity of the soul—an isolated monad only according to the Sāṁkhya, but the ground and origin of all existence according to the Śaṅkaran Vedānta.

For the monist, then, the *unio mystica* must appear as the last stage in the progression of the soul from this world of duality towards ultimate reality which is indivisibly one; and, avowedly, theistic mystics often seem to corroborate the monist's thesis. So one of the Ṣūfīs is represented as saying: 'Lovers do not attain to the

[1] *Br*Up., 2.4.14.

reality of love until the one says to the other, "O thou I".'[1] Statements such as this—of which Ḥallāj's 'I am the Truth' and Abū Yazīd's 'I am He' are only the most famous—would tend to support the monistic point of view: and it is an odd paradox that Ṣūfism, whose major premiss is the absolute distinction between God and man, should arrive at a conception of mystical experience that seems to be identical with that of the monistic Hindus who start from the totally contrary premiss that man is in some sense God. Both define it in terms of absolutely undifferentiable unity, the destruction of man's humanity (*bashariyya* or *nāsūt* in Muslim terminology) and the perdurance of God or the Absolute. In such a state, since there is consciousness of eternal being, and since all consciousness of the ordinary empirical self (the *ahaṁkāra* of the Hindus) has disappeared, and since, according to Muslim theology, there is no eternal being other than God, one can only cry out with Ḥallāj, 'I am the Truth'. The human soul does not become God but is completely annihilated, and God's own self-consciousness alone remains. This is the position adopted by Ghazālī in his later works, and it appears to be indistinguishable from that of Śaṅkara.

There is, however, an important difference between the two, and that is that in the case of the Ṣūfīs, as of the Christian mystics, the means of realizing divinity is love, whereas in the case of the strict Vedāntins and the followers of the Sāṁkhya-Yoga it is simply the acquisition of the intuitional truth that the soul, which, for the Vedāntin, is identical with the godhead, is eternal. Neither in the Upaniṣads nor in the Sāṁkhya-Yoga does love play any part at all. The Bhagavad-Gītā, however, describes both the Yogic way of 'becoming Brahman' and the lover's way of entering into God, though it scarcely attempts to correlate the two. Rāmānuja, however, pursues the arguments of the Gītā to their logical conclusion, and reaches a conclusion that is diametrically opposed to that of Śaṅkara. Like all Hindus he takes the immortality of the soul for granted, that is, he assumes that the human soul is, of its nature, eternal, a being that exists outside space and time, and that it is

[1] Sarrāj, p. 384.

possible for the soul to realize itself as such. This, however, is not the *final* goal of human existence, but only a halfway house; for it is only when the soul has shaken off all the fetters that bind it to what E. G. Browne called 'a miserable actuality',[1] when it has completely freed itself from all desires for what is other than God that it can make itself acceptable to God. 'Liberation' is the end of the first phase only, not the final end which is communion with God. On realizing himself as a spiritual, that is, an extra-temporal being, man can then take the additional step of entering into a personal relationship with God. This does not mean that he becomes God, because as an eternal being he is only a minute fraction of God, but he can fully enjoy his eternal relationship with God, for he is of like nature to him, or, in the language of Christian and Muslim mystics, he is made in his image. The mysticism of love, then, is not, as Śaṅkara would have it, merely a lower and less sure way of achieving liberation. It is a stage in the spiritual life which can lead to communion with the source of all life in an ecstasy of love. However, it is perfectly possible to take this first step without advancing to the second. It is possible to 'become Brahman' without for that reason entering into loving communion with God; and this is, in fact, what the monistic mystics do. Divested as they are of all their mortal trappings they are content to rest in the quiet contemplation of their own souls; having reached the immortal they can conceive of nothing beyond. They are blinded by their own self-sufficiency, for having conquered desire they cannot rekindle desire itself and direct it to its proper goal which is God.

Rāmānuja divides reality into three categories, the objective world, the spiritual world of eternal beings which consists mainly of human souls, and God who is the source and origin of both. God is not identical with Brahman, but the author of Brahman, Brahman being the sum-total of eternal substances, the 'category of soul' or *ātmatattva*. Thus to become Brahman, for Rāmānuja, means no more than to realize your own immortality. Brahman is not the world-soul as it is for Śaṅkara, it is that which is unconditioned by space and time, the state of being as opposed to

[1] E. G. Browne, *A Year amongst the Persians*, 3rd ed., London, 1950, p. 136.

becoming which the individual soul is of its very nature at liberty to enjoy. God, on the other hand, is the originator of eternal being just as he is the creator of the world. He is Lord alike of the spiritual and the material world.[1]

In admitting a plurality of souls Rāmānuja, of course, stands much nearer to Muslim orthodoxy than do any of his predecessors. Yet even within Islam we find the same dispute as to whether there is a plurality of souls or merely one great soul corresponding roughly to the Hindu view of Brahman as normally understood. The dispute is carried on not by the theologians, for whom, of course, souls are created and separate, but by the philosophers who allowed themselves more liberty, Avicenna maintaining that souls were individual and Averroes holding that all souls would be merged into one great soul at death. Again Rāmānuja's interpretation of Brahman as the sum-total of individual souls is paralleled in Ṣūfism. Ghazālī, following Avicenna, makes a clear distinction between what he calls 'the world of creation' and the 'world of the Word' (*'ālam-i amr*),[2] the one being composed of all that has extension, size, and quantity, the other being made up of spiritual essences which cannot be measured: from this world the human souls derive. Ghazālī's scheme is almost identical with that of Rāmānuja except that, for Ghazālī, souls, although not subject to time or space, are nevertheless created. This was denied by some Ṣūfīs,[3] whose position thereby became precisely that of Rāmānuja.

Again the Indian and Muslim traditions agree on the necessity of killing desire if the liberation of the eternal spirit is to be achieved. Ṣūfism, however, it must be confessed, does not neatly divide mystical experience into two separate stages as Rāmānuja does: the idea of the liberation of the soul from its bondage to time and space does not come naturally to it. It does, however, see the soul as the mirror of God[4] and regards the cleansing of the mirror of the soul as an essential preliminary to the subsequent love-duet with God. Desire (*shahwa*) is destroyed in order that 'yearning' (*shawq*) may be born: desire for all that is not God must be destroyed in order

[1] See below, pp. 69ff.

[2] *KS.*, i, 12; Ṣabrī, p. 23.

[3] Sarrāj, pp. 222–3; Qushayrī, p. 45.

[4] See below, p. 158.

that the way may be cleared for an all-devouring passion directed exclusively towards God.

Hindu mysticism differs from both the Christian and Muslim varieties in that it accepts the eternity of the soul as a fact of experience. Whether there is only one world-soul or a plurality of individual souls, it is taken for granted that this soul or souls exist(s) in an element which is unaffected by change. Since they exist outside time, it is as impossible for them to be born as it is for them to die: what is born and dies is something other than they with which they are temporarily connected. Hence the overwhelming preoccupation with liberation. Now it is also a fact of experience, it would seem, that a man, on tasting the experience of liberation, tends to interpret this as meaning that, by the mere fact of knowing that he is eternal and immortal and of experiencing an undifferentiated unity, this experienced immortality which deprives all that comes to be and passes away of all significance and reality, must be identical with the immortality enjoyed by the supreme immortal Being himself, and that the experience of undifferentiated unity must mean that he is in fact 'Being itself, One without a second'.[1] This, according to Rāmānuja, is an error: the unity realized is the unity only of the single soul.

Theistic systems, since they do not admit that the soul exists eternally, independent of time and space, very rarely make this cut-and-dried distinction between the realization of the eternity and oneness of the soul, the subsequent love affair with God, and the final state of union with him. In our later lectures we shall have occasion to try to unravel the positions they actually took up on this all-important question. Just now I would confine myself to quoting the opinion of a modern Jewish mystic who claims, from his own experience, to have established the falsity of the monist position. Although I have twice quoted this passage in published work, it seems to me so vitally important and so relevant to our present context that I make no apology for quoting it again:

Sometimes I hear it said [writes Martin Buber], that every *I and Thou* is only superficial, deep down word and response cease to exist, there is

[1] *Ch*Up., 6.2.2.

only the one primal being unconfronted by another. We should plunge into the silent unity, but for the rest leave its relativity to the life to be lived, instead of imposing on it this absolutized *I* and absolutized *Thou* with their dialogue.

Now from my own unforgettable experience I know well that there is a state in which the bonds of the personal nature of life seem to have fallen away from us and we experience an undivided unity. But I do not know—what the soul willingly imagines and indeed is bound to imagine (mine too once did it)—that in this I had attained to a union with the primal being or the godhead. That is an exaggeration no longer permitted to the responsible understanding. Responsibly—that is, as a man holding his ground before reality—I can elicit from those experiences only that in them I reached an undifferentiable unity of myself without form or content. I may call this an original pre-biographical unity and suppose that it is hidden unchanged beneath all biographical change, all development and complication of the soul. Nevertheless, in the honest and sober account of the responsible understanding this unity is nothing but the unity of this soul of mine, whose 'ground' I have reached, so much so, beneath all formations and contents, that my spirit has no choice but to understand it as the groundless. But the basic unity of my own soul is certainly beyond the reach of all the multiplicity it has hitherto received from life, though not in the least beyond individuation, or the multiplicity of all the souls in the world of which it is one—existing but once, single, unique, irreducible, this creaturely one: one of the human souls and not the 'soul of the All'; a defined and particular being and not 'Being'; the creaturely basic unity of a creature, bound to God as in the instant before release the creature is to the *creator spiritus*, not bound to God as the creature to the *creator spiritus* in the moment of release.[1]

The last phrase 'bound to God as in the instant before release the creature is to the *creator spiritus*' would appear to correspond to what Junayd means when he says that God demands of man 'that he should return at last to his first state, and be as he was before he was',[2] that is, a single idea within the divine mind. Buber is in fact describing precisely the Vedāntin experience of *mokṣa* or liberation, but he interprets it not as Śaṅkara does, that is, as the realiza-

[1] Martin Buber, *Between Man and Man* (Eng. trans.), London, 1947, pp. 24–5.
[2] Qushayrī, pp. 135–6.

tion of self as the primal being or the 'soul of the All', but as Rāmānuja does, that is, as the realization of one's own personal 'pre-biographical unity', as eternal and, to that extent only, divine.

The types of mysticism which we have distinguished in this lecture are most clearly exhibited in the Hindu tradition, and I shall try to outline their development up to the time of Rāmānuja in the next three lectures. The types are (i) the pantheistic or pan-en-henic in which the human personality seems to comprise all existence, the 'I am this All' of the Upaniṣads; (ii) the realization of undifferentiated unity, however philosophically interpreted; and (iii) the loving dialogue with God which results in transforming union, to use the Christian phrase.

Though it would seem that this classification of mystical experiences is perfectly valid, it should always be remembered that the one type is always liable to slip over into one of the other forms. To the rational consciousness it is clear that the sensation of 'being the All' is the exact opposite of the sensation of being an absolute monad in splendid isolation *from* the all, but it is doubtful whether many Ṣūfīs, particularly when writing in Persian, ever felt this. Only a minority of mystics sees, with Martin Buber, that to 'reach the undifferentiable unity' of one's own being is probably something quite different from the transforming union in God. The distinction is undoubtedly made most clearly in India, not indeed in the Upaniṣads or even in the Gītā, but in the later philosophers and some of the classical 'schools' of Indian philosophy. Indian religion is unique in that it makes mystical experience the very basis of religion; and both the Vedānta and the Sāṁkhya are attempts to explain mystical experience in ontological and psychological terms. Hence a far clearer picture of the facts of mystical experience emerges from the Hindu tradition than it does from the Muslim, and it is only when we have formed a clear picture of the varieties of mystical experience as they appear in India that we will be able to approach the far more amorphous Ṣūfī phenomenon. For Indian mysticism is unique in that it develops freely and unhampered by any dogmatic restraints.

Ṣūfism, on the other hand, is not only hampered by a fundamentally uncongenial dogmatism, it is very largely an imported growth.[1] Strongly influenced at first by Christian monasticism in which God's love for man and man's love for God are the essential elements, it later, in my view, becomes the unconscious victim of Vedāntin ideas transmitted by Abū Yazīd of Bisṭām and possibly also by Ḥussayn b. Manṣūr al-Ḥallāj and Abū Sa'īd ibn Abī'l-Khayr. In any case it was Abū Yazīd who introduced seemingly monistic ideas into Ṣūfism, alleging, as he did, that the soul is, at its deepest level, identical with God ('I am He'). Strangely enough none of the Ṣūfīs, however outwardly orthodox, ever repudiated this extraordinary man; and since they accepted him, they found themselves faced with the same problem that was later to confront Rāmānuja in India. How they dealt with this problem will be the principal theme of our last four lectures.

[1] See *Encyclopaedia of Islam*, s.v. *taṣawwuf*; Margaret Smith, *Early Mysticism in the Near and Middle East*, London, 1931.

II

In Search of an Absolute

We saw in our last lecture that three kinds of mysticism can be distinguished, of which only one is concerned with the soul's relations with God. If, however, we identify mysticism with an experience of union with God as Christians usually do, then Hindu mysticism will appear very odd indeed; for by the time of the Upaniṣads, with which this lecture will be principally concerned, the idea of God as distinct from the universe had almost entirely disappeared. In the Qur'ān, Islam claims, God gives his final revelation to man, and it is one of complete transcendence. God is removed from man by so immeasurable a distance that it seems impossible to establish any relationship with him except through worship 'in fear and trembling'; and thus, for the early Ṣūfīs, there could be no relationship with God unless God, in his mercy, calls man towards him. It is man's duty to prostrate himself before God, and it would be sheer presumption to approach him except as a slave or chattel. If relationship there is to be, then it is God who must make the first move. This is vividly illustrated by the traditional account of the conversion of one of the earliest Ṣūfīs, Ibrāhīm bin Adham, who, like the Buddha, was said to have been the son of a prince. One day he was out hunting when he heard an unseen voice saying: 'Ibrāhīm, was it for this that thou wast created?' This phrase was repeated three times until Ibrāhīm, again like the Buddha, gave up all his worldly goods on the spot, giving the horse he was riding to a shepherd who happened to be there in exchange for his coarse woollen cloak.[1] The story illustrates clearly enough how the early Ṣūfīs regarded the religious

[1] Abū 'Abd al-Raḥmān al-Sulamī, *Ṭabaqāt al-Ṣūfiyya*, Cairo, 1953/1372, p.30: Abū Nu'aym al-Iṣfahānī, *Ḥilyat al-Awliyā*, Cairo, 1932–8, vii, 368: Farīd al-Dīn 'Aṭṭār, *Tadhkirat al-Awliyā*, ed. R. A. Nicholson, London/Leyden, 1905–7, i, 86.

life. The decision to leave the world and devote oneself to God's service comes not from man, but is dictated or suggested by God. The resemblance between the legends of the 'conversion' of the Buddha and that of Ibrāhīm bin Adham are all circumstantial and on the surface: the actual motive for renouncing the world could scarcely be more different. What started the Buddha on his great quest for Enlightenment was the sight of old age, disease, and death, the grim facts of this earthly life which his father had hitherto successfully debarred him from seeing. What persuaded Ibrāhīm bin Adham to abandon the world, on the other hand, was what he believed to be the voice of God.[1] God, for the Muslim, was, as always, the first to act in drawing man towards himself.

Hinduism, on the other hand, was not supplied by its sacred book with any clear picture of a transcendent God. The religion of the Vedas is a polytheism which develops along henotheistic lines, to use the convenient phrase coined by Max Müller. Of the great Vedic gods Varuṇa might have developed into an Indian counterpart of the Ahura Mazdāh of Zoroastrianism, the one true God who utterly transcends his creation; but in fact he did not. Not only he but all the other gods lost in importance, and, during the period of the *Brāhmaṇas*, the correct performance of an incredibly complex system of sacrifices ousted the gods from the centre of the religious stage. Although, as has been repeatedly pointed out, there was an increasing tendency to identify the gods one with another and to see in each and all of them an aspect of some supreme power, the mere fact that they had all of them individual characteristics of a mythological nature disqualified each from becoming the undisputed Creator and Lord of creation. In his thought-provoking book *Patterns of Comparative Religion* Professor Mircea Eliade maintains that the purpose of myth and ritual is to abolish what he calls 'profane time' and to situate man in an eternal setting.

Every myth [he writes], whatever its nature, recounts an event that took place in *illo tempore*, and constitutes as a result, a precedent and

[1] 'Take God as your companion and leave men on one side': Sulamī, op. cit., p. 37.

pattern for all the actions and 'situations' later to repeat that event. Every ritual, and every meaningful act that man performs, repeats a mythical archetype; and . . . this repetition involves the abolition of profane time and [the] placing of man in a magico-religious time which has no connection with succession in the true sense, but forms the 'eternal now' of mythical time. In other words, along with other magico-religious experiences, myth makes man once more exist in a timeless period, which is in effect an *illud tempus*, a time of dawn and of 'paradise', outside history. Anyone who performs any rite transcends profane time and space; similarly, anyone who 'imitates' a mythological model or even ritually assists at the retelling of a myth (taking part in it), is taken out of profane 'becoming', and returns to the Great Time.[1]

Ritual is the enactment of myth, but in India the old Rig-Vedic myths would appear to have lost their savour: new myths appear concerning the origin of the world and its perpetual renewal, and the whole elaborate system of sacrifice which forms the subject-matter of the *Brāhmaṇas* is a re-enactment of the creative process. To take part in the rite is to take part in creation and the ever-renewed life of nature itself. Participation in a rite which centres round the creative self-immolation of the Primal Person—be he Puruṣa or Prajāpati or some other—means that the participant himself dies as the One, gives birth to the many, and is reconstituted as the One; he identifies himself with the world process as a whole, and by so doing he enters into what Eliade calls 'sacred time', which is eternity. Thus on the one hand religious interest is transferred from a pantheon that had become largely irrelevant to an absorption in the sacrifice representing the world-process itself, and on the other hand to speculation on what it was that gave myth, prayer, spell, and ritual worth and significance. By the beginning of the Upaniṣadic period the word that had superseded all others to denominate this power was *brahman*.

The etymology of this word is still disputed, but the development of the idea seems fairly clear. Originally it seems to have meant prayer, and, by extension, a spell: later it is used as an

[1] M. Eliade, *Patterns in Comparative Religion* (Eng. trans.), London, 1958, pp. 429–30.

equivalent for the three Vedas, and still later as the sacred power underlying any sacred action.[1] By the time of the earliest Upaniṣads it had come to mean that mysterious power by which the universe coheres; for in the thought of the *Brāhmaṇas* the sacrifice had come not only to represent the world-process but also, in the minds of the sacrificers, to be identical with it. The idea that the macrocosm and microcosm are one was already there in embryo.

The earliest Upaniṣadic speculation is still very much bound up with the sacrifice. To realize this we have only to look at the opening of the *Bṛhadāraṇyaka* and at the endless and, to us, dreadfully tedious series of cosmic and ritual identifications that go to form the greater part of the first half of the *Chāndogya* Upaniṣad. 'Verily, the dawn is the head of the sacrificial horse; the sun, his eye; the wind, his breath; the universal fire his open mouth. The year is the body (*ātman*) of the sacrificial horse; the sky, his back; the atmosphere, his belly; the earth, the underpart of his belly.'[2] And so on. Similarly too with the *sāman* or sacred chant, every syllable not only represents some natural phenomenon but actually *is* it. Thus 'the sound *hā-u* is the world; the sound *hā-i* is the wind; the sound *atha* is the moon; the sound *iha* is oneself; the sound *ī* is fire; the sound *ū* is the sun; the sound *e* is the invocation; the sound *au-ho-i* is the All-Gods; the sound *hiṅ* is Prajāpati; sound itself is breath; *yā* is food; voice is Virāj (the first principle); and the sound *huṁ* is the undefined'.[3] These identifications, which seem incredibly strange to us, are not only made between sacrificial beasts and sacred words on the one hand and cosmic phenomena on the other. In the earlier Upaniṣads the various organs of the human body too are identified with cosmic forces or objects in the external world: man and the universe are thus brought into a magico-religious relationship which is, however, not yet interpreted as actual identity. Thus we read in the *Chāndogya*: 'One should reverence the mind as Brahman—thus with reference to the self.

[1] See H. Grassmann, *Wörterbuch zum Rigveda*, s.v. *bráhman*: A. B. Keith, *The Religion and Philosophy of the Veda and Upanishads*, Cambridge, Mass., 1925, ii, 445–8. For an extensive survey of the whole problem of *bráhman* see J. Gonda. *Notes on Brahman*, Utrecht, 1950.

[2] *Br*Up., 1.1.1.

[3] *Ch*Up., 1.13.1–3.

Now with reference to the divinities—One should reverence space as Brahman. . . . That Brahman has four quarters. One quarter is speech, one quarter is breath, one quarter is the eye, one quarter is the ear. Thus with reference to the self. Now with reference to the divinities. One quarter is fire, one quarter the wind, one quarter the sun, one quarter the points of the compass'.[1] So we find human speech identified with fire, breath with the wind, the eye or sight with the sun, and the ear or hearing with the points of the compass. Each human faculty answers to a cosmic phenomenon; each is a quarter of Brahman, and the total man is therefore identical with the total Brahman which here obviously means the sum-total of existence. This form of microcosm-macrocosm speculation is typical of much early Upaniṣadic thought; and it contributed undoubtedly to the *ātman-brahman* synthesis that is rightly considered to be the dominant teaching of these astonishing treatises. By the *ātman-brahman* synthesis is meant, of course, the identification of the innermost essence of man with the unchanging ground of the universe.

In the passage we have just quoted Brahman, which in this instance is the All, appears in the human being as mind and in the external universe as space, that in which all things move and have their being, the very condition of physical life itself. The use of space as a symbol of deity is appropriate and it appears again in the far more advanced thinking of the Bhagavad-Gītā:[2] 'As the great wind that goeth everywhere abides ever in space, so do all creatures abide in me; understand this.'

This equation of Brahman with space is worth considering a little more closely, for in another passage from the same Upaniṣad we read: 'That which is known as Brahman is surely this space which is outside a man; and this space which is outside a man is surely this space which is within a man. And that space which is within a man is surely that space which is within the heart. This is the plenum and is not subject to change (*apravartin*).'[3] Now, quite obviously, what the author of the Upaniṣad is trying to express is what is usually known as the union of opposites. Outside space,

[1] *Ch*Up., 3.18.1–2. [2] BG., 9.6. [3] *Ch*Up., 3.12.7.

that is, the infinitely great, is said to be identical with 'the space within the heart', the infinitely small: in other words there exists a mode of existence in which space, without which no purely physical life can be conceived, is itself transcended. This is no longer space, it is what the Muslims call *lā-makān* 'not-space', the characteristic of the '*ālam-i amr* or 'world of the Word'[1] which is not subject to extension, magnitude, or measurement, that world which we usually call the spiritual world. To transcend space and time means to transcend form; the 'plenum' which is infinity in space is also infinity in time, and to neither do the ordinary categories of thought apply. 'Where one sees no other, hears no other, knows no other, that is the plenum (*bhūman*), but where one sees another, hears another, and knows another, that is a little thing; for the plenum is immortality, a little thing is mortal.'[2] Thus to recognize the identity of the infinitely great with the infinitely small, that is, to experience the transcending of space itself means immortality. For the human consciousness so liberated neither time nor space have any meaning, and death becomes, as Tennyson once said, 'an almost laughable impossibility', and 'loss of personality (if so it were) . . . no extinction but the only true life'.[3]

The same theme is more fully expanded in the eighth chapter of the *Chāndogya* Upaniṣad: 'In this city of Brahman (the body) there is a small lotus, a dwelling; within that a minute inner space. Now what is within that should be the object of our quest; that is what we should try to understand.'[4] Should the pupil ask why, he should be given the following answer: 'Even as great as is this [external] space, so great is the space within the heart. Within it are concentrated both heaven and earth, both fire and wind, sun and moon, both lightning and stars, [both] what one possesses in this world and what one does not possess: everything is concentrated within it.' Thus the human heart is regarded as comprising the whole wide world; 'within and without are one' as the Ger-

[1] See above, p. 16.
[2] *Ch*Up., 7.24.
[3] See Zaehner, *Mysticism, Sacred and Profane*, pp. 36–7.
[4] *Ch*Up., 8.1.1.

man philosopher Karl Joel once said.[1] And this feeling of oneness in which 'one sees no other, hears no other, knows no other', and in which space has ceased to have any meaning, means too that time is conquered and that man himself is therefore immortal. For, as the Upaniṣad goes on to say:

> If they should say, 'If this whole world (*idaṁ sarvam*) is concentrated within this city of Brahman, all creatures and all desires, what remains of it when it grows old and perishes?' Then he should reply: 'That does not grow old when [the body] grows old, nor is it slain when [the body] is smitten. This is the real city of Brahman, in this are all desires concentrated: this is the soul (*ātman*) from which all evil falls away, ageless, deathless, devoid of sorrow, hunger, and thirst, whose desire is the Real, whose conception is the Real.'[2]

Man is, then, both an immortal spirit and, as microcosm, the faithful image of the entire universe. 'Know', says Origen, speaking at a totally different time as well as in a totally different context, 'that you are another world in miniature and that within you are sun, moon, and stars.'[3] Not only is man as an eternal being, capable of transcending time and space, the *imago Dei*, he is also the *imago mundi* in that all time and space are concentrated in the point without magnitude which is within his heart. In that 'secret abode' the infinitely great and the infinitely small meet: zero meets infinity, and the result is the undifferentiated One.

This remarkable passage, however, unlike many we shall have occasion to quote, is not pure pantheism, for it distinguishes clearly between the apparent 'city of Brahman', the body, and the real 'city of Brahman', the soul: the first is perishable and the second eternal, the first mortal and the second immortal. My soul is not 'this All', that is, the universe which, vast as it is, is yet conditioned by space and time, it *comprises* the All because what is literally measureless can be said to comprise all that can be measured either in space or in time. In theistic terms this means that man's 'finest essence', which is physically nothing, is identical with

[1] Zaehner, op. cit., p. 38.
[2] *Ch*Up., 8.1.4.
[3] *Hom. in Leviticum*, 126.5.2 *apud* Jung, *Collected Works*, xvi, 196.

God from whom everything proceeds in so far as he, despite the changes he initiates, yet remains himself exempt from all change: so too the human soul, as distinct from body, mind, and emotions, remains eternally the same. The identification of the soul with Brahman therefore means that they are the same in so far as they are both beyond space and time and change. It does not necessarily mean any more than this.

Brahman, however, is more than an eternal essence: it is also the source of creation and all change. The Supreme Being, then, by whatever name he is called—Brahman, Puruṣa, Ātman, Prajāpati—is regarded as having both a perishable and an imperishable side. The idea goes back to the famous *Puruṣasūkta* or 'Hymn of the Primal Man' where the Supreme Being is thus described:[1]

> Puruṣa is this all, whatsoever was and is yet to be; he is the Lord of immortality which he outgrows by food. So far does his greatness extend, and greater still is Puruṣa. All creatures form one-quarter of him; three-quarters of him are what is immortal in heaven.

Here, then, the Supreme Being is composed of two clearly differentiated parts, a smaller part—one-quarter of him—being the whole phenomenal universe which is subject to change, and the larger—three-quarters of him—being the spiritual world which is exempt from change. In the process of emanating the universe he 'outgrows himself', he assumes a dual nature, for, though still remaining free from change, he has at the same time become subject to change, which he himself has inaugurated:[2] having emanated the world he enters into it.[3]

Thus the Primal Being is twofold, 'the formed and the formless, the mortal and the immortal, the stationary and the moving, the actual and the yon'.[4] In the external universe the formed Brahman is whatever is distinct from wind and atmosphere, and its essence is the sun. Wind and atmosphere constitute the formless Brahman, and their essence is called the 'Person in the [sun-]

[1] Rig-Veda, X, 90, 2–3. [2] Cf. *Maitrī* Up., 7.11(8). [3] *Aitareya* Up., 3.11–12.
[4] *Br*Up., 2.3.1.

disk'. Similarly in the human being the 'formed' is all that is other than breath and the space within the *ātman*, presumably meaning 'body' here; its essence is the right eye. Breath and space within the body, on the other hand, are the formless and immortal, and their essence is 'the Person in the right eye'. The 'Person in the sun-disk' and the 'Person in the right eye', the eternal outside man and the eternal within him are identical. In this passage, however, there is no attempt to identify the mortal parts of the two.

Now, the process by which the authors of the Upaniṣads reached the conclusion that man's immortal soul is identical with the immortal substrate of the changing universe would seem to be twofold. On the one hand, by intensive introspection, they succeeded in discovering the immortal 'ground' of their own souls, what Martin Buber calls the 'original pre-biographical unity'; on the other, they concluded both from the creation-hymns of the Rig-Veda, especially the *Puruṣasūkta* (X, 90), the *Hiraṇyagarbha* hymn (X, 121), and the *bhāvavṛttam* hymn (X, 129), and from their own reasoning that the material world too had an eternal and unitary subtrate. This aspect of the Upaniṣads is closely paralleled in pre-Socratic Greek philosophy: both are preoccupied with the search for a first cause, and both at first reach equally naïve results. The Greeks, however, seem to have been the more naïve, for their identifications of the first cause with air, water, or fire are quite arbitrary and are certainly not based on observation.

The Indians, on the other hand, in their search for the unitary principle of organic life, became intensely interested in two very concrete manifestations thereof—food and breath. 'This whole world is surely just food and the eater of food', we read,[1] and 'Brahman is food'.[2] Obviously if we translate *brahman* as 'God', this statement will have an absurd ring. Basically, however, it is not absurd, for life can indeed be reduced to these terms. You cannot live unless you eat, and you cannot eat unless you take other lives whether animal or vegetable. The process of eating and being eaten constitutes the unity underlying the diversity of physical existence, it is the unchanging law underlying the ever-changing

[1] Ibid., 1.4.6.

[2] *Taitt*Up., 3.1(2).

phenomena: it is Brahman, and to realize oneself as food and the eater of food is very bliss: as a most surprising passage in the *Taittirīya* Upaniṣad puts it:

> O rapture, O rapture, O rapture!
> I am food, I am food, I am food!
> I am an eater of food, I am an eater of food, I am an eater of food!
> I am a maker of verses, I am a maker of verses, I am a maker of verses!
> I am the first-born of the universal order,
> Earlier than the gods, in the navel of immortality!
> Whoso gives me away, he, verily, has succoured me!
> I who am food, eat the eater of food!
> I have overcome the whole world![1]

This extraordinary paean of joy is only comprehensible to us if we understand it as an expression of the transcending of the finite personality in a cosmic process. Eating and being eaten represent life in death, and death in life, the abolition of the individuality in the unending life of the Primal Man of the *Puruṣasūkta*, who, though sacrificed, continues to live as the All. Food, then, is seen as the Absolute as manifested in the material world.

Of even more importance, however, was the Upaniṣads' preoccupation with breath. This, however, is scarcely surprising, for breath is a symbol used in almost all religions to represent the eternal; and we ourselves all too easily forget that our own word 'spirit' is simply the Latin for breath. Breath, of course, is life: and the symbol is an obvious one, for where there is no breath, there there is no life. Therefore, in the *Bṛhadāraṇyaka* Upaniṣad the 3306 gods are in the final analysis reduced to only one, and that is breath, and 'that they call Brahman'.[2]

These identifications of Brahman with physical processes or objects are not of merely academic interest as showing how an idea developed. They are essential to a proper understanding of the nature of Brahman as it develops in the Upaniṣads and the Bhagavad-Gītā. It is true that the distinction between the formed

[1] Ibid., 3.10(6).
[2] *Br*Up., 3.9.9.

and the formless Brahman is liable to be swallowed up in a full-blooded and omnivorous pantheism in which everything is indiscriminately identified with everything else, but in the later writings, notably in the *Muṇḍaka* and the Gītā, the distinction between the higher and lower Brahman is clearly made; Brahman is both the absolutely changeless eternal with which the human soul is identical at least in so far as it shares with it a mode of being that is beyond space and time, and it is also the changeless law behind the changing phenomenal world. In the terminology of Śaṅkara it is both Brahman and *māyā*, or in that of the Sāṁkhya it is both Puruṣa (whether understood as one great spirit or as a plurality of them) and *prakṛti*; it is, in Western terminology, both pure spirit and primal matter. Whatever it is, it is certainly not God as we understand him. It is true that in the countless creation myths of the earlier Upaniṣads the First Principle, under whatever name he appears, is the origin of the universe and that he pervades the universe or actually is it, but no clear distinction between God and the universe is made. The later Upaniṣads, on the other hand, show two distinct tendencies. First there is a tendency to think of the Supreme Principle in personal terms, and secondly there is a tendency towards pure monism. The monist position distinguishes itself from the pantheistic in that it concedes reality only to the undifferentiated One, which, it is claimed, can be experienced in trance. This One is both the liberated human soul and the unknowable godhead from which the 'All' proceeds—the All, in so far as it manifests itself in multiplicity, being illusory; 'he goes from death to death who sees diversity here'.[1] Pantheism, on the other hand, identifies the human soul not only with the ground of the universe but with the universe itself in all its diversity. The clearest statements of this position are in *Chāndogya* 7.25 and *Kauṣītakī* 1.6, the first of which runs as follows:

'That [the Plenum, *bhūman* here standing for Brahman] indeed is below. It is above. It is to the West. It is to the East. It is to the South. It is to the North. Indeed it is this whole universe.

[1] *Br*Up., 4.4.19: cf. *Kaṭha* Up., 4.10,11.

'Next the instruction with regard to the ego (*ahaṁkāra*). I am below. I am above.' And so on as above.

'Next the instruction with regard to the soul (*ātman*). The soul is below. The soul is above,' etc.

Here the universe, the individual soul, and the *ātman*, meaning certainly in this context 'the universal soul', are all identified. The person who realizes this, being the All, knows all: he is therefore omniscient. This sense of 'being the All', common among nature mystics seems to be what Jung means by 'positive inflation' and what the Muslim mystic Qushayrī understood by the technical term *basṭ*, 'expansion'. In an illuminating passage he warns against it:

> The man subject to expansion [he says] experiences an expansion great enough to contain [all] creation; and there is practically nothing that will cause him fear. . . . [This expansion] makes him quiver with joy, yet unsettles him. . . . There is the greatest danger in this mood, and those who are open to it should be on their guard against an insidious deception.[1]

In the Yoga system this would correspond to the stage of complete omniscience which is said to precede the achievement of *kaivalyam* ('isolation'), in which all differentiation between subject and object is obliterated. 'Just as the effulgence of the sun is visible before the sun actually rises,' writes Bhojarāja, following Vyāsa, in his commentary on the *Yogasūtras*,[2] 'so does the preliminary illuminative knowledge which has all things as its object arise before the [supreme] knowledge of the difference [between the eternal and the temporal and the consequent isolation of the former from the latter] supervenes. This being so, he knows everything without recourse to any other form of Yogic concentration.' Today we find it impossible to pay serious attention to claims to omniscience made by Yogins or anyone else, yet one has only to read the third chapter of the *Yogasūtras* to see how literally the author believed that Yogic techniques could produce omniscience in the literal sense of that word. The claim, however, becomes comprehensible in the light of the experience of nature mystics of

[1] Qushayrī, p. 33. [2] 3.33.

all ages and places. The sensation of 'being the All' is a well-attested phenomenon, impossible though it may be to explain it rationally; and since to know something in its entirety is, according to Upaniṣadic thought, to be it, to 'be all' necessarily involves knowing all.

What, however, is interesting and somewhat surprising is that the *Yogasūtras* should regard this stage of omniscience as being less perfect than the final state of undifferentiated oneness which is the total isolation of the immortal soul not only from this world and from the body with all its physical and psychic faculties, but also from all other souls including God.

In the Upaniṣads themselves this realization of the total undifferentiated unity of the soul forms the theme of the very late *Māṇḍūkya* Upaniṣad. This Upaniṣad is the climax of a whole series of speculations on the nature of dreams and sleep.[1] Because dreams are the product of the dreamer's mind, they are regarded as being more real than the ordinary waking state; for the real is the undifferentiated One, and whereas the objective world does not appear to the normal waking consciousness as being the product of the subjective mind, dreams undoubtedly are. Moreover, in deep dreamless sleep there remains only what the *Māṇḍūkya* calls a unified state. If, however, the macrocosm and microcosm are one, what does the subjective state of dreamless sleep correspond to in the objective world? Dream, which is an emanation of the dreamer's own mind, corresponds to God's emanation of the phenomenal world. Dreamless sleep, by the same analogy, must then correspond to God, 'the Lord of all, the knower of all, the inner controller, the womb of all, the origin and end of creatures'. But beyond dreamless sleep there is a fourth state which the *Māṇḍūkya* characterizes as being a state of complete, undifferentiated oneness 'devoid of duality': 'it causes the phenomenal world to cease'. This is the soul, the self, the *ātman*. So in the last analysis, according to the *Māṇḍūkya*, the 'Lord of all', that is God, is merely an emanation from the undifferentiated One which is at the same time the human soul. The difference between the *Māṇḍūkya* and

[1] *Br*Up., 4.3.9–33: *Ch*Up., 8.10–12: *Praśna* Up., 4.5–6, etc.

the *Yogasūtras* is that whereas the latter interpret liberation as the self-isolation of one individual soul in what Buber calls 'an original pre-biographical unity', the *Māṇḍūkya* interprets it as the realization of the unfractionable unity of Being as such, of which the omniscient Lord is but an emanation—and, necessarily, an illusory one since to admit his reality would be to admit duality, and this is not tolerable to the mystic who has realized, as he thinks, the absolute One 'without a second'. If he is that One, then, obviously, worship offered to another being can only be a meaningless folly: indeed the perfected ascetic is expressly advised by Gauḍapāda, in his *Kārikā* on the *Māṇḍūkya*, to 'refrain from prayer, public worship, and funeral processions',[1] that is, from any religious act whatever. These, certainly, are not condemned, but they are regarded merely as a useful *askesis*, like the practice of Yoga, which will help the soul at a certain stage of its development to draw nearer to its final goal which is to realize itself in the absolute oneness of its own eternity.

God, in the *Yogasūtras*, plays a similar but different rôle: he is primarily an object of contemplation, and not a person with whom union is sought. Along with a strict bodily discipline and the repetition of spells, devotion to God is considered to be efficacious as a step towards final liberation[2] which is the complete isolation of the individual soul from all that is other than itself, and this means the total suppression of all discursive thought.[3] God or the Lord is thus described in the *Sūtras*:

> The Lord is a special type of soul which is untouched by care, works, the fruits of works, or desire. In him the seed of omniscience is perfect. He is the *guru* even of the ancients since he is not limited by time.[4]

God, then, is the only existing soul that has never been involved in the process of transmigration: he dwells in permanent isolation, and is permanently unaffected by care, activity, or desire, the characteristics of our mundane existence. He is omniscient and the instructor of the ancient sages. He dwells outside time. The 'isolation' of God, however, seems to be qualified, for as '*guru* of the

[1] 2.37. [2] *YS.*, 2.1. [3] Ibid., 1.2. [4] Ibid., 1.24–26.

ancients' he is their instructor and therefore involved in action of some kind. True, he, like the God of the Bhagavad-Gītā, remains totally unaffected by his teaching activity and indifferent to its results, but he does nonetheless help souls still bound in matter to achieve liberation. Indeed, according to the commentaries, God would seem to differ from other souls in that he is, in fact, permanently in contact with matter in its most subtle form. In the Sāṁkhya-Yoga, as is well known, matter is thought to be compounded of three 'strands' or *guṇas*—*sattva*, *rajas*, and *tamas*, sometimes translated as goodness, passion, and dullness: these roughly correspond to the three constituents of the soul associated with the intellect, anger, and desire which feature in Plato's *Republic*, which were taken over by the early Muslim philosophers, adapted by Ghazālī and transmitted through him into the mainstream of Ṣūfī thought. The God of the *Yogasūtras* is permanently united to the quality of *sattva* in its most abstract form which is pure wisdom, and through it he is able, by his will, both to sustain the world and to cause both the union of individual souls with matter and to assist them to liberation from matter. Whether or not Vyāsa and Bhojarāja's interpretation of the *Sūtras* represents the mind of the author or not, it is impossible to say, but it does seem to attribute to the Lord a degree of involvement in the world that is surprising in the context of the *Sūtras*; for in this respect God, though omniscient and permanently unaffected by change, would appear to be inferior to the ordinary liberated soul, for liberation means, according to the definition of the *Sūtras* themselves, the total isolation of the soul in its eternal essence. God, though unaffected by the world, is nonetheless, through his association with the quality of *sattva* and through his very omniscience, permanently aware of the world and to that extent committed to it: for it will be remembered that in the *Yogasūtras* omniscience is considered to be merely an incidental stepping-stone on the way to the goal of final isolation.

Such then would appear to be the theology of the *Yogasūtras*. What of the cult of the deity in practice? Devotion to the Lord is described as the third main method in the Yoga technique. The first of these is bodily discipline or asceticism. From this results 'the perfection of the bodily senses from impurity and decay. From the study of scripture (the repetition of spells—*svādhyāya*) results the cognition (*samprayoga*) of the deity of one's choice. From devotion to the Lord results the perfection of concentration (*samādhi*).'[1]

These are, then, the three main stages in the Yoga technique of concentration. First the body must be brought under control, then follows the repetition of a sacred formula, through which the deity invoked in the formula becomes present to the mind, and thirdly by concentration on God one becomes like him, that is, perfectly recollected. The juxtaposition of *iṣṭa-devatā* 'the divinity of one's choice' and *īśvara* 'the Lord' calls for comment. Do the two words mean the same thing or not? Now, according to the theology of the *Yogasūtras*, there is only one Lord, and it is therefore unlikely that he would be referred to as the 'divinity of one's choice'. Such divinities would, then, appear to be merely a focus for what is called 'one-pointed' concentration, the mental counterpart of the muttered spell. 'Devotion to the Lord', on the other hand, leads directly to *samādhi* because the object of contemplation is the eternal exemplar of the perfectly liberated and isolated soul, who, though aware of matter, is nonetheless totally unaffected by it. The Yogin's aspiration is not, like the Vedāntin's, to become what, for them, he eternally is, that is, the Absolute, but to become *like* God who is forever unaffected by change.[2] Bhojarāja goes further than the *Sūtras* in that he says: 'Devotion to the Lord produces actual *samādhi* because the divine Lord, being well-disposed, removes [all] cares which stand in the Yogin's way and awakens *samādhi* in him.'

I was wrong, I now consider, when I said in my *Mysticism, Sacred and Profane* (p. 127) that 'when the Yoga introduces the idea of the Lord . . ., he is introduced for no other purpose than to help the soul towards isolation'. This is true enough so far as it goes, for concentration on the Lord *does* help the soul towards isolation, but the object of contemplation is not simply, I now consider, a 'deity

[1] Ibid., 2.43–45; cf. Bhojarāja's commentary.

[2] Cf. Vyāsa on *YS*, 1.29. 'As the Lord is a pure, serene, isolated *puruṣa* free from defect, so does [the Yogin] understand that the [individual] *puruṣa* who accurately understands (?) the *buddhi* is like him.'

of one's choice' but God as defined in the first chapter of the *Sūtras* themselves.

To sum up: the Sāṁkhya-Yoga admits of no Absolute One. Reality is interpreted along dualistic lines. There is the world of pure spirit (corresponding to the '*ālam-i amr* of Ghazālī) on the one hand composed of an infinity of eternal substances called *puruṣas* or persons, that is, human souls and one special soul, God, and the world of coming-to-be and passing away, *prakṛti* or Nature (the '*ālam-i khalq* of Ghazālī) on the other. The conjunction of soul and body is an unnatural conjunction, and the goal of the soul is to shake itself free from the trammels of matter and to become what it is, a pure and isolated spirit. God differs from human souls in two respects: first he is from all eternity unaffected by matter, he is forever beyond space and time. On the other hand, unlike the liberated soul, he remains eternally aware of the phenomenal world, though without thereby being in any way affected or diminished by it. As such he is the sole effective object of contemplation, for by meditating on him who is forever beyond space and time, the bound soul can realize its own true nature which is also beyond space and time. Some relationship between God and the world is, however, recognized, and this has to be: for if, like the liberated human soul, God were completely isolated in his own essence, he would not even be a possible object of contemplation, nor would he be able in any way to assist the soul out of bondage. It is very doubtful whether the additional attributes attributed by Bhojarāja to the Lord reflect the ideas of the *Sūtras* themselves, namely that he supports the world by his will and that he is the cause of the soul's involvement in matter as well of its release.[1] Such ideas can be directly traced to the *Śvetāśvatara* Upaniṣad. For Patañjali, however, it would rather appear that God is the divine archetype of the soul by the contemplation of whom the soul can itself become what it always is, immortal. The Yogin's aim is neither deification nor participation in the divine essence: it is rather the fulfilment of the promise of the serpent to Eve in the Garden of Eden that 'you shall be as gods';[2] and in so far as the

[1] Bhojarāja on 1.25.

[2] Genesis 3.5.

Yogins reach a state in which they realize their own immortality in a condition in which time and space are no more, like gods they are, and the serpent spoke true.

Before proceeding to consider the development of theism in the Upaniṣads themselves, let us first compare the Yoga and Vedānta views concerning final liberation and God. Let us, then, first take the points on which they agree. First they are at one in their view that liberation means the isolation of the eternal from the contingent, and that this is an experience of undifferentiable oneness. Secondly they are agreed that, from the empirical point of view at least, there is such a thing as the Lord. Thirdly, they agree that contemplation of this Lord is an effective method of bringing about one-pointed concentration of mind, the goal of which is in each case the experience of absolute oneness, in which the second, that is, the Lord vanishes away. Where they differ is on the matter of what this absolute oneness consists in. For the Vedāntin the One is . . . the One—without a second: for the Sāṁkhya-Yogin it is an undifferentiated monad, self-sufficient, but only one among endless other monads, distinct from them and distinct from God. For the Vedāntin God is, from the absolute point of view of the One, an illusory being; for the Sāṁkhya-Yogin he is real and can and does actively promote the liberation of souls. Though veiled from their sight after liberation, he nonetheless exists though there is no contact with him. In the Vedāntin hierarchy of being only the One exists absolutely: the Lord and all that proceeds from him are produced by cosmic 'illusion' or 'ignorance', and the proof of this is mystical experience which, it is maintained, is at its highest the realization of the absolute unity of being; beyond this, therefore, it is ontologically impossible to go. The Sāṁkhya-Yoga too defines liberation as 'isolation' and, though it admits the existence of God, it refuses to concede that there can be any form of existence beyond the self-isolation of the eternal soul in its undifferentiated oneness. The Vedāntin appears to be the more consistent, for in the Yoga system God ceases to be relevant once liberation has been achieved, and devotion to God is only practised before liberation, not after; for in neither system is there any inkling that communion with God is possible. Both see the goal beyond which all further spiritual experience is impossible as being the 'undifferentiable unity of myself without form or content', as Buber puts it. God is thereby excluded from man's extra-temporal experience.

We must now consider how the idea of deity developed in the Upaniṣads themselves. As we have seen, there are plenty of passages in the Upaniṣads which are fully pantheistic. There are others, however, which draw a distinction between the human person and the universe on the one hand and the supreme principle on the other. Prominent among these is the concept of the Inner Controller in the *Bṛhadāraṇyaka*[1] who is regarded as being essentially other than all things in the phenomenal world. 'He who, dwelling in the earth, is yet other than the earth, whom the earth does not know, whose body the earth is, who controls the earth from within, he is your soul, the inner controller, the Immortal.' So too is this Inner Controller other than water, fire, the atmosphere, wind, sky, sun, the points of the compass, the moon and stars, space, darkness and light, other than the whole objective universe, then. And as far as the human personality is concerned, it is other than breath, speech, sight, hearing, the mind, the sense of touch, and understanding, distinct, then, from all man's physical and psychical faculties. It is, in reality, the only percipient: 'He is the unseen seer, the unheard hearer, the unthought thinker, the ununderstood understander.' This Inner Controller, who is plainly akin to our own conception of God, however, is still identical with the human soul at its deepest level; it is the imperishable (*akṣara*) across which all space is woven;[2] it is the eternal conceived of either as God, from whom the perishable world proceeds, or as the Eternal Being as he is in his essence. In earlier Upaniṣadic thinking the human soul is roundly identified with this Imperishable, and it is not considered possible that there can be any higher form of being. Sometimes, however, this Being is spoken of as the Lord. He is the Soul, the Immortal, Brahman, and the All, yet he is also overlord and king of all things, and in

[1] *Br*Up., 3.7. [2] Ibid., 3.8.11.

him all creatures, all gods, all worlds, all vital breaths, and all souls converge as spokes converge on the hub of a wheel.[1] In this passage which is of vital importance in the development of early Hindu thought the purest pantheism is combined with a recognizable theism. The author states that God or rather the *ātman*, the Universal Soul *is* not only all things but that it is also the Lord of all things including human souls; yet these themselves appear to be identified with the ground of all the objective world in the whole of this section. A point of departure, however, towards a theistic interpretation of existence has been made, and we shall perhaps not be guilty of reading into this passage what is not there if we say that human souls are considered as being identical with God in so far as they are, like him, eternal, but as logically posterior to him in that they proceed from him as their first cause. The human soul is co-eternal with God in that it has its being outside time, but logically it is posterior to him. The procession of the Holy Ghost from the Father (and the Son) is a good parallel from Christian theology: it is an operation that takes place outside time in eternity, and Father, Son, and Holy Ghost are con-substantial and co-eternal, though logically distinguishable. So too, in this passage from the *Bṛhadāraṇyaka* Upaniṣad, it would appear that the relationship of the soul to God is one both of co-eternity and of logical posteriority, identical as to the essence but at the same time distinct from God in that he is the centre and circumference of all individual souls, the hub and felly of the wheel of which they are the spokes. These ideas will reappear in Ṣūfism despite their obvious incompatibility with orthodox Muslim belief. Ṣūfism, indeed, tends ever more strongly to bring God and the human soul together, so violently did they seem to be separated in the Qur'ān, while Hinduism, in what is really its major trend, seeks to draw God out from the soul and the universe so that the soul, even in its lonely eternity may experience a spiritual relationship with Another—a relationship which the experience of an absolutely undifferentiable state would seem automatically to exclude.

[1] Ibid., 2.5.15.

III

God and Brahman

In our last lecture we considered the theology, if we may use the term, of the earlier Upaniṣads and the *Yogasūtras*. From the early Upaniṣads no clear picture emerges; yet although there are a great number of passages in which a complete identity between Brahman, soul, and the external universe is asserted, there is also another tendency which seeks to identify God conceived of as the unmoved mover, to use the Aristotelian phrase, with the deepest ground of the human soul. The classic formulation of this view is perhaps that of the so-called *Śāndilya-vidyā* of the *Chāndogya* Upaniṣad:

> All this [world] is Brahman [the Upaniṣad declares]. Let one venerate it in all quietness as *tajjalān* [a mystical code-word which the commentators understand as meaning 'that from which one is born, into which one is dissolved, and in which one breathes and acts']. . . . He who consists of mind, whose body is breath, whose form is light, whose conception is the real, whose self is space, through whom are all works, all desires, all scents, all tastes, who encompasses all this [world], who does not speak and has no care, he is my self within the heart, smaller than a grain of rice or a barley corn, or a mustard-seed or a grain of millet or the kernel of a grain of millet; this is my self within the heart, greater than the earth, greater than the atmosphere, greater than the sky, greater than these worlds. All works, all desires, all scents, all tastes belong to it; it encompasses all this [world], does not speak and has no care. This my self within the heart is that Brahman. When I depart from hence, I shall merge into it. He who believes this will never doubt.[1]

The purport of this and similar passages seems to be that at the deepest level of existence there is a formal identity between the

[1] *Ch*Up., 3.14.

human soul 'within the heart' and the 'soul of the All'. Both the body and the external universe are subject to coming-to-be and passing away: but the soul, the inner controller of both, is not so conditioned. Soul and God are therefore identical in that they enjoy an existence beyond space and time, and this is the only sense, perhaps, in which they can be regarded as being identical. The emphasis is, however, certainly anthropocentric. The self within the heart, a fine point without magnitude, is the same as the spirit who 'encompasses all this [world]'; the human 'self', which is by definition eternal, is the focal point of the whole universe as it is of the human body. Indeed, the universe seems to be regarded as an extension of the body. The senses and the objects of sense are regarded as being two aspects of the same thing. The world is the human personality as seen from outside, the senses the human personality as seen from the inside: both the external and the internal personality depend on the immortal substrate of both, and whatever of reality they may have, they derive from what is alone real, the immortal self.

We have seen how in the *Bṛhadāraṇyaka* Upaniṣad, the self or soul is referred to not only in pantheistical terms, as the immortal, Brahman, the All, but also as the 'overlord of all things and the king of all things'. The eternal as such, then, is the Lord of all contingent being, but no distinction is yet drawn between the eternal element in the human soul which is 'more minute than the minute' and that other eternal, God, who is 'greater than the great'.[1] This distinction, though just discernible in the later Upaniṣads, does not clearly emerge until the latter part of the Gītā. The later Upaniṣads, however, do show an increasing preoccupation with the nature of God, and this is evidenced by the reappearance of the word *deva* in the sense of 'God' rather than in the sense of *a* god. This is something quite new, and it shows that the authors of the later Upaniṣads are beginning to think monotheistically, they are beginning to think of a Supreme and active Being who is distinct both from the soul which is, by definition, inactive and the ever-active and ever-changing external universe.

[1] *Kaṭha* Up., 2.20: *Śvet*Up., 3.20.

By whom impelled, [by whom] sped forth does the mind soar forth?
By whom enjoined does the first breath go forth?
By whom impelled this speech do people utter?
The eye, the ear—what god enjoineth them?'[1]

This is the question which the *Kena* Upaniṣad seeks to answer. Now, what is a source of endless confusion in the earliest Upaniṣads is their readiness to make positive and contradictory statements about almost everything. The resulting picture is one of complete pantheism in which all is ultimately identifiable with everything else. The *Kena* and the *Īśā*, on the other hand, seem to feel that the earlier equations and identifications are over-simplifications, and that ultimately you can say nothing intelligible about the Supreme Principle at all. All you can say about him can only be an approximation to the reality, for, in the last resort, he is unknowable. From your experience of what you yourself are, and from speculation about the outside world, you may obtain some idea about him, but this will only be a partial and approximate affair. 'If you think, "I know well,"—well, you may know a very little,—a form of Brahman, [only] that [much] of it that you yourself are, or that [much] of it which is in the gods.'[2] Brahman as such is just not accessible to the mind, it can only be apprehended by a spiritual awakening, a *pratibodha*. 'It is conceived of [only] by one who has no conceptual thought about it (*yasyā'mataṁ tasya matam*). Those who think about it do not know it. It is not known to those who busy themselves with knowledge, but it *is* known to those who are not concerned with knowledge. It *is* known and conceived of when there is an awakening, for immortality is experienced. By the soul one attains virtue, by knowing immortality. If one knows it here, that is truth (*satyam*); if one does not know it here, great is the destruction. Discerning it in all creatures the wise, on departing this world, become immortal.'[3]

Brahman, then, is absolutely unknowable to the mind. It can only be apprehended by an 'awakening', an intuition, that is, from an agency other than yourself, since to wake up is not an act of one's own volition. The agent of awakening is not mentioned

[1] *Kena* Up., 1. [2] Ibid., 9. [3] Ibid., 11–13.

here, but the thought that lies behind this passage is more positively stated in two passages from the *Muṇḍaka* and *Kaṭha* with which we shall be dealing shortly. Brahman is immanent in all things as well as in oneself, and it is by contemplating him in creatures that one realizes him as the immortal within oneself. This is a long step beyond pantheism: there is no longer any identification of the soul with the All. The soul participates in Brahman, but it is not identical with it (*yad asya tvam*, 'what of him thou art'), and Brahman is *in* all creatures (*bhūteṣu bhūteṣu*), but it is not identical with them. It is unknown and the 'other'—'other than the known and other than the unknown',[1] to be discerned but never wholly understood;[2] it transcends both the objective world (the All) and the *ātman*. If one discerns it as the immortal substrate of all creatures, then one realizes one's own immortality. This does not necessarily mean that one 'becomes Brahman', for Brahman is unknowable, it means simply that one realizes the immortality of 'that of Brahman' which is oneself. The *Kena* Upaniṣad is as vague as is Buddhism as to how the released state is conceived. Like Buddhism it is content to describe it as the 'immortal' or 'deathless' (*amṛtam*), and the reader is at liberty to interpret this in any way he pleases: it may mean that the soul enjoys solitary isolation, or that it realizes itself as Brahman, the sole-existing One, or that it is merged in Brahman as the waters of a river are merged into the great ocean.[3] The *Kena* Upaniṣad, however, prefers not to analyse the experience, but merely to assert that it is one of deathlessness; and it is achieved by the contemplation of the deathless in all creatures, of the solidarity of all contingent things in one immortal substrate. For the *Kena*, then, Brahman is both the external universe, the 'mortal', and the soul, the 'immortal'. It is the ground in which two different modes of existence, Nature and the soul, the *puruṣa* and *prakṛti* of the Sāṁkhya system meet; yet though it is in them, it is other than they. It is both immanent and transcendent. This is, perhaps, the first clear statement in the Upaniṣads of the transcendence of the Supreme Principle.

[1] Ibid., 3. [2] Ibid., 13.

[3] *ChUp.*, 6.10.1: *Muṇḍaka* Up., 3.2.8: *Praśna* Up., 6.5. Cf. *Udāna*, p. 55.

But this principle, if it is transcendent, must also be Lord. 'This whole universe *must* be enveloped by a Lord,' the *Iśā* Upaniṣad begins, 'whatever moving thing there is in this moving world'. This Lord, it transpires, is the One who, however, is identical neither with the soul nor with the universe. Its nature can only be expressed in paradox. It does not move, yet it is swifter than mind. Standing still, it overtakes others as they run. 'It moves, yet it does not move. It is far, yet it is near. It is within this All, yet it is outside it.'[1] The Lord and the One, moreover, is also the *ātman*, for the Upaniṣad goes on to say: 'He who contemplates all beings in the Self and the Self in all beings, does not shrink from him. To him who discerns aright, all beings have become the Self in him; then what delusion, what sorrow is there for one who contemplates the unity?'[2] One may equally translate the first half of the sentence as 'in him all beings have become the self of him who discerns aright', and this would apparently take us back to a purely pantheistic position; but even if we do so, there is still a difference, for this is no longer a simple identification of everything with everything else: it is a unity in diversity, for the unity is *in* him, it is not simply he. The Supreme Being is thus both Lord, and the One, and the *ātman*, but *ātman* here used apparently in the sense of the 'soul of the All', not of the released individual soul, with which it does not seem to be identical.

This, however, is the great difficulty in any objective attempt to interpret the Upaniṣads, for we can never be certain in what sense a given word is used. We can never be sure whether *ātman* means what was later called the *paramātman*, that is God, or the *pratyagātman*, the individual released soul, or indeed the mind or the body. Yet in the *Iśā* it seems clear that the *ātman* is primarily used as a synonym for God, not for the individual, eternal soul. God manifests himself both in the temporal and in the eternal, and, as in the *Kena*, is other than both. 'Into blind darkness enter they who worship non-becoming; into darkness greater than that enter they who rejoice in becoming. For they say, "Other is it [the Absolute] than

[1] *Iśā* Up., 5.
[2] Ibid., 6–7.

origin, and other than what has no origin".'[1] God, then, pervades both the world of space and time *and* the spiritual world outside place and time, though he is distinct from both.

These two short Upaniṣads adumbrate a world-view that only becomes explicit in the *Śvetāśvatara* Upaniṣad and the Gītā, the view that there is a being that is beyond and distinct from the two categories of existence which are seen more and more as the fundamental pair of opposites, namely, eternal, unchanging being on the one hand, what Rāmānuja calls *ātmatattva* or 'category of soul', and all becoming that is subject to origin, change, and dissolution on the other. God, in the later theology, is regarded as the source of both, more ultimate, then, than the 'imperishable' (*akṣara*) itself. Liberation means always the realization of the self as an imperishable being, and the general tenor of the Upaniṣads is that the 'imperishable' is one, is Brahman, and that Brahman is totally undifferentiated. Perhaps the best simile of what is understood by the soul's liberation is that of the *Kaṭha* Upaniṣad 4.15:

> As pure water poured into pure becomes like unto it (*tādṛg*),[2]
> So does the soul of the discerning sage become [like unto Brahman].

Thus there is a loss of what is normally described as personality in an eternal mode of existence. This is certainly not the *kaivalyam* of the *Yogasūtras*, nor is it union with God who stands outside the eternal mode of existence though pervading it. It is what the Ṣūfīs call *fanā*, the destruction of the purely human personality in the eternal (*baqā*), all sense of a separate individuality being lost; in Ṣūfī terms it is the destruction of man's *bashariyya* or *nāsūt* in his *rubūbiyya* or *lāhūt*, his divinity. But even in the more extreme forms of Ṣūfism there is a distinction between *lāhūt*, what is inherently divine in man, and God himself. So in Hinduism it came to be felt that there might be something beyond Brahman. In this connexion it may not be unprofitable to consider the concept of *akṣara*, the Imperishable Brahman in the Upaniṣads.

[1] Ibid., 9–10 (Renou), 12–13 (Hume). § 16 (Hume), in which the Supreme Person is again roundly identified with the individual soul, seems to be quite discontinuous with the rest of the Upaniṣad, and may be an addition.

[2] Scarcely 'the very same' as Hume translates.

It first appears in the *Bṛhadāraṇyaka* 3.8. Gārgī asks the sage Yājñavalkya: 'That which is above the sky, that which is beneath the earth, that which is between these two, sky and earth, that which people call the past, the present, and the future—across what is that woven, warp and woof?' What kind of being, Gārgī is asking, is it that transcends all spatial and temporal categories? To this Yājñavalkya replies 'Space'. Gārgī remains unsatisfied and asks on what space is woven, warp and woof.

'That,' says Yājñavalkya, 'Brāhmans call the Imperishable. It is not coarse, not fine, not short, not long, it does not glow nor does it adhere; it is neither shade nor darkness, air or space. Unattached it is, without taste, smell, eye, ear, voice or mind, without energy (*atejaskam*), without breath or mouth, without measure, without inside or outside. It eats nothing nor does anyone soever eat it.' This Imperishable, then, is a being about which nothing can be truly predicated because any predication would bring it down to the ordinary categories of human thought which are conditioned by space and time, whereas the Imperishable is beyond both. In the later Upaniṣads and particularly in the *Śvetāśvatara* it was sharply divided off from the *kṣara* or 'perishable'; but in the *Bṛhadāraṇyaka* the 'imperishable', though devoid of mind (*manas*), energy (*tejas*), or measure, is yet the measure of all things; for it is 'at the behest of the Imperishable' that 'the sun and moon stand apart, . . . that the earth and sky stand apart, . . . that the moments, hours, days, nights, fortnights, months, seasons, and years stand apart'. The Imperishable, then, though devoid of qualities in itself, is at the same time that which keeps the perishable world in being, and though previously described as without eye, ear, or mind, it is nonetheless 'the unseen seer, the unheard hearer, the unthought thinker, the ununderstood understander. Other than it there is naught that sees. Other than it there is naught that hears. Other than it there is naught that thinks. Other than it there is naught that understands. Across this Imperishable, Gārgī, is space woven, warp and woof.' Thus the Imperishable is seen here not simply as an Absolute without any quality, but also as the upholder of the universe and the sole true percipient. It is very much more than the *akṣara* of the *Muṇḍaka* and *Śvetāśvatara* Upaniṣads and the Gītā. It corresponds almost exactly to the God or Lord described in these later treatises; and it is this perpetual shifting of the meaning of words which makes any coherent interpretation of the Upaniṣads wellnigh impossible, for the terminology of the later Upaniṣads begins to use Sāṁkhya categories which do not agree with the terminology of the earlier treatises. This is particularly true of the *Śvetāśvatara*.

The *Muṇḍaka* Upaniṣad takes up the thought of the passage from the *Bṛhadāraṇyaka* which we have just analysed. Here it is again the Imperishable that is the source of all things.

That which is invisible, impalpable, without family, without caste,
Without sight or hearing, without hand or foot,
Eternal, all-pervading, present everywhere, exceeding subtile,
That is the Imperishable (*avyaya*) which the wise perceive as the source of creatures.

As a spider emits and draws in [its threads],
As herbs arise on earth,
As the hairs of the body and head [arise] from a living person,
So from the Imperishable arises everything here.[1]

This theme is again taken up in 2.1.1:

As from a blazing fire sparks
Issue forth in their thousands with [individual] forms,
So from the Imperishable, my friend, beings manifold
Are born and thither also they return.

The Imperishable, then, is here regarded as the source of all being and, one would think, the first cause. It is, moreover, also Brahman, the immortal and the real (2.2.1). It is

Manifest, yet hidden: 'moving in secret' is its name,
The great abode. In that is placed
What moves and breathes and winks.
What that is, know as Being and Not-Being,
An object of desire, higher than understanding,
Best of creatures.

[1] *Muṇḍaka* Up., 1.1.6–7.

It is the last word that is astonishing in the context, for Brahman, the imperishable being, is here referred to as a creature—the best of creatures, certainly, but a creature (*prajā*) none the less. This could be interpreted simply as loose phraseology, but there is other evidence in the Upaniṣad to show that the Imperishable Brahman is regarded as being subordinate to another principle, Puruṣa, the Supreme Person.

> Heavenly, formless is the Person,
> He comprises without and within, unborn is he:
> Without breath, without mind, effulgent,
> Higher than the high Imperishable.[1]

And this superiority of the Person to Brahman is confirmed in a later passage[2] where he is described as the Maker, Lord, and Person whose womb is Brahman. This would appear to be the sense of *brahmayoni* rather than 'the source of Brahman' as it is generally translated, or 'who has his source in Brahman'[3] (giving precisely the opposite meaning!); for Bhagavad-Gītā, 14.3 is clearly a development of this same idea, and there it is for once unambiguously stated that 'the great Brahman is my womb; therein I plant my seed. From that is the coming-to-be of all contingent beings'. Brahman, then, is the *materia prima* which is regarded as being constant through change, and Puruṣa, the great Male, is its Lord and the agent which forms it.[4] This at any rate can be deduced from this passage (3.1.3). But it would be useless to insist that this distinction is maintained throughout even so short an Upaniṣad as the *Muṇḍaka*. There seems to be no difference between the Imperishable Brahman of the first *Muṇḍaka* and the Puruṣa of the first *khāṇḍa* of the second. Both seem to be based on *Bṛhadāraṇyaka* 3.8; both are eternal, and both are the source of all things.

In the second *khāṇḍa* of the second *muṇḍaka* the Puruṣa is again quietly forgotten, and the *ātman* takes its place. The *ātman* too is 'he on whom the earth, the sky, and the atmosphere are woven, and the mind together with all senses'.[5] He is 'the bridge of immorta-

[1] Ibid., 2.1.2. [2] Ibid., 3.1.3. [3] So Max Müller.
[4] *kartṛ*: *Muṇḍaka* Up., 3.1.3. [5] Ibid., 2.2.5.

lity', and he is also 'the more minute than the minute . . . set down in the secret place [of the heart]'.[1] Yet here again a distinction *is* made, for whereas the Imperishable Brahman is 'without sight or hearing',[2] and the Puruṣa is 'without life-breath or mind',[3] the *ātman is* to be 'known by thought'[4] because it *does* possess a mind.[5] This is important, for it explains how the *ātman* can choose its devotees; for we read in 3.2.3:[6]

> This *ātman* is not to be obtained by instruction,
> By intellect, or much lore heard;
> He is to be obtained by him whom he chooses.
> To such a one the *ātman* reveals his own form [*tanūm*].

The *ātman* is here regarded as a personal force which chooses whomsoever it will. Liberation is no longer regarded as something that can be attained by one's own effort; it depends on the grace of the *ātman*. The *ātman*, moreover, though it is 'he on whom, the sky, the earth, and the atmosphere are woven', is in the preceding verse spoken of as the arrow which should be shot into the target which is Brahman: it is then the means by which one obtains Brahman, not Brahman itself. This explains why it is also called the 'bridge of immortality'.[7] Moreover, the *ātman* itself disappears in the featureless Brahman when the final goal is reached.

> Those ascetics whose firmly determined aim is the knowledge of the Vedānta,
> Whose being is purified by the Yoga of renunciation,
> They at the end of time, surpassing death,
> Are all liberated in the Brahman-worlds. . . .
>
> Gone are [all] deeds and the *ātman* which consists of knowledge;
> All become one in the Imperishable (*avyaya*) beyond.

[1] Ibid., 3.1.7.
[2] Ibid., 1.1.6.
[3] Ibid., 2.1.2.
[4] Ibid., 3.1.9.
[5] Ibid., 2.2.7.
[6] This stanza is also found in *Kaṭha* Up., 2.23.
[7] *Muṇḍaka* Up., 2.2.5.

As rivers flowing into the ocean
Disappear, leaving behind them name and form,
So too the one who knows, released from name and form,
Draws near (*upaiti*) to the divine Person beyond the beyond.[1]

Now it must be admitted that in the *Muṇḍaka* the descriptions of Brahman, Puruṣa, and *ātman* do not vary greatly; and it is quite legitimate to see in them all the supreme principle, for the descriptions of them resemble each other closely. This, however, should not blind us to the distinctions, and it is important to consider what these are, for they are further developed in the Bhagavad-Gītā and are the first steps in the change of orientation from pantheism to a recognizable form of theism. Brahman is the source of all phenomenal being, it is imperishable; but Puruṣa, the personal God, is 'beyond the imperishable',[2] he is *parāt param* 'beyond the beyond'.[3] The *ātman*, on the other hand, though all-pervading is nonetheless only the arrow aimed at the target Brahman. It is *vijñānamaya* 'possessed of knowledge', but it must ultimately disappear and become one with the imperishable Brahman.[4] Yet even in the *Muṇḍaka* Upaniṣad this sublime union of all souls in Brahman, if such it is, is not regarded as union with God. The 'one who knows' and is released from 'name and form' and has in very deed become Brahman,[5] does not thereby become Puruṣa or God, he is merely in a position to draw near to God, for the word *upaiti* means no more than this. Further it is perhaps worth pointing out

[1] Ibid., 3.2.6–8.
[2] Ibid., 2.1.2.
[3] Ibid., 3.2.8.
[4] Ibid., 3.2.7. The sense of *ekībhavanti* is not absolutely clear. The phrase occurs in *Br*Up., 4.4.2 ff. where it refers to a dying man whose senses become one, that is, are extinguished in the heart. Here the meaning appears to be 'he is becoming a unified or unitary being, one in himself'. *Praśna*, 4.2, however, is closer to our passage. In it the rays of the setting sun *ekībhavanti* in an orb of brilliance, i.e. the setting sun which no longer appears to emit rays. Our passage can, then, either mean 'All individual souls become unified [in themselves, i.e. integrated] within [the sphere of] the imperishable beyond', or 'All individual souls become one in the imperishable beyond', i.e. one with it. Both senses are permissible, and the phrase is probably deliberately ambiguous. 'All become unified in the imperishable beyond' would probably best render the meaning of the text.
[5] Ibid., 3.2.9.

that this is precisely the word used for a pupil approaching his master for instruction[1] and that this is by far the commonest meaning of the word in the Upaniṣads. The purport of all this seems to be that the released soul who has realized his essential unity with all things in Brahman, the Imperishable ground of all being, is then and only then fit to approach God. All things proceed from Brahman as sparks from a fire, and all things return to him as rivers to the sea; things, then, are one in the sense that they are all made of one substance, and the realization of this causal oneness in which all sense of individuality is lost, is regarded by the author of the Upaniṣad as being a necessary preliminary in any approach to him who is beyond the beyond, who is beyond immortality. The means of attaining to oneness with Brahman are described by the *Muṇḍaka* as the Yoga of renunciation, and it is with this Yoga that the first six chapters of the Gītā are concerned. The thinking of the Gītā begins where the *Muṇḍaka* leaves off.

The Gītā, however, differs from the *Muṇḍaka* in that Buddhist influence would appear to have affected it. Thus we find the Buddhist term *nirvāṇa* appearing in conjunction with Brahman,[2] and *nirvāṇa* is, of course, a Buddhist, not an Upaniṣadic conception. Similarly the term *brahmabhūta*[3] would seem to be directly borrowed from Buddhism, for the term in this form is not found in the Upaniṣads, although the form *brahma bhavati*[4] is twice attested. In Buddhism, on the other hand, it is a common term for one who has attained liberation or enlightenment.[5] Buddhism, however, while accepting the term, never attempted to define what was meant by it any more than it attempted to define *nirvāṇa* more exactly than as the 'deathless', that is, a state beyond space and time. The simile of the ocean, however, is applied to *nirvāṇa* in the *Udāna*[6] just as it is to Brahman in the Upaniṣads. It seems, then,

[1] *Ch*Up., 4.4.3: *Kauṣītakī* Up., 1.1: *Br*Up., 2.1.14, 15: 6.2.7: *Praśna* Up., 1.3: 6.1.

[2] BG., 2.72: 5.24–26.

[3] Ibid., 5.24: 6.27: 18.54.

[4] *Br*Up., 4.4.25: *Muṇḍaka*, 3.2.9.

[5] E.g. *Dīgha Nikāya*, iii.84: *Majjhima*, i.111: iii.195, 224: *Saṃyutta*, iii.83: iv.94: *Anguttara*, ii.206: v.226: *Suttanipāta*, 561, 563.

[6] p. 55.

fairly safe to conclude that when the Gītā uses the word *brahma-bhūta* it meant that the soul was merged in a world-soul and not, as Rāmānuja held, that it simply realized its own essence. Both the Buddhist usage and the *Muṇḍaka* passage on which the *brahma-bhūta* passages of the Gītā seem to be based, bear this interpretation out.

As we have seen, the *Muṇḍaka* introduces two new ideas into Brahmanical thought. It not only makes a distinction between the *ātman*, Brahman, and Puruṣa or God, but it also introduces the idea of divine election, though it is the *ātman*, not God, who is here the agent of election.

The *Śvetāśvatara* develops the idea much more fully. God is there the origin and Lord of both the perishable and the imperishable (*kṣara* and *akṣara*),[1] over the world of coming-to-be and passing away and over the world of eternal values, over what the *Śvetāśvatara* Upaniṣad calls 'ignorance' and 'knowledge'. This equation of 'ignorance' with 'becoming' and 'knowledge' with 'being' was later worked up in a grandiose manner by Śaṅkara into his famous doctrine of cosmic ignorance as the ultimate source of phenomenal being. The idea was already present in the *Īśā* Upaniṣad (9, 13) where ignorance and knowledge are concepts parallel to, but not identical with, 'becoming' and 'not-becoming'. In both the *Īśā* and the *Śvetāśvatara* 'being' and 'becoming' are categories of existence. The Imperishable Brahman is the category of being, but it is also the source of the category of becoming; but, in the *Śvetāśvatara* at least, God is supreme over both aspects of Brahman, and he is responsible for the conjoining of the two as well as for their separation: this constitutes his supernatural power or *māyā*.[2]

In the *Śvetāśvatara* the figure of God stands out from all that is other than he far more clearly than in any other Upaniṣadic literature, yet even in this Upaniṣad liberation is not considered to be union with God. God can be contemplated and known, and such knowledge brings liberation,[3] but knowledge of him does not mean union with him.[4] Liberation is described as either to be

[1] 1.10: 5.1. [2] *Śvet*Up., 4.9–10. [3] Ibid., 1.11: 2.15: 4.16:5. 13: 6.13.
[4] See my *At Sundry Times*, pp. 111–12.

merged in Brahman,[1] as realization of oneness,[2] as isolation,[3] or as access to Brahman.[4] The reason why the author does not speak of union with God but rather prays God to give him access to Brahman, is probably that his God, though he is Lord of both the finite and the infinite in a way that the God of the *Yogasūtras* is not, is nevertheless seen against a Sāṁkhya-Yoga background, and union with him is therefore not considered possible. Moreover, the emphasis is still all on intellectual contemplation, and there is no suggestion that God is a legitimate object of love. Liberation is interpreted as either a merging into Brahman as in the *Muṇḍaka* or as isolation as in the *Yogasūtras*. The two are not considered incompatible. In the words of the *Muṇḍaka* 'All become unified in the Imperishable beyond'.

It is always unsafe to generalize about the Upaniṣads, so contradictory are they of themselves and so maddeningly imprecise is their terminology. Yet it is nonetheless not wholly false to say that in the verse Upaniṣads there is a just perceptible movement away from a monist-pantheistic view of the universe towards a more overtly theistical one. God begins to detach himself from the universe and to take on personal characteristics. The theology of the *Śvetāśvatara* would appear to be approximately this:

God is the supreme Lord of the universe, and all the universe proceeds from him 'in whom this whole universe comes to be and dissolves'.[5] The created world which emanates from him is Brahman (which already in the *Muṇḍaka*[6] is called the best of *creatures* (*prajānām*)); and Brahman is twofold,[7] the imperishable and the perishable. The imperishable is what the Buddhists understand by *nirvāṇa*, an eternal mode of existence, but it is also the unchanging ground of the changing universe. It is both the unchanging *per se*, the state of being experienced by the liberated soul, and the *materia prima* of the universe which, though constantly taking on different forms remains, as *materia prima*, always the same. As the *Chāndogya* puts it: 'Just as everything made of clay can be known in one lump of clay—any new form it takes being but a verbal

[1] *Śvet*Up., 1.7. [2] Ibid., 2.14. [3] Ibid., 1.11. [4] Ibid., 6.10. [5] Ibid., 4.11. [6] 2.2.1. [7] *Śvet*Up., 1.10: 5.1.

distinction, a name—the reality is clayness',[1] so too primal matter preserves an unchanging identity beneath the world of change. This dualism is reflected in the life of the individual being: to the 'perishable' aspect of the universe corresponds the soul that is still in bondage to matter, to the 'imperishable' the released soul. The bound soul is steeped in ignorance, the released one is the possessor of saving knowledge, ignorance and knowledge being identified with becoming and being respectively.[2] God is the ruler of both and therefore committed to the world of becoming as much as to that of being. *Māyā* is God's power active in Nature,[3] what we would call the laws of Nature, God's creative power from which he is inseparable,[4] and this power in turn is identified with Nature as such.[5]

Both the *Śvetāśvatara* and the Gītā introduce Sāṁkhya terminology into the already sufficiently confused vocabulary of the Upaniṣads, but this should not blind us to the fact that neither in the Upaniṣads nor in the Gītā is there an absolute duality between the imperishable and perishable, the *puruṣa* and *prakṛti* of the Sāṁkhya, for both are combined in the 'imperishable infinite city of Brahman',[6] and the ruler of the city is God. From the individual's point of view liberation means crossing over from one side of the city to the other, a transition from the status of a slave to that of a lord, and this high estate can be reached by meditating on the Lord of lords.[7] In this sense liberation means to become *like* God, not to unite with him, but to resemble him in his immortality and freedom.

Hindus reverence the Vedas and more particularly the Upaniṣads, the end of the Veda or Vedānta, as revealed truth, the *brahman* or sacred word of the Supreme Spirit. By revelation we in the West understand a revelation by God of his own nature: we expect revelation to have a positive content. The Upaniṣads, however, reveal a God who is essentially a *deus absconditus*, ever elusive to the human mind. The real message of the Upaniṣads is not so much the identity of *ātman* with Brahman, which amounts to a

[1] *Ch*Up., 6.1.4. [2] *Śvet*Up., 5.1. [3] *Śvet*Up., 4.9–10.
[4] Ibid., *devātma-śakti*, 1.3. [5] Ibid., 4.10. [6] Ibid., 5.1. [7] Ibid., 1.11.

tautology—for either word is used to mean almost anything—as that the human soul is immortal: its being is bound by neither space nor time:

> Unborn, constant, eternal, primeval this
> Is not slain when the body is slain. . . .
>
> More minute than the minute, greater than the great
> Is the soul that is set in the secret place of a creature here.'[1]

The Gītā, though it does not enjoy the status of *śruti*, is a revelation in quite another sense; it is a revelation of the nature and attributes of God and of his relationship to man. The God of the Upaniṣads, like the God of the *Yogasūtras*, though real and the source of reality, is yet not the object of man's desire; he is only the object most worthy of his contemplation: 'By knowing God one is released from all fetters.'[2] The God of the Gītā is quite different; he is a God of love and grace whom it is possible to know at least in part, and so to love him.

In these lectures I shall have no time to undertake any detailed analysis of the Gītā. All I shall have time to do is to analyse its theology, to enquire into the relationship between God and Brahman, and the relationship between liberation and the new and totally different concept of the love of God. Rāmānuja divides the eighteen chapters of the Gītā into three parts of six chapters each. The subject-matter of the first is psychology; it concerns itself with the nature of the soul. The second section is concerned with theology, the nature and attributes of God, and the last is devoted to miscellaneous topics, the full and 'most mysterious' doctrine of all being summed up in the conclusion of the last chapter.

Rāmānuja, like all the ancient commentators, treats the Gītā as a united whole. Modern commentators, on the other hand, have all been struck by the contradictions that are everywhere apparent in it. Some, like Garbe and more radically Otto, have sought to construct an original Gītā which would be coherent in itself from what seems to be an extraordinary hotch-potch of mutually

[1] *Kaṭha* Up., 2.18, 20.

[2] See above, p. 53 n. 3.

exclusive doctrines. Others, like Hill and Edgerton, are happy to accept the contradictions as they stand on the grounds that what seems self-contradictory to us has never been felt to be so by the Hindus. In these lectures I have no alternative but to treat the Gītā as a single whole.

Now in trying to establish that there is a real distinction between God and Brahman in the Gītā, one is immediately faced with the problem of the terminology used. *Ātman*, for instance, is indisputably used to mean both the 'immortal soul' which cannot die and what we would call the 'ego', concepts that correspond quite exactly to the *rūḥ* 'spirit' and *nafs* 'carnal soul' of the Ṣūfīs. Indeed, in BG. 6.5–6 the word *ātman* seems to indicate not only both these, but also the human person as such. The passage runs as follows:

uddhared ātmanā'tmānaṁ
nā'tmānam avasādayet.
ātmaiva hy ātmano bandhur,
ātmaiva ripur ātmanaḥ.

bandhur ātmā'tmanas tasya
yenā'tmaivā'tmanā jitaḥ;
anātmanas tu śatrutve
vartetā'tmaiva śatruvat.

Without any explanatory footnote Edgerton translates as follows:

One should lift up the self by the self,
And should not let the self down;
For the self is the self's only friend,
And the self is the self's only enemy.

The self is a friend to that self
By which self the very self is subdued;
But to him that does not possess the self, in enmity
Will abide his very self, like an enemy.

This translation, as it stands, is meaningless, and those of Otto, Hill, and Radhakrishnan are better only in so far as they employ a capital S to distinguish the two senses of 'self'. There is, however, a further difficulty, for not only is the word *ātman* used in its usual two senses, that is, to mean the 'immortal soul' on the one hand and as a reflexive pronoun on the other; it is also used in the sense of the 'lower self', the 'animal soul' as exemplified in *kāma-krodha* 'desire and anger'. As Radhakrishnan points out, the idea is already present in the *Dhammapada*,[1] where it is stated that 'the self is the lord of self', meaning that the 'immortal soul' is lord of the total human personality or of the ego.[2] This triple ambivalence of the word *ātman* is extremely confusing, but it is common both to the Gītā and the twelfth book of the *Mahābhārata*.[3] It is, however, no longer mysterious if we set it alongside the parallel Muslim development where different words are used to indicate the three different meanings. Against the background of Muslim terminology which expresses the same ideas with greater clarity, we should translate:

> [A man] should uplift himself by his spirit: he should not degrade himself. Spirit is man's friend, the animal soul his enemy. Spirit is the friend of him who has himself conquered the animal soul; but as an enemy would spirit behave to him who is spiritless.[4]

When translated thus the meaning of the text becomes perfectly clear.

The case of *ātman*, however, is only one case of a word being used to indicate two or more totally different things. The word *brahman* is another case in point. In chapter 5.16–end it is obviously used in the sense of 'an eternal mode of existence', 'world-soul', or 'impersonal Absolute'—the exact nuance cannot be allowed to detain us now—whereas in § 10 of the same chapter it means 'Nature' or *prakṛti*,[5] and it is in this sense that the word is used in

[1] § 380.

[2] On 'self' in Buddhism see my *At Sundry Times*, pp. 98–103. The ego, for the Buddhists, is, of course, considered to be an illusion. There is no continuity in the human personality, and a man is not the same today as he was yesterday. To speak of an 'ego' is, then, a concession to popular terminology.

[3] E.g. 6509, 6558, 8748, 8802, 8962, etc.

[4] That is, denies spirit. Cf. *Iśā* Up., § 3 which speaks of 'slayers of the *ātman*' meaning those who stifle it: see Hume's note *ad loc.*

[5] See below, p. 67.

14.3 where Krishna says: 'The great Brahman is my womb, in him I place my seed.'

Again even the word *īśvara*, 'the Lord', is not exempt from confusion, for in 15.8 it is used to mean the individual soul which is here expressly stated to be *part* of God. This, incidentally, amounts to proof that when the *Śvetāśvatara* Upaniṣad (1.11) speaks of the soul achieving 'lordship' at death, it does not mean that it becomes *īśvara* or God *tout court*, as might otherwise be supposed, for the same Upaniṣad (4.10) also says that 'the whole world is pervaded by beings that are part of him', that is, individual souls. *Aiśvaryam* is no more used in an absolute sense there than is *īśvara* in BG, 15.8. The one case proves the other, and the achievement of lordship means no more than the passage from the condition of being a bondsman to matter to the complete freedom of the spirit. Similarly in the fifth chapter of the Gītā which superficially appears to be devoted to the exaltation of the impersonal Brahman above the Lord, it is said that the Lord (*prabhu*) does not initiate agency and actions in this world, nor does he receive anyone's good or evil deeds, but this must refer to the soul 'embodied in the city of nine gates' mentioned in § 13, that is, the individual incarnate soul, not the universal Lord who is Krishna.

With these qualifications in respect of terminology in mind we are now in a position to consider the respective rôles of God and Brahman in the first chapters of the Gītā. Rāmānuja is quite right in maintaining that the main theme of these chapters concerns the soul and the methods by which it can obtain liberation. One of the arguments Krishna uses in his attempt to persuade Arjuna to go into battle is that, since the soul is immortal, it cannot be affected by the death of the body; and for this purpose he relies on the authority of the *Kaṭha* Upaniṣad.[1] But it is not clear whether the Gītā is here thinking in terms of a plurality of souls, or one world-soul, or both. In 2.12 Krishna says: 'Never was there a time when I was not, nor thou, nor these lords of men, nor shall we ever cease to be, all of us, henceforward', and he thereby seems to assume the eternal existence of a plurality of souls. Nor is this necessarily

[1] BG., 2.19 = *Kaṭha* Up., 2.19.

contradicted by § 17 which speaks of an indestructible neuter something by which the whole world is pervaded.[1] This is elsewhere identified with God 'in the form of the unmanifest'[2] or with the Supreme Person,[3] a confusion which I have sought to explain elsewhere.[4] § 18 then goes on to say that 'bodies which belong to an (or the) eternal soul come to an end'; and it is quite impossible to say whether the author is here speaking of the neuter principle which pervades the whole universe or of the individual soul spoken of a few verses earlier, since the relevant words are in the genitive case in which masculine and neuter are not distinguished. However, the word used for soul is *śarīrin-*, 'embodied one', and this is exactly parallel to the *dehin-* of identical meaning which appears in § 13. Hence we must conclude that the author here admits of a plurality of souls on the one hand and an indestructible something which pervades the whole universe on the other; and that, of course, is Brahman. The co-existence of a plurality of individual souls and a world-soul, however, is not necessarily self-contradictory; and, given the two concepts, liberation can be taken to mean either the realization of one's own unitary being within the universal 'soul-stuff' of Brahman, or merging into Brahman, both of which are admitted by the *Śvetāśvatara* Upaniṣad; or again it may be taken to mean actual identity with Brahman.

The various means of achieving this state—*jñāna*, *yoga*, and *sannyāsa*—need not detain us, for they all have this in common, that they aim at a complete detachment from and indifference to all that is not the immortal soul. This is achieved primarily by the conquest of desire and anger,[5] as well as of the delusion that the soul or *ātman* is in any sense an agent;[6] for if liberation into a timeless state is to be achieved, it is essential to realize that the soul cannot be an agent, since action can only take place in time.

Now in the first six chapters God is scarcely spoken of in relation to liberation except as an object of contemplation; and he is to be contemplated as the Supreme Being who, although he is not for a minute idle in his ordering of the world, is nonetheless, in the

[1] Or 'by whom all this world is woven'. See my *At Sundry Times*, pp. 124–5.
[2] BG., 9.4. [3] 8.22. [4] See *At Sundry Times*, ibid. [5] 3.37 ff. [6] 5.8.

ground of his being, wholly unsullied by what he does. The conception is not very different from that of *īśvara* in the *Yogasūtras* except that the God of the Gītā is God in every sense of that word, the Eternal, who creates, sustains, and reabsorbs the universe. 'Know,' Krishna says, 'that though I am the doer of this, I am eternally a not-doer. Actions do not stain me, for I have no yearning for their results.'[1] Thus by contemplating the God whose action keeps the world in being, yet who eternally remains changeless in his essence, the devotee realizes that he himself, constantly involved in action though he may be, is at the root of his being eternally at rest. Contemplating God thus he will 'see all things without exception in his own soul, and then in [God]'.[2]

Man 'arafa nafsa-hu, fa-qad 'arafa rabba-hu, says a well-known Ṣūfī tradition attributed to the Prophet: 'Who knows himself, knows his Lord', and this text forms the subject-matter of the first book of Ghazālī's *Kīmiyā-yi Sa'ādat* with which we shall be dealing later. By seeing oneself as the microcosm of the divine, one comes to know the divine itself. To realize one's own immortal soul as eternal and yet as active in and through the body, controlling it through its link with matter, yet forever unaffected by what it does, is to understand *in parvo* the relationship of God to the world. Such a man cannot be afflicted by pleasure or pain, for they will not touch his deepest essence. That this is really the meaning of the Gītā seems clear from the fact that in this passage self-realization is regarded as being prior to knowledge of God: the liberated soul sees all things first in himself and *then* in God. The same idea is repeated in 6.29–30. 'The man who is integrated by Yoga discipline[3] sees his *ātman* as being in all things and all things in his *ātman*,[4] considering all things indifferently (*samadarśanaḥ*). For him

[1] 4.13–14. [2] 4.35: cf. 6.29–30.

[3] *yogayuktātmā* would seem to mean what we would call an 'integrated personality' in the Jungian sense of a personality no longer centred on the ego but on what Jung calls the 'self' which has its being outside time. See my *Mysticism, Sacred and Profane*, pp. 109–10 and *At Sundry Times*, p. 77.

[4] This state would appear to be what the *Yogasūtras* call *sarvaviśayaṁ jñānam*, the intuitive knowledge of all things which is said to precede the final isolation of the soul. See above, p. 33.

who sees me everywhere and all in me, I am not lost, nor is he lost to me.' Here again it is the realization that one's soul, because it is eternal and beyond space and time, must somehow comprise all that is conditioned by space and time, that leads on to the understanding of God in whom all things move and have their being. The next verse makes this point abundantly clear. '*By analogy with oneself*', it says, 'he who sees the same everywhere (*sama-*, that is, "changeless, spiritual being") whether it be [manifested in] pleasure or pain, is deemed the highest Yogin.' *Sama-* is used in the Gītā to mean what is unaffected by pleasure and pain or any of the other opposites,[1] and is once equated with Brahman.[2] Brahman, then, in these contexts means that which, itself being changeless, is unaffected by change or by anything that goes on in the phenomenal world. It is in fact the quality of eternity in both God and human souls. In this state the soul is freed from all desire and has no consciousness of 'I' or 'mine': it is the state of Brahman.[3] Similarly in the fifth chapter the man who has achieved complete indifference to all earthly things, is established in Brahman, he goes to the *nirvāṇa* of Brahman and actually becomes Brahman;[4] and only by becoming Brahman can he then approach God. By analogy with the experience of his own soul man is now in a position to understand the nature of God.

The state of becoming Brahman is achieved in both the fifth and sixth chapters by intense Yogic concentration and introspection, the mind being subjected entirely to the *ātman* or immortal soul.[5] This is endless bliss,[6] and the Yogin who achieves it is the highest of his kind.[7] He is superior to the ascetic, the *jñānin* or gnostic, as well as to the more humble mortal who performs his religious duties conscientiously; for he has realized the eternal nature of his soul—he has become Brahman which is at the same time his inmost soul. But, says Krishna in the last verse of Chapter VI: 'Of all Yogins I consider him to be the most integrated (*yukta*) who worships me with faith, his inner soul lost in me.'

It would, then, seem clear that in the Gītā itself, and not only in

[1] 2.38, 48: 4.22: 12.18. [2] 5.19. [3] 2.71–72. [4] 5.24–26: 6.27.
[5] 6.18, 26. [6] 6.28. [7] 6.32.

Rāmānuja's commentary, liberation is seen not as an end in itself, but as a stage on the way to union with God. It is the essential purification that must precede any approach to God, the *zuhd* or ascetic preparation that must precede the mystic's *qurb* or 'drawing nigh' to God. Brahman, then, even in the first six chapters of the Gītā, is not the ultimate reality. It is rather what the Buddhists understand by the word—an eternal mode of existence in which all liberated souls share, and it is no accident that the Gītā so often falls back on Buddhist terminology. In our next lecture we shall have to consider how the Gītā and Rāmānuja conceive of the liberated soul's relationship with God.

IV

The God of Love

We saw in the last lecture that, in the first six chapters of the Gītā, liberation was regarded as 'becoming Brahman', which seems to mean, as it does in Buddhism, to enter into an eternal form of existence. The term *brahman* seems to be formally equated with the Buddhist *nirvāṇa* in the compound *brahma-nirvāṇa*.[1] We shall now have to consider first the relationship of Krishna as God to Brahman as the impersonal Absolute, and secondly his relationship to the released soul which, as *brahma-bhūta*, has already realized itself as Brahman.

The general impression conveyed by the last two-thirds of the Gītā is that God both is Brahman and is yet higher than it. Let us see whether a closer examination of the text enables us to be more precise.

We must first consider one passage in which God would appear to be only an aspect of Brahman:

> Brahman [the text reads], is the supreme Imperishable; it is called Nature in its relationship to the human person (*adhyātmam*); as the creative force known as *karma* it causes the conditions of contingent being to come into existence. In its relationship to contingent beings it is what is subject to coming-to-be and passing away (*kṣaro bhāvaḥ*). In its relationship to the gods it is Puruṣa. In its relationship to sacrifice I am it here in the body.[2]

[1] BG., 2.72: 5.24, 25, 26.

[2] BG., 8.3–4. *Adhyātmam*, *adhibhūtam*, and *adhidaivatam* are all common Upaniṣadic terms meaning 'with reference to the human person', 'with reference to creatures or contingent beings', and 'with reference to the gods'. See Jacobi's *Concordance*, ad loc. Here they would seem clearly to be used adjectively agreeing with *brahman*. To translate them as if they were independent substantives as Edgerton, Hill, and others, following the Indian commentators, have done is quite contrary to the Upaniṣadic use of the words, and seems quite unjustified. The

In this passage, then, it would appear that God is merely Brahman in its relationship to the religious cultus; he is not identical with the supreme Imperishable, but only one aspect of it. This single instance of the subordination of God to the 'supreme Imperishable', Brahman, however, seems contrary to the main trend of the Gītā, and is probably to be interpreted against the background of 10.20 ff. in which Krishna describes himself as the best of each category of being, by which, presumably, he means that it is he who, by entering each category of being, gives it value. Moreover Krishna, as personal God, is the only true object of worship, and even worship offered to false gods is acceptable to him;[1] he is, then, in a very special sense the 'supreme Imperishable' in its relationship to sacrifice.

There are, moreover, a number of passages in which God seems to be merely a personalized version of Brahman. Thus, like Brahman, he is *sama*-,[2] unaffected by change and emotion, and as such devoid of love or hatred. Again he is formally addressed as the 'supreme Brahman, the supreme abode'[3] although Brahman itself is elsewhere referred to as God's supreme abode or law.[4] Like Brahman again he is the All,[5] devoid of qualities, and the *ātman* established everywhere.[6] Thus even in the Gītā Indian religion remains rooted in pantheism; and God, like Brahman, therefore, must not only be the cause of all things, he *is* also all things. What is surprising rather is not that he is sometimes identified with Brahman, but that in several passages at which we must now look, he is raised far above it.

We have just said that although Brahman is described as God's 'supreme abode or law (*dhāman*)', God is himself thus described.

evidence of the Upaniṣads is overwhelmingly strong and totally against any such interpretation. *Adhiyajño* agrees grammatically with *aham* in the usual way, but still refers to Brahman. 'I am Brahman in relationship to the sacrifice' is what Krishna is saying. *Adhyātma*- is in fact used in the sense indicated 37 times in the Upaniṣads, *adhibhūta*- 4 times, and *adhidaivata*- 14 times. The three occur together in *Br*Up., 3.7.14–15 from which this passage from the Gītā no doubt derives. *Adhidaivatam* and *adhyātmam* are regularly contrasted (12 times). *Adhiyajña* is an innovation in the Gītā.

[1] 9.20–27. [2] 9.29; 13.27. [3] 10.12; cf. 15.6
[4] 8.21; cf. 15.6. [5] 11.40. [6] 13.32; cf. 10.20.

This contradiction is only apparent; for in 8.21 Brahman, 'the unmanifest beyond the unmanifest', is described by *Krishna* as his 'supreme abode', whereas it is *Arjuna* who in 10.12 and again in 11.38 addresses Krishna as 'the supreme abode'. This merely shows that Krishna is propounding a doctrine that is totally new to Arjuna, one that at first he is unable to understand; for what God is asking him to believe is that he, the incarnate personal God, is higher and more fundamental than what had hitherto been universally accepted as the ultimate principle. For Arjuna Brahman was the ultimate ground of the universe, to which personal beings including the highest could only be subordinate; and Brahman, in the Upaniṣads, is that from which everything proceeds. He simply does not understand the new doctrine, and, in addressing Krishna as 'the supreme Brahman and the supreme abode', he acknowledges him as the ground of all being as taught in the Upaniṣads, the highest conception open to him. It is only after he has seen God in a vision specially vouchsafed to him that he is able to exclaim: 'And why should they not worship thee, for thou art more venerable than Brahman, thou, the original creator. O infinite Lord of the gods, in whom the world dwells, thou art the Imperishable, Being, Not-Being, and what is beyond both.[1] Thou art the primeval God, the ancient Person, thou art the supreme bourn of this universe; the knower and what is to be known art thou, the supreme abode; by thee is this universe pervaded,[2] O infinite in form.'[3]

Arjuna here, after he has been terrified by the vision of God as devouring Time,[4] acknowledges him as 'more venerable than Brahman' and as what is beyond being and not-being, that is, totally inaccessible to conceptual thought. This does not prevent him from again calling him 'the supreme abode', for that is traditional terminology for the highest principle, and as the greater than Brahman he includes Brahman as the whole includes the part, for as Krishna had already said of himself: 'I have established

[1] *Tatparam*, so Rāmānuja. *Tat param* 'that supreme' could equally be read.

[2] See above, p. 60, n. 1.

[3] BG., 11.37–38. [4] 11.32.

the whole universe with one single fraction of myself, and so abide.'[1]

Throughout the Gītā we are confronted with two principles which together constitute the whole of what we would call created existence, that is, all that has being of any kind and is other than God. The two principles are the eternal and the temporal, the static and the dynamic, the world of pure spirit and the world of thought, emotion, volition, sensation, and matter, the ideal and the phenomenal. Sometimes Sāṁkhya terminology is used, and we meet with the familiar *puruṣa* and *prakṛti*: elsewhere we meet with the two natures (*prakṛtis*) of the Lord,[2] or two 'unmanifests',[3] or again two *puruṣas*.[4] In Rāmānuja's theology the two together constitute Brahman, 'the body of the Lord', and this seems to be the consistent view of the Gītā itself.

In 7.5 ff. we are introduced to the two natures of the Lord. The lower consists of the elements, mind, consciousness, and the ego; the higher is *jīvabhūtam*, organic life, we might translate, which is the womb or origin of all beings. This 'womb' of all things is elsewhere identified with Brahman,[5] and not only is it the origin of the world, it also keeps it in existence.[6] This Brahman, as origin and final resting-place of all phenomenal being, is the *mūla-prakṛti* or 'primal matter' of the Sāṁkhya, but not the 'primal matter' of Aristotle, for it is a living and dynamic force, instinct with energy even when it is at rest. It is much more 'matter' as interpreted by Marx and Engels, the 'most important of the inherent qualities' of which 'is motion, not only mechanical and mathematical movement, but still more impulse, vital life-spirit, tension'.[7] The two *prakṛtis* of the Lord are not, then, equivalent to the *puruṣa* and *prakṛti* of the Sāṁkhya, they are rather (i) living matter at rest, and (ii) living matter in motion. They are two aspects of the same thing—matter in the Marxian, not in the Aristotelian, interpretation of the word. Both constitute what is elsewhere called the 'unmanifest', the *avyakta*.

[1] 10.42. [2] 7.5 ff. [3] 8.18 ff.
[4] 15.16. [5] 14.3. [6] 7.5.
[7] K. Marx and F. Engels, *The Holy Family*, ed. Moscow, 1956, p. 172.

But here again there are two *avyaktas*, not one. The lower one corresponds to the lower 'nature' of the Lord; from it all beings derive, and into it they are dissolved;[1] but 'beyond this unmanifest there is another unmanifest, an eternal mode of being (*bhāva*) which does not perish when all contingent beings perish. This unmanifest is called the imperishable; it is [also] called the highest course. Once this is attained, men do not return [to the phenomenal world]. That is my supreme abode. That is the *puruṣa* beyond, attainable by exclusive devotion, in which [all] contingent beings dwell, by which this universe is pervaded.'[2]

This 'eternal unmanifest', being God's 'supreme abode', is, of course, Brahman. Brahman, then, is also the *paramā gatiḥ*, 'the highest course'[3] to which the liberated man attains. It is both *puruṣa* and *prakṛti*, 'soul' and 'Nature' as commonly understood—the unmanifest 'life-spirit' in matter and changeless being.

Both God and Brahman are referred to as 'what does not perish when all [other] beings perish',[4] and both are the unchanging substrate of the universe. 'When a man sees the various states of contingent beings as abiding in one [essence], . . . then he attains to Brahman':[5] similarly in the theophany of Chapter XI Arjuna is said to have seen 'the whole world abiding in one [essence] yet divided manifold[6] in the body of the God of gods'.[7] This does not mean that, even in Chapter XIII which is the most confused in the whole Gītā, God and Brahman are identical. Rather Brahman is the one essence in which all creation abides, and as such he is the body of God only, not his *ātman* or soul. This concept Rāmānuja was to develop much more fully later.

[1] BG., 8.18.

[2] 8.20–22.

[3] The words *para-* and *parama-* present the translator with a problem. The usual translations 'highest' and 'supreme' will hardly do since the 'highest course' is in fact itself transcended by God. Rāmānuja glosses: *ātma-svarūpaṁ viśayebhyaḥ param*, 'having the nature of soul, beyond sense objects'. Perhaps 'supra-sensory' would be as good a translation as any.

[4] Of God, see 13.27.

[5] 13.30.

[6] Cf. 13.16 of Brahman.

[7] 11.13.

We saw that in 8.22 the 'imperishable unmanifest' is identified with the '*puruṣa* beyond'. Elsewhere[1] the 'perishable' and the 'imperishable' are spoken of as two *puruṣas*, the higher of which is the *kūṭastha*- imperishable, 'the imperishable who stands on high', that is, the absolutely unchangeable: but the Gītā goes on to say: 'The supreme Person is another, it is called the supreme soul (*paramātmā*) who, entering the three worlds, supports them, the undying Lord.'

Thus the Gītā seems to be quite consistent in its analysis of being: it is only the terminology that varies, and that does vary quite inordinately. Being is divided into two categories which may conveniently be classed as what is liable to change and what is not. One is 'absolutely unchangeable, unmoving, firm', the 'undefinable unmanifest',[2] the other is the world of becoming. The unchanging side of being, however, pervades all that comes to be and passes away, and all things can therefore be said to exist in and through it. What is new in the Gītā's teaching, however, is that there exists a being still higher, whose dwelling or law (*dhāman*) eternal being is, and who is at the same time the source of that law which in its turn emits and reabsorbs all contingent being. Though he too pervades all things eternal and temporal, he transcends them all, for he is their overseer:[3] though pervading them he at the same time stands apart from them, contemplates them and approves of them. He is the foundation of both eternal and temporal being: 'I am the foundation of Brahman, of the immortal and the imperishable, of the eternal law, and of absolute bliss'.[4]

Thus God is absolutely transcendent, but he is also absolutely immanent. Just as he is the foundation of Brahman, so does he indwell the soul, just as the soul indwells the body,[5] and it is he who, abiding in the human heart, causes creatures to act by his supernatural power (*māyā*).[6] Thus in the Gītā Krishna, as God, asserts his supremacy over the impersonal and indescribable Brahman, to become which or to realize oneself as which had been the aim of the Upaniṣadic sages. God, though taking over all the

[1] 15.16. The idea is based on *Muṇḍaka* Up., 3.1.2–3. [2] 12.3.
[3] 9.10: 13.22. [4] 14.27. [5] 17.6: cf. 13.31. [6] 18.61.

attributes of Brahman, nevertheless transcends Brahman as a personal God who wills and thinks and becomes incarnate.

It is now time to consider this new theory of a personal God existing beyond the impersonal Brahman in relationship to the soul in search of liberation and to liberation itself.

Liberation is either described in quite general terms, or in relation to Brahman, or in relation to God. It means reaching the beyond (*param*),[1] the state beyond (*paraṁ sthānam*)[2] or the 'course beyond' (*parā, paramā gati-*)[3] or highest goal as Edgerton translates, which, as we have seen, is a synonym for Brahman. It is an 'imperishable abode' (*padam avyayaṁ*)[4] or one 'free from defect'[5] or again 'supreme success' (*saṁsiddhiṁ paramām*).[6] Sometimes it is referred to as *sukham* 'what is pleasant',[7] or 'what is supremely pleasant',[8] very often as 'peace' or 'cessation' (*śānti-*)[9] which is once equated with 'supreme *nirvāṇa*'.[10] If we accept Rāmānuja's interpretation of *para* as meaning 'beyond the senses', we obtain a clear picture of 'liberation' as being a state of absolute rest and quiet bliss in which there is neither change nor suffering, perfect and timeless peace. This is the condition of Brahman (*brāhmī sthitiḥ*);[11] and so it can be said that the liberated man not only goes to the eternal Brahman[12] or achieves contact with it,[13] it is also conformed to the nature of Brahman (*brahma-bhūyāya kalpate*),[14] becomes very Brahman,[15] and enters the *nirvāṇa* of Brahman.[16]

But what are the liberated man's relations with the Lord? Twice he is said to approach him[17]—and again the Upanisadic word for a pupil approaching his *guru* is used—or more plainly he goes to him.[18] Or again he participates in him through worship[19]—for the sense of participation must still be present in the root *bhaj-* since not only does the worshipper participate in the Lord, but the Lord also participates in him.[20] Thus he is made fit for deification (*mad-*

[1] 3.19. [2] 8.28. [3] 6.45: 8.13: 9.32: 13.28: 16.22. [4] 15.5.
[5] 2.51. [6] 8.15. [7] 5.21. [8] 6.21, 27.
[9] 2.70, 71: 4.39: 5.12, 29: 6.15: 9.31: 18.62. [10] 6.15.
[11] 2.72: cf. 5.19, 20. [12] 4.31: 5.6: 8.24: 13.30. [13] 6.28.
[14] 14.26: 18.53. [15] 5.24: 6.27: 18.54. [16] 5.24–26: 2.72.
[17] 9.28: 10.10. [18] 4.9: 7.23: 9.25, 34: 18.65. 7.19 (*prapad-*). Cf. 7.18 (*āsthitaḥ*).
[19] 7.28: 15.19. [20] 4.11.

bhāvāyo'papadyate),[1] approaches God's nature,[2] or simply goes to it.[3] Once indeed the worshipper is actually said to enter into God.[4] Such, then, is the bare evidence of what the Gītā conceives the relationship of the liberated soul to God to be.

There is one striking difference between the passages that refer to Brahman and those that refer to God: for whereas the liberated man actually becomes Brahman, he merely approaches God, and once only, right at the end of the Gītā where Krishna is expounding to Arjuna 'the most secret doctrine of all', does he speak of his devotee entering into him.

Rāmānuja claims that *ātmabodha* or 'self-realization', so far from being man's highest goal, is, on the contrary, only a prelude to *bhakti*, loving devotion to the Lord. We must now examine the Gītā itself to see whether the text bears him out.

The first six chapters, as we have seen, are mainly concerned with the realization of the self which is identical with Brahman. When God is mentioned in connexion with liberation, it is usually as the object of meditation, and it is only when he is thus meditated on that he can be approached. This is fully in accord with the Hindu belief that you go to or become what you worship, the worshipper of the gods going to the gods, and the worshipper of Krishna, the true God, going to him,[5] for 'what a man's faith is, so is he'.[6] Yet in Chapters V and VI which are directly concerned with the achievement of liberation, God, like the *īśvara* of the *Yogasūtras*, is little more than an object of meditation; he is not yet the higher than Brahman but the only eternally released soul. This seems clearly to be the case in Chapter VI where the meditation on God precedes the intense concentration on the self which leads to liberation. The peace that inheres in God and ends in *nirvāṇa* is contemplated *before* the soul achieves the *nirvāṇa* of Brahman. This is because the God of the sixth chapter is not the living God of the later chapters, but merely the supreme object of contemplation. By contemplating God as the examplar of all released souls because he has never been bound by matter, the soul is then

[1] 13.18. [2] 14.19. [3] 4.10: 8.5–7.
[4] 18.55. [5] 7.23: 9.25. [6] 17.3.

enabled to plunge into its own essence and to realize that itself, at its deepest level, is not bound by matter. This, and not 'the peace that inheres in God', he considers to be 'the ultimate bliss attainable to consciousness and beyond sense' . . . a bliss 'which once attained, he thinks there is no other boon beyond'.[1] This is 'supreme bliss', and the Yogin has now become Brahman.[2] He has found what Martin Buber calls 'the original pre-biographical unity' of the soul in which 'the soul is bound to imagine that . . . it has attained to a union with the primal being or the godhead'.[3] Than this, the Yogin considers, there can be nothing higher; it is the ultimate bliss, and God, his perfect exemplar, therefore fades from his vision. Thus in Chapters V and VI Krishna describes how the Yogin and Sannyāsin attain to liberation which consists in the realization of one's own inmost soul as being eternal, *brahma-bhūta*, that is, existing outside time. Contemplation of God as *the* Eternal Being is useful to obtain this result, but it does not necessarily bring you any nearer to God himself. It is only in the later chapters that man's relation to God is considered, the final relationship between the released soul and God only being described at the very end of the book. The relationship between loving devotion and the state of liberation is, however, touched upon long before this. 'Men who are liberated from the delusion of the pairs of opposites, worship me with firm resolve',[4] Krishna says, and thereby implies that liberation is no more than a necessary first step on the path of the worship of God. Again it is only after one has integrated oneself that one can advance towards God;[5] and even more clearly we read: 'Thou who hast integrated thyself with the Yoga of renunciation, when liberated, wilt draw nigh to me.'[6]

The whole doctrine is clearly summed up at the end of the eighteenth chapter where it is made quite clear that 'to become Brahman' is only a first step on the way to God.

With consciousness cleansed [it says], integrated, restraining himself with firmness, abandoning the objects of sense, sounds and the rest, casting aside desire and hatred, cultivating solitude, eating lightly, with

[1] 6.21–22. [2] 6.27. [3] See above, pp. 17–18.
[4] BG., 7.28. [5] 9.34. [6] 9.28.

voice, body, and mind restrained, ever intent on the Yoga of meditation, cultivating passionless detachment, abandoning the ego, force and pride, desire, anger, and possessiveness, regarding nothing as his own, becalmed, thus is he fitted for becoming Brahman. Having become Brahman, his soul is serene; he neither grieves nor desires. Indifferent to all beings, he receives the supreme devotion to me. Through devotion he comes to know me, who and how great I am in my very essence. Then, knowing me in my essence, he forthwith enters into me. Though he be ever engaged in works, relying on me, he reaches the eternal undying state by my grace.[1]

The Yogin or mystic can, then, reach the condition of Brahman entirely by his own efforts: having purified his soul of all dross, he realizes it as immortal. This is the necessary prerequisite for the reception of the divine grace which leads first to a knowledge of God, and then to communion with him. The Yogin renounces all things in order to find his own soul. This in itself is pleasing to God, even if he has no conception of Krishna as the omnipotent, omniscient Lord; for 'even those who revere the undefinable Imperishable, the unmanifest, omnipresent and unthinkable, the absolutely changeless, immovable and fixed . . . reach me indeed'.[2]

This is 'the most secret doctrine of all', that after liberation man will not only experience immortality as Brahman, but will then, and only then, come to know God and to participate in his life. Yet there is a secret doctrine even higher than this, and that is that God loves man: 'Because I greatly desire thee, therefore will I tell thee thy salvation. Think upon me, worship me, do sacrifice to me, do me reverence. Then shalt thou come to me. This I promise thee truly: for thou art dear to me.'[3]

Thus in the Gītā we see mysticism developing in a way that seems to be the direct opposite of the way it develops in Islam. For Indian mysticism starts from the actual experience that the human soul, when stripped to its ultimate nakedness, is immortal because it has its being outside time. Speculative philosophy then busied itself with this empirical fact; some philosophers alleged that in liberation the soul did nothing more than realize its own individual

[1] 18.51–56. [2] 12.3–4. [3] 18.64–65.

immortality, others maintained that the soul became merged into the infinite as a river is merged into the sea without, however, becoming actually identical with it, and others again declared that the absolutely undifferentiated oneness that the soul experiences in this state meant that the soul was nothing less than the Absolute. The Gītā, which claims to be the revelation of an incarnate God, can admit either the first or the second hypothesis, it cannot admit the third: for it teaches that liberation does not mean the final isolation or destruction of individual personality, much less does it mean that man has realized himself as God, it only means he has realized his own immortality, and that is only the essential preliminary to communion with God. Thus while it is perfectly possible to speak of a man as *brahma-bhūta* 'become Brahman', he can never be *mad-bhūta* 'become Me or God'. He attains, it is true, to *mad-bhāva* 'a divine mode of existence', but there is all the difference in the world between sharing in a divine mode of existence and actually being God: for Brahman in these passages means, as it does in Buddhism from which the expression *brahma-bhūta* seems to derive, a divine mode of existence, whereas God is a Person who is beyond the eternal as much as he is beyond the temporal, and the last message of Krishna to Arjuna is that God loves him and that he is to be entered through love. This is possible, for man himself is said to be a particle of God.[1]

The idea of God's love for man is present for the first time in the Gītā, though it cannot be said that it is prominent in it. Indeed, it must have been extraordinarily difficult for any thinker in the Upaniṣadic tradition to conceive how God, whom at first he regarded as a kind of personalized super-Brahman, unaffected by change, though ultimately causing it, could possibly be subject to feeling of any kind. This traditional view of the supreme Being is still reflected in 9.29 where God, like Brahman, is described as *sama-* 'alike' or 'indifferent' to all creatures; he neither loves nor hates any of them. This is the traditional view, and it is only gradually that the later chapters modify it. In the later part of the book, however, we are told that it is out of compassion for those

[1] 15.7.

who meditate lovingly on him that God, while ever remaining impassive in his own eternal nature, destroys the darkness born of ignorance which prevents them from realizing their own eternal souls.[1] It is he who raises souls in bondage out of the 'ocean of the round of death',[2] although it is he himself who 'sets all things in motion as if fixed in a machine'.[3] God's compassion, indeed, seems strangely at variance with his 'lower nature' which forever keeps the wheel of *saṁsāra* going. He reminds us of the 'necessary being' of Avicenna who is obliged by his own nature to create.[4] Krishna too keeps creation going like a vast machine, the wheel of Brahman of the *Śvetāśvatara* Upaniṣad, but what he incessantly does through his 'lower nature' or supernatural power (*māyā*) he undoes by his grace. God is forever retrieving particles of his higher nature from enslavement in his lower nature, but this constitutes no absolute dualism as in the Manichaean system which is in some ways comparable, for *sub specie aeternitatis* God remains always impassive and one, but in so far as he ensnares creation within his 'lower nature', he is eternally performing a kind of cosmic Yoga, striving to integrate in his eternal essence those particles of him which are temporarily lost. *Pralaya* or the return of the cosmos to its primal state of unity is God's *samādhi* just as liberation for the individual soul is the integration of all the bodily faculties in the 'pre-biographical unity' of the immortal soul. Man, then, aspiring to liberation is merely imitating God's ever-recurring tendency to absorb what he emanates back into himself; and it is because the aspirant for liberation is in this respect imitating a necessary tendency in God that God holds him dear; for it is not the man who loves his neighbour that the Lord esteems, but rather the man who has reached what St. François de Sales called 'la sainte indifférence', 'undisturbed by the world, . . . uninvolved in any enterprise, . . . unaffected by love or hate, . . . treating friend and foe equally, . . . content with his lot, . . . compassionate and friendly to all though caring for none'.[5] None of

[1] 10.11. [2] 12.7. [3] 18.61.

[4] See L. Gardet, *La Pensée religieuse d'Avicenne*, Paris, 1951, pp. 48 ff.

[5] BG., 12.13–20.

this advances us very far beyond the Upaniṣadic view of God or Brahman—God merely puts the seal of his approval on the classical ideal of utter detachment from all worldly things. There is no positive content in this *prīti*, this affection, whatever: it is certainly not what we mean by love.

Now, it would seem that Krishna, when he is imparting a new doctrine in the Gītā, indicates this by referring to it as *guhyatama-* 'most secret'. Thus the doctrine proclaimed in Chapter IX, which first introduces *bhakti* and presents Krishna as the sole true object of worship, is described as *guhyatama-*. Again the quite new doctrine that God transcends Brahman, the 'absolutely changeless and imperishable', and as *puruṣottama*, the 'absolutely supreme Person', transcends all other beings described as 'Person' including the 'primal Person' of the *Puruṣasūkta*, is once more described as *guhyatama-*. When the author comes to the end of Chapter XVIII, having twice used the superlative, he is somewhat at a loss to find words for a doctrine he considers even more amazing than all that had gone before. The purport of this doctrine which, in order to emphasize its yet greater importance, he calls *guhyād guhyatama-*, 'more secret than the secret', is that the soul, after it 'becomes Brahman' at liberation, has yet further joys to experience, for though already enjoying the bliss of its eternal being, it will now enter into its Lord. Yet even this is not Krishna's 'most secret doctrine of all'[1] which is his 'ultimate word'. This, his absolutely final word, because the most secret of all, is that Arjuna is not only beloved (*priya-*), but is also positively desired (*iṣṭa-*) by him. This, the closing section of the last chapter of the Gītā, forms the culmination of the whole book, the purpose of which would thus seem to have been fourfold—first to demonstrate that there exists a personal power beyond even the impersonal and 'imperishable eternal', second that the proper relationship of man to God, whether in bondage or in the freedom of liberation, is one of humble adoration, thirdly that liberation, 'to become Brahman', is not the ultimate aim of existence but is only the essential purification of the human soul that precedes its approach to God,

[1] 18.64.

fourthly that the proper relationship between the human soul and God is one of love.

It is perhaps not unprofitable to compare this 'most secret of all' doctrines proclaimed by the Gītā to the 'secret doctrine' of Ghazālī 'to explain which would be unlawful innovation (*bid'at*)'.[1] For Ghazālī this secret doctrine would appear to be the actual identity of the human soul with God, the *Anā'l-ḥaqq*, 'I am the Truth', of Ḥallāj. For the author of the Gītā the *ahaṁ brahmā'smi*, 'I am Brahman', of the Upaniṣads was already a commonplace. What for him is secret and therefore new was that though the human soul is Brahman, that is, eternal in essence as a river and the sea are both one as being water, it is distinct from God who is beyond Brahman and therefore for the first time has the opportunity of loving him and being loved by him. Ghazālī, on the other hand, for fear of being convicted of fearful heresy, dare not say what he believes to be true, namely that he has found the One which is beyond the creator God and with which the human soul is, in the last analysis, identical. In sharp contradistinction to him the author of the Gītā says—and he can scarcely believe it—that there is indeed a loving God *beyond* the undifferentiated unity of Brahman. The Hindus knew, from the immemorial practice of Yoga techniques, that it can be shown to be a fact of experience that the human soul has changeless being outside time, and they speculated on the relationship of this state of being to the Brahman which they regarded as being the changeless substrate of the external world, but it is only in the Gītā that they reach the conclusion, through a divine revelation, that there is a Person who transcends even the eternal Brahman and the eternal soul. The Muslims were taught, again through divine revelation, that there is a personal God and he is alone eternal, yet this seemed to be proved false by the basic experience of their own mystics who claimed to have passed out of time. Thus, since they had no concept corresponding to Brahman or *nirvāṇa*, they could only conclude that man, in his deepest ground, *was* God. How they related their experiences to their theology will be the subject of our last four lectures.

[1] *KS.*, ii, 898.

In orthodox Islam, as opposed to the philosophers and those later Ṣūfīs who were influenced by the Neo-Platonism of the philosophers, there was, as we have seen, nothing that corresponded to the Hindu conception of Brahman. Hinduism, however, starts with the idea of an impersonal Absolute, Brahman, and only later advances towards the idea of a personal God. Even in the Gītā the distinction is so ambiguously made that most modern scholars have seen no clear distinction between the two. For Śaṅkara Brahman was the One, the Absolute, and absolutely indivisible; and God, the Lord, in his system, corresponds almost exactly to the Nous of the Neo-Platonists. He is the 'mass of wisdom' of the *Māṇḍūkya* Upaniṣad (§ 5) which is at the same time the 'Lord of all' and the 'knower of all'. In both systems God is the first and only product of the One, for, according to them, from One only one can proceed. For Śaṅkara, however, Brahman, the One, alone truly exists, and the mystic, in en-stasy, as Louis Gardet calls it, experiences this one absolutely undifferentiated being, apart from which, he now thinks he realizes, nothing at all, not even God, can claim existence: he is Brahman in the fullest sense. From the absolute point of view God does not exist, but from the relative point of view he is seen to be the first evolute from the One, the creator and sustainer of the world and omnipotent Lord. But even from the relative point of view he must be regarded as subordinate to the wholly undifferentiated and inactive Brahman. In this Śaṅkara faithfully follows the *Māṇḍūkya* Upaniṣad and interprets all other Upaniṣadic texts in this sense. For him, it is clear, the experience of liberation is one of absolute unity—a unity, indeed, so absolute that all else must be seen as illusion. 'The soul', and here I must quote Buber again, so extraordinarily relevant is what he says in this context, 'willingly imagines *and indeed is bound to imagine* (mine once did it) that it has attained to a union with a primal being or the godhead.' Rāmānuja, like Buber, utterly denies that any such inference is justifiable.

For him, as for the Sāṁkhya, there exist an unlimited number of individual souls, the sum-total of which constitutes Brahman.[1]

[1] Rāmānuja (R.) on BG., 8.3.

Liberation means no more than the soul's realization of its own true nature which is eternal—what Buber calls the 'original unity' of oneself which 'is hidden unchanged beneath all biographical change'. Rāmānuja interprets liberation as the *Yogasūtras* do, as the isolation of the soul in its essence: he does not interpret it as meaning a merging into Brahman as a vaster spiritual unity, for Brahman is merely the 'soul-thing'[1] or 'category of existence which characterizes the soul'. For Rāmānuja what we call created or contingent being and what Avicenna would call possible being is neatly divisible into the spiritual and the material, the eternal and the temporal, or, to use the Indian terminology, the imperishable and the perishable. The first consists of souls, the second of matter in the Marxian sense of that word, namely, the subtrate not only of all change and motion, but also of all thinking and feeling. Soul and matter, however, are both dependent on God as our own bodies are dependent on our souls. Together, then, they may be regarded as the body of God,[2] and this view of the relationship of the created all to God is consistently maintained by Rāmānuja throughout his writings. Alternatively the two categories of created being are thought of as the intelligent or conscious (*cit*) and the non-intelligent (*acit*),[3] and these may exist independently or apart. Thus the kingdom of God is divided into three different abodes, corresponding perhaps to the three steps of Viṣṇu, the abode of unconscious matter, the abode of conscious spirit and the abode of beings which are a compound of the two.[4] The three abodes, then, are spirit, matter, and beings partaking of both, which, in Rāmānuja's scheme of things, means liberated souls, inanimate matter, and living human beings and animals.

The soul of its nature is eternal and timeless[5] and not susceptible to change. Being a purely spiritual thing, it is indivisible[6] and of the same substance as God:[7] it is pure consciousness (*cit*) and as such unthinkable.[8] Its essence is knowledge and bliss.[9] But because it is all these things, it should not be supposed that souls, when

[1] *ātma-vastu-*: R. on BG., 5.19.
[2] R. on BG., 3.30, etc.
[3] R. on BG., 2.17, etc.
[4] R. on BG., 8.21: 15.17.
[5] R. on BG., 2.20, etc.
[6] R. on BG., 2.18.
[7] R. on BG., 4.35.
[8] R. on BG., 2.25.
[9] R. on BG., 6.44.

liberated from their corporeal tenement, are all identical. The world is not pervaded by one world-soul, but is inhabited by a multitude of individual souls. Thus when the Gītā speaks of seeing all things in one's self, it does not mean that one's own soul comprises all creation as the pantheists would hold, but that there exists 'an identity between yourself and other creatures when divested of all material adjuncts (*prakṛti*) in that they all have one form—consciousness'.[1] This is all that is meant when it is said that Brahman is the same in all creatures;[2] it merely means that as 'soul-thing' it is the stuff of all souls. Similarly when it is said that the soul is omnipresent,[3] it means no more than that it is more subtile than all the evolutes of Nature and only in this sense can it be said to pervade them. Rāmānuja does not seem to use the obvious argument that the soul is omnipresent because it is literally immeasurable, not thinkable in spatial terms. 'Seeing all things in one's soul and one's soul in all things',[4] which is a common experience of nature mystics and has been fully dealt with by William James in his *Varieties of Religious Experience* in his chapter on mysticism and by myself in *Mysticism, Sacred and Profane*, does not mean that one's soul and the All are, in some inexplicable way and at the deepest level of consciousness, identical; it means that one sees one's soul as having the same 'form' as all ensouled things: there is identity of spiritual essence but diversity of persons, if we may apply Christian terminology to a very different set of ideas. Thus 'when one has experienced one soul, one has experienced the whole soul-stuff (*ātma-vastu-*) because there is an identity of substance between them (*tatsāmyāt*)'.[5]

It is true that souls are eternal and as such have their being outside space and time, and this much they have in common with God; but this participation in the divine nature is not apparent to them so long as they inhabit a body. The soul's connexion with the body is not illusory as Śaṅkara held, but real,[6] and is caused by God's *māyā* which does not mean 'illusion',[7] but God's mode of operation throughout the material universe.[8] The embodied

[1] R. on BG., 4.35. [2] Cf. BG., 5.19. [3] BG., 2.24. [4] Ibid., 6.29.
[5] R. on BG., 6.29. [6] R. on BG., 7.14. [7] Ibid. [8] R. on BG., 18.61.

human soul is not created, for the idea of creation out of nothing is foreign to all Hinduism; from all pre-eternity it has been transmigrating from body to body, and it is only on liberation that its links with matter are finally severed. With liberation it enters into a new form of existence; it passes from that 'abode' or section of the kingdom of God in which the conscious and the unconscious are combined, into the 'highest abode'[1] of God which is Brahman, where all is pure consciousness and timeless bliss. This is *ātma-darśana*- the 'vision or direct experience of the soul'[2] which, by making the soul aware of its own timeless substance, enables it to realize timeless substance itself, that is, Brahman as such.

We have seen that the soul's connexion with a body is regarded as existing from pre-eternity, and it is important here to distinguish between our two uses of the word 'eternity'. It can either mean time without beginning and without end or it can mean a state of being where time simply does not exist. These two modes of existence for which we indiscriminately use the word 'eternity' are, of course, totally distinct and very nearly mutually exclusive. The first the Indians call *saṁsāra*, the second *brahman* or *nirvāṇa*: God alone, according to Rāmānuja, transcends them both. The soul imprisoned in *saṁsāra* must strive to be liberated therefrom, but it may well be asked how it ever became so enmeshed since God is all-powerful and, according to Rāmānuja, full of loving-kindness.[3] God, it is said,[4] 'is the cause of the emanation of the souls of the gods, etc., but the principal cause of the diversity that exists among the gods and other creatures is the different potencies engendered by the past actions of already emanated souls'. This is a *regressus ad infinitum*, for creation, in the Hindu system, is cyclic. The world is for ever and ever emanated from and reabsorbed into the deity or, in Rāmānuja's system, into the body of the deity. Are the 'potencies engendered by past actions' to be regarded as derived from God or not? If so, God must be responsible for any evil thing those potencies may lead to: but Rāmānuja will not have this, because his God is wholly devoid of any evil quality.[5] As

[1] BG., 8.21: 10.12. [2] R. on BG., 2.53, 60, etc. [3] See R. on BG., 6.47.
[4] R. on BG., 4.14. [5] Cf. R.'s introduction to BG.

there is no beginning to *saṁsāra*, there never was a time when human souls were not conditioned by these 'potencies engendered by their past actions',[1] and these are only indirectly related to God, who surveys impassively the development of the potentialities of Nature which he himself had set in motion.[2] The implication is that these potentialities planted in embodied souls by God in pre-eternity were free to develop as they wished, and that God is thereby not responsible for their development in *saṁsāra*. 'Nature, which depends on me,' says Rāmānuja's commentary, 'is in accordance with the *karma* of souls; I, whose will is [always] true, survey it as an overseer, [but it is] Nature which produces the world of moving and unmoving creatures. The world is kept going by reason of my supervision of it in conformity with the *karma* of souls. My lordly power . . . consists in my sovereignty, my willing what is real, and my freedom from cruelty and all defects whatsoever.'[3] Although the Gītā says time and again that God, through the intermediary of the three *guṇas* or 'strands' that pervade all Nature,[4] is the sole real agent, Rāmānuja exempts him from all responsibility for evil by attributing it to the 'potencies engendered by the past actions' of embodied souls. *Mutatis mutandis* this is not unlike the Christian doctrine of original sin.

The *Yogasūtras* and Buddhism had taught that liberation is within the grasp of everyone if he will but make the effort. Rāmānuja denies this, saying that without divine grace it would not be possible to make the immense effort required to conquer the lower self,[5] and the Yogin who seeks liberation without first fixing his mind on God is heading for mental breakdown.[6] God is no longer simply an object, the contemplation of which will help one to liberation; it is God who enables the Yogin so to concentrate the mind by purifying it with his saving touch.[7] True, there are people whose spiritual development is such that they can of their own resources enjoy the experience of their own immortal souls,[8] but this must be considered as the result of God's grace in former

[1] *prācīna-karma-śakti-*. [2] BG., 9.9. [3] R. on BG., 9.10.
[4] BG., 3.15–30. [5] R. on BG., 2.61–62. [6] R. on BG., 2.63.
[7] R. on BG., 6.15. [8] R. on BG., 3.17.

lives. No man attains even to the fruition of his own soul without the action of the divine mercy: without that he is forever caught in the relentless machine of God's *māyā*.[1]

Māyā is the power by which the soul is bound to the body, and since *māyā* belongs to God, he is the cause of bondage as well as of liberation. But Rāmānuja also calls it God's wisdom (*jñāna-*) and his will (*saṅkalpa-*);[2] more often he thinks of it as a divine game[3] which he plays without deriving any benefit from it for himself.[4] That Rāmānuja, along with the later sacred texts of the Hindus, should regard the whole world-process of bondage and release as a 'game' which the deity plays with individual souls, may seem surprising; but it should be remembered that the final upshot of this game is not only the perfect bliss which liberation brings, but also beyond this the even intenser happiness of union with an absolutely perfect being who at the same time loves you with a consuming passion.

For Rāmānuja God is the fully personalized Viṣṇu who is also *parabrahman*, the supreme Brahman; he is possessed of all desirable qualities in their perfection, and the traditional epithet *nirguṇa*, 'without qualities', applied to the Absolute and also to God *qua parabrahman* is explained as 'devoid of evil qualities'.[5] As well as being omnipotent and omniscient he is compassionate and tender in his love for men.[6] So far from being impassive, he cannot bear separation from his elect. 'Since I cannot bear to be separated from those [who love me],' Krishna is made to say, 'I choose them out. I bring to fruition their acts of devotion designed, as they are, to enable them to possess me. I remove whatever obstacles are in their way and inspire them with intense love for me.'[7] Thus God first helps man to achieve his own liberation which enables him to enjoy the timelessness of his own soul—and this is a godlike condition (*mad-bhāva-*), on the attainment of which he may be led to think that he himself is God so profound and seemingly final is the bliss that he enjoys.[8] This, however, is not the end, for God who

[1] BG., 18.61. [2] R. on BG., 4.6. [3] R. on BG., 7.14. [4] R. on BG., 7.12.
[5] R.'s introduction to BG., etc. [6] See R. on BG., 6.47, etc. [7] R. on BG., 8.14.
[8] Cf. BG., 6.22 'Once he has possessed himself of [the vision of the soul], he thinks there can be no higher boon'.

himself is 'that desire which is not opposed to righteousness',[1] rekindles the fire of desire in the tranquil soul and causes it to be directed exclusively to him. This is something quite new in Hindu mysticism, for hitherto the eradication of desire in any form had been regarded as a *sine qua non* without which liberation could never be achieved. The idea that, after the soul had liberated itself from every attachment, had realized its total autarchy and independence of all things, and had thus achieved a state of bliss beyond which it cannot even conceive that there might be something yet more exquisite—the idea that after all this the soul should once again be set aflame with a passion of longing, must have been regarded almost as madness by the earlier mystics who regarded it as an indisputable axiom that liberation is the final goal beyond which it is impossible to go. Having become Brahman, which hitherto had been synonymous with the highest principle, the eternal, unchanging source of all things, what further step could there possibly be? The whole position of the Brahmavādins is challenged by Rāmānuja: their interpretation of liberation as meaning that the soul realizes itself as the One and unfractionable spiritual Being, is false. The soul may think that, in realizing its own 'undifferentiable unity', it thereby realizes itself as the One and the All. This, according to Rāmānuja, is a vulgar error, for the soul realizes itself as one single *śeṣa* or fraction of an infinite Being that vastly transcends it and which is its sovereign Lord (*śeṣin*),[2] to whom it owes its very existence. Once the liberated soul becomes conscious of God, on the other hand, it is once again galvanized with desire. Already it has become 'like God', it now yearns to be united with God himself in a transport of passionate love, and it is quite unable to bear separation from him for a single moment.[3] The mystic no longer attaches importance to his godlike condition which has transported him outside time nor to the sense of power that he derives therefrom, he is interested in one thing only and that is God.[4] Through God's grace he can now possess God as a lover possesses his beloved; from utter detachment he falls again into an attachment more passionate than anything he had known

[1] BG., 7.11. [2] R. on BG., 9.4. [3] R. on BG., 6.47. [4] R. on BG., 8.14.

before, his 'mind cleaves to God', and without him he is no longer secure in his own immortal soul,[1] and thus he at last becomes united to his immortal Lord. And even after fruition this love never leaves him, for 'once one has achieved possession of God, this never fails'.[2] To know, to love, and to be united with God is man's final goal. Liberation, indeed, is an excellent thing, but compared to the love of God it is as a mustard-seed beside Mount Meru,[3] and the cultivation of one's own immortal soul is contemptuously dismissed as fit for those only who do not know how to love.[4]

The kernel of Rāmānuja's teaching, then, is this: to realize the nature of one's immortal soul as being unconditioned by time and space and to see all things in the soul and the soul in all things, is inherent in all men naturally, and it is a godlike state. But this is not to know God: to know God is to love him, and without a passionate and all-consuming love there can be neither communion nor union with the beloved. Any mystical state which is one of undifferentiated oneness is the experience that one individual soul enjoys of its own individual self: it has nothing to do with God. Thus in any form of mystical experience from which love is absent, there can be no question of God: he is absent too. To interpret the experience as being identical with the One or the All is absurd; beguiled by the beauty and apparent infinity of its own deep nature, the liberated soul—so Rāmānuja holds—mistakes the mustard-seed for Mount Meru, the drop for the sea.

[1] R. on BG., 8.15.
[2] R. on BG., 9.2
[3] R. on BG., 6.47.
[4] R. on BG., 12.11–12.

V

Vedānta in Muslim Dress

IN our brief study of Indian mysticism we saw how slowly it advanced towards the idea of a personal God who was distinct from the human soul, and how, even in its theistic development, it did not at first move forward from a passive contemplation of the Lord in his solitary perfection to an active love of him. In religions which are fully monotheistic from the start the clear distinction which we have been able to draw between the mysticism of the complete isolation of the soul in its timeless and eternal ground, that of merging in the All as a drop of water in the sea, and that of a loving communion and union with God, cannot always be drawn with anything like precision: for whereas the Indian sage starts from the timeless essence of the human soul, which he claims is a fact verifiable by experience, the monotheist starts with the idea of a transcendent God who is creator of all things including the human soul, who is made known by revelation, who operates in time, and who demands from man absolute obedience to the laws he has revealed. Of the monotheistic creeds it is only Christianity that builds a bridge between God, the Eternal, and man, the temporal, in the shape of Jesus Christ, the God-Man, who in his dual nature is fully representative of both kinds of existence. Man is brought into relationship with God through Christ who, by his sacrifice on the Cross, demonstrates God's indefectible love for man. For the Christian to partake of eternity means to participate in the being of God, and this is achieved by the grace of God which raises man up in passionate longing from his merely human estate to a divine form of existence in which he is fitted to share in God's nature and to love him as the source of his being and his Redeemer.

Since the proper relationship between God and man is one of love, and since God is himself defined as love, it follows that the soul that has been purified of sin can enjoy a relationship with God so close as almost to amount to fusion. The creature abandons himself entirely to the will of God and allows God to act through him: there is a complete unity of will though not of essence. In the state of transforming union the mystic will feel himself so transfused and penetrated by the love of God that he interprets this complete alteration of his being as meaning that he now is, in a sense, God by participation, so completely has he abandoned all thought of self. The resulting experience may then be expressed in almost monistical terms, yet the monotheistic mystic is always aware that however transfused and transformed he may be, he never can become identical with God if only for the simple reason that he can never attain omnipotence and omniscience.

Obviously the layman who is a stranger to mystical experience is in no position to distinguish between the various 'states' of the mystic; but comparison between the Indian experience and that of the monotheistic mystics should put us on our guard. Above all the Indian contention that the human soul is, at least potentially, an extra-temporal being should be taken at least as seriously as the monotheistic assertion that there is no eternal being but God. In fact it must be taken rather more seriously, for whereas there is overwhelming evidence that human beings can, and do, from time to time succeed in transcending time itself and realize a form of being in which death is 'an almost laughable impossibility', it will never be possible to prove to the sceptic that the God of mystical experience is other than an ever-recurring element eternally present in the constitution of man himself. Thus Jung, following Leuba, persists in regarding all mystical manifestations as being due to the activities of what he calls the archetype of the self which, like the Indian *ātman*, is the true centre of the human personality. This term includes 'the totality of the psyche in so far as this manifests itself in an individual. The self is not only the centre, but also the circumference that encloses consciousness and the -un conscious; it is the centre of this totality, as the ego is the centre of consciousness'.[1] The Indian *ātman* too is the centre and circumference of the personality, the hub and the felly, as the *Bṛhadāraṇyaka* Upaniṣad puts it:[2] and both the Upaniṣad and Jung would agree that this 'self' is identical with the 'God' of mystical experience, and cannot be distinguished from him empirically.[3] Yet though Jung goes all the way with the Upaniṣads in that he speaks of the self as the 'One who dwells in [man], whose form has no knowable boundaries, who encompasses him on all sides, fathomless as the abysms of the earth and vast as the sky',[4] he does not draw the metaphysical conclusion that the Upaniṣads in the main do, he does not identify the 'form that has no knowable boundaries' within with infinity without. For him every man has within him his own infinity, and this is in no way correlated with that of his neighbour or with a God external to man (if such a God exists). Each soul is a cosmos unto itself, not *the* cosmos. In this respect Jung aligns himself with the Sāṁkhya-Yoga and Rāmānuja: human souls have a common 'infinite' and eternal substrate, what Rāmānuja calls the category of *ātman*, but they are nonetheless separate ontologically—microcosms, each a universe of its own with its own presiding deity, the *ātman* or soul of each single individual.

In the Indian tradition Rāmānuja was the first to claim unequivocally that the realization of the *ātman* within one, 'the One who dwells within, whose form has no knowable boundaries', is not only not the realization of the One God who is the creator and sustainer of the universe, but only the first stage from which it is possible to approach him. For him the experience of release, in which the soul drops out of time, was a reality, but Krishna, as the living God and Lord, was also a reality, and the two realities had to be brought into relation. For Śaṅkara and the monists the transcending of time and the realization of undifferentiable unity which accompanies it, represented man's final goal beyond which it was

[1] C. G. Jung, *The Integration of the Personality* (Eng. trans.), London, 1940, p. 96.
[2] 2.5.15.
[3] C. G. Jung, *Answer to Job* (Eng. trans.), London, 1954, p. 177.
[4] Ibid., p. 180.

impossible to proceed, because man is not only his own microcosmos, he is the cosmos *tout court*, or rather the eternal substrate of an unreal because perishable cosmos which is an illusory projection of himself. Beyond this sole self-existent reality, plainly, no further progress would be possible. Rāmānuja concedes that with liberation one realizes oneness and eternity, but he insists that the soul must be shaken out of this passive contemplation of self and brought into the presence of God, who is other than self, by means of a passion of love.

Jung, I think, is therefore wrong when he says that we cannot distinguish between the archetype of the self and the God-image, by which he means God as he makes himself known in mystical experience; for in that type of experience in which God and the soul are regarded as separate beings the relationship between the two is always one of love, whereas in the Yogic type of mysticism of both the *Yogasūtras* and the first six chapters of the Bhagavad-Gītā there is no question of the love of one person for another, but only an *askesis* of self-integration and self-realization in which there is no union of one with another, but only the extrication of an eternal element in the soul from all that is not eternal. Yoga is the realization of a single spiritual essence and in the Gītā means exactly what Jung means by integration (the word *yoga* itself means 'joining'), whereas mystical union in the Christian sense is the union of one spiritual essence with another, the most natural simile for which is that of sexual union. Hence in Christian and most of Muslim mysticism love is the highest manifestation of man's relationship to God and without it no union is possible, whereas in Yogic mysticism release is not achieved by love, but by intensive introspection and the mastering of sense and mind. The achievement of the Bhagavad-Gītā was that it brought the God who is the object of meditation into relationship with the God who is the object of passionate love, but between meditation on God, which is merely a means of achieving liberation and the leap towards the God who is the object of the soul's desire, the Gītā places release. In Christian and Muslim mysticism this stage is never made quite clear, for the idea of liberation is foreign to both systems. The Ṣūfīs, however, were plainly familiar with the experience, and Qushayrī speaks of the Ṣūfī who is *ibn waqti-hi*, 'the man of his time',[1] for whom the future does not exist, hence 'he neither fears nor sorrows'. This presented them with a problem, for if it is possible to experience a form of existence in which there is no time, does it not follow that the soul itself is uncreated since creation implies the existence of time? This view was already present in Sarrāj's time[2] and was rejected by the orthodox as being plainly heretical. In rejecting this view, which is basic to all Indian mysticism, however, the Ṣūfīs caused themselves unnecessary difficulties, for it is perfectly possible to admit that the soul may reach a state of consciousness in which past and future become meaningless without drawing the conclusion that what experiences this timeless state of being is necessarily uncreated; for the nature of such timeless existence is wholly outside the scope of our ordinary categories. Ghazālī, as we have seen, attempted to solve the problem by positing a world of spiritual substances not susceptible to measurement alongside the corporeal world. Such substances would necessarily transcend not only space but also time since time itself is, according to Aristotle and the Muslim philosophers, the measurement of motion. Thus by rejecting, at least in their exoteric teaching, any possible connexion between God the Eternal Creator, and his creation, which has its being in space and time, they deprived themselves of any rational explanation of the experience of transcending time: they could only say that creaturely existence was thereby annihilated and that God alone remained. This is, in fact, a rather silly quibble, for there must be consciousness of the experience, otherwise it would not be an experience, and consciousness is individual since it occurs in one person at any given time and place. The Ṣūfī in ecstasy was forced by the logic of his own position, to say, with Ḥallāj, *Anā'l-ḥaqq*, 'I am the Truth or God', because he had passed beyond time, and in his theology there is no timeless entity but God. They were not in a position to make the distinction between an

[1] Qushayrī, p. 119.
[2] Sarrāj, pp. 222–3.

extra-temporal soul and an extra-temporal God which came quite naturally to Rāmānuja.

Islam, we would have thought, was not a congenial soil in which a mystical tradition of any kind could take root. Ṣūfism met with the hostility of the orthodox theologians from the beginning, and both Dhū'l-Nūn of Egypt and Abū'l-Ḥussayn al-Nūrī[1] are said to have been arraigned before the Caliph on suspicion of heresy. The theologians maintained that there could be no love between God and man because there can only be love between like and like, and God is totally unlike any created thing:[2] when the Qur'ān speaks of love, then it means no more than obedience. Yet the idea that not only is love between God and man possible, but also that it can be experienced here and now, very much made its way into Ṣūfism, and it is already fundamental in Rābi'a, Muḥāsibī, and Dhū'l-Nūn,[3] who flourished at the end of the second and the beginning of the third centuries of the Hijra. For Dhū'l-Nūn love is an intense yearning of the soul, and he is not afraid to use the word *shawq* meaning 'passionate longing' to make his meaning clear. 'There are four doors [to wisdom],' he says, 'first fear, then hope, then love, then passionate longing',[4] and the way to win God's approval is to shape one's character in conformity with his 'beautiful attributes'.[5] This enables the soul to enjoy the fellowship of God which is eternal bliss;[6] but such fellowship cannot be achieved by man's own unaided efforts, for it is God who chooses his lovers from pre-eternity:

> Special souls has he chosen for his love;
> These did he choose before time ever was.
> He chose them before he brought forth his creation,
> And they are depositories of wisdom and manifestation.[7]

The soul so chosen renounces its own will and its very self entirely, it loves God's will only, however much suffering it may

[1] See above, p. 3.

[2] *KS.*, ii, 943.

[3] See the articles on the latter two in Abū Nu'aym's *Ḥilyat al-Awliyā*, ix, 331–95, x, 3–4 and 73–110.

[4] *Ḥilya*, ix, 378. [5] Ibid., p. 376. [6] Ibid., p. 360. [7] Ibid., p. 355.

be caused thereby. So great is its love for him that there is no room for the love of any thing beside him: 'not even the measure of a grain of mustard-seed remains empty of him, and nothing remains in them but he'.[1] This does not mean that the individual mystic as such ceases to exist as some Ṣūfīs were later to maintain: for 'nothing that God sees can die any more than anything that sees God can live. For God's life is abiding (*bāqī*), and abiding in it is he who sees it'.[2] Dhū'l-Nūn, then, like Rāmānuja regards passionate longing as the means by which the soul journeys to God; and, again like Rāmānuja, though with more certain an emphasis, he insists that the initiative must, in the last instance be God's. Moreover, he is chary of using words for 'union' to denote the soul's relationship to God; he prefers to speak of the vision of God.

For Muḥāsibī too it is God who kindles the fire of love in man's heart. 'Passionate longing wells up in the heart', he says, 'only through the light of [God's] love; and when God kindles this lamp in the heart of one of his servants, it can only burn on in the ravines of the heart if the heart itself craves light from him.'[3] The mystical union is the result of God's grace in the first instance, and its continuance is only made possible by the willing acceptance of his grace on the part of man; but all the early Muslim mystics agree that the acceptance of grace implies a total abandonment of self and an exclusive devotion to God to the complete exclusion of all created things.

In her book, *Early Mysticism in the Near and Middle East*, Dr. Margaret Smith has shown how indebted early Muslim mysticism is, with its overwhelming emphasis on the love of God, to the thought of the great Christian mystics of a slightly earlier time, and, in view of the grave suspicion with which this doctrine of love was regarded by the orthodox theologians, her conclusions cannot be seriously disputed. What, however, is much more disputable is the possible influence of Indian mysticism on Ṣūfism.

Dhū'l-Nūn and Muḥāsibī, as we have seen, never tire of speaking of God's love for man and man's love for God, but they avoid using the word *tawḥīd*, 'union', to indicate the mystical union.

[1] Ibid., pp. 353. [2] Ibid., p. 373. [3] *Ḥilya*, x, 78.

Dhū'l-Nūn, after describing the flight of the soul in passionate longing to God in which 'it passes through the realm of *malakūt* (spirit) more swiftly than the blowing of the wind', says only that the soul is then 'God's and with God'.[1] Yet at the very time that Dhū'l-Nūn had brought this doctrine of intense mystical love to perfection, very different accents began to be heard in the village of Bisṭām in Western Khorasan. Here was born and flourished a man who was to change the whole tenor of Ṣūfism for better or for worse, for it was he who, for the first time in Islam, dared to make himself equal with the deity: it is he who first said, 'I am He'. The question which scholars have asked themselves for upwards of a century is, did he say this of himself or was it suggested to him by another?

R. A. Nicholson long ago pointed out that Abū Yazīd of Bisṭām might have derived his quite new doctrine of *fanā*, by which he understood the total destruction of the empirical self in God, from his teacher, Abū 'Alī al-Sindī.[2] This view, which was hotly defended by Max Horten,[3] has recently been rejected as not proven by Professor A. J. Arberry.[4] We must, then, once again re-examine the evidence presented both from the Hindu and the Muslim side.

Nicholson maintained that the fact that Abū Yazīd's reputed master was a man from Sind[5] accounted for the doctrines in Abū Yazīd's recorded sayings which seemed to him to be 'certainly' of Indian origin. Arberry, however, considers that the term 'Sindī' may refer to a village called Sind in Khorasan which is recorded by the geographer Yāqūt. Theoretically, of course, it might, but it is rather difficult to believe that the Sind referred to is any other than the province of that name. However that may be, it would seem that this Abū 'Alī was a convert to Islam from another religion, for Abū Yazīd says of him: 'I used to keep company with Abū 'Alī al-Sindī and I used to show him how to perform the obligatory

[1] Ibid., ix, 364.

[2] R. A. Nicholson, *The Mystics of Islam*, London, 1914, p. 17.

[3] *Festgabe Jacobi*, Bonn, 1926, pp. 397–405: *Indische Strömungen in der islamischen Mystik*, I, Heidelberg, 1927, pp. 17–25.

[4] A. J. Arberry, *Revelation and Reason in Islam*, London, 1957, p. 90.

[5] Loc. cit.

duties of Islam, and in exchange he would give me instruction in the divine unity (*tawḥīd*) and in the ultimate truths (*ḥaqā'iq*)'.[1] Abū Yazīd, then, represents himself as learning the 'ultimate truths' about the divine unity from a man who did not even know how to perform the obligatory duties of a Muslim. It seems, then, fairly clear that this man, Abū 'Alī al-Sindī, was a convert from another faith.

What the 'ultimate truths' he taught were are plainly reflected in the sayings of Abū Yazīd with which Sarrāj particularly concerns himself. The most remarkable of these is perhaps the following:

> Abū Yazīd is reported to have said [Sarrāj tells us]: 'Once [God] raised me up and placed me before him, and said to me: "O Abū Yazīd, verily my creation longs to see thee." And I said: "Adorn me with thy unity and clothe me in thine I-ness and raise me up unto thy oneness, so that when thy creatures see me, they may say: 'We have seen thee (i.e. God) and thou art that.' Yet I (Abū Yazīd) will not be there at all." '[2]

Here there is one phrase—'Thou art that'—that is wholly unintelligible in the context. So unintelligible is it indeed that Nicholson, rather than commit himself to writing what seemed to him nonsense, translated: 'and that only Thou mayst be there, not I'. Farīd al-Dīn 'Aṭṭār paraphrased the phrase in Persian as follows: 'Adorn me with thy unity so that when thy creatures see me and look upon thy handiwork, they will have seen the Creator.'[3] 'Aṭṭār thus gives us his own interpretation of what he thinks the phrase ought to mean: the mysterious 'that' is used to mean God. The pronoun 'that' (*dhāka*), of course, is never used in Arabic to mean 'God'. If a pronoun is used, it is always *hūwa*, 'he'. Nicholson's mistranslation of the phrase is proof enough that the phrase 'Thou art that' in the context is wholly unintelligible. The pronoun 'that' (*tat*), however, *is* regularly used in Sanskrit as a synonym for Brahman. We have only to think of the phrase *oṁ tat sat* or the *etad vai tat* ('This is truly that') of the *Kaṭha* Upaniṣad. 'That', indeed, for the Hindu is the normal way of referring to

[1] Sarrāj, p. 177. [2] Ibid., p. 382.
[3] *Tadhkirat al-Awliyā*, i, 174. See Appendix B, I, §§ 320–6.

Brahman as the Absolute, and the phrase *takūnu anta dhāka* is, in fact, a literal translation of the famous phrase of the *Chāndogya* Upaniṣad, *tat tvam asi*, 'Thou art that', which forms the concluding phrase to this most famous of all the *mahāvākyāni* or 'great utterances' of the Upaniṣads. 'That which is the finest essence—this whole [world] has it as its soul (*ātman*). That is Reality. That is the soul. That art thou.'[1] This, presumably, is one of the 'ultimate truths' that Abū Yazīd learnt from his master, Abū 'Alī al-Sindī, and the proof that the phrase is borrowed from a Vedāntin source seems to me to be that, whereas the phrase is utterly foreign to anything Islam had ever taught, in Hinduism it is so commonplace as almost to be banal, so universally familiar would it be to anyone schooled in the teachings of the Upaniṣads. It should further be stressed that the phrase is peculiar to the Vedānta, it is not Buddhist, nor is it paralleled in any other mystical system; you meet with no such bald identification either in Neo-Platonism or in Taoism, or anywhere else. Moreover, the phrase came to the knowledge of Abū Yazīd at a time when the great Śaṅkara had just revived and systematized the Vedānta in its most extreme form in India itself.

Now what distinguishes the unadulterated Vedānta of Śaṅkara from both the Upaniṣads and the *viśiṣṭādvaita* or 'non-duality with a difference' of his successor, Rāmūnuja, is that he concedes reality to the *ātman-brahman* only and dismisses the whole phenomenal world as *māyā*, which for him means 'illusion'. This again is unmistakably reflected in another of the sayings of Abū Yazīd:

'As soon as I reached [God's] unity' [he says], 'I became a bird whose body was of oneness and whose wings were of everlastingness, and I went on flying in the atmosphere of relativity for ten years until I entered into an atmosphere a hundred million times as large; and I went on flying until I reached the expanse of eternity and in it I saw the tree of oneness.' Then [says Sarrāj], he described the soil [in which it grew] its root and branch, its shoots and fruits, and then he said: 'Then I looked, and I knew that all this was deceit.'[2]

[1] *Ch*Up., 6.8 ff.

[2] Sarrāj, p. 384.

This tree seems to be none other than the cosmic tree of the *Kaṭha* Upaniṣad[1] and the Bhagavad-Gītā. Abū Yazīd is represented as describing the soil from which it grew, its roots, branches, shoots, and fruit, but Sarrāj does not tell us how he described them. The Gītā, however, does describe them, root, branches, shoots and all. This is what the Gītā says:

With roots above and branches below the imperishable fig-tree has been declared. Its leaves are the Vedic hymns. Whoso knows it knows the Veda. Below and above extend its branches nourished by the qualities (*guṇas*), and the objects of sense are their sprouts. Below are extended the roots from which arise actions in the world of men.[2]

Thus we can be fairly certain that when Sarrāj says that Abū Yazīd described 'its root and branch, its shoots and fruits', he described these in accordance with the original. This is already striking, but there is more to it than this, for this selfsame tree appears in the *Muṇḍaka*[3] and *Śvetāśvatara*[4] Upaniṣads, and in the latter case it is brought into connexion with *māyā*. This is how the passage reads:

Two birds, closely linked companions, cling to the same tree. One of them eats its sweet fruit, while the other looks on without eating. On the same tree a person, sunken and deluded, grieves at his impotence; when he sees the other, the Lord contented, and his greatness, his grief departs. . . . From that (Brahman) the Master of *māyā* emits the whole [world],—metres, sacrifices, ceremonies, ordinances, the past, the future, and what the Vedas proclaim. In it, by *māyā* the other (the individual) soul is confined. Now one should know that the phenomenal world is *māyā* and that the great Lord is the master of *māyā*.

The two birds are the same as the two persons, the one grieved because bound to matter, the other contented because it enjoys

[1] 6.1.

[2] BG., 15.1–2. Cf. also Śaṇkara's *Viveka-cūḍāmaṇi*, 145: 'Of the tree of *saṁsāra* (phenomenal existence) [the quality of] darkness is the seed, mistaking the body for one's self is the sprout, attachment the tender leaf, action its water, the body the trunk, the vital functions the branches, the senses its twigs, sense-objects its flowers, pain its fruit.' Cf. also *Mahābhārata*, xii, ch. 254.

[3] 3.1.1–3. [4] 4.6–10.

perpetual liberation. What binds the former is *māyā*, God's mysterious power which is at the same time identical with Nature or the phenomenal world. *Māyā*, however, also means 'deceit',[1] and this is precisely how Abū Yazīd describes his own tree of oneness. The Arabic word *khud'a* is in fact an exact and literal translation of the Sanskrit *māyā* which both means 'deceit' and God's mysterious power by which he creates. For Śaṅkara, however, *māyā* meant simply 'illusion', and the word *khud'a* is therefore wholly apposite. We have only to compare the dictionary translations of the two words to see how exactly they correspond. For *māyā* Monier-Williams gives for the classical usage 'illusion, trick, artifice, deceit, deception, fraud, juggling, sorcery, witchcraft', and so on, while for *khad'a* Lane gives 'a single act of deceit, delusion, guile, circumvention or outwitting'. The two words could scarcely correspond more exactly. Moreover, to the best of my knowledge, the world is not described as *khud'a* in any other Ṣūfī text, it does not come naturally and only makes sense if it is seen to be a translation of *māyā*. When the Ṣūfīs speak of the unreality of the world, they speak of it as a dream,[2] or a game,[3] not as deceit.

I have pointed out elsewhere how practically everything in this particular saying of Abū Yazīd can be explained from Indian sources, all of which stand close to the *Śvetāśvatara* Upaniṣad,[4] and I do not wish to repeat my arguments here. I would merely emphasize that in these two sayings of Abū Yazīd there occur two phrases which are simply unintelligible unless viewed against a Hindu Vedāntin background. 'Thou art that' is meaningless in the context unless one is familiar with the *Chāndogya* Upaniṣad, and the reference to the world as 'deceit' is wholly unnatural in Arabic and only appears natural if one knows the various meanings of the word *māyā* in Sanskrit. There is no need to stress the simile of the bird in Abū Yazīd's saying and the two birds in the Upaniṣadic

[1] So clearly in *Praśna* Up., I.16 where it is coupled with *anṛta*- 'unrighteousness'.
[2] E.g. *KS*. ii, 983, 984: Rūmī, *Masnavī*, iv, 3654.
[3] E.g. Rūmī, op. cit., iv, 3666.
[4] See *Indo-Iranian Journal*, i, 294–7.

passage, for the simile of a bird in flight is also a favourite of Dhū'l-Nūn's[1] and may derive from him.

Perhaps of all the sayings of Abū Yazīd that shocked his pious contemporaries, the most shocking was *subḥānī, mā a'ẓama sha'nī*, 'Glory be to me, how great is my glory'.[2] It is very possible, however, that Abū Yazīd never went further than to say *subḥānī*, which is all that Sarrāj[3] records, while Sahlajī reports no less than three versions of this particular logion, and it is therefore probable that the second phrase is in each case a gloss. Besides 'How great is my glory' we also have 'How great is my sovereignty (*sulṭānī*)',[4] and, more striking still, 'I am the Lord Most High',[5] the last of which is also reported as a separate saying.[6] Now *subḥānī*, 'Glory be to me', is absolutely blasphemous to Muslim ears, and nothing remotely comparable is recorded of any of the Ṣūfīs who preceded Abū Yazīd, and once again we find the explanation of it in a Hindu source: for the Sanskrit equivalent of these words occurs in the *Bṛhatsannyāsa* Upaniṣad,[7] where we read *mahyam eva namo namaḥ*, 'Homage, homage to me'.

There is, however, yet another parallel between the sayings of Abū Yazīd and the Upaniṣads. Of Abū Yazīd it is recorded that he said: 'I sloughed off my self as a snake sloughs off its skin: then I looked into my self and lo! I was He.'[8] In this case it is quite true that the metaphor of sloughing off the self as a snake sloughs off its skin might derive from sources other then the Vedānta, for it occurs in the very first stanza of the Buddhist *Suttanipāta*, but the combination of the simile with the statement 'I am He' points to only one possible source. This source is the Vedānta or, more specifically *Bṛhadāraṇyaka* Upaniṣad 4.4.7, 12 where we read:

'As the sloughed off skin of a snake lies on an ant-hill, dead, cast off, so does this body lie. But this incorporeal, immortal spirit is

[1] Abū Nu'aym, *Ḥilyat al-Awliyā*, ix, 364, 385.
[2] Sahlajī, p. 78.
[3] Op. cit., p. 390. Sarrāj is our earliest source (d. A.D. 988).
[4] Sahlajī, p. 111.
[5] Ibid., p. 68.
[6] Ibid., p. 103.
[7] See F. O. Schrader, *The Minor Upaniṣads*, Madras, 1912, i, 257.
[8] Sahlajī, p. 77.

Brahman indeed, is light indeed. . . . If a man should know himself (his *ātman*) and say: "I am He", what could he possibly wish for or desire that would make him cling to the body?'

Once again the resemblance is too close to be fortuitous: there is the same simile of the snake sloughing off its skin and the same conclusion framed in the same words ('I am He', *ayam asmi* in Sanskrit = *anā hūwa* in Arabic) and expressing in the shortest compass the basic doctrine of the non-dualist Vedānta, that is, the absolute identity of the human soul with the Absolute. Moreover, there is further evidence that this logion of Abū Yazīd is directly borrowed from the passage from the *Bṛhadāraṇyaka* we have just quoted, for the saying is preserved not only by Sahlajī but also by Bīrūnī[1]—but with a significant variant; for whereas Sahlajī uses the same word (*nafsī*) for the self sloughed off and the self into which Abū Yazīd looks and which he discovers to be 'He', that is God, Bīrūnī uses *nafsī* in the first instance and *dhātī* ('my essence') in the second.

We saw in an earlier lecture how the Sanskrit word *ātman* is used not only as a reflexive pronoun, but is also pressed into service to mean the immortal soul whether of the individual or the world, that soul as conjoined with a body, and what the Muslims call the *nafs* or lower soul; and we saw that the same ideas appeared in Ṣūfism, but that the Arabic terminology was far more clear and varied. Both accounts of this saying of Abū Yazīd would appear again to be translated from a language which makes no verbal distinction between the concept of *nafs* or 'lower soul' and that of *dhāt*, the eternal spiritual essence of man. Once again, then, the problem finds its solution in the Sanskrit language where *nafsī* and *dhātī* can only be represented by the one word *ātman*- 'self'. Thus we have no less than four instances in the sayings of Abū Yazīd of words or phrases which are either nonsensical or blasphemous or both in the Arabic-Muslim setting, but which are closely paralleled in Sanskrit Vedāntin texts where alone they fit. Thus not only are Abū Yazīd's ideas pure Vedānta, the very words and phrases he uses only make sense when seen in a Sanskrit context.

[1] *India*, ed. Sachau, p. 43; translation, i, 87–88.

Thus the evidence for Vedāntin influence on Abū Yazīd is not merely the fact that his master was a man from Sind, but the inexplicability of many of his utterances except against a Vedāntin background. It is this internal evidence that makes it overwhelmingly probable that Abū Yazīd's master, Abū 'Alī, was a native of what everyone normally understands by Sind and not of a village in Khorasan: for wherever this man, Abū 'Alī, came from, the 'ultimate truths' he seems to have imparted to Abū Yazīd are pure Vedānta and nothing else. It thus seems reasonably certain that Abū Yazīd was directly influenced by a totally alien stream of mysticism and that it was through him that Vedāntin ideas became part and parcel of later Islamic mysticism.

Abū Yazīd was not an educated man[1] and showed the greatest contempt for book-learning.[2] It is therefore probable that his master, Abū 'Alī, instructed him verbally, and Abū Yazīd himself may have been quite ignorant of the origin of those outrageous theories he made so thoroughly his own. This would seem to be the usual way in which foreign ideas percolated into Islam, and we may assume that just as the sayings of Christ and St. Paul passed into Islam, presumably by word of mouth, and were then transmuted into traditions of the Prophet,[3] so did logia from the Upaniṣads and other Hindu writings pass into Islam by the mouth primarily of Abū Yazīd.

It is known that Buddhist material passed into Islam in a literary form, and Dr. D. M. Lang has done much to illuminate the filiation of these ideas, often through a Manichaean medium.[4] Apart from the various versions of *Barlaam and Josaphat* we find the celebrated Buddhist story of the blind men and the elephant from the *Udāna* reappearing in Tawḥīdī[5] and Ghazālī,[6] and later in

[1] Sahlajī, p. 53.

[2] Ibid., p. 116.

[3] See *Indo-Iranian Journal*, i, 287–8.

[4] D. M. Lang, *The Wisdom of Balahvar*, London, 1957, pp. 24–29.

[5] *Kitāb al-Muqābasāt*, Cairo, 1929, pp. 259–60. Cf. Fritz Meier, 'Das Problem der Natur im esoterischen Monismus', *Eranos Jahrbuch*, xiv (1946), pp. 174–80. Dr. S. M. Stern had kindly drawn my attention to this passage before I had seen Meier's article.

[6] *KS.*, i, 50–51.

Sanā'ī[1] and Jalālal-Dīn Rūmī.[2] The point of the story is that just as the blind men each feel only a part of the elephant, and thereby run away with the idea that their partial experience is the whole truth, so do the various religions possess only partial truth, yet all claim, in their blindness, to possess the whole. This condemnation of all dogmatism which is fundamental to Buddhism suited the book of the later Ṣūfīs very well, since as time went on they became increasingly impatient of the dogmatics of the theologians. The Buddhist origin of the story was, however, quite forgotten.[3]

Buddhism, however, was not an esoteric creed, and there is thus nothing surprising in the transmission of Buddhist ideas into Islam through literary channels. The doctrines of the Upaniṣads on the other hand were regarded as being highly secret and not lightly to be divulged to unauthorized persons; and it is highly significant that Bīrūnī, in his study of India, was unable to obtain access to them. It does then seem an odd chance that these very doctrines should have made their way into Islam—assuming of course that our theory is correct—through the collaboration of a convert from Hinduism and the grandson of a Zoroastrian who shouted them from the housetops, so intoxicated with this heady wine was he.

Among the sayings of Abū Yazīd there are also some which bear a strange likeness to Buddhist texts. Thus he is reported as saying:

You see how rivers flow with a plashing, chattering sound, but when they draw near to the sea and mingle with it, their plash and chatter is stilled, and the sea has no experience of them nor do they increase in it; nor if they were [again] to emerge from it, would they have the slightest effect on it. Man is like the torrent and the sea; for the torrent, so long as it is alone, bustles along in its course and makes loud its chatter, but when it draws near to the sea and mingles with it, its bubbling and

[1] *Ḥadīqat al-Ḥaqīqa*, Tehran, 1329, A.H. (solar), p. 69.

[2] *Maṡnavī*, iii, 1259 ff.

[3] In this case the story probably passed through the Buddhists of Central Asia, for it occurs in Khotanese. See M. Leumann, 'Das nordiranische (sakische) Lehrgedicht des Buddhismus' in *Abhandl. für die Kunde des Morgenlandes*, Leipzig, 1933–6, II, 122, p. 24. Reference kindly supplied by Professor H. W. Bailey.

chatter are stilled, and the sea has no experience of it, nor does it increase or decrease though [the torrent] were turned back [again].[1]

This seems clearly to be based on *Udāna*, p. 55, which reads as follows:

Just as—whatsoever streams flow into the mighty ocean and whatsoever floods fall from the sky, there is no shrinkage nor overflow seen thereby in the mighty ocean, even so . . . though many monks pass finally away into that condition of *nirvāṇa* which has no remainder, yet there is no shrinkage nor overflow in that condition of *nirvāṇa* seen thereby.

The parallelism is surprisingly exact, but the simile of rivers flowing into the ocean is to be found in almost all forms of mysticism, whether pantheistic or theistic, and should not for that reason be unduly stressed. Abū Yazīd's borrowings from Vedānta are, however, in quite another class since closely parallel passages are found nowhere else except in the Upaniṣads and are utterly characteristic of them.

Now it would be interesting to trace the development of Abū Yazīd's ideas from a form of mysticism that was not noticeably different from that of his predecessors to the extreme Vedāntin position expressed in those sayings of his which we have quoted. More particularly would it be interesting to know at what stage of his career he met Abū 'Alī of Sind. The only clue we have to this is the following. Abū Yazīd is said by Sarrāj to have rebuked Abū 'Alī for the performance of a miracle[2] on the grounds that the performance of miracles is evidence of distraction from the serious business of pure mystical experience. Elsewhere he is said himself to have been favoured with miracles in his early life though even then he set no great store on them.[3] It seems then fair to conclude that his association with Abū 'Alī was not a youthful one; and this would go a long way to explain the very marked difference that can be detected both in his sayings and in the accounts of his attitude towards the religious law and practice of Islam.

To present a clear picture of Abū Yazīd's teaching, let alone of

[1] Sahlajī, p. 124. [2] Sarrāj, p. 325. [3] Ibid., p. 324.

any consistent development within it, is, however, impossible. The traditions attributed to the Prophet, even when accepted as genuine by the foremost traditionalists, are frequently suspect. So too, in the case of the sayings of the early Ṣūfīs, we would be well advised to preserve a healthy scepticism as to their authenticity, since they were never subjected to the kind of control which, in the course of the early Muslim centuries, became *de rigueur* in the case of the sayings of the Prophet. The need for caution becomes apparent when we compare the early works on Ṣūfism with each other, and a glance at Zhukovsky's index to Hujwīrī's *Kashf al-Maḥjūb* will suffice to convince us that the attribution of a given saying to a given Ṣūfī was often more or less haphazard. Even Rābi'a's description of the two loves the soul entertains for God which Dr. Margaret Smith has made famous,[1] is attributed to a chance acquaintance of Dhū'l-Nūn by the *Ḥilyat al-Awliyā* of Abū Nu'aym al-Iṣfahānī.[2] In the case of Abū Yazīd the sayings attributed to him by our earliest source, Abū Naṣr al-Sarrāj, may perhaps be accepted with a certain degree of confidence, for they were accepted as genuine by Junayd who wrote a commentary on them and who died about half a century after him:[3] but the recently published selection of his sayings which are certainly the work of Sahlajī[4] must be treated with some reserve. It is an honest enough attempt, indeed, to record all the sayings attributed to the master in Sahlajī's own day,[5] but that day was some two hundred years after the death of Abū Yazīd, and there was thus plenty of time to elaborate freely on the original deposit. This process of free elaboration reaches its finest flower in the *Tadhkirat al-Awliyā* of Farīd al-Dīn 'Aṭṭār, and it is in itself of very considerable interest, for it shows how the later Ṣūfīs attempted to explain or explain away utterances which were in no way reconcilable with orthodoxy.

[1] *Early Mysticism in the Near and Middle East*, p. 223: cf. Abū Ṭālib al-Makkī, *Qūt al-Qulūb*, Cairo, 1932, iii, 84.

[2] *Ḥilya*, ix, 348.

[3] Sulamī (*Ṭabaqāt al-Ṣūfiyya*, p. 156) gives the date of Junayd's death as A.H. 297 and that of Abū Yazīd as either 261 or 234. Sahlajī gives the latter date only.

[4] See *Indo-Iranian Journal*, i, 290, n. 14.

[5] On Sahlajī's date see *Indo-Iranian Journal*, loc. cit.

There was, however, one very simple expedient to which the ecstatic Ṣūfī could resort if he wished to avoid a head-on collision with authority, and that was to let it be understood that he was mad. This Abū Yazīd himself did when he was accused of neglecting certain of his religious duties,[1] and many of the curious who had gathered round him were content to dismiss his claims to be God as the result of madness. 'Abū Yazīd has gone mad,' they said with a shrug and left him.[2] This too was the impression of an emissary whom Dhū'l-Nūn had sent to wait upon the great man.[3] Shiblī was later to resort to the same expedient[4] and it was Ḥallāj's refusal to do so that cost him his life. It is quite possible that Abū Yazīd may have derived this idea from India too, for we read in the *Nāradaparivrājaka* Upaniṣad that the perfected Sannyāsin should behave like an idiot.[5] In any case the device was to become a common one among the later Ṣūfīs, and in 'Aṭṭār's *Muṣībat-nāma* the word *dīvāna*, 'madman', became a synonym for an ecstatic mystic. Abū Yazīd was responsible for a lot of the less immediately attractive features of Ṣūfīsm.

The dichotomy between those sayings of Abū Yazīd in which he explicitly identifies himself with God and the more conventional sayings which are attributed in equal number to him, can perhaps be explained by comparison with the case of Abū Sa'īd ibn Abī'l-Khayr with whom he has much in common. We are told[6] that for forty years the latter indulged in the fiercest austerities and strictly observed the religious law, but that once he had achieved what the Hindus called liberation and he himself sometimes calls 'freedom',[7] he considered that he had passed beyond the law and fully demonstrated this conviction by his outrageous behaviour. So too, perhaps, in the case of Abū Yazīd we may attribute the

[1] Sahlajī, p. 95.

[2] Ibid., p. 122.

[3] Qushayrī, p. 38.

[4] Sarrāj, p. 50.

[5] F. O. Schrader, *The Minor Upaniṣads*, i, 184 and 147.

[6] In the *Asrār al-Tawḥīd fī Maqāmāt al-Shaykh Abī Sa'īd*, by Ibn Munawwar, ed. Tehran, 1332, A.H. (solar).

[7] See below, p. 120.

more conventional sayings to the time when he was still on the path and his extravagant claims to be identical with God to the period when he considered he had entered in unto the 'truth', as the Ṣūfīs would say.

If my contention that Abū Yazīd had direct access to Vedāntin teachings is right, his case is full of interest, for it will show us how a man brought up in a monotheistic tradition and a school of mysticism that regarded the love of God leading to the contemplation of his holiness as the highest goal of man, managed to adapt his theology and mystical practice to a system, the cornerstone of which is that the human soul is identical with God. 'I sloughed off my self as a snake sloughs off its skin, and I looked into my essence and saw that "I am He".'[1] This must describe an experience that Abū Yazīd believed he actually had had, and which the Vedāntin terminology he had learnt from his master seemed accurately to describe. Prominent, if not overwhelming, must have been the experience of passing beyond space and time, later described by Abū Sa'īd in the words, 'For me there is no space, neither below nor above, neither right nor left, there is no [such thing as] direction'.[2] The same experience is interpreted by Abū Yazīd as being everywhere at the same time. 'This servant', he says, 'is with God in all places and no place is devoid of him.'[3] This means that he is present in any place he pleases, for he has altogether passed beyond place and space. The experience is expressed by the Upaniṣadic phrase 'I am this All', and since the All is, for Abū Yazīd, also God, he must therefore *be* God. In such a state when the mystic sees himself divested of all human attributes and adorned with divine ones, he is almost bound to think he is God, for in Islam no clear distinction is drawn between God and what the Gītā calls *mad-bhāva-*, 'the mode of existence in which God has his being'. This is scarcely surprising, for the Gītā itself is far from clear on this point, and it took a Rāmānuja to draw what was for him a vital distinction. Abū Yazīd, on the contrary, discards his experiences of divine love as being merely a prelude to the experience of absolute unity, for when all is one, plainly there can be

[1] See above, p. 98. [2] *Asrār al-Tawḥīd*, p. 115. [3] Sahlajī, p. 75.

no room for love, the nature of which is a mutual outpouring between two persons.

Abū Yazīd has made himself so notorious by his identification of himself with God that we tend to forget that he has some very beautiful things to say about the love that is possible between the Creator and his creature. 'The perfection of the mystic', he says, 'is that he should burn in his love for his Lord,'[1] and 'the reward the mystic receives from his Lord, and his perfection, is to burn in God and for God (*la-hu*).'[2] Or again he marvels at God's loving condescension to his creature: 'There is nothing marvellous in my love for thee, for I am a poor slave; but there *is* something quite marvellous in thy love for me, for thou art a mighty king,'[3] and not only a mighty king, but also the perfect object of love, 'for it is impossible to know thee', he says, 'and not to love thee.'[4] Moreover, this love has no end because you cannot exhaust the unfathomable riches of an infinite Being, and the lover's 'thirst is never quenched, his tongue hangs out, and he says, "Is there yet more"'.[5] The intensity of this passionate longing to be with God entails an equally passionate desire to conform oneself so utterly to God that one regards one's own creaturely existence as a hindrance in the way, for, to live the divine life, self must be utterly annihilated. In a characteristic passage he says: 'The man who is advanced [on the mystic path] is lashed with the whip of love, slain with the sword of passionate longing, propped up against the gate of awe.'[6] In assessing the monistic utterances of Abū Yazīd this is the background against which we must see them, for it would be quite unrealistic to treat the two as unrelated phenomena.

There is one saying of his, however, which quite contradicts this exaltation of passionate love, and that is: 'Those who follow the way of love are screened [from God] by their [very] love.'[7] This is a complete denial of all that has gone before and so radical a reversal of the mysticism of love that is the hall-mark of Abū Yazīd's contemporaries and predecessors that we are driven again

[1] Sahlajī, p. 81. [2] Ibid., p. 135. [3] Ibid., pp. 109, 122. [4] Ibid., p. 122.
[5] Ibid., p. 136. [6] Sarrāj, p. 227. [7] Sahlajī, p. 133.

to suspect the intervention of an outside influence; and once again no rational explanation is forthcoming unless we accept a direct Vedāntin influence on Abū Yazīd personally. What, then, was the attitude of the contemporary Vedānta in India to worship and devotion to God?

The *Sannyāsa* Upaniṣads, Gauḍapāda's *Kārikā* to the *Māṇḍūkya* Upaniṣad, the *Laws of Manu*,[1] and Śaṅkara himself, all speak of the liberated man as having passed beyond all the rites of religion. Śaṅkara, however, does strongly recommend an intense and loving devotion to God and was himself the author of many strikingly beautiful hymns to both Viṣṇu and Śiva, but always he insists that these are merely convenient rungs on the ladder to the One. Once a man has realized himself as the One, all else falls away from him; all else, including devotion to a deity, is seen for what it is, and in the eyes of the liberated soul, which is now the One without a second, what it is is pure illusion; it is nothing. Imagine the impact of such a doctrine on one of Abū Yazīd's highly emotional temperament, nurtured as it had been on a mysticism of passionate love.

His ecstasies which take him out of space and time now appear to him in the light of an alien philosophy. Now there is no longer any blasphemy in saying, 'I am He', for that is the 'ultimate truth' he had learnt from his master. However, the God he had known, the Allah of the Qur'ān, was a very different God from either Viṣṇu or Śiva: he was an intensely personal God, and with him, Abū Yazīd had thought, he had had relations of loving intercourse, but now he feels able to say that love itself is a screen. Having reached this supreme eminence, he, like his Indian teachers, now considered himself beyond the religious law, beyond all ritual acts of piety. He does not go to Mecca, Mecca comes to him.[2] He who once denied all value to miracles unless the worker of miracles scrupulously followed every jot and tittle of the law,[3] he who had bitterly accused himself for stretching his legs in a mosque,[4] and refused to concede sanctity to a venerable Ṣūfī who had spat in a mosque,[5] now considers that acts of worship are merely ordained

[1] vi, 95–96. [2] Sahlajī, p. 124. [3] Sarrāj, p. 324. [4] Ibid., p. 201. [5] Sahlajī, p. 65.

for those who are incapable of mystical experience,[1] while he himself has reached a stage in which he makes all the acts of worship ever offered in all the heavens and all the earth a pillow on which to to rest his cheek.[2] He no longer considers himself bound by worship, or asceticism, or mystical knowledge itself, and loses his temper when his deficiency in the first two is mentioned, claiming that he himself is the source of all three.[3] Meditation too was a hindrance, for only when he had given it up did he realize his identity with God.[4] Reading the Qur'ān and other religious observances were all very well for the ordinary believer, but the perfected mystic had passed beyond all this as he had passed beyond all reason.[5] His growing contempt for all organized religion and for Islam in particular is best exemplified in the terse comment he is alleged to have made when passing a Jewish and a Muslim cemetery. Of the Jews he said, 'They are pardoned', of the Muslims, 'They are duped'.[6] And this is the man whose orthodoxy Junayd sought so ardently to defend!

Just as he came to believe himself to be exempt from the law of the Prophet, so did he come to regard himself as being superior to the Prophet himself. He had indeed said that the Prophet was endowed with knowledge that even the angels did not possess[7] and confessed that between even his own most exalted state and that of the Prophet there were a thousand degrees that separated the former from the latter,[8] but once that he had convinced himself that he was very God, he had no hesitation in saying: 'Verily all creatures are beneath the banner of Muhammad, but, by God, my banner is more exalted than the banner of Muhammad. My banner is of light, and beneath it are all the prophets that have ever appeared among Jinn and men.'[9]

Such a complete change in the character of a man and, through the man, of the movement of which he formed part, was not, I think, possible without a powerful influence from outside, and the only influence that fully explains the sayings attributed to Abū

[1] Ibid., p. 135. [2] Ibid., p. 133. [3] Ibid., p. 111. [4] Ibid., p. 124, cf. p. 80. [5] Ibid., p. 95. [6] Sarrāj, pp. 392–3. [7] Sahlajī, p. 88. [8] Ibid., p. 66. [9] Ibid., p. 111.

Yazīd is that of the extreme non-dualist Vedānta which Śaṅkara had revived in India only a short time before Abū Yazīd appeared on the scene. Not only do some of his sayings show an unmistakable Vedāntin origin, but his whole mode of life, his new-found contempt for religious forms which was the natural result of the conviction that he *was* God, are exactly paralleled in the Vedānta of Śaṅkara; for it is that philosophy alone which considers all worship and all religious law to be of value only to the man who has not reached liberation, and to be deliberately disregarded by the liberated. The liberated man abandons all but the Self:[1] the Self is Brahman, and since the Muslims had no concept comparable to Brahman, the self therefore must be God. So Abū Yazīd had no choice but to exclaim, to the outraged horror of the orthodox, 'I am He'. So did Indian monism make its way into the Muslim creed which should have abhorred it.

[1] *Nāradaparivrājaka* Upaniṣad, E. O. Schrader, *The Minor Upaniṣads*, i, 199

VI

Self-Deification

In our last lecture we saw that in Abū Yazīd of Bisṭām Indian mysticism for the first time makes itself felt in Islam; and even if we reject the evidence as mere coincidence, we cannot deny that, with Abū Yazīd, a wholly new way of expressing mystical experience passes into Islam. Prior to Abū Yazīd the essence of the mystical approach to God had been *takhalluq bi-akhlāq Allāh*, 'conforming oneself to the character of God'[1] so that man becomes a mere instrument of God's will: God acts through the perfected mystic, but does not destroy his personality. The idea is expressed in a probably spurious but endlessly quoted tradition: 'When my servant draws ever nearer to me by performing works of supererogation, then do I begin to love him; and once I have started to love him, I become his ear by which he hears and his eye by which he sees.'[2] God displaces the human personality, but does not destroy it. When this has happened, what remains of the human personality is completely 'deified', to use the expression of St. John of the Cross. 'Love between two [persons] is not sound,' says Sarī al-Saqatī, Junayd's master, 'until the one can say to the other, "O thou I".'[3] Here, it must be supposed, it is God who addresses the soul, for the human soul, in so far as it is created and human, is now totally displaced. All this was thoroughly familiar to Abū Yazīd, but he goes much further. Transforming union, for him, does not only mean that God uses the perfected soul as the instrument through which he acts, but also that the soul actually becomes God.

[1] E.g. Abū Nu'aym, *Ḥilyat al-Awliyā*, ix, 376.

[2] The earliest quotation of this tradition by a Ṣūfī known to me is by Junayd. See *Islamic Quarterly*, i, 80.

[3] Qushayrī, p. 146.

Now in the Vedānta a distinction is always drawn between Brahman, the One, who is the eternal impassive ground of all action and change, and Īśvara, the Lord, who is the omnipotent, omniscient God who creates the universe by his *māyā*. In the Upaniṣads and the Gītā the relationship between the two is anything but clear, but in the completely non-dualistic Vedānta standardized by Gauḍapāda and Śaṅkara it is made perfectly plain, as it was already in the *Māṇḍūkya* Upaniṣad, that the Lord is only the first emanation from the Absolute Brahman. In the sphere of relativity he is absolutely supreme, but in his relationship to the Absolute he is non-existent except that in so far as he is an emanation of the Absolute, he also is the Absolute just as, in the last analysis, all human souls are. *Quâ* Lord and agent, however, and as operating in time, he is as unreal as are unliberated souls; in fact he is the *māyin*, the Lord of *māyā*, and as such the author of the whole unreal universe, the creator of unreality or *avidyā*, 'cosmic nescience', as Śaṅkara prefers to call it. Thus as the author of unreality he is distinct from human souls who are the victims of that very unreality with which he envelops them, but as himself identical with Brahman because proceeding from him he is identical with them too.

Śaṅkara's dates are given by Surendranath Dasgupta[1] as 788–820, and the revival of monistic thought by Gauḍapāda within Hinduism is thought by him to be datable at 'about the period A.D. 780'. Rāmānuja's dates are much later and are given by the same authority as 1017–1137.[2] According to Sahlajī[3] Abū Yazīd died in 234/848 at the age of seventy-three, though Sulamī gives an alternative date 261/874.[4] Abū Yazīd, then, was only slightly the junior of Śaṅkara, and the 'ultimate truths' he would have learnt from his Sindī master would therefore be the Vedānta according to Śaṅkara, not the Vedānta according to Rāmānuja who was yet to be born. Since it is fatally easy to confuse all types of mysticism under one head, Abū Yazīd was bound to go a step beyond the older Ṣūfīs; he was bound to identify his former experience of

[1] *A History of Indian Philosophy*, i, 418. [2] Ibid., iii, 100, 104.
[3] p. 63. [4] See above, p. 103, n. 3.

loving communion with the Vedāntin experience of identity with the Absolute. From identity of will he jumps forward to the idea, wholly revolutionary in Islam, of identity of essence.

Islam has no concept corresponding to the Brahman of the Vedānta. Allah, like the Yahweh of the Old Testament, is essentially an active God, he is not the timeless Absolute of philosophy. He is a God who deals with men, not something in which the soul can be absorbed. Islamic mysticism, however, taking over many of its leading ideas from Christianity, sees in God the eternal Beloved who draws the soul towards himself in an ecstasy of love, and in the ultimate phase of this love God can say to the soul *Yā anā*, 'O thou I'. However, he always remains an operating, active God, who leads the soul to himself. The Īśvara of the *Yogasūtras*, of the *Śvetāśvatara* Upaniṣad, and of the first chapters of the Bhagavad-Gītā, on the other hand, leads the soul on not to union with himself, but to 'isolation' or *brahmabhūya*, 'the conditīon of Brahman', 'pure' existence in which the distinction between subject and object is lost, and time and space are thereby transcended. Abū Yazīd could scarcely have been aware of the distinction which Rāmānuja was later to make between *mad-bhāva*, 'a divine state of being', and the personal encounter with God himself, since the distinction had never yet been clearly formulated. *Any* experience, then, which took him outside time and space and beyond all differentiation he would interpret as identity of essence with God: for him there was neither morning nor evening. 'Morning and evening are only for those who are still subject to attributes,' he says, 'and I have no attributes.'[1] 'Attributes' (*ṣifa*) corresponds to the Sanskrit *nāma-rūpa*, 'name and form', and Brahman is devoid of these. But Ṣūfī theology too was beginning to interpret God's *tanzīh*, his total unlikeness to all created things, as meaning that, in his essence (*dhāt*) as opposed to his attributes, he was quite unqualifiable, but they did not separate the essence from the 'essential' attributes which inhered in his essence. When Abū Yazīd says *Anā hūwa*, 'I am He', and so reproduces, almost certainly without knowing it, the *ayam asmi* of *Bṛhadāraṇyaka* Upaniṣad 4.4.12, he is

[1] Sahlajī, p. 70.

not merely saying that he is Brahman, that is, in some sense identical with a passionless, featureless, qualityless Absolute; he is saying, so far as his audience is concerned, that he is the Muslim God, the Merciful, the Compassionate, the Ruler of the Day of Judgement. This, of course, was not only blasphemy but nonsense.

Abū Yazīd, however, did not shrink from the consequences; and if only a fraction of the sayings attributed to him by Sahlajī is authentic, it is quite plain that he claimed to be God in all respects.

The original form in which Abū Yazīd made formal claim to identity with God is probably in the saying which is quoted by both Bīrūnī and Sahlajī: 'I sloughed off my self as a snake sloughs off its skin, and I looked into my essence (or self) and lo, I was He.'[1] This is likely to be original both because we have it from two wholly unconnected sources, and because it reads as a paraphrase of *Bṛhadāraṇyaka* Upaniṣad, 4.4.7, 12. The phrase, however, also appears in the form 'I am Thou',[2] and in order, presumably, to make clear his position of absolute monism, as 'I am I'.[3] The passage where this last phrase occurs alone is absolutely astonishing. Abū Yazīd, in his quest for God, reaches his throne, finds it empty, and therefore takes possession of it himself. Then he says: 'I plunged into the oceans of *malakūt* (the realm of pure ideas) and the veils of deity (*lāhūt*) until I reached the throne, and lo, it was empty; so I cast myself upon it and said, "Master, where shall I seek thee?" And the veils were lifted up,[4] and I saw that I am I, yea, I am I. I turned back into what I sought, and it was I, no other, into which I was going.' The phrase 'I am I' is combined with 'I am He' in another saying: 'I am not I, I am I, for I indeed am He, I am He, I am He, He.'[5]

Once again these sayings which to Muslim ears were either heinous blasphemy or plain lunacy, are absolutely typical of the

[1] See above, p. 98.

[2] Sahlajī, pp. 109, 119.

[3] Ibid., p. 128.

[4] Arberry, *Revelations and Reason in Islam*, p. 96, translates: 'He (God) unveiled.'

[5] Sahlajī, p. 111. Arberry (ibid., p. 98) translates this apparent gibberish thus: 'I am not I I I because I am He I am He I am He He.'

Vedānta. When the mystic affirms 'I am I', he uncompromisingly affirms the sole existence of the One, which must be 'I', whatever else it may be, for 'I' is the subject of all experience. Again 'I am not I' means 'I am not R. C. Zaehner, height 5 ft. $6\frac{1}{2}$ in. as described in my passport or *Who's Who*'; that is not me, but only my *nāma-rūpa*, my 'name-and-form'. And it is for such elementary confusions as these that Śankara gently chides his pupil in the *Upadeśasāhasrī*.[1] I am not the psycho-physical frame my soul inhabits, nor the mind which has laboriously elucubrated these lectures; no—as both the Vedānta and Abū Yazīd teach, 'I am He'. But 'He', for Abū Yazīd, is no unqualifiable Absolute, it is the Allah of the Qur'ān, and so it is only natural that Abū Yazīd should see himself as occupying the throne of Allah. In Hindu terminology he sees himself not only as Brahman but as Īśvara too, so he has no scruple in exclaiming, 'I am the Lord Most High',[2] or more preposterously still: 'Verily, I am—there is no God but me, so worship me.'[3] Here he claims explicitly to be the Allah of the Qur'ān, not merely the 'Truth' as Ḥallāj was to do, nor the Lord, terms which are applicable to what is other than God. He uses the one Name of God which, as he himself points out, God shares with no created thing.[4] In this he goes beyond the Vedānta, for in that system the soul does not become identical with the Lord who is the creator of the universe, but passes clean beyond him into the wholly undifferentiated Brahman. As ruler of the world and as the supreme object of worship, the Lord is the sole author of *māyā*, and the liberated soul can never be identified with him *in this capacity*, for 'occupation with the affairs of the world' (*jagad-vyāpāra-*) is the exclusive privilege of the Lord, not of any individual soul, bound or released. This, at any rate, appears to be the clear sense of *Brahmasūtras* iv. 4.17–21 and of Śaṅkara's commentary thereon.

Abū Yazīd, however, was no scholar, and, for him, to be Brahman could only be interpreted in Muslim terminology as meaning to be God, both in his essence and in his attributes, whereas the Vedānta teaching is rather that the liberated soul *is*

[1] 1.10. [2] Sahlajī, p. 103. [3] Ibid., p. 122. [4] Ibid., p. 83.

God in his essence but not in his attributes: it is the One, but not the Creator of heaven and earth. This distinction seems occasionally to have been dimly apparent to Abū Yazīd as the following saying shows:

> The first time I made the pilgrimage I saw the House (i.e. the Ka'ba), and the second time I made it I saw the Lord of the House, but not the House, but the third time I made it I saw neither the House nor the Lord of the House.[1]

This presumably means that once the mystic has achieved a condition in which he is devoid of all attributes, he passes beyond the personal God into a purely featureless form of existence, the '*nirguṇa* Brahman' or 'Brahman without quality' of the Vedānta. It seems that it is to a misunderstanding of this idea that we must attribute this utterance of our hero: 'By God's life, my onset is more violent than God's.'[2] This is a comment on the Qur'ānic passage: 'Verily the onset of thy Lord is violent',[3] which then goes on to proclaim the greatness of God as creator:

> It is he who originates and restores,
> And he is the forgiving, the loving,
> The occupant of the throne, the glorious,
> The doer of what he intendeth.

God's *baṭsh* or 'onset' is thus interpreted as his creative activity, and in saying that his own onset is greater than God's Abū Yazīd would seem to mean that he is greater than the Creator in that he has pierced clean through beyond the distinction between Creator and created into the Absolute One. Yet not only is he God and what is beyond him, he is also the archetype of all creation, for he also claims to be the 'guarded Tablet',[4] the uncreate source of all revelation. His self-deification, then, is more absolute than any but the most extreme positions taken up by the Vedāntins.

Now it can be readily imagined that this new type of mysticism introduced into the main current of Ṣūfism must have caused some alarm to those whose principal preoccupation was to gain recognition from the theologians for the orthodoxy of the Ṣūfī movement.

[1] Ibid., p. 79. [2] Ibid., p. 111. [3] Qur'ān, 85.12. [4] Sahlajī, pp. 80, 113.

Yet there is no evidence that Abū Yazīd was ever made to suffer for his beliefs beyond being seven times expelled from his native Bisṭām.[1] This is in sharp contrast to the fate of Ḥallāj who was executed for making a claim that was identical with that of Abū Yazīd—he claimed to be God (*da'wat al-rubūbiyya*).[2] This Abū Yazīd had done time and time again, both explicitly[3] and implicitly, yet no action was taken against him. This may perhaps be explained by the fact that he was assumed to be mad and therefore left in peace. The indifference of orthodoxy, however, is less surprising than the fact that, unlike Ḥallāj, he was not disowned by any of the Ṣūfīs either in his own day or after his death. Junayd, who had refused to have anything to do with Ḥallāj although he continued on close terms with Shiblī whose views were indistinguishable from those of Ḥallāj, did not repudiate Abū Yazīd, which he might easily have done, but wrote a commentary on his ecstatic sayings, the object of which was apparently to clear him of the charge of heresy. No Ṣūfī before Abū Yazīd had dared to make claims such as he did, yet once they had been made, they were never challenged by Ṣūfīs who considered themselves orthodox. On the contrary they were commented on and in the process of time distorted so as to correspond with the individual views of the commentators. This universal acceptance of Abū Yazīd as one of the greatest of the Ṣūfī 'saints' did more than anything else to smooth the way for Vedāntin ideas in a movement which had hitherto regarded the mystic's goal as being union with God, not outright identification with him.

It now remains for us to examine how later commentators explained or explained away the more outrageous claims of this outrageous man, and more particularly how they built out of his sayings the story of his *mi'rāj* or 'ascension' into the world above, how they modified it, and how they fitted it into their own scheme of things. Whether Abū Yazīd himself did not feel in his more

[1] Ibid., p. 48.

[2] See L. Massignon, *Al-Hallaj, Martyr mystique de l'Islam*, i, 138 ff.

[3] Sahlajī, pp. 79, 82: 'The most accurate definition of the mystic is that the attributes of Truth and the mode (*jins*) of lordship flow in him.'

sober moments that he had perhaps overstated the case is not absolutely clear, but one saying of his seems significant in this connexion. 'After attaining the ultimate', he says, 'the mystic's portion is always to return to one thing—asking for forgiveness.'[1] And this doubt that perhaps the Vedāntin interpretation of his experiences was not the true one is borne out by the sobriety and humility of what purport to be his last words; for at the solemn hour of death he makes no extravagant claim to deity, nor does he disdain to address a God with whom he had claimed identity and whom he had once believed he had transcended, he confesses only to his own hopeless imperfection. 'I have never meditated on thee', he says, 'but that I was distracted, nor hast thou laid hold upon me but that I was languid.'[2] These sayings would seem to indicate that Abū Yazīd himself was more doubtful of the authenticity of his claims than some later Ṣūfīs showed themselves to be.

His case is indeed strangely similar to that of Rimbaud which I have dealt with at some length elsewhere:[3] he too had scaled the heavenly ladder and surveyed all creation from the heights of his ecstasy, but he too had to descend and 'ask pardon for having fed himself on lies'. I personally prefer to think that Abū Yazīd too, who esteemed himself so little as a man, saw that to claim to be God—to be Allah, that is—is really absurd. In justice to him whom posterity remembers for saying, 'Glory be to me, how great is my glory', we must record that he is also reported to have said: 'So long as a man thinks that any creature exists worse than himself, he shows pride.'[4]

There can be little doubt that Abū Yazīd was subject to severe fits of depression as well as of elation so intense that he believed himself to be God. In a depressive phase he is alleged to have remained perfectly silent for thirteen years, his chin resting on his knees and no syllable escaping his lips except an occasional 'Ah'.[5] A man whose dismal lot it was to be his companion during these years was told that this was the period of his *qabḍ*, his

[1] Sahlajī, p. 122. [2] Sarrāj, p. 210.
[3] My *Mysticism, Sacred and Profane*, pp. 61–83. [4] Sahlajī, p. 133.
[5] Ibid., p. 141.

'constriction' or depression as we would call it, and that things would have been very different had he had the good fortune to be with him during his *basṭ*, his 'expansion' or elation.

The alternation of extreme elation and intense depression is known to psychology as a manic-depressive psychosis, and the fact that Abū Yazīd was indeed considered by his contemporaries to be mad would indicate that he may very well have suffered from this affliction. The Ṣūfī technical terms *qabḍ* and *basṭ* are variously explained, but Qushayrī's description of them is worth recalling when we remember that he was a contemporary of Abū Sa'īd ibn Abī'l-Khayr, a fervent admirer of Abū Yazīd's[1] who attached the greatest importance to *basṭ* or the 'expansion' of the personality for its own sake. Qushayrī is represented by Abū Sa'īd's biographer as being envious of him, and endless anecdotes are told of how the great Shaykh of Mayhana humbled him. When Qushayrī describes *basṭ* and its evil effects, then, we may be sure that he had Abū Sa'īd in mind.

Expansion and contraction [Qushayrī says] are two [emotional] states which supervene when a man has passed through the states of fear and hope. Contraction in the adept corresponds to fear in the beginner, and expansion to hope. The difference between fear and hope on the one hand and expansion and contraction on the other is that fear is confined to something in the future, be it the loss of a beloved object or the onslaught of something perilous. So, too, hope refers to the attainment of a desired object in the future, to the removal of an obstruction, or to the end of an unpleasantness for the beginner. Contraction, however, means something actually present at the time: so also expansion. The subject experiencing either fear or hope has his mind fixed on the future, whereas those who experience expansion and contraction are presently and actually the prisoner of an overwhelming obsession (*wārid*). The experiences of persons affected by expansion and contraction will vary according to their respective [spiritual or emotional] states. One kind of obsession brings on contraction, but even so the appetite for other things remains; for the mood is not exhaustive. But there are also contracted persons who have no appetite whatever for

[1] He is said to have made a pilgrimage to his tomb. See Ibn Munawwar, *Asrār al-Tawḥīd*, p. 151.

anything except their obsession, for they are entirely devoted to it to the exclusion of everything else. . . . Similarly the expanded man experiences an expansion great enough to contain [all] creation; and there is practically nothing that will cause him fear. He is so 'expanded' that nothing will affect him in whatever state he may be. . . . One of the proximate causes of contraction is that the mind is attacked by an obsession, the cause of which is the presentiment of damnation and a mysterious intuition that such punishment is deserved. Inevitably contraction will gain possession of the mind. The occasion for the [opposite] mood is a presentiment of drawing near to or of approaching some sort of favour or welcome; then the mind will experience expansion. . . .
Expansion comes suddenly and strikes the subject unexpectedly, so that he can find no reason for it. It makes him quiver with joy, yet scares him. The way to deal with it is to keep quiet and to observe conventional good manners. There is the greatest danger in this mood, and those who are open to it should be on their guard against an insidious deception. . . . Both conditions, that of expansion as well as that of contraction, have been considered by those who have investigated the truth of these matters to be things in the face of which one should take refuge in God, for both must be considered to be a poor thing and a harmful one if compared with the [spiritual states] which are above them, such as the [apparent] annihilation of the servant [of God] and his gradual upward progress in the truth.[1]

In this remarkable passage Qushayrī obviously has his rival Abū Sa'īd in mind, for the latter seems to have regarded 'expansion' almost as an end in itself,[2] for in that state he felt that he was God, and since God was all[3] he too was all. This is obviously what Qushayrī is referring to when he speaks of 'an expansion great enough to contain [all] creation'. Such ideas are, he says, 'an insidious deception' and extremely dangerous. Qushayrī, however, was a voice crying in the wilderness: Abū Yazīd had injected into the body of Ṣūfism a dose of the Indian Vedānta that was soon to transform the whole movement. It was now within the power of every Ṣūfī to realize himself as God, and this entitled him to live

[1] Qushayrī, pp. 32–33.
[2] Ibn Munawwar, op. cit., p. 60, etc.
[3] *hama ū'st*: ibid., pp. 300, 318, etc.

in total disregard of the Muslim religious law. We have seen how Abū Yazīd saw himself as superior to the Prophet and beyond the law, and this was only natural: for if it is true that his master came to Islam from the Vedānta, then he would have learnt that the laws of all religions are intended only for those souls which have not attained liberation, but in no wise apply to those who have found release, for the released soul cannot possibly derive any benefit from them.[1] Abū Sa'īd was to put this doctrine into practice in no uncertain way, and it is not without significance that he should use the word *āzādī*, 'freedom' or 'liberation' to mean the ultimate state of the mystic when he loses all sense of an independent ego. 'In this state', he says, 'a kind of helplessness overcomes the servant [of God], and his desires fall away from him. The servant (or perhaps 'the bondsman' in this context) becomes free (*āzād*) and at rest (*āsūda*). Thus he desires only what God will desire. The bondsman is finished with and reaches [his] rest. All is He, and you are no one at all.'[2] As far as I know the word *āzādī* (or Arabic *ḥurriyya*) is not used before Abū Sa'īd to mean 'release' or 'liberation' into a purely spiritual mode of being. The exact correspondence of the term with Sanskrit *mukti* or *mokṣa* is striking, and the mention of 'rest' (*āsāyish*) in this connexion cannot fail to call to mind the Sanskrit *śānti*, 'rest' or 'peace' which is the fruit of liberation. This may be coincidence, but it is nonetheless striking.

The seed that Abū Yazīd had sown bore a rich fruit, and the extravagant antinomianism of Abū Sa'īd is a typical specimen of what the Vedānta looks like in Muslim dress. But not all the Ṣūfīs went the way of Abū Sa'īd: the majority, of whom Junayd is regarded as the founding father, strenuously clung to the outward observance of the law, whatever their inward experience may have led them to believe. Junayd, indeed, who accepted Abū Yazīd as an authentic exponent of true Ṣūfī doctrine, wrote a commentary on his ecstatic utterances; and the fragments of this work which have come down to us merit our attention.

[1] Cf. Śaṅkara on *Brahmasūtras*, iii, 4.15–19.

[2] Ibn Munawwar, op. cit., p. 300. Cf. p. 328: 'God created thee free, so be as he created thee.' Cf. also p. 25 where 'freedom' is identified with madness.

Abū Yazid's apparently blasphemous 'Glory be to me, I am the Lord Most High' Junayd seeks to explain away as meaning that the vision of God's glory had completely annihilated him and that he was speaking 'in accordance with what had annihilated him, for, being *in* God, he was diverted from the contemplation of him. He bore witness to none other than God, described him, and spoke through him.'[1] This is in conformity with Junayd's own theory of *fanā* or 'annihilation' in which he would maintain that man's purely human attributes are literally obliterated, and nothing remains but God and the soul's relationship to him. He conceded that 'some of Abū Yazīd's utterances, in their force, their profundity, and extreme significance, were drawn up from an ocean to which he alone had access and which was appropriated to him alone'. 'I saw', Junayd continues, 'that the utmost limit of his [spiritual] state . . . was one which few could understand from his own words when they heard them and which few could interpret because only those who knew the [hidden] meaning of his sayings and had access to the source of his inspiration could bear with him.'[2] But, he goes on to say, 'he was drowned in what he experienced and missed the highest truth (*ḥaqīqat al-ḥaqq*), for he did not enter into it. [He described] spiritual realities (*ma'ānin*) which submerged him in accordance with the occasions on which such immersion occurred, each experience differing from the others. . . . He had [indeed] spoken truly about the science of Union except that his words were only beginnings of what might be expected from one who is of the elect.'

In this passage Junayd concedes that Abū Yazīd had spoken truly of union, that his experiences were peculiar to himself, and that each differed from the next. This, however, only represented a beginning on the road to the mystic's true goal. What Junayd means by this it is difficult to say, but he must be referring to the sayings of Abū Yazīd which immediately follow in the text, and all of these refer to a complete loss of personality at the height of the mystical experience, in which the senses cease to function, and 'there is nothing left in existence, nor is there experience of

[1] Ṣahlajī, p. 68.

[2] Sarrāj, p. 381.

anything lost . . . nor any time to be reckoned with'.[1] This experience which Junayd describes as *al-fanā 'an al-fanā*, 'annihilation following on annihilation', he would seem to regard as being a mere beginning. The explanations of Abū Yazīd's other sayings—'and these too are difficult', as Sarrāj encouragingly says[2]—confirm his general view. When Abū Yazīd askes to be clothed in God's I-ness and raised to his Oneness so that when creatures see him, they may say, 'We have seen thee', yet he would not be there at all,[3] Junayd says that 'this is the way a person talks whom [God] has not clothed with the realities of the ecstasy of isolation in perfect and true union; [had God done so], he would have been content with the [spiritual] clothing he might have received and dispensed with what he [actually] asked for, but [the mere fact] that he asked for this [at all] shows that he was near to attaining his goal; but a person who nearly gets to a place is not the same as one who is [actually] in it: it is the difference between having something actually in one's power and the mere desire to be in such a position (?).'[4] Junayd avoids the awkward phrase 'Thou art that', and contents himself with saying that there is no evidence that Abū Yazīd ever actually attained to what he prayed for, though he does not deny that his prayer could have been granted.

His meaning, however, is made rather more clear in his commentary on Abū Yazīd's claim to have become a bird which flew to the field of eternity without beginning where he saw the tree of oneness, all of which he condemned as 'deceit', a word which, as we have seen, translates the Sanskrit *māyā*. This is the original seed from which the so-called *mi'rāj* or 'ascension' of Abū Yazīd was later to develop, and Junayd's commentary on it will not be without interest. 'When [Abū Yazīd] says,' Junayd comments, ' "I entered into his unity," this represents his first glimpse of unity. He describes what he observed there, he describes the furthest point he was capable of attaining, the ground of his own finite roots.[5] All this is only one path among many[6] for those who are

[1] Ibid., p. 388. [2] Ibid., pp. 338-9. [3] See above, p. 94. [4] Sarrāj, p. 382.

[5] Lit. 'the abiding-place in the end (limitation or completion) of his firm-rootedness (*al-mustaqarr fī tanāhī rusūkhi-hi*)'. [6] Reading *ṭuruq*.

called to attain the true experience (*'ilm*) of union.' Further, when Abū Yazīd speaks of 'an atmosphere a billion times as large', he is referring to something infinitely greater; he is in fact describing an infinite form of existence unconditioned by space. 'Then', says Junayd, 'he described what was there, and this was still not the reality he was seeking, nor the final and all-comprising goal; no, this is only part of the way.'[1]

Again when he comments on another of the sayings of Abū Yazīd which we have not quoted, but which is usually considered as an extreme example of the *via negativa* or 'way of denudation', Junayd lets himself go on his favourite conception of *fanā*, the total destruction of all purely human characteristics in the encounter with God and points out that this means the transcending of time: for 'his mentioning ten years refers to his *waqt* (i.e. 'time' in the technical sense of a mystical state). It [really] has no meaning, for all times disappear in this condition; and when time is obliterated . . . ten, or a hundred, or more years all mean exactly the same.' Having transcended time, then, Abū Yazīd goes on to say: 'I now contemplated Union, which meant that [all] created things had utterly disappeared from [the ken of] the mystic and the mystic had utterly disappeared from [the ken of all] created things.' This means, says Junayd, that 'in his contemplation of union certain knowledge arose in him that all created things whatsoever are totally absent from God Most High, and that he is isolated in his majesty from his creation. These words of Abū Yazīd are well known as referring to the bringing of the man desired [by God] into the presence of what he is trying to express (i.e. God).'[2]

Sarrāj is right: 'Junayd's comments too are difficult except to those who are familiar with them.'[3] However, his meaning seems

[1] Sarrāj, pp. 384–5.

[2] *idkhāl al-murād fi-mā urīda min-hā*. *Murād*, contrary to the usual usage, appears to refer to the mystic, not to God, just as *maṭlūb* throughout Junayd's commentary on the *shaṭḥiyyāt* of Abū Yazīd is used of the mystic and not of God who is represented as the seeker, not the sought. *Murād* is also used in this sense by Ḥallāj (see Massignon, *Al-Hallāj*, p. 517).

[3] Sarrāj, pp. 388–9.

to be this: Abū Yazīd describes the state of complete negativity in which all sense of self, all feeling, and all sense of loss of self even—everything is lost: time and space are transcended, and for Abū Yazīd, if not for his commentator, there is awareness of nothing but an undifferentiated oneness in which all created things including the empirical self utterly and completely disappear. This condition Abū Yazīd attributes to himself, but Junayd attributes it to God. In fact this *tajrīd* ('separation') and *tafrīd* ('isolation') must be identical with the condition aimed at by the Sāṁkhya-Yoga—the total isolation of the soul within itself. Abū Yazīd interpreted this as meaning that the soul *is* God: Junayd saw in it rather a state in which the soul in isolation contemplates the isolation of God, exactly as the Sāṁkhya-Yoga does. In neither is there any ardent desire for union with God. Between the two Junayd appears to make a distinction—but we shall necessarily be returning to Junayd who is perhaps the most intriguing of all the Muslim mystics. Before we return to him, however, we must consider Abū Yazīd's so-called *mi'rāj* or ascension, Junayd's views on which we have just considered.

The word *mi'rāj* which had hitherto only been applied to the Prophet's supposed ascension into the highest heaven, is, so far as I know, first applied to Abū Yazīd by Hujwīrī (*c*. 470/1077). The kernel of the episode he calls the *mi'rāj* is the saying recorded by Sarrāj in which Abū Yazīd says that he 'became a bird', and after flying through all eternal modes of existence and seeing the tree of Oneness, he realized it was all 'deceit'. We saw that the Arabic word *khud'a* most probably represented the Sanskrit *māyā* and how the whole saying could be explained as a rearrangement of different Hindu texts. We also had occasion to remark how unnatural the word *khud'a* appeared in the context. Thus it is not altogether surprising to find that Hujwīrī has radically altered the whole meaning of the saying while preserving the formal structure of the episode. This is how Hujwīrī's account runs:

My inmost soul (*sirr*) was rapt into the heavens, but it looked at nothing [on the way]. Heaven and hell were displayed to it, but it paid no attention to anything; and it was drawn up beyond [all] contingent beings and all that veiled him from its sight. And I became a bird and flew continuously in the atmosphere of [God's] essence (*hūwiyyat*) until I overlooked the broad plain of oneness in which I saw the tree of eternity without beginning. When I looked [upon it all], all of it was I. I said: 'O Lord God, so long as a sense of "I" remains, there is no way from me to thee, nor have I any means of passing beyond the selfhood of self. What shall I do?' [Then] the command came [saying]: 'O Abū Yazīd, thou canst not escape from thy consciousness of being a "thou" except by following our beloved; wipe thine eye with the dust of his feet as with a collyrium and never cease to follow after him.'[1]

This, says Hujwīrī, is known as the *mi'rāj* of Abū Yazīd.

The central portion is based on the saying as preserved by Sarrāj with slight differences. In Sarrāj it is 'the atmosphere of quality' through which Abū Yazīd flies; in Hujwīrī it is an 'atmosphere of [God's] essence'. In Sarrāj the field is of eternity without beginning and the tree is of oneness; in Hujwīrī the field is of oneness and the tree is of eternity without beginning. These differences are of minor importance: what is important is that the climax of the experience has completely changed. In Sarrāj Abū Yazīd looks and realizes that 'all this is deceit', whereas in Hujwīrī he looks and 'all of it was I'. The substitution of the one phrase for the other is not at all easy to explain except on polemical grounds; for in Hujwīrī the pantheistic vision is represented as being a literally infinite expansion of the ego, not as a release *from* the ego. This blessed release which is seen as a release from the classic pan-en-henic experience in which the mystic sees himself as the All, can only be effected by following the path laid down by the Prophet. This point is made unmistakably clear by Hujwīrī in that he produces God himself to condemn an experience which, so far from being *fanā* or any loss of self, is, on the contrary, a colossal exaltation of self.

'Aṭṭār, too, though he follows Sarrāj in the details in which Hujwīrī differs from him, adopts Hujwīrī's dénouement—'everything I saw was I'.[2] How is this to be explained?

[1] Hujwīrī, *Kashf al-Maḥjūb*, ed. V. Zhukovsky, Tehran reprint, 1336 A.H (solar), p. 306. Cf. Appendix B, I, §§ 342–409.

[2] *Tadhkirat al-Awliyā*, i, 175.

We have seen that, in so far as Abū Yazīd follows the Vedānta, he accepted two main propositions—the soul is identical with Brahman (which he translates as 'God'), and the whole phenomenal world is an illusion. In the place of the latter proposition Hujwīrī makes him say that he is the All—a genuine enough Upaniṣadic proposition which, however, cannot be found in this form in our most reliable sources, Sarrāj and Sahlajī. The nearest approach to it is perhaps the saying: 'My likeness is as the likeness of the dark (? *muṣṭalam* for *muẓlim*?) ocean, which has neither beginning nor end.'[1] Furthermore his claim to be present in all places with God[2] almost amounts to the pantheistic identification of the human soul with the All. It is therefore possible that both versions are genuine. If so, there is once more so close a Hindu parallel that we must consider whether this is not yet another direct loan from the Vedāntin tradition. Thus in the Gītā[3] we read:

> He whose self is integrated by Yoga sees himself as being in all creatures, and all creatures in himself.

And this is immediately followed by a promise by Krishna that he will not abandon the man 'who sees *me* everywhere and sees all in *me*'. Here God and the liberated soul are apparently regarded as being co-terminous and as comprising all things. Abū Yazīd identifies himself with God time and time again, and if the saying recorded by Hujwīrī is genuine, it would amount almost to a translation of this Gītā passage. For, given the difference of context, there is very little difference between '*I looked*, and all that was I' and 'he sees himself as being in all creatures and all creatures in himself'.

Whether or not Abū Yazīd was familiar with this passage from the Gītā it is impossible to say, but we can be fairly certain from the tenor of his other sayings that if he spoke of seeing all things as himself, he accepted the corollary of seeing all things in God, because he *was* God. Hujwīrī, however, and, following him, 'Aṭṭār,

[1] Sahlajī, p. 99. [2] Ibid., p. 75. [3] 6.29.

add a postscript to the saying which is certainly not original. The two accounts differ very greatly in emphasis, but each serves a polemic purpose. According to Hujwīrī Abū Yazīd has reached that stage, so common in nature mysticism and constantly recurring in the Upaniṣads, in which the self expands to such an extent that it appears to include all things. This is that dangerous condition of *basṭ* described by Qushayrī: in its extreme form it amounts to self-identification with God, but it is still *self*-identification, and so Abū Yazīd is himself made to appeal to God to deliver him from his 'self' which has now come to comprise the whole world. God then, like any orthodox theologian, bids him have recourse to the law of his beloved, the Prophet. This is significant, for it means that Hujwīrī regarded all claims to be the 'All' or to be God as dangerous illusions, though he did not condemn them. It is very unlikely indeed that he had any direct knowledge of Indian mysticism, but his terminology is nevertheless extremely reminiscent of that of the Hindu mystical classics. 'There is no way to thee with my I-ness, there is no passage for me from the selfhood of my self,' Abū Yazīd is represented as saying. If we put this into Sanskrit, the 'I-ness' or ego will appear as *ahaṁkāra*, and so long as that exists there is no way to God. There is nothing remarkable about this, for all types of mysticism agree that the 'ego' must be either disciplined, suppressed, or simply annihilated. But, having got rid of the ego, there remains the 'selfhood of self', the *khudī-yi khud* of the Persian text, that is, in Sanskrit, the *ātman*. Hujwīrī, then, takes up a position that seems almost identical with that of Rāmānuja. It is not enough for a man to 'see himself as being in all creatures and all creatures in himself': he must be delivered from his second self, his transcendent self or *ātman* too, and he must be delivered by God. For Hujwīrī this means a return to the Prophet as the source of revelation.

'Aṭṭār is more subtle. At the end of his *mi'rāj* Abū Yazīd is represented as saying:

I saw Abū Yazīd. Whatever I saw, all that was I. Then did I traverse four thousand deserts, and reached the end. . . . Then I went on for a while in that infinity, so that I said: 'Nobody has ever reached a point higher than this, and it is not possible that there is any stage more lofty than this.' And when I looked closer, I saw that my head was laid at the feet of one of the prophets. Then I realized that the journey's end of the saints is only the starting-point of the prophets. To the final stage of the prophets there is no end.'

Abū Yazīd, then, like the Yogin of the sixth chapter of the Bhagavad-Gītā, reached a state in which he thought that 'there was no bourn beyond it',[1] but, according to Rāmānuja in India and 'Aṭṭār in Persia, they were perfectly wrong. To realize oneself as infinite, that is, as unconditioned by space and time or, as 'Aṭṭār puts it, 'to journey in infinity' is not the end but only the beginning of the mystical life. This too must be what Junayd meant when he said that Abū Yazīd's words were 'only beginnings' and that he had 'missed the highest truth'.[2]

How or when the legend of the *mi'rāj* of Abū Yazīd started we do not know. Hujwīrī's version of it we have already discussed, but it is only with Farīd al-Dīn 'Aṭṭār that it attains the proportions of a fully-fledged legend.[3] 'Aṭṭār's version is a hotch-potch compounded out of various sayings recorded by Sahlajī, the main portion being based on a text which appears on pp. 138–41 of Badawī's edition of the latter and which has been translated by Professor Arberry in his *Revelation and Reason in Islam*, pp. 99–103. Another and totally distinct version, however, exists, and was published by Nicholson in *Islamica*, vol. ii, pp. 402–15. This version, however, is without interest from the point of comparative mysticism since it is a more or less conventional account of the mystic's journey through the seven heavens, and is designed to confirm the claims of the Prophet through the mouth of Abū Yazīd himself who had vaunted his own superiority to him. Sahlajī's version, however, if genuine, gives us a better idea of how Abū Yazīd or, more probably, a later compiler of his sayings, interpreted his experiences than can his isolated sayings, because it appears as a consecutive narrative.

[1] BG., 6.22.

[2] See above, p. 121.

[3] For parallel accounts of the *mi'rāj* see Appendix B, I.

From the ecstatic utterances of Abū Yazīd which we analysed in our last lecture it seemed fairly clear that he was reproducing in Arabic phrases and ideas that are directly traceable to the Upaniṣads. The Upaniṣadic relationship of the soul to the supreme principle is what Martin Buber called an I/It relationship, and necessarily so, since Brahman is wholly impersonal. The Muslim mystics' relationship to their God, however, had always been essentially an I/Thou relationship in which there always was a distinction of persons. So too Sahlajī's anecdote which forms the basis of the greater part of 'Aṭṭār's account of Abū Yazīd's *mi'rāj* takes the form of a dialogue between Abū Yazīd and God.

This dialogue falls into four parts, the close of each section being marked by the words *inqaṭa'a ḥujjat Allāh 'alāya*, 'So did God's testimony against me conclude'. God indeed is tempting Abū Yazīd with all the 'consolations' that the mystic could legitimately desire: he is putting him to the test to see whether his claim to desire nothing but God himself is true. The first three sections represent different degrees of contemplation, as the use of the word *naẓartu*, 'I looked', clearly shows: the final section only deals with what the author conceives to be true union.

The ascension starts with Abū Yazīd contemplating God with 'the eye of certainty after he had turned me away from all that was not he and illumined me with his light, . . . and showed me his essence (*hūwiyya*)'. Then Abū Yazīd contemplates his ego through God's own essence, his own excellencies through God's, and so astonished is he at this vision of himself that he exclaims, 'Who is this?' and God replies, 'This is not I nor other than I. There is no God but me.' God then transforms his ego into his own essence and shows him that essence in isolation. Abū Yazīd then enjoys the vision of God, as it were, through God's eyes and in God, and this results in complete loss of consciousness. God restores him to consciousness and gives him 'wisdom from his wisdom, and a tongue from his loving-kindness, and an eye from his light', and Abū Yazīd, completely overwhelmed by his experiences (as well he might be), exclaims, 'What have I to do with thee?' God replies, 'I am thine through thee'. This is the first temptation to which, in some other of his sayings, he succumbs—it is the temptation to believe that one has pierced beyond God who is active in the world to an utterly immutable Absolute beyond. Abū Yazīd does not succumb: 'Do not beguile me with myself,' he says: he does not want himself, but only God without any sense of himself at all. God then bestows himself on him, and Abū Yazīd communes with him with no sense of ego left. God then tells him he is bound to observe his commands and prohibitions, but tempts him again by telling him that he (God) praises and thanks him for observing them. Again Abū Yazīd does not fall into the trap. 'Bestow the thanks for it upon thyself,' he exclaims, for 'thou dost command and thou art the commanded.' So ends the first temptation, and the lesson learnt is that Abū Yazīd exists only through God and that 'He is He', that is, God alone exists as the source of all existence.

In the second phase Abū Yazīd is illumined with God's essence (*dhāt*), not merely his light, and contemplates him 'with the eye of bounty (*faḍl*)'. God tells him to ask of his bounty what he will, again putting temptation in his way. Abū Yazīd, however, is not deluded: 'Beguile me not with thy grace and generosity, nor with thy bounty, for bounty proceeds from thee for ever and to thee does it return. . . . Thou art the desirer and thou the desired.' God then praises Abū Yazīd for speaking the truth, and Abū Yazīd replies by extolling God as Truth indeed. 'Thou [too] art nothing but the truth. By the Truth hast thou spoken,' says God again, tempting him, but Abū Yazīd hotly denies it. 'No,' he says, 'Thou art the Truth, and thy word is truth, and through thee is truth truth. Thou art thou, there is no God but thee.' Asked again what he is, Abū Yazīd replies, 'I am through thee.' Well, says God, 'If thou art through me, then I am thou, and thou art I.' Again Abū Yazīd does not fall into the trap. 'Do not beguile me with thyself [so that I swerve] away from thee,' he says. This, the second of the great temptations is to mistake what is 'through God', that is, the divine mode of existence into which God may transform human nature, for God himself. Abū Yazīd now sees himself as being 'with God'—he enjoys companionship with him—and 'through' him—his existence is sustained by him.

Here follows what may be an interpolated passage, for it is closely akin to the two sayings from Sarrāj we had occasion to quote in the last lecture.[1] God provides Abū Yazīd with wings of 'glory and majesty', but even when so equipped he is unable to come to the end of God's glory and majesty. Terrified, he then cries out for help and implores God to save him from God himself by God's power: he implores the divine mercy to save him from the divine wrath, as 'Aṭṭār interprets it. 'I had no power to bear with him,' cries Abū Yazīd, 'except [it came] through him.' God then views him with the eye of munificence, strengthens him with his strength, adorns him, and crowns him with the crown of his generosity. He isolates him in his own isolation, makes him one by his own oneness, and gives him attributes 'which none share with God'. Then God says to him: 'Make thyself one with my oneness, and isolate thyself by my isolation. Lift up thy head in the crown of my generosity, glory in my glory, exult in my exultation, and go forth with my attributes to my creatures that I may see my selfhood (*hūwiyya*) in thy selfhood—whoso sees thee, sees me, and whoso seeks thee, seeks me, O thou, my light in my earth and my ornament in my heaven.' This terrible invitation to claim absolute divinity and proclaim it to the wide world Abū Yazīd again rejects. 'Thou art the sight in my eye and my knowledge in my ignorance,' he exclaims. 'Be thyself thine own light that thou mayst be seen by thyself.' Once again God is well pleased with him, for he has resisted the temptation and bids God be isolated in his own isolation and oned in his own oneness. 'Do not busy me with thyself [so that I swerve] away from thee.' This last temptation, to which in some of his other sayings he completely succumbs, he here successfully overcomes.

Abū Yazīd now dwells with God in God's isolation, but without being 'isolated' himself. Then his own attributes are obliterated in God's. He now contemplates God through God's very essence (*dhāt*), and God addresses him with his own divine name, and communes with him in his oneness. He tempts him again saying, 'O thou I,' but Abū Yazīd will say nothing but 'O thou'.

[1] See above, pp. 94–5.

So ends yet another temptation—the temptation of completely identifying oneself with God. Once again Abū Yazīd loses consciousness and remains for a time 'without soul or body like one who is dead'.

God then revives him with divine life[1] and repeats the *mīthāq* verse of the Qur'ān—'Whose is the kingdom today?' to which Abū Yazīd replies, 'God's, the One, the Overwhelming', thereby admitting his absolute dependence on God. This done, God goes on to say: 'I have made thee to live with my life, made thee to reign over my kingdom, named thee with my name, given thee to rule with my rule, caused thee to understand my choice, and conformed thee (*wāfaqtu-ka*) to names of lordship and attributes of eternity.' Again Abū Yazīd is nonplussed. What does he mean? 'I do not understand what thou wantest,' he says, 'I belonged to myself, yet thou wast not satisfied; and I belonged to thee through thee, and still thou wast not satisfied.' God replies, 'Belong neither to thyself nor to myself. Verily, I was thine when yet thou wast not: so be mine [as] when thou wast not. And belong to thyself even as thou wast, and be mine even as thou wast.' Abū Yazīd, understandably confused, replies: 'How shall this be to me except through thee?' Then God looks on him with the eye of power, annihilates him with his own Being, and 'manifests himself' in him 'in his essence'. 'And I existed *through* him,' Abū Yazīd stolidly repeats. This is the end of this remarkable dialogue. The conclusion is no less remarkable, and I must quote it in full:

And the Word became one, and the All through the All became one. And he said to me, 'O thou,' and I said to him, 'O I.' And he said to me: 'Thou art the alone.' I said: 'I am the alone.' He said to me: 'Thou art thou.' I said: 'I am I. But if I were I as an ego, I would not have said "I". But since I never was "I" (an ego), be thou thou, yea, thou.' He said: 'I am I.' My speaking of him as "I" is like my speaking of him as "he"—denoting unity. And my attributes became the attributes of lordship, and my tongue a tongue proclaiming the divine unity, and my attributes—He, that is: he is he, there is no God but he. Whatever was, was what it was by his[2] Being; and whatever is, is what it is by his

[1] Reading *ḥayyāti-hi* for *ḥayyātī*. [2] Reading *mā* for *mim-mā*.

Being. My attributes were the attributes of lordship, and my traces the traces of eternity, and my tongue a tongue proclaiming the divine unity.'

Now, whatever this may signify, it is certainly not the straight monism of the Vedānta. It is precisely what Massignon calls transforming union in the case of Ḥallāj: every temptation to identify himself with God is resisted by Abū Yazīd, and it is only when he formally confesses the absolute sovereignty of God in the words of the Qur'ān that God exalts him and clothes him with 'the attributes of lordship'. Then Abū Yazīd can, at God's bidding, affirm again his own individuality, not as an ego, but as 'the alone' (*al-fard*), an individual substance wholly transformed by the essence of God. He is what he is through him who supremely is; and in so far as he is, and only in that respect, is he God. The meaning of 'The Word became one' is, presumably, that all creation is subsumed in the creative word *kun*, 'Be', and that Abū Yazīd realizes himself as that word and thereby sees himself in all created things, but all this is possible to him only through God's will and power.[1] Wholly overcome, Abū Yazīd, like an hypnotic patient, automatically repeats the words God dictates to him.

'Aṭṭār's interpretation is different, for, as we have seen, he ends up his account of the *mi'rāj* with Abū Yazīd claiming to be the All. It would, then, seem probable that the *mi'rāj* recorded by Sahlajī is either not a genuine utterance of Abū Yazīd since it avoids the explicit monism of many of his utterances, or else it represents a later modification of the earlier 'Vedāntin' sayings in a form rather more acceptable to current Ṣūfī thought. Personally I would favour the former view since the whole passage avoids any explicit identification of the mystic with God rather too carefully. The author chooses his words with considerable skill. The final 'Whatever is, is what it is, through [God's] Being', has a philosophical ring which would seem alien to the untutored mind of Abū Yazīd.

Before closing this lecture I should like to record 'Aṭṭār's interpretation of Abū Yazīd's *mi'rāj*. As we have seen, he says that Abū

[1] See further below, p. 140.

Yazīd reached a state than which he could conceive none higher: he had reached eternity. 'Aṭṭār, however, here tacks on another saying of Abū Yazīd, also recorded by Sahlajī,[1] in which he is represented as being unable to approach the Prophet because he sees 'a hundred thousand seas of fire without end and a thousand veils of light', and had he put his foot into the first sea, he would have been burnt up. So he is made to say: 'Although I had reached God, I had not the courage to approach Muhammad.' 'That means', says 'Aṭṭār, 'that anyone can reach God in accordance with his own capacities, for God is with all things.' By this he appears to mean that all can find identity with the 'All', and all can experience the eternity of their own being, but this is only the beginning of a deification that can never be complete, and a 'deified' Muhammad would be as vastly superior to a 'deified' Abū Yazīd as is, to use the Indian metaphor, Mount Meru to a mustard seed.

Abū Yazīd, then, by introducing Vedāntin ideas into Ṣūfism, confronted the more orthodox Ṣūfīs with the problem of how to explain in terms that are not crassly heretical, the conviction that many of them secretly shared with him, namely, that the soul, at the end of its journey, actually *is* God. We have seen some of the explanations that were offered: none, however, could be wholly satisfying, for the Ṣūfīs did not admit the existence of what Rāmānuja called the 'category of *ātman*'—a mode of existence which is divine in that it takes account of neither space nor time, but which is not itself the ground of being. We will be considering in the next lecture how Junayd and Ghazālī tackled this problem.

[1] p. 86.

VII

The Teaching of Junayd

'UNION means to isolate eternity from origination':[1] so did Abū'l-Qāsim al-Junayd of Baghdad define *tawḥīd*, which can mean either the affirmation of the divine unity or the mystic's experience in ecstasy of that unity or union. That a word meaning 'union' should be used to mean its precise opposite, that is, the isolation or separation of two distinct and incompatible elements, may seem surprising. Exactly the same development, however, is observable in the Indian tradition; for the word *yoga*, which means 'joining' or 'uniting', comes to mean, in the philosophy of the Sāṁkhya-Yoga, the dis-joining or dis-uniting of *puruṣa* from *prakṛti*, of the eternal soul from the psycho-physical apparatus to which it is temporarily attached. In Buddhism the word still means 'conjunction', and more specifically the four fetters of craving, false views, becoming, and ignorance, which enslave the immortal spirit to the body and the world.[2] In the Bhagavad-Gītā the word, when applied to a spiritual discipline, means almost exactly what Jung calls 'individuation' or 'integration of the personality': the *yoga-yuktātmā* is the integrated personality, the man who has subjected his senses, conquered desire, subjected his mind to the *ātman* or permanent spiritual essence and thereby brought it to rest.[3] For the Yoga of the Gītā is nowhere near so radical as that of the classical Sāṁkhya-Yoga; it is a true integration, not a total isolation of the soul from matter. Only in the classical Yoga is the word used in a sense precisely opposite to its etymology. 'The aim

[1] Qushayrī, p. 3.

[2] See *The Pali Text Society's Pali-English Dictionary*, ed. T. W. Rhys Davids and William Stede, s.v. *Yoga*.

[3] BG., 6.25–27.

of . . . [this] *yoga*', Hiriyanna says, 'is very different from that of Upanishadic *yoga*. It is not union here, but separation. There, it is believed, the individual self unites with or merges in the absolute self by means of *yoga*; but here, where no such self is acknowledged, it comes to be by itself, through extrication from Prakṛti. Thus *yoga* which means "union" there, comes to mean "disunion" (*viyoga*) here.'[1]

Similarly in Islam, the word *tawḥīd*, which means 'uniting' or 'affirming unity', comes to mean with Junayd 'isolation' or 'separation'. In the Sāṁkhya-Yoga the 'isolation' or 'separation' is the isolation of the immortal and timeless soul from its bodily frame: in Junayd it is the separation of God who is alone eternal from the created universe. Commenting on one of Abū Yazīd's sayings Junayd had said that 'all creatures whatsoever are totally absent from God Most High, and he is isolated in his majesty from his creation'.[2] Abū Yazīd had in fact said no such thing: he had said that it was from the mystic, the '*ārif*, not from God, from whom all things were absent. Junayd applies to God what Abū Yazīd and many others had applied to the soul in ecstasy, thereby apparently raising an insuperable barrier between God and the human soul. This he did in order to appear as more orthodox than the orthodox themselves.

Junayd flourished at a time of crisis for Ṣūfism. Dhū'l-Nūn of Egypt had already been arraigned before the Caliph Mutawakkil on the suspicion of heresy, and his own close friend Nūrī only escaped execution by his sublime offer to lay down his life to save his friends or at least to postpone the hour of their imminent death.[3] Junayd, in common with most Ṣūfīs, regarded Ṣūfism as being an essentially esoteric doctrine which it was not lawful to divulge to the uninitiate. He was not then at all pleased when Ḥallāj, whom he had refused to accept as a disciple,[4] started to

[1] H. Hiriyanna, *The Essentials of Indian Philosophy*, London, 1949, p. 122; cf. *Mahābhārata*, III, ch. 212, l. 13,992, *taṁ vidyād brahmaṇo yogaṁ viyogaṁ yoga-sañjnitam*.

[2] See above, p. 123.

[3] See above, p. 3.

[4] See L. Massignon, *Al-Hallaj, Martyr mystique de l'Islam*, p. 52.

preach the most secret doctrines in public. The result he is alleged to have foreseen in that he dismissed Ḥallāj with these terrible words—'What a gibbet you will befoul [with your blood]!'[1] Himself of a retiring disposition[2] he wished to develop his doctrine out of the public eye. Yet despite his shyness and reserve he came to be regarded as the founding-father of all the Ṣūfī brotherhoods. There is scarcely a spiritual pedigree that is not traced back to him, and this is true not only of the avowed exponents of his doctrine, the orthodox Sarrāj, Qushayrī, and Hujwīrī, but even of so wild a follower of the 'intoxicated' discipline of Abū Yazīd as Abū Sa'īd ibn Abī'l-Khayr.[3] In Ṣūfī circles his prestige was unchallenged for it was he who was considered to have formulated the Ṣūfī doctrine in terms that could not give offence to the orthodox.

Of his works, some of which still survive in manuscript,[4] only one consecutive fragment has been published so far,[5] and it is not easy to form a consistent view either of his doctrine concerning God or of his interpretation of mystical experience from those sayings of his which are scattered throughout the early treatises on Ṣūfism from Sarrāj to 'Aṭṭār, but the essence of his doctrine which is uncompromising in its transcendentalism, may perhaps be deduced from his definitions of *tawḥīd*, both in its theological and its mystical aspects, which Sarrāj and Qushayrī have preserved.

Massignon sums up Junayd's doctrine as a 'coherent but empty monism',[6] but this is a generalization which, like all generalizations about individual Ṣūfīs will not stand up to the facts. Consistency was achieved by Indian thinkers like Patañjali because they

[1] Id., *Quatre Textes inédits, rélatifs à la Biographie d'Al-Ḥosayn—ibn Manṣoūr al-Ḥallāj*, Paris, 1914, p. 45*.

[2] Cf. Abū Nu'aym, *Ḥilyat al-Awliyā*, x, 255. Muḥāsibī had the greatest difficulty in getting him to go out at all.

[3] Ibn Munawwar, *Asrār al-Tawḥīd*, p. 27.

[4] Listed by Massignon, *Al-Hallaj* . . ., p. 35.

[5] From the *Kitāb al-Fanā*: see Ali Abdel Kader, *Islamic Quarterly*, i, 71–89.

[6] Massignon, ibid., p. 38. A. Abdel Kader has already corrected this too facile generalization in his 'The Doctrine of Al-Junayd' (*Islamic Quarterly*, i, 167–77) and 'Al-Junayd's Theory of *Fanā*' (ibid., pp. 219–28). He sums up Junayd's doctrine in these words: 'The worshipper loses the characteristics of his worldly individuality, returning into his eternal primeval self in God.'

were *primarily* concerned with the nature of the human soul and a mystical experience which consisted in an undifferentiable unity, they were not delving into the nature of a transcendent God and the relationship of that God to an originated and dependent human soul. In any case Junayd's definition of *tawḥīd*, which is to isolate the eternal from the contingent, is not monism but as frank a dualism as the Indian Sāṁkhya. Junayd's problem was rather how to build a bridge between the two orders of existence without impairing the transcendence and absolute unity of God.

Despite his theological definitions Junayd, like all the Ṣūfīs before him, starts with the assumption that love of God is not only possible, but the one sure way by which the soul can reach God. Qushayrī tells us that when Junayd was still a youngish man, the youngest of a group of Shaykhs in Mecca who were discussing love, he was asked what his opinion on the subject was.

> He cast down his head and tears began to flow. Then he said: '[The lover is] a servant [of God] who departs from himself, who cleaves to the recollection of his Lord, who undertakes to discharge his duty towards him, who contemplates him in his heart, whose heart has been set ablaze by the lights of his essence (*hūwiyya*), who drinks a pure draught from the cup of his love, to whom the Almighty reveals himself, and for whom he draws aside [all] veils that conceal him in his hidden remoteness. And if he speaks, it is by God [that he speaks], and if he makes public discourse, it is of God [that he discourses], and if he is active, it is by God's command, and if he is silent, it is with God; and he [exists] through God, belongs to God, and [dwells] with God.'[1]

The assembled Shaykhs started to weep, found nothing wanting in the definition, and bestowed on him the title of the 'Crown of the Mystics'.

The doctrine, then, that won Junayd such signal approval from his elders was neither a rigid monism nor an absolute dualism of God and his creation which he elsewhere seems to have proclaimed: on the contrary it is a doctrine of a *deus absconditus* who gradually reveals himself as the dispenser of the cup of love and the kindler of the fire of yearning in the heart. How is it, then, to be recon-

[1] Qushayrī, p. 147.

ciled with his definition of *tawḥīd* as 'the isolation of eternity from origination'?

Massignon is right when he says that Junayd pays attention above all to the Qur'ānic conception of the *Mīthāq*, the covenant by which human souls swore fealty to God before he created their bodies: all that individual man has of reality is reduced to this primordial confrontation of his essence, which is still a simple divine idea, with the divine essence itself.[1] In the Qur'ān the *Mīthāq* passage reads as follows:

> [Recall] when thy Lord took from the children of Adam, from their loins, their posterity and made them testify as to themselves: 'Am I not your Lord?' and they said: 'Yea, we testify'—lest ye should say on the day of resurrection: 'Of this we have been neglectful.'[2]

This may not seem a particularly sure foundation on which to base so novel an idea as that of the eternal existence of human souls as ideas in the divine mind; for the passage tells us little more than that souls pre-exist their bodies. However that may be, Junayd developed the doctrine that the supreme aim of the mystic was 'to be as he was before he was', that is, as an idea in the mind of God. This, in theory, preserved the absolute unity of God, yet made it possible for there to be a relationship between God and the soul. His affirmation of the unity of God for exoteric purposes is absolutely orthodox, his mystical interpretation of it is only apparently so. For exoteric purposes he defines *tawḥīd* as 'to declare the isolation of the Unified One by affirming his unity in perfect oneness, [to declare] that he is the One who neither begat nor was begotten, who knows neither opposite nor equal nor any like unto him, than whom none is worshipful. He cannot be compared to anything, nor qualified, nor pictured, nor likened to anything—one God, eternal, individual (*fard*). There is nothing that is like unto him. He is the seer, the hearer.'[3] Such is Junayd's declaration of the divine unity.

Tawḥīd as it affects the mystic is, however, thus described: it

[1] Massignon. *Al-Hallaj*, p. 36.
[2] Qur'ān, 7.171 (Bell's translation).
[3] Sarrāj, pp. 28–29: Qushayrī, p. 4.

means that '[God's] servant should be before God the Glorious like a [lifeless] body on which the different modes of his ordaining are exercised in accordance with the ordinances of his power, in the depths of the oceans of his unity: such a man will be naughted to self and to any claims creatures may have upon him and any response he may make to them. [He will exist] by the truths of God's unique Being in the reality of his nearness to him. All sensation and movement will be lost when God faces him with what he desires of him—and that is that he should return at the end to his first state, and be as he was before he was.'[1]

'Deification', then, for Junayd means to become, so far as one is able, once again an idea in the divine mind. If the divine word is 'Be', the word of the human heart which, in Ṣūfism as in the Upaniṣads, is regarded as the organ of spiritual enlightenment, is 'union'.[2] This strange idea is reproduced in Sahlajī's account of Abū Yazīd's *mi'rāj*, on which we commented in our last lecture: 'And the Word became one, and the All through the All became one. And he said to me: "O thou", and I said to him, "O I". And he said to me: "Thou art the alone". I said: "I am the alone".'[3] The doctrine that seems to underlie both these passages is that with the creative word *kun* 'Be' human souls which had previously been ideas in the divine mind take on a separate consciousness, but when the heart utters its own word *tawḥīd* 'union', it again becomes integrated into God as his idea, and God can once again address it as 'O thou I', and it can in its turn say 'O I' in recognition of its divine origin. Sahlajī's version of Abū Yazid's *mi'rāj*, then, is so very consistent with the thought of Junayd, and is so very much at variance with the common run of the utterances of the ecstatic of Bisṭām that I am strongly inclined to think that it is a remodelling of material stemming directly or indirectly from Abū Yazīd in accordance with the personal theology of Junayd.

Yet the demand that Junayd attributes to God that the soul 'should be as it was before it was' does not mean its total extinction,

[1] Sarrāj, p. 29: Qushayrī, p. 135.

[2] Qushayrī, p. 6.

[3] See above, p. 132.

but rather a new life, not indeed as God, but in and through God: for, for Junayd, Ṣūfism means 'that God causes you to die to self and to live in him'.[1] *Fanā* means the destruction of the creaturely life of the flesh and participation in the divine. On the way to this end, however, there are various stages: first the soul is chosen by God, then it is voided of self and 'isolated' in its commerce with God (*taqallubi-hi la-ka*). This twin operation is the first step of all which annihilates all trace of succession in time (*mā tarādafa*).[2] At this stage, then, the soul leaves the temporal world and enters into the eternal. Now at this stage God isolates the soul in itself in what Junayd calls 'the first stage of utter isolation', and this is for once more or less clearly described by this exceedingly abstruse writer. Writing to a friend he says:

> May God encompass thee as he encompasses those of his lovers whom he claims as his own, may he confirm thee and us on the paths of his good pleasure, may he conduct thee into the pavilion of his intimacy, and exalt thee in the gardens of the riches of his bounty. May he protect thee in all circumstances as an embryo in its mother's womb. Then may he perpetuate for thee the life that is appropriated [for thee] from eternal (timeless) life for ages everlasting, and may he isolate thee in himself (*bi-hi*) from what is thine and in thyself from what is his, until thou art isolated through him (*bi-hi*) for all eternity. Then there shall be neither thou nor thine, nor knowledge of him, but God will be alone.[3]

This prayer of Junayd for his friend falls into two distinct halves. In the first he prays that God may exalt and protect him like 'an embryo in its mother's womb', that is, wrapped away from all created things *in* God, but this is only the preparation for the break through the time barrier. This, the entering into a different kind of existence, is marked by the emphatic *thumma* 'then'. Once the time barrier is passed Junayd prays that his friend may firmly remain in this timeless state in the life 'that is appropriated [for thee] from eternal life for ages everlasting'. Like Rāmānuja Junayd sees the human soul in eternity as having its own pre-ordained share of eternal life. This he describes as the isolation of the soul in God

[1] Qushayrī, p. 126. [2] Sarrāj, p. 241. [3] Ibid. pp. 242–3.

from what belongs to the soul, and in itself from what belongs to God. Now, this seemingly obscure phrase is not comprehensible unless we compare it to the parallel development in India. What *belongs* to the soul is its former life in space and time, *bashariyya*, or the human personality as commonly understood. The soul is now isolated in, or, more accurately, through or by means of God, from its whole psycho-physical life, and this means isolation in itself or by itself from what belongs to God, that is, from all created things, both those that are bounded by time and space and those that are not, that is, other human souls as well as the angels. The soul is now isolated in itself in and through God (for the Arabic preposition *bi-* has both meanings); and this is exactly what Rāmānuja means by liberation. In his system the soul first realizes itself as eternal and therefore as sharing in the nature of God: 'It sees [God] in all soul-stuff (*ātma-vastu-*) and all soul-stuff in God', and God does not conceal himself from the man who perceives the true nature of his soul because he has the same mode of existence (*tat-sāmyāt*).[1] The soul's vision of its eternal self leads on to the vision of God; but at the stage of liberation, before the fire of love is kindled, the soul is isolated in itself, but in and through God: it contemplates the extra-temporal existence it has from God, but as yet it neither knows nor loves God. So too Junayd says, 'There shall be neither thou nor thine'—for the empirical ego has been done away with—'nor knowledge of him, but God will be alone'. The soul is here left in its own eternity in separation from God whom it contemplates in a state of blind annihilation. So far does Junayd take us in this passage, and it is precisely the stage of 'liberation' as understood by Rāmānuja. But this is not the end.

The soul has now passed out of time and is isolated in its own essence: it has reached the *kaivalyam*, the isolation that is the goal of the Sāṁkhya-Yoga. But so far from this being the end, it is only the 'first stage of isolation in separation and the reality of true isolation (*kā'in al-tafrīd*)'.[2] And so [the text goes on to say], 'when the soul is thus separated, [God] overwhelms, and annihilates the

[1] Rāmānuja on BG., 6.30. [2] Sarrāj, p. 241.

overwhelming of, what the soul in contemplation had previously experienced from God after all consciousness of creaturely existence had been destroyed. At this stage the full reality (*ḥaqīqat al-ḥaqīqa*) [of the mystical experience that the soul now possesses] comes to pass from God to God; and during this process, through the certain knowledge [the soul has] of that final stage which leads to the experience (*'ilm*) of union, there is a movement towards the experience of isolation in separation.'

These are dark words indeed, but they seem to mean that God, having allowed the soul to contemplate and to savour its individual and pre-ordained parcel of eternal life, overwhelms and annihilates this new and timeless particularism—that of the immortal *ātman* rather than that of the mortal ego, and sweeps it into the life of divine relationships where all commerce is 'from God to God', and, as a result of this, the soul obtains an infused knowledge of the absolute transcendence of God. It is in God and with God, and yet it knows that God in his 'isolation' and 'separation' is forever distinct from him. The Gītā is trying to express the same idea when it says that the soul is only a part of God,[1] and 'Aṭṭār when he says that 'the soul can attain to God [only] in accordance with its own capacity'.[2] Junayd himself, marvelling at the communion that he knows takes place between human souls and God—the souls originated though not in time, and God, the eternal origin of all—exclaims: 'When is he who has no peer and like unto whom there is nothing united with one who has peers and who is like others? Ah! this, but for the grace of the Gracious One, this is a strange fancy, ununderstandable, unimaginable, incomprehensible except as a pointer to a certain truth and as confirmation of the Faith.'[3]

Human souls were in origin ideas of God, and, for Junayd, when the pre-existent souls affirm the sovereignty of God, they at the same time accept suffering for themselves, for, in enunciating the word *balā*, they were not only saying 'Yes', they were also

[1] BG., 15.7.
[2] 'Aṭṭār, *Tadhkirat al-Awliyā*, i, 175. See above, p. 134.
[3] Qushayrī, p. 6.

affirming their acceptance of their own 'testing' or 'suffering', for the word *balā* means both 'yes' and 'testing'. The Qur'ānic story of God's covenant with man Junayd brings together with the Qur'ānic verse, 'Has there come upon man a period of time when he was not a thing mentioned',[1] and relates it to the mystical 'mentioning' of or meditation (*dhikr*) on the attributes of God.

May the truth of election [he writes to a friend] make thee die to the outward appearances of imperfection, and may the Truth, working secretly, save thee from considering thine own advantage and distract thee from the consideration of thy self and thy mystical experiences, and busy thee with the glorification of God during the time thou devotest to meditating on him. Then may he bring it to thy mind that it was he who bore thee in mind in pre-eternity before the time of testing and before the conditions of testing [were created].[2]

Dhū'l-Nūn had already used the idea of man existing in some form before he became a 'thing mentioned'—'Thou didst originate me in thy mercy before I was a thing mentioned,'[3] he says—but Junayd goes further, for he maintains that the human soul was for all eternity 'mentioned' by God—there never was a time when it was not present to his mind. For all eternity, then, the soul is in loving communion with God, and God's covenant with man, which for Muḥāsibī was a thing of joy,[4] spelled, for Junayd, rather a 'testing' by suffering. The separation from God which the pre-existent souls confirmed by their acknowledging him as their Lord, is itself the source of suffering—and suffering willingly accepted or, better still, joyfully embraced is one of the ways in which God leads the estranged soul back to himself. 'The mystic', Junayd says, 'knows full well that God does not afflict him out of

[1] Qur'ān, 76.1.

[2] Sarrāj, p. 242.

[3] Abū Nu'aym, *Ḥilyat al-Awliyā*, ix, 332.

[4] Ibid., x, 76: 'He made himself known to them (the souls), guided them to his obedience, and showed them love, independent though he was of them. And he deposited love for him in the hearts of his lovers. Then he clad them in shining light [which appeared] in their speech out of the fullness of the love for him they bore in their hearts. And after he had done this for them, he presented them to the angels, rejoicing in them.'

hatred or in order to punish him. Whatever affliction falls to his lot from God he sees as the purest love between himself and God. It is only sent upon him that he may restore his soul to God out of his full free choice. And when he discovers this and things like this, it is small wonder that his soul flies to God in passionate longing and turns away from its familiar haunts with passion[ate loathing].'[1]

To become fit for union with God the mystic must 'conform to, or live in harmony with, God under all circumstances'[2] so that God's attributes replace his.[3] Then he is in a position to 'taste of the cup of [God's] love, and vital force (*'aysh*) will be joined to vital force, life to life, and spirit to spirit'.[4] Junayd, of course, as a Muslim, wholeheartedly believed in the truth of his religion as officially expounded. Because he admired Abū Yazīd as a genuine mystic, though only a beginner, he sought to soften down the harshness of his utterances, but he would not countenance any infringement of the religious law. He claimed that Ṣūfism depended on the Qur'ān, the religious law, and the Traditions,[5] and that all ways were barred to those who did not follow in the footsteps of the Prophet.[6] Any form of quietism was thus abhorrent to him, and when asked to comment on the proposition that 'those who have knowledge of God reach a state in which they leave behind them good works and the fear of God', he left his interlocutor in no doubt at all as to where he stood. 'This', he said, 'is the doctrine proclaimed by those who teach "the dropping of works". In my opinion it is a monstrous doctrine. A fornicator or a thief is better off than people who talk like that.'[7] 'Those who know God', he goes on to say, 'take their works from God and return to him with them. Were I to live for a thousand years, I should not abate one jot from the doing of good works unless some insuperable obstacle were put in

[1] Sarrāj, p. 305.
[2] Ibid., p. 217.
[3] Ibid., p. 59: Qushayrī, p. 145.
[4] Sarrāj, p. 242.
[5] Qushayrī, p. 19.
[6] Ibid.
[7] Sulamī, *Ṭabaqāt al-Ṣūfiyya*, p. 159: Qushayrī, p. 19.

the way.'[1] For Junayd life on earth was deadly serious—it was a testing—and by obeying God's commandments and doing good a man conformed himself to God and offered up his actions back to God. Junayd thus continues the deep moral seriousness of his Ṣūfī predecessors, and separates himself sharply off from those gay, free spirits who, like Abū Sa'īd ibn Abī'l-Khayr, were later to flout the law and indulge in the silliest extravagances on the grounds that their exalted spiritual state put them beyond the law. It is a tribute to the spiritual stature of Junayd that even Abū Sa'īd should trace his spiritual ancestry back to him.

Before leaving Junayd a few words must be said about his *Kitāb al-Fanā* which Abdel Kader has recently published.[2] Like all Junayd's writing it is purposely difficult and obscure, for he knew that his doctrines, if clearly formulated, could scarcely be accepted by the orthodox theologians.

In this fragment of the *Kitāb al-Fanā* Junayd attempts to describe what happens to the soul in its encounter with God. His conception of the love of God had little of tenderness in it, for he never forgets for a moment the awful majesty of God. The 'intimacy' that the soul enjoys with God, which the Ṣūfīs call *uns*, he characteristically defines as 'the cessation of shyness without the loss of awe'.[3] The first step towards union, then, he sees as the creature's encounter with the irresistible might and majesty of God, in which the creature is swept away, crushed, and annihilated like a straw in a hurricane.

Using the Covenant verse from the Qur'ān as his text Junayd says that God 'addressed [the human souls] when they did not [yet] exist except in so far as he "existed" them (*wujūdi-hi la-hum*); for he was [eternally] "existing" [his] creation in a manner that was different from his "existing" individual souls (*anfus*), in a manner that he alone knows. . . . He was "existing" them, encompassing them, witnessing them in the beginning when they were no thing apart from their eternal being [in which] state they were from all pre-eternity—and this is the divine (*rabbānī*) existence and divine (*ilāhī*) awareness which is proper to him alone. Therefore did we

[1] Qushayrī, ibid. [2] See above, p. 137. [3] Sarrāj, pp. 65–66.

say that when he "existed" man, causing his will to flow over him as he wished, [endowing him] with his most exalted attribute in which none can share, this [form of] existence was without doubt the most perfect and the most efficacious.'[1]

When I last translated this passage,[2] I took *shāhid* to mean 'calling to witness' in accordance with the tenor of the Covenant verse in the Qur'ān. It must, however, mean 'witness', for Junayd himself elsewhere defines the word as meaning 'the Truth (i.e. God) witnessing in your heart and most secret places and taking cognizance thereof'.[3] The phrase *wajada li-* I would now translate as to 'exist' something in a transitive sense, a usage that is current among some French Catholic existentialist writers. To cause to exist is *awjada* in Arabic, and it would seem that Junayd uses *wajada li-* to indicate something more subtle, more immediate, more 'existential', if you like, than this. What he means, I think, is this: in his timeless eternity God contemplates or witnesses, 'mentions' or thinks, encompasses or comprehends all human souls (*arwāḥ* not *anfus*) in one single existential act of witnessing, thought, and comprehension: in this single act he 'exists' them. The term denotes the logical priority of God over all souls, but a community of substance, and the 'substance' in this case is eternal extra-temporal being. The moment of creation in time is called *fanā'i-him 'an baqā'i-him*, 'their annihilation out of or after their eternal being', that is to say, their entry into time from eternity. This takes place 'in the beginning' and marks the entry of the soul into space and time. The existence of the soul (*rūḥ*) in eternity is divine, *rabbānī* and *ilāhī*, and is simply not comparable to the existence of the lower soul or *nafs* in this world: it is the most perfect existence a human being can enjoy, and it is totally devoid of humanity as we understand it (*idh lā ṣifata bashariyyatin*) since 'it proceeds from God and his overwhelming power.'[4] In itself it too overwhelms all purely human characteristics, but 'what souls have

[1] *Islamic Quarterly*, i, 80.

[2] In my *Mysticism, Sacred and Profane*, p. 166.

[3] Sarrāj, p. 229. Perhaps I would not have made this mistake if I had recalled that in India too God is the *sākṣin-*, the eternal witness in the heart.

[4] *Islamic Quarterly*, i, 80.

of eternity' is an existence derived from another; and to express this idea Junayd says they are 'clad' in it. It constitutes a bliss which is quite incomprehensible: it is a free gift of God, and 'generosity as applied to God is not what we usually mean by generosity'. The relationship between God and immortal souls must therefore always remain unknown to any but God—or rather, as Junayd says elsewhere, to any but God and any individual soul which God deigns to raise up to him; for 'sincerity is a secret between God and his servant which no angel may know that he should record it, nor devil that he should defile it, nor desire that it should divert it'.[1] God's relationship with the soul in eternity is not an I/It relationship, to revert to Martin Buber's terminology, but an I/Thou relationship of such personal intensity that none but the soul and God can have any knowledge of it. This existence in God which is eternal, manifests itself in time through the bodily apparatus, and, in the words of the Tradition: 'When my servant constantly draws near to me by works of supererogation, then do I love him, and once I have started to love him, I become his eye by which he sees, his ear by which he hears, his tongue by which he speaks, and his hand by which he grasps.'[2]

This tradition, which Junayd whole-heartedly accepts, opened the door to every kind of excess since any lunatic who considered he had fallen under the control of a higher power, could claim that his actions were no longer his but God's; and it is no accident that Abū Sa'īd ibn Abī'l-Khayr's initiation into the higher mysteries should have been at the hands of one of these '*uqalā'-i majānīn*, these 'madmen who are yet sane', whom God had personally freed from his commands and prohibitions.[3] This kind of thing Junayd had foreseen, and he therefore lays down that absolutely no one has a right to make such claims for himself: hence his insistence that under no circumstances may the obligatory duties of the religious law be neglected. For man lives both in eternity with God and in time with the world. His *rūḥ*, immortal soul or *ātman*,

[1] Qushayrī, p. 96.

[2] This is the full version of this exceedingly popular Ṣūfī tradition. See Sarrāj, pp. 383–4.

[3] Ibn Munawwar, *Asrār al-Tawḥīd*, pp. 24–25.

being eternal cannot directly act, but his *nafs*, which for Junayd seems to mean the whole of the human psyche which operates in time, can and does, though neither the *nafs* nor the senses have any awareness of the soul's timeless bliss.[1] What is present to the one is absent from the other and *vice versâ*.

We have seen that Junayd considered the sign of spiritual progress to be the gradual replacement of human qualities by divine ones. Most Ṣūfīs would have agreed with this, but they believed that this could only be effected by the actual destruction of the *nafs*. Sahl ibn Abdullah of Ṭustar who was famous for his austerities, said: 'Know that this is a time in which no one can attain salvation except by slaying his *nafs* in sacrifice by fasting, long-suffering, and gruelling toil.'[2] In a similar vein Abū Sa'īd al-Kharrāz recommends that the *nafs* be melted by obedience, killed by showing enmity to it, sacrificially slaughtered by despairing of all that is not God, and murdered by the shame one feels before God.[3] Such drastic measures do not commend themselves to Junayd. For him the *nafs* is rather a disease that may yet be cured: once it ceases to be a slave to the lusts of the flesh and opposes them, 'its disease becomes its cure'.[4] The relationship of the eternal soul to the temporal one is, then, for Junayd, analogous to the relationship of God to the eternal soul—the junior partner must in each case be brought into conformity with the senior, and, as far as the lower soul is concerned, this is achieved by conforming to the religious law.

Junayd, shy and retiring though he was, squarely faced the fact that even the mystic has to live in this world, and though, in ecstasy, the soul may transcend the senses and time, it nevertheless has to return to both; and this constitutes the torment (*'adhāb*) of the soul.[5] But there are torments and temptations besides this, and the worst of these temptations is that the soul should enjoy itself in isolation apart from God.

The two words that Junayd continually uses in the *Kitāb al-Fanā* to express God's relationship to the soul are *isti'thār* and

[1] *Islamic Quarterly*, i, 81. [2] Sulamī, *Ṭabaqāt al-Ṣūfiyya*, p. 209.
[3] Sarrāj, p. 264. [4] Qushayrī, p. 71. [5] *Islamic Quarterly*, i, 81.

istīlā', 'appropriation' and 'supremacy' or 'overwhelming'. When once the soul has communed with God in the manner that God has 'appropriated' to it, it returns again to the world and experiences torment, the 'pang of loss' which stimulates it to an 'intensity of effort'.[1] It now makes demands on (*ṭālaba*) God of a kind that God alone has a right to make, for such souls 'now dwell in power and have attained to the reality of high favour [with God]. He dwells in them and occupies them, and, thanks to him, all that ever was or was not in the order of contingency (*ṣifa*) wells up within them.' They then 'become satisfied with what had already appeared to them, lose all sense of destitution, and abandon all sense of judgement. They preen themselves on the victory [they think they have obtained] by their own efforts and power and overweening pride. But [in truth] they had been looking on things with what [in them] was theirs, without passing upwards to what is God's, and so they induce distinction and separation because they see and experience with their own two eyes, whereas God overwhelms with his two commands. And when God's manifestations appear to them, [God] causes them to take refuge from him in their own [attributes] so that they exult and glory in their isolation. At this stage they go forth without any repining (?) towards him, preferring [to him] that in which their joy is isolated, playing the wanton with him, so sure are they of his forbearance. They do not see that return will be demanded of them and that an account will be exacted from them. When this happens, it is God's guile that encompasses them in a manner they do not understand.'

Though the style is obscure, the purport of this passage seems to be clear enough. The mystic is represented as first experiencing communion with God in which an eternal and unique relationship is established between the extra-temporal soul and God who is its ground and source: God's rôle is to elect and overwhelm, the soul's to be elected and overwhelmed. Once the mystic is restored to the world of space and time, it strives to re-establish the *rapport* by its own unaided efforts. The mystic's own striving (or what he conceives to be such, for God controls him all the time) brings him

[1] Ibid., p. 82.

to a point where he thinks he can do without God: both his sense of creatureliness and his judgement forsake him, and he prefers to enjoy the isolation of his own soul to the timeless relationship he had enjoyed with God. This is God's *makr*, the quality of guile by which he leads the mystic astray. The mystic thinks he has achieved all this by his own efforts, whereas it is really God putting him off the scent. In the Indian tradition Rāmānuja too warns against this danger. 'The consciousness of a man whose mind is not fixed on God', he says, 'and who, in subduing the senses, relies entirely on his own efforts, cannot succeed even if his mind is directed exclusively to the *ātman*.'[1] Thus, in their different traditions and against their different theological backgrounds, Rāmānuja and Junayd agree that even the soul's realization of itself in apparent isolation from God cannot be attained without the divine intervention. For Junayd this monistic trance is the ultimate temptation, the snare with which God trips up the spiritually proud.

According to Junayd God may now shatter this rapture of self-regarding isolation by re-asserting his authority. The impact causes these souls 'to be distraught for life eternal': it causes acute suffering and makes them realize that they have lost God. None of their acquired mystical habits (*mawāṭin* and *amākin*) will avail them now, they are overcome with misery at their disloyalty to God. God, on his side, makes them long and thirst for him with an unquenchable thirst, makes them taste again utter denudation (*faqr*), and gives them strength to endure suffering for his sake. The last veil is lifted, and God torments them, but they do not shrink away. 'And how should any veil divide them from him?' Junayd asks, 'For they are his captives, imprisoned before him, and even as they are afflicted, they find favour with him in that they are destroyed in what is manifested to them. They no longer aim at looking after themselves, content with God's love and their dependence on him and their nearness to him. In the swiftness of their awakening they behold the myriad glances that proceed from him so that the very destruction [of their human, individuality] is [itself] drowned in the tide that flows over them in

[1] Rāmānuja on BG., 2.66.

eternal Being and violent suffering, until their very suffering is turned to joy, and their abiding in it brings delight in God, for they see that he is near to ward off their suffering and to draw its sting. Then the soul no longer turns away from the burden of suffering out of faint-heartedness, nor is it grieved by it nor chafed. These are the [real] heroes of mystical experience because God has revealed his secrets to them, and they have taken up their abode in his omnipotence (*qahr*), awaiting his command, that God [himself] may fulfil a deed performed.'

I hope I may be forgiven for having quoted Junayd's *Kitāb al-Fanā* at some length. I have thought it right to do so, for here even more than in the epistles quoted by Sarrāj, Junayd's analysis of mystical experience seems to be particularly penetrating. His main line of thought may be summed up as follows.

The relationship between God and the *rūḥ* or higher soul is an eternal one in which God is *mustaulī*, 'absolutely predominant' and *musta'thir*—he appropriates each elected soul to himself in a manner that is peculiar and individual to each and every soul so elected. In mystical experience this relationship will be revealed to the soul in a flash of intuition in which it not only realizes that it has its being outside time, but that it has forever a unique relationship with God. When the vision passes the soul suffers bitter anguish and therefore strives to attain this state again by its own efforts. What it achieves, however, is not a relationship with God of any kind, but a total isolation or en-stasis in itself. In this state it thinks itself independent of God, loses all sense of awe, and behaves with coquettish boldness towards him: this is what Junayd elsewhere calls *awwal tafrīd al-tajrīd*,[1] 'the beginning of' or 'first' 'isolation in separation', and this is the trap which God sets for the soul. It explains, among other things, how Abū Yazīd could have brought himself to believe that his 'onset was more violent than the onset of God'.[2] God, however, now visits the mystic, thus drunk with spiritual pride, again: and his soul, confident though it is in its timeless being, is utterly humbled, made to suffer agonies, but made also, in and through its very agony, to thirst for God who,

[1] Sarrāj, p. 241. [2] See above, p. 115.

it now sees, is its only true goal and perfect satisfaction. The suffering of the soul is then transmuted into joy, and its spiritual life is now enriched beyond the original happiness it had enjoyed when 'it was not', that is, when it was only an idea in God's mind. Finite existence has thus taken nothing away from it, but, on the contrary, has added what was lacking before, the joy-in-agony of loving and being loved by God. The path that one must tread to reach this state is long and perilous, or, to quote the words of this spiritual genius for the last time: 'The journey from this world to the next is easy and simple for the believer, but to separate oneself from creatures for God's sake is hard, and the journey from self to God is exceedingly hard, and to bear patiently with God is the hardest of all.'[1]

'*Tawḥīd* means to isolate eternity from origination.' These were the words of Junayd with which we introduced him; and I hope that our analysis of the few writings of his which remain to us may have made the meaning of this pregnant saying a little more clear. The soul is God's idea and, as such, eternal; it is dipped in time and returns to him enriched by the experience of suffering for his sake. For a Muslim the idea is daring, and the orthodox school of Ṣūfīs of whom Junayd was the founder, adopted other formulas to explain the nature of the soul. Of Junayd's successors in 'orthodox' Ṣūfism Ghazālī was without doubt the most influential as well as the most prolific; and we must now consider his view both on the nature of the soul and the nature of mystical experience.

In Ghazālī we will look for the deep concentration of thought that we found in Junayd in vain; for, in my opinion at least, Junayd was a spiritual genius of the very first rank and was rightly hailed as the 'Crown of the Mystics'.[2] Ghazālī was essentially the popularizer of other men's ideas, and in his mystical writings he bothered very little about consistency. 'When we come to the

[1] Qushayrī, p. 85.
[2] See above, p. 138.

books of Shaykh Abū Ḥāmid al-Ghazālī,' writes the twelfth-century Andalusian philosopher Ibn Ṭufayl, 'so far as he addresses himself to the general public, he binds in one place only to loose in another, pronounces certain doctrines heretical at one time only to adopt them later.'[1] As an example Ibn Ṭufayl quotes his condemnation of the philosophers for denying the resurrection of the body in the *Taḥāfut* and his blithe acceptance of the same doctrine in the *Mīzān al-'Amal* where he quotes it as being the considered opinion of the Ṣūfī Shaykhs. Such contradictions are to be found throughout the enormous output of Ghazālī and do not seem to have troubled this supposedly logical thinker unduly. Manichaean and Platonic conceptions of the nature of the world jostle each other happily, and no attempt is made to reconcile them. This confusion of thought which is characteristic of Ghazālī is due to the fact that for the first time in the 'orthodox' Ṣūfī tradition Ṣūfism and philosophy meet. Ghazālī was not, as is often alleged, a synthetizer: he borrows from both Ṣūfism and philosophy, combines the two in a loose and incoherent mixture, but makes no attempt to construct a logical system out of the ingredients he has selected. His mystical reading included the *Qūt al-Qulūb* of Abū Ṭālib al-Makkī, Muḥāsibī, and the recorded fragments concerning Junayd, Shiblī, and Abū Yazīd al-Bisṭāmī.[2] His own brand of Ṣūfism is, in fact, based largely on Muḥāsibī and Makkī, and there is no evidence that he ever even understood the crucial problem which had exercised Junayd as it was later to exercise Rāmānuja in India—namely, how is the mystic's claim to have reached a state of undifferentiable oneness in isolation to be reconciled with a theistic view of the universe?

Before Ghazālī Ṣūfism had not been seriously interested in metaphysics. It approached the mystical element in religion not *via* theology but by the direct road of moral discipline and self-purification. The greatest exponent of this method is certainly

[1] Ibn Ṭufayl, *Ḥayy bin Yaqẓān*, ed. A. Ḥakīm, Beyrout, 1954, p. 8.

[2] *Al-Munqidh min al-Ḍalāl*, ed. M. M. Jaber, Cairo (undated), p. 43: translation by W. Montgomery Watt as *The Faith and Practise of Al-Ghazālī*, London, 1953, p. 54.

Muḥāsibī who, in his remorseless analysis of motive and the secret sins of the soul, bears more than a superficial resemblance to St. François de Sales in the mystical flowering of the Counter-Reformation in the West, whereas Junayd, with his profoundly penetrating analysis of the stages the soul goes through in its return journey to God, may not ineptly be compared with St. John of the Cross. Ghazālī's writing on the ascetical preparation for the mystical encounter are very largely dependent on Muḥāsibī, whereas his ideas on the nature of mystical experience seem to be based on Abū Yazīd, Ḥallāj, and Abū Sa'īd ibn Abī'l-Khayr rather than on Junayd. We shall have to return to this in our next and last lecture.

Like practically all mystics Ghazālī considers man to be of a dual nature: he is composed of a mortal body and an immortal soul. His mature views on the relationship between the body and the soul, and the soul and God, are given in the first book of the *Kīmiyā-yi Sa'ādat*, one of his latest works.[1] His starting-point is the celebrated tradition—*man 'arafa nafsa-hu fa-qad 'arafa rabba-hu*—'Who knows himself knows his Lord': so he proceeds first to analyse human personality and then, by analogy, he analyses the relationship of God to the world. As his text for the nature of the soul he takes the Qur'ānic text: 'And they will ask you concerning the spirit; say, the spirit is *min amri rabbi-hi*.'[2] This phrase, as it stands, is exceedingly obscure and may mean either 'is of the affair of his Lord', i.e. God's business, or 'derives from the command of his Lord'. Now, as has often been pointed out before, 'the semi-personal and changing sense of *amr* [in the Qur'ān] . . . strongly suggests the *mēmrā* of the Talmud which, as a substitute for the name of Yahweh, gives the appearance of being a person or at least an intermediary force between God and the world, without being either in reality'.[3] This personification of the divine command or Word is a commonplace of Isma'īlī theology: for it is made to correspond to the Neo-Platonic Nous, the *'aql al-kullī* or

[1] Written after the *Mishkāt al-Anwār* which it mentions on p. 50.

[2] Qur'ān, 17.87.

[3] T. O'Shaughnessy, S.J., *The Development of the Meaning of Spirit in the Korān*, Rome, 1953, p. 39.

'universal intelligence' of Avicenna. It is the exteriorization of the *deus absconditus*, the unqualifiable One of the Neo-Platonists. 'All created things and all creation subsist totally in the *amr* of God,' writes Nāṣir-i Khusraw, the famous Isma'īlī apologist of the eleventh century,[1] 'and nothing is either prior or posterior to it': it is an effect of God, the One, just as writing is the effect of the scribe, in other words it is the creative power of God—the exact equivalent of the Hindu *śakti* or *māyā*—and as such the real creator. Proceeding without intermediary from God it still remains one with God, but 'being perfect in act and potency, it is in truth the creator and the agent'.[2] Thus the impassive godhead is preserved in its absolute unity while creation is the work of the *amr* which, as its sole effect, is both identical with it and distinct. The *amr* or command is also called the 'Word'—the creative word of the Qur'ān, *kun*, 'Be'.[3] Thus the 'Word' of the Isma'īlīs corresponds exactly to the *Īśvara* or 'Lord' of the Śaṅkara Vedānta, the 'Lord of *māyā*'[4] and the *śakti* of the *Śvetāśvatara* Upaniṣad.

The God of Isma'īlī metaphysics is the One of Plotinus which, being absolutely one, cannot be the source of multiplicity: hence the necessity for the creative Word which faces both ways, so to speak—one with the One as its sole effect when it faces inward, but the cause of all multiplicity when it faces outward. The One of Plotinus, however, is very different from the Allah of the Qur'ān, and it therefore seems surprising that Ghazālī should see fit to introduce the idea of the creative Word into Ṣūfism. His interpretation of the Qur'ānic *amr*, however, is not identical with that of the Isma'īlīs, though, in the *Risālat al-Ladunniyya*[5] where he con-

[1] Nāṣir-i Khusraw, *Kitāb-i Gushā'ish wa Rahā'ish*, ed. S. Nafisi, Leiden, 1950, p. 6.

[2] Ibid., pp. 6–7. [3] Ibid., p. 86. [4] *Śvet*Up., 4.10.

[5] The authenticity of this work is disputed by Asín Palacios (*Espiritualidad de Algazel*, iv, 388) on the grounds that much of it re-appears in the *Risāla Fī'l-Nafs wa'l-Rūḥ* of Ibn al-'Arabī. It is true that the *Risālat al-Ladunniyya* is more explicitly Neo-Platonist than any of Ghazālī's other works, but the theology of the *amr* and *rūḥ* are fully developed in the *Kīmiyā-yi Sa'ādat*, and the *Risālat-al Ladunniyya* may well represent a very late stage in Ghazālī's thought. The close resemblance to Ibn al-'Arabī's treatise can best be explained by the fact that plagiarism was not at the time regarded as being particularly reprehensible.

sciously tries to adapt Neo-Platonism to 'orthodox' Ṣūfism, it is very nearly so.

We saw that in India the various philosophical schools attempted to explain the nature of the universe against the background of the experience of liberation. Liberation reveals that there is, in addition to the world of space and time, a world where the soul passes beyond both. The experience of liberation is both for the Sāṁkhya-Yoga and the Śaṅkara Vedānta one of undifferentiated oneness: there is no experience of anything but oneself. Gauḍapāda and Śaṅkara held that this experience meant that the released soul was in fact the ground from which all existence in time and space grew, and, because it must have been plain even to them that in fact they were not the creator of the world, they had to take the further step of declaring the world to be illusory. Abū Yazīd, in introducing these ideas into Islam, made the mistake of identifying the qualityless Brahman with the Allah of his own creed. The fact is, however, that the God revealed in the Qur'ān simply is not the God of the mystical experience of Abū Yazīd. Junayd squarely faced this issue. He did not make the mistake of dismissing Abū Yazīd as a madman or his experiences as either illusory or of diabolic origin: he accepted them as genuine experiences of what Louis Gardet calls *an* absolute, or what I would prefer to call, with Buber, the 'pre-biographical' unity of the soul—he accepted them and assigned them their due place in what he conceived to be the soul's ascent to God. For him each soul is unique, and its relationship with God is therefore unique too. His theology is therefore a theology of eternal relationships, and within this frame he logically accounts for the soul's delusion that it is God when all it really is, is itself in its 'pre-biological unity'. Abū Yazīd's experiences which had seemed to raise the mystic beyond the God of the Qur'ān, were deflated and put where they belonged. The majesty and uniqueness of God were thereby preserved intact.

Ghazālī, in his handling of the esoteric doctrine of the *amr*, seems to do so against the background of the claim of Abū Yazīd and others that the mystic in ecstasy actually realizes himself as

God. This appears fairly clearly in the *Mishkāt al-Anwār* in which the mystic is said to see that nothing at all exists except God. The corollary of this is, of course, that creation is illusory; and, like Śaṅkara and Plotinus, Ghazālī is forced to introduce a secondary figure as the creator God of what is from the absolute point of view an unreal universe. This is presumably the secret doctrine 'to explain which would be reprehensible innovation (*bid'at*)'.[1] So, in his works written for the general public other theories of the relationship of the soul to God, and the soul to the body appear.

In the *Kimiyā* Ghazālī divides existence into two separate compartments, the '*ālam-i amr*, 'the world of the Word', and the '*ālam-i khalq*, 'the world of creation'.[2] The latter is the material universe characterized by extension, quality, and quantity, the former is the spiritual, ideal, or intelligible world consisting of souls which are not subject to spatial categories but which are nevertheless created: moreover, it would appear that, like the *ātman*-Brahman of Śaṅkara, they are devoid of quality, they are not in any way definable, and there is no answer to the question: 'What is the soul like?'[3] Similarly, since they are not subject to extension, they are indivisible monads,[4] very much like the *puruṣas* of the Sāṁkhya-Yoga, except that for Ghazālī they are usually though not always created.

The soul is a spiritual essence like that of the angels, and 'its descent into this world is alien to the nature of its essence';[5] further it is the mirror of God[6] and as such enters into a mysterious *rapport* with the 'Preserved Tablet' which is the mirror of God in

[1] *KS.*, p. 898.

[2] *KS.*, p. 12. Ghazālī borrows the idea of the '*ālam al-amr* and the '*ālam al-khalq* from Avicenna. See F. Dieterici, *Alfārābī's philosophische Abhandlungen*, Leiden, 1890, pp. 69, 72 (Arabic text). Dr. R. Walzer tells me that the treatise *Risāla Fuṣūṣ al-Ḥikam* where the passages occur is not by al-Fārābī but by Avicenna. He has also drawn my attention to a similar passage in the *Risāla fī Māhiyyat al-Ṣalāt* (published in M. A. F. Mehren, *Traités mystiques . . . d'Avicenne*, Leiden, 1894, fasc. iii, p. 33 (Arabic text)).

[3] *KS.*, p. 44.

[4] Ibid., p. 45.

[5] Ibid., p. 78.

[6] Ibid., p. 75.

the cosmos.[1] According to a well-known tradition based on Genesis 1.27, 'God created man in his own image',[2] and the soul's relationship to the body must therefore reflect the relationship of God to the world. The soul in the body is like a king in his kingdom and the lower faculties are his functionaries, the two prime instincts of the lower soul, anger and desire, being likened to the chief of police and the chief tax-gatherer respectively.[3] Similarly in the macrocosm God is the king and as such he corresponds to the soul or heart of man:[4] both God and the soul are *munazzah*, 'devoid of qualities', and as such unimaginable and inconceivable, yet both hold sway in their own kingdoms.

In the first book of the *Kīmiyā-yi Sa'ādat* Ghazālī is careful to point out that the 'world of the Word', though in no way commensurable with the 'world of creation', is nonetheless created, yet in the third book he allows himself to say that the soul (which is part of the world of the Word) 'is a substance that exists of itself'.[5] Ghazālī is indeed always betraying himself by these apparent slips of the pen, and it is highly probable that his own inner convictions were far nearer to the Isma'īlī metaphysics than he would have cared to admit. In the *Risālat al-Ladunniyya* where he claims to expound the beliefs of the 'Ṣūfī elect', he speaks a very different language. As in the *Kīmiyā* the soul derives from the *amr*, Word, or Logos of God, but God does not create it out of nothing: 'he *manifested* the substance of the soul from his one, perfect Word which brings about perfection and benefit'.[6] The Word is unique: it is the 'power' or 'potency' (*quwwa*) of God, known in philosophy as the first intelligence and in the Qur'ān as the Tablet or Pen. So too the soul is a 'durable and permanent substance not subject to decay', 'a singular perfect substance that is alive by its own essence'.[7] The body is described both in the *Kīmiyā*[8] and the

[1] Ibid., p. 22.
[2] Ibid., p. 45.
[3] Ibid., pp. 14–15.
[4] Ibid., pp. 44–45.
[5] Ibid., p. 734.
[6] *Risālat al-Ladunniyya* in Ṣabrī, p. 23.
[7] Ibid., p. 25.
[8] p. 36.

Risāla[1] as the mount or the instrument of the soul, but in the *Risāla* we also meet with the wholly Manichaean idea of the body being composed of darkness and the soul of light.[2] As usual no attempt is made to reconcile the two points of view.

Similarly in his view of the world Ghazālī is wildly inconsistent, although it should be pointed out that he draws a distinction between the '*ālam*, the orderly cosmos which reflects the creative activity of God, the contemplation of which may bring one nearer to the Creator,[3] and the *dunyā*, the sublunary world as it affects man. But in his judgement of the *dunyā* or sublunary world we see the same gaily eclectic tendency at work. As a journey,[4] hotel,[5] ship,[6] or even a dream,[7] it would seem to be relatively harmless, but this can scarcely be said of it in its capacity as the 'prison of the faithful',[8] as a sorcerer,[9] harlot,[10] a refuse dump,[11] or a devouring flame.[12] So too it is the enemy of God,[13] and 'God created nothing on the face of the earth [*sic*] more hateful to himself than the world, and when he created it he never so much as looked at it',[14] so man should shrink from it as from a corpse.[15] This, however, does not prevent this same world from being created for man as a provision.[16] Little inconsistencies like these Ghazālī easily takes in his stride.

The almost paranoiac hatred of the world that Ghazālī sometimes displays must derive directly or indirectly from a Manichaean source, and the contemplation of the filthiness of the body which he commends as a salutary exercise[17] must ultimately go back to Buddhism.[18] This exercise, however, in no way precludes the grateful meditation on the marvellous mechanics of this same vile body.[19] Rarely has the reputation of a thinker of repute rested more securely on the absence of adequate translations of his works.

Professor Arberry doubts 'whether [Ghazālī] was himself a

[1] p. 26. [2] p. 23. [3] *KS.*, pp. 789 ff., 921. [4] Ibid., p. 67.
[5] Ibid., pp. 68, 621. [6] Ibid., p. 69. [7] Ibid., p. 622.
[8] Ibid., pp. 84, 548. [9] Ibid., pp. 66, 616. [10] Ibid., pp. 67, 616.
[11] Ibid., p. 617. [12] Ibid., p. 619. [13] Ibid., p. 616.
[14] Ibid., p. 617. [15] Ibid., p. 622. [16] Ibid., p. 789.
[17] Ibid., p. 720. [18] Cf. especially *Visuddhi-Magga*, ch. vi.
[19] *KS.*, p. 791.

mystic at all in the strict sense of the term'.[1] Ghazālī's interpretation of mystical experience in both the *Kīmiyā* and the *Mishkāt al-Anwār*, however, show a relative consistency that we look for in vain in his metaphysical writing, and it is likely that Ghazālī may have had a purely monistic experience in which all disappeared except the 'One', for this would account for the difference between his esoteric doctrine (which is purely monistic) and his more 'popular' work which tries to follow orthodox lines. In our last lecture, then, we shall have to consider the nature of the experiences he describes, and pass in review the theories of some of his successors who perhaps gave rather more thought to these difficult matters than did the illustrious philosopher of Ṭūs.

[1] A. J. Arberry, *Revelation and Reason in Islam*, p. 108.

VIII

Ghazālī and After

GHAZALĪ'S prestige as a philosopher and theologian was immense, and his doctrinal formulation of Ṣūfism was bound profoundly to influence the whole future development of the Ṣūfī movement. In the years of his retirement from which none of the blandishments of Sanjar's Grand Vizier, Fakhr al-Mulk, could withdraw him,[1] he must have written his last great work, the *Kīmiyā-yi Sa'ādat*. This and the short treatise, the *Mishkāt al-Anwār*, were singled out for criticism by his enemies,[2] for these works contain propositions which were unlikely to find favour with orthodoxy. These propositions were (i) that the formula 'There is no God but God' was a definition of the divine unity only fit for popular consumption, whereas the 'privileged', the *khawāṣṣ*, preferred the formula 'There is no He but He', (ii) that light in its reality is God, and (iii) that the soul of man is a stranger in this world and originated in the world above. In defence of these propositions Ghazālī wrote the *Faḍā'il al-Anām*, though he evinced little hope of convincing his critics. 'Nowadays', he writes, 'if anyone [ventures to] speak the truth, the very walls rise up in enmity against him.'[3] Yet he can scarcely have been surprised at the criticisms levelled against him, for he confesses that in the *Kimiyā* he was adumbrating doctrines 'to explain which would be heresy'[4] and 'pure infidelity'.[5]

Now, to judge from the *Kīmiyā* it would appear that Ghazālī held two doctrines, the precise formulation of which would constitute heresy or worse: the first concerns the indwelling of God in creatures, and the second the denying not only to God but to the

[1] *Faḍā'il al-Anām*, ed. M. Ṣābitī, Tehran, 1333 A.H. (solar), p. 15.
[2] Ibid., p. 17. [3] Ibid., p. 15. [4] *KS.*, p. 898. [5] Ibid., p. 745.

human soul as it is in its essence of any attributes whatever. Thus he says that the soul, as king of the psycho-physical body, is *bī-chūn* and *bī-chigūna*, that is, absolutely unqualified, 'exactly as the king of the world (God) is *bī-chūn* and *bī-chigūna*'.[1] This, he admits, is the Mu'tazilite doctrine of *ta'ṭīl*,[2] the denying to God in his essence of any attribute whatever; but the whole doctrine would become clear, he says, if 'one were openly to proclaim the peculiar nature of the soul in its secret essence (*sirr*); but this is not permitted'. The doctrine, however, is already formulated, though not precisely, in the tradition, 'Verily God created Adam in his own image'.[3] From the two passages from which we have been quoting it seems fairly clear that the secret doctrine Ghazālī speaks of is that the soul, in its total denudation of all qualities, is identical with God, and there are passages in the *Kīmiyā* and the *Mishkāt* which show that this conclusion is correct.

The second secret doctrine is usually called *ḥulūl* and was particularly associated with Ḥallāj; and this again is justified not only by the *imago Dei* tradition but also by the tradition we have already quoted with reference to Junayd: 'When a servant of mine draws near to me, then do I accept him as my friend, and once I have befriended him, I become his, ear, his eye, and his tongue.'[4] This doctrine of the indwelling God receives additional confirmation from a tradition which purports to be God's words to Moses, but which is in fact based on Matthew xxv. 36–40. 'O Moses,' so the tradition runs, 'I was sick and thou visitedst me not.' [Moses] replied: 'Thou art the Lord of the whole world, how shouldst thou be sick!' [God] said: 'Such-and-such a servant of mine was sick; and hadst thou visited him, thou wouldst have visited me.'[5] It seems slightly ironical that the words of one who had claimed to be God's only-begotten Son should be used by a man who had earned himself the title of the 'Proof of Islam' in support of the heretical doctrine that God indwells all men—a doctrine, moreover, the originator of which had, like Jesus, died upon a cross.

[1] Ibid., p. 45. [2] Ibid., p. 79. [3] Ibid., p. 45.
[4] Following the Persian version as given in the *KS.*, p. 952.
[5] *KS.*, ibid.

Ghazālī knew full well what he was doing: his 'secret doctrines', when clearly formulated, were plain infidelity, they were *ittiḥād* and *ḥulūl*, the doctrine that the soul is identical with God and the doctrine that God indwells the soul.[1] 'It is all very difficult to explain,' as Ghazālī rightly adds.

There is a well-known passage in the *Mishkāt al-Anwār* which very clearly shows what Ghazālī's secret doctrine was.

> The mystics [he writes], after their ascent to the heavens of reality agree that they saw nothing in existence except God, the One. Some of them attained this state through discursive reasoning, others reached it by savouring it and experiencing it. From these all plurality finally fell away. They were drowned in pure isolation: their reason was lost in it, and they became as if dazed in it. They no longer had the capacity to recollect aught but God, nor could they in any wise remember themselves. Nothing was left to them but God. They became drunk with a drunkenness in which their reason collapsed. One of them said, 'I am God (the Truth)'. Another said, 'Glory be to me! How great is my glory!' while another said, 'Within my robe is naught but God.'

So much for the experience; and now Ghazālī proceeds to rationalize it along more or less orthodox lines:

> But the words of lovers when in a state of drunkenness [he writes], must be hidden away and not broadcast. However, when their drunkenness abates and the sovereignty of their reason is restored—and reason is God's scale on his earth—they know that this was not actual identity, but that it resembled identity as when lovers say at the height of their passion:
>
> 'I am he whom I desire, and he whom I desire is I;
> We are two souls inhabiting one body.'
>
> For it is not impossible that a man should be confronted by a mirror and should look into it and not see the mirror at all, and that he should think that the form he saw in the mirror was the form of the mirror itself and identical with it: or that he should see wine in a glass and think that the wine is just coloured glass. And he gets used to this [way of thinking] and becomes fixed in it, and it overwhelms him so that he says:

[1] Ibid., p. 745.

'Thin is the glass and clear is the wine;
The two are alike—mutual resemblance.
It is as if there were only wine, and no glass at all,
Or as if only glass, and no wine there.'

But there is a difference between saying, 'The wine is the wine-glass', and saying, 'It is as if it were the wine-glass'. Now when this state prevails it is called 'annihilation' with reference to the person who is experiencing it, or even the annihilation of annihilation, for [the mystic] is annihilated so far as he himself is concerned, and annihilated too so far as his own annihilation is concerned: he is not conscious of himself in this state, nor is he conscious of his own unconsciousness; for were he conscious of his own unconsciousness, he would be conscious of himself. This condition is metaphorically called *ittiḥād* with reference to the man who is immersed in it, but in the language of truth [it is called] *tawḥīd* (union).[1]

And to conclude we have the usual maddening sentence: 'Beyond these truths there are further mysteries the penetration of which is not permissible.'

From this passage it is plain that Ghazālī takes Abū Yazīd, Ḥallāj, and Abū Sa'īd ibn Abī'l-Khayr as his models, for he uses the slogans *Anā'l-ḥaqq*, *Subḥānī*, and *Mā fī'l-jubbati illā'llāh* with which these persons had become identified as the supreme examples of mystical truth. They it was who had reached the 'reality of realities',[2] the realization of the identity of the soul with God, or, as he here puts it, 'the annihilation of the soul and the sole vision of God'. The whole passage, however, is full of contradictions.

In the introduction to the passage we have quoted the human soul is first said to have been only on loan, then it is described as the 'property' of God, and lastly as pure not-being. What being it has it derives from its relationship to God. Amplifying the last proposition that man *per se* is pure not-being, Ghazālī proceeds to appeal to mystical experience in justification of the metaphysical doctrine he is here advocating. The experience, we are told, con-

[1] *Mishkāt al-Anwār* in Ṣabrī *Al-Jawāhir al-Ghawālī*, pp. 122–3: tr. W. H. T Gairdner, *Al-Ghazzālī's Mishkāt al-Anwār*, Lahore, 1952 (reprint), pp. 106–8.

[2] Ibid., p. 121: translation, p. 103.

sists in *seeing* nothing in existence except God, and the seer then becomes drowned in 'isolation', by which he apparently means God's isolation. This is clearly the experience which Junayd had defined in the case of Abū Yazīd as 'the first isolation', the soul's enjoyment of *its own* timelessness and seeming infinity. Ghazālī, however, interprets it here as meaning the identity lovers are alleged to feel at the height of their passion, and as evidence of this unity he quotes a verse of Ḥallāj which affirms the meeting of *two* souls in one body! He thereby confuses the doctrines of *ḥulūl* and *ittiḥād* which he appears to think are the same. He further alleges that the mystic, once his ecstasy is over, *knows* that what he experienced was not actual identity, whereas the reverse seems to be true. Neither Abū Yazīd nor Abū Sa'īd, let alone the extreme Vedāntins, ever doubted that what they had experienced really *was* identity, and this is almost certainly what Ghazālī himself believed, as we shall see. His 'as if' is simply begging the question since he is unwilling to reveal 'mysteries' which it is not 'lawful to penetrate'.

Now in the *Mishkāt* he says that the type of mystical experience enjoyed by Abū Yazīd and Ḥallāj is called '*tawḥīd* in the language of truth'. *Tawḥīd* in the context is probably meant to mean no more than the 'affirmation of the divine unity', but in the *Faḍā'il al-Anām*, which is a commentary in Persian on the *Mishkāt*, he reveals at last the 'secret doctrine' of *tawḥīd*. Here he argues that two things can never become one: for either both exist, in which case they are not identical; or one exists and the other does not, in which case again there is no identity; or they both do not exist, and in that case there is no identity either. So 'perfect *tawḥīd* means that nothing exists except the One'.[1] Here at last Ghazālī forgets to worry about the orthodoxy he usually chooses to parade, and declares himself a non-dualist of whom Śaṅkara himself might have been proud. *Ātman* is Brahman, and Brahman is *ātman*; the soul is God, and God is the soul. This is his 'secret doctrine' and his 'reality of realities'. Yet the *fanā* he speaks of is the first *fanā* of Junayd, the destruction of *bashariyya*, of all the human qualities

[1] *Faḍā'il al-Anām*, p. 24.

that bind the soul to a body, all its mental, emotional, and sensitive apparatus. The terms *ittiḥād* and *ḥulūl*, which imply an original duality, are thus seen as not being extreme enough, and the metaphors Ghazālī uses in the *Kimiyā* and elsewhere like the comparison of God and the soul to the sun and its rays,[1] are mere approximations to the full monistic truth.

In his treatment of *dhikr* Ghazālī puts forward the same interpretation of *fanā*: in the last stage of the meditation on the name of God all disappears except the object of meditation, God. In this passage, however, Ghazālī, very surprisingly, takes up not so much a Vedāntin approach as a Sāṁkhya-Yogin one. The person engaged in meditation 'forgets both himself and all that is, except God. He now enters on the beginning of the Ṣūfī path. It is a condition called "annihilation" or "not-being" by the Ṣūfīs. That is to say, all that is becomes non-existent as a result of his [one-pointed] meditation, and that too becomes non-existent because [the mystic] has forgotten himself as well. And just as God possesses universes of which we have no knowledge and which, as far as we are concerned, do not exist, so our existence is [simply] that of which we have consciousness and about which we have information. When someone forgets these worlds which constitute created being, they cease to exist, and when he forgets his own selfhood, he too ceases to exist so far as a self is concerned: and since he is left with nothing but God, his existence *is* God, neither more nor less (*va bas*). And just as you survey heaven and earth and all that in them is and only see part of it, you will say that the universe extends just so far as this and that this is all. So too does this man (the mystic) also see nothing but God, and he says, "All is He and apart from him there is nothing at all".'[2]

Ghazālī here seems to be making a dangerous admission from the monist's point of view. You are, he says, what you are conscious of: therefore if, by one-pointed meditation on God, you put yourself into a trance and are aware of nothing but the object of your meditation, you *are* God. God, therefore, is simply a sub-

[1] *KS.*, p. 964, etc.

[2] Ibid., p. 206.

jective state from which all external impressions conveyed by sense or imagination have been obliterated and in which space has been transcended.[1] He is, in fact, the soul *bī-chūn* and *bī-chigūna*—the One who is not affected by space, time, and causation. In this passage Ghazālī as good as says that God is what your meditation makes him. He, however goes further than this and says that, having discovered in yourself that nothing exists except God, you then discover that God is also all things, by which he presumably means that you see all things *sub specie aeternitatis* because you are no longer in space and time.

And this brings us back again to the sixth chapter of the Bhagavad-Gītā. There the technique is identical with the Ṣūfī *dhikr* except that the object of meditation is there, most significantly, the self; all thought is made subject to the self so that a state of mindlessness ensues,[2] and then it is that one sees all things in the self and the self in all things.[3] Realizing an extra-spatial and extra-temporal existence in yourself you project it on to the objective world. Ghazālī thus identifies a subjective condition of undifferentiable unity with God and then projects this condition on to all created things: so it is that he takes up the slogan of Abū Sa'īd, 'All is He'. Thus he succeeds in combining a rigid monism with a full-blooded pantheism. He gives the sanction of his authority not only to Abū Yazīd's 'Glory be to me', but also to Abū Sa'īd's 'All is He'.

Junayd, it will be recollected, had laid down that Abū Yazīd 'had spoken truly about the science of union except that his words were only beginnings of what might be expected from one who is of the elect'.[4] He had pointed out that beyond the first 'isolation in unity'—which is the unity and isolation of the soul only, not of God, there lay the path of suffering and love which was the only way out from the self-isolated soul to God. Ghazālī too says that beyond the realization that the soul is God (as he thinks) the soul can enter into yet higher states. After realizing himself as God what further experience, one wonders, can the mystic possibly enjoy?

[1] Ibid., p. 745. [2] BG., 6.25–27. [3] Ibid., 6.29. [4] See above, p. 121.

'When he has reached this stage', Ghazālī informs us, 'the form of the spiritual world (*malakūt*) begins to reveal itself to him and the souls of angels and prophets begin to appear in comely forms, and that which is willed by his Divine Majesty begins to show forth. Grand mystic states appear which it is impossible to describe.' This, surely, is downright frivolous. Here is a man with a world-wide reputation as a philosopher, who after making the tremendous claim that he has, in some sense, *been* God, is conscious of no bathos in referring to visions of lesser beings as if this were a yet deeper plunge into the unseen. In the Indian tradition which can claim rather more expertise in these matters than can Ghazālī visions of this kind are regarded as being premonitory signs that *precede* the vision of the 'self' or the achievement of isolation: they are ancillary to the achievement of oneness and of no value in themselves.[1] St. Teresa too was not so naïve as to attach undue importance to her visionary experiences, but it is precisely these experiences of hers and of St. Catherine of Genoa that enabled Leuba to build up his thesis that mysticism can be explained in terms of pure psychology without any reference to God as a reality distinct from the soul. Had he been an Orientalist Ghazālī would have furnished him with additional ammunition.

In another extraordinary passage Ghazālī says that 'man is of the substance of the angels and one of the works of Divinity, as it is said, "Say: The soul is of the command of my Lord".[2] So because of the exceedingly intimate relationship that exists between the soul and [God's] Dominion (*rubūbiyyat*), to seek dominion is man's very nature, and everyone has a secret desire to say with Pharaoh, "I am your Lord, the Most High". So everyone naturally loves dominion, and the meaning of dominion is this that all is He and nothing else whatever exists beside him'.[3]

Junayd had issued a solemn warning against all those who thought themselves 'endowed with the attributes of Lordship' or

[1] See *Śvet*Up., 2.11–15: *Yogasūtras*, 3.32 where 'vision of those who have reached the goal' ranks as one of the supernatural powers that precede the achievement of isolation.

[2] See above, p. 155. [3] *KS.*, p. 660.

divinity. Ghazālī, on the other hand, sees in this 'claim to Lordship' man's *natural* expression of his divinity. He thereby puts the seal of his approval on yet another of the Ṣūfīs' aberrations that had come into existence since the time of Junayd, the fatuous claims of self-deified Ṣūfīs to display not only the essence of God but both his beautiful and his majestic attributes. Shaykh Murshid Abū'l-Isḥāq al-Kāzarūnī, for example, had been particularly fond of displaying the divine jealousy because 'all the movements, repose, and dealings of the particular favourites and elect of God are the movements, repose, and dealings of God', as this man's biographer solemnly assures us.[1] His kingdom on earth was some four hundred square parasangs around Kāzarūn, and in this territory he would not tolerate the presence of rival Shaykhs. One Shaykh who presumed to defy this ban was summarily told that if he wished to call the people to God, he should call them to minister to Shaykh Murshid,[2] since for four hundred square parasangs around Kāzarūn he *was* God. Such claims as these Ghazālī would, no doubt, have had no difficulty in accepting.

Another proof that, in his later life, Ghazālī had become a convinced monist is his attitude to personal relationships. 'If you ever see anyone at peace (*rāḥat*)', he says, 'you will understand [him] only when all of you passes away in him, and all becomes his glory, so that duality ceases and unity appears. He remains, and you do not; or he passes away in you, and you remain and he does not. Or else both of you pass away in God and pay no attention to yourselves, and that is perfection. From this oneness there is perfect repose. In short, so long as duality persists, no repose is possible for repose is [only] in unity and oneness.'[3] The doctrine when applied to personal relationships seems even more preposterous than when it is applied to God. We have again reached the position originally formulated in the *Kauṣītakī* Upaniṣad: 'Thou art the soul of every single being. What thou art, this am I. . . . Thou art this All.'[4]

Thus, in the *Kīmiyā-yi Sa'ādat* Ghazālī lends the immense

[1] Maḥmūd bin 'Uthmān, *Firdaus al-Murshidiyya fī Asrār al-Ṣamadiyya*, ed. I. Afshār, Tehran, 1333 A.H. (solar), p. 439.

[2] Ibid., p. 444. [3] *KS.*, p. 705. [4] *Kauṣītakī* Up., 1.6.

weight of his authority to two doctrines which fly in the face both of the letter and of the spirit of orthodox Islam, the doctrine that the soul and God are one thing, and the doctrine that God and the universe are co-terminous. By ruling that the desire for Lordship, that is, the divine omnipotence, is inherent in man by nature because he is the image of God, Ghazālī smoothed the path for all the pathological excesses that were later to bring Ṣūfism into disrepute. And not only this, for it was he too who first introduced Neo-Platonic ideas into Ṣūfism, so that after him the Universal Intelligence and the Universal Soul became *de rigueur* for any Ṣūfī writer in poetry or prose. The reason why Ghazālī should have done this at the end of his life would appear to be that once he had adopted a fully monist position, he felt the need to justify it philosophically, and the current Neo-Platonism deriving from the so-called *Theology of Aristotle* lay ready to hand. 'God', for him, now meant timeless being experienced in ecstasy, and such unqualifiable being, he felt, could have no part in becoming, let alone originate it. Hence his adoption of Neo-Platonic ideas in the *Risālat al-Ladunniyya* and his introduction of the mysterious figure of the *Muṭā*', the 'Obeyed One', into the *Mishkāt*.

The *Mishkāt* ends with a description of those 'who are veiled by the lights' themselves: these form the highest grade of the mystical hierarchy, and are divided into three sub-categories. The first of these recognizes God as 'transcending the ideas of his attributes'[1] and as Mover of the heavenly spheres. The second, dissatisfied with the plurality inherent in the spheres, realizes that there is a single sphere beyond these, and it is this sphere only which the Lord moves; thus he is removed from all contact with multiplicity. For the third category even this will not do, and they therefore assert that the Prime Mover's communication of movement to the supreme sphere is an act of worship rendered by an angel to the *Muṭā*', the 'Obeyed One', who himself imparts motion not by direct effort but by his simple command. The 'command' is of course the Qur'ānic *amr* (identified in the *Risālat al-Ladunniyya*[2]

[1] *Mishkāt*, p. 145 (text): p. 170 (translation).
[2] p. 25 (in *Al-Jawāhir al-Ghawālī*, ed. Ṣabrī).

with the Neo-Platonic Universal Intelligence), God's creative Word;[1] and the *Muṭā'* is therefore the Allah of the Qur'ān. The fourth and highest category, however, realizes that this *Muṭā'*, because he is still endowed with attributes, cannot be Absolute Being (*wujūd al-ḥaqq*) itself; his relationship to Absolute Being is rather that of the sun to pure light in the abstract (*al-nūr al-maḥḍ*). Thus they rise beyond the Mover and the spheres and the Obeyed One who orders their movement to a Being utterly devoid of any kind of attribute or quality whatever. This Being is seen by the mystic for whom all else is utterly annihilated although he himself as the contemplating agent remains; but beyond these are the *khawāṣṣ al-khawāṣṣ*, the cream of the mystical aristocracy, who are 'blotted out and *disintegrated* (*talāshū*) in their essence',[2] so that the One alone remains.

Ghazālī's terminology is interesting; for this final state is represented as a *disintegration* of personality into the One, not a controlled process of integration as in the Yoga of the Bhagavad-Gītā. In the terminology of Jungian psychology this is the overwhelming of the thinking ego by the collective unconscious which is by definition without form, and Ghazālī is doing what Gauḍapāda and Śaṅkara had done before him in India—he is constructing a metaphysical system out of a psychological experience: because he has experienced undifferentiable oneness, therefore nothing exists except the One. If this is so, then absolute Being must be denied to the Allah of the Qur'ān, but even Ghazālī shrinks from going quite so far as this. So he introduces the mysterious 'Obeyed One' as a substitute for Allah.

This idea he derives from the *Ṭāsīn al-Sirāj* of Ḥallāj[3] where 'the lamp that proceeds from the light of the unseen' is the pre-existent and eternal Light or Reality of Muhammad. This Light is 'more eternal than eternity itself' (*aqdam min al-qidam*), it pre-exists the Pen, is the 'Lord of creation', is superlatively unique and

[1] 'There are mysteries in the doctrine of this *amr* and what it actually is, which are beyond the range of most minds,' adds Ghazālī, *Mishkāt*, ibid.

[2] *Mishkāt*, p. 146 (text).

[3] L. Massignon, *Kitâb al Ṭawâsîn*, Paris, 1913, pp. 9–15.

superlatively existent.[1] Before time was heard of, he was *madhkūr*, a clear reference to Qur'ān 76.1[2] which we have already come across in our discussion of Junayd. Thus Ḥallāj transfers the Logos theory as applied to Christ lock, stock, and barrel to the person of Muhammad. The Light of Muhammad is the divine Word, God's *dhikr* of himself, his meditation or thinking of himself, which becomes hypostatized as a being separate from him though one with him in substance. This idea Ghazālī adopts, but for Ḥallāj's Muhammad he substitutes the less personal Obeyed One. There can, however, be no doubt that the Obeyed One of the *Mishkāt* is either Muhammad or Gabriel, for obviously Ghazālī does not pick the word at random, but is referring to some passage in the Qur'ān. Luckily the word *muṭā*' occurs only once in that book, in Sūra 81.21:

> It is verily the speech of a noble messenger,
> Powerful, beside Him of the Throne established,
> Obeyed (*muṭā*') there and trustworthy.

According to the commentators this 'noble messenger' is Gabriel, but in this passage it must surely refer to Muhammad[3] as 'transcendent prophetic spirit'. He thereby becomes identified with the 'Lord' who is 'the mover of the universe by way of command',[4] that is, by the creative word *Kun*, 'Be'. Muhammad, then, *is* God, the active Creator, the Allah of the Qur'ān, while Allah as highest principle becomes the undifferentiable One that the mystic

[1] Ibid., p. 11.

[2] 'Has there come upon man a period of time when he was not a thing mentioned.'

[3] Elsewhere (*Fayṣal bayn al-Islām wa'l-Zandaqa* in *Al-Jawāhir al-Ghawālī*, p. 85) Ghazālī himself identifies the *Muṭā*' with Gabriel. Perhaps, then, in this passage too the *Muṭā*' as divine mediator should be understood as Gabriel. Against this must be set the fact that in the *Mishkāt* (p. 110) Muhammad is explicitly called 'the light of lights' and is identified with the 'transcendent prophetic spirit' as source of light (p. 119). The *Muṭā*' *qua* 'transcendent prophetic spirit' is equally applicable to Muhammad and Gabriel, but since Gabriel plays no part in the *Mishkāt* it would seem reasonable to conclude that in *that* work it refers to Muhammad *qua* 'transcendent prophetic spirit' unless, as Dr. W. Montgomery Watt suggests (JRAS, 1949, pp. 5–22) the third chapter of the *Mishkat* is spurious, which seems unlikely.

[4] *Mishkāt*, p. 145 (text): p. 171 (translation).

claims to experience in trance. Muhammad, then, is exalted *above* the Logos and assumes the functions of the God the Father of Christianity—and in this respect Ghazālī goes further than Ḥallāj. Muhammad is the Light of lights[1] who illumines both himself and the darkness of not-being which is outside himself.[2] He is in the spiritual world what the sun is in the material world, and he derives his light from the 'absolutely pure light'[3] which is the One. He is, then, God as he manifests himself in his creation—and this is the third major heresy that Ghazālī sanctioned in Islam: the Prophet is exalted to the rank of the creator God.

In the *Mishkāt al-Anwār* Ghazālī's novel notion of Muhammad as the Obeyed One is not integrated into the Neo-Platonic scheme of the *Risālat al-Ladunniyya*, nor can it very well be, for the Obeyed One is set above the Neo-Platonic Universal Intelligence which is the Qur'ānic *amr* and is therefore yet another intermediary set between the many and the One. Ghazālī must be more monist than Plotinus himself, for the One may not even utter the creative word 'Be' lest its absolute oneness be impaired. Taking the *Mishkāt* and the *Risālat al-Ladunniyya* together it can be said that the hierarchy of being envisaged by Ghazālī in his last period was (i) the One, (ii) the eternal pre-existent Muhammad (the Obeyed One), (iii) the *amr* as Universal Intelligence, and (iv) the *rūḥ* as Universal Soul. The one *is*, the Obeyed One *commands* with the Word 'Be', and the Word once spoken becomes the Universal Intelligence, and this, in turn, emanates the Universal Soul which is the female creative principle whose relationship to the Universal Intelligence is that of Eve to Adam.[4]

The introduction of Neo-Platonic ideas into Ṣūfism from philosophy was, of course, made much of by Ibn al-'Arabī who systematized them into something very like Śaṅkara's version of the Vedānta. Most of the Persian mystical poets after Ghazālī pay lip-service to them, but in so far as they are still interested in mystical experience rather than this new theosophy, they appear to resent

[1] Ibid., p. 110 (text); p. 75 (translation).
[2] Ibid., p. 119 (text): p. 97 (translation).
[3] Ibid., p. 145 (text): p. 172 (translation).
[4] *Risālat al-Ladunniyya*, p. 35.

the intrusion of the Universal Intelligence and the Universal Soul into their scheme of things. Ḥallāj's deification of Muhammad, however, was readily accepted. Sanā'ī, for example, represents the Universal Intelligence and Universal Soul as being helpless before the Qur'ān,[1] while the former bows down in worship before the pre-existent Muhammad[2] and is devoid of honour until it confesses itself his servant.[3] Nevertheless Ghazālī's late and tentative flirtation with Neo-Platonism did much to change the nature of the Ṣūfī movement. Formerly it had concerned itself almost entirely with the practice of mysticism, it had concerned itself little with theory; and when it did so, it was interested in the theory as it affected the practice itself, not with the metaphysical constructions which were supposed to tally with mystical experience. Muḥāsibī had laid the foundations of Ṣūfī ethics and Ghazālī follows him closely in those sections of the *Kīmiyā* (which are little more than abbreviated versions of his earlier and much more voluminous *Iḥyā*) in which he deals with ethics. Junayd had analysed mystical experience itself with extraordinary subtlety, but his thought was not fully understood. Only Qushayrī among his disciples seems to have grasped the import of his teaching, and to this we owe his earnest warning against the dangers that can follow on an expansion of the personality[4] which will lead the mystic to believe that he is God or the All. Ghazālī was hardly of the spiritual calibre to understand Junayd's teaching: yet he can scarcely be blamed for that, for not only was Junayd's writing purposely obscure, his doctrine was also one that mystics who have only had an experience of undifferentiated oneness find it almost impossible to accept. As Buber has pointed out, it is fatally easy, indeed almost inevitable, to mistake the 'pre-biographical unity' of one's own soul for Being itself. The mistake is, however, only made by the mystics who are—as they are bound to be—conditioned by their own religious beliefs. The Upaniṣads taught that the human soul is eternal, infinite, Brahman, the One, and the All,

[1] Sanā'ī, *Ḥadīqat al-Ḥaqīqa*, Tehran, 1329 A.H. (solar), p. 172, l.6, reading *'ājiz*.

[2] Ibid., p. 202. [3] Ibid., p. 207. [4] See above, pp. 118–9.

and mystical experience was accordingly interpreted on those lines. The Bhagavad-Gītā did something to redress the balance, but it needed the religious genius of a Rāmānuja to distinguish between 'the category of Brahman' and the God who stands beyond Brahman and who cannot be approached except with the deepest humility and with a passionate love.

In Islam mysticism developed along lines closely comparable to the early experience of Christianity. God could and should be approached with reverence and love; he was always the 'other' and his relationship with the soul was a two-way affair in which the initiative necessarily lay with God. This attitude of humbly waiting upon God which is characteristic of the earliest Ṣūfīs, was very soon wrecked by the introduction of such artificial aids towards ecstasy as music, dancing, and, of all things, the contemplation of beautiful boys. Junayd had set his face against all these practices as had many other Ṣūfīs, but the tide could not be turned because experience taught that ecstasy in which a man could for a moment get outside not only himself but also time and space, could be obtained by the use of music and dance. Ṣūfism thus became much more interested in ecstasy as such than in finding the living God. Preoccupied with 'states' and 'stations' they began to lose sight of the goal, the personal God who kindles the human heart to a new life in himself.

It was Abū Yazīd who, as we have seen, introduced Vedāntin ideas into Ṣūfism and who, by identifying his own subjective state in ecstasy with the Muhammadan God, caused theological havoc in the Ṣūfī movement. It was left to Ghazālī to sketch out the broad outlines of the new theology of the One and the many, but the implications of permanent self-deification had already been illustrated in practice by his predecessor Abū Sa'īd ibn Abī'l-Khayr.

If we are to believe Abū Sa'īd's biographer, Ibn Munawwar, the former, after he had attained to what he thought was complete deification at the age of forty,[1] considered himself to have passed quite beyond the law. He ranked his own sayings at the same level

[1] Ibn Munawwar, *Asrār al-Tawḥīd*, p. 58.

as the Qur'ān, saying that what had been revealed to Muhammad was only part of the full revelation, whereas what God had revealed to his Ṣūfī servants was boundless and would never come to an end.[1] Similarly with Tradition: in the past transmitters of the Traditions of the Prophet had been careful to present a plausible pedigree (*isnād*) for any saying of the Prophet, true or spurious, which they wished to pass on to others. Abū Sa'īd, however, claimed that Tradition, like the allegedly unrevealed portion of the heavenly Qur'ān, could be directly transmitted to the Ṣūfī 'saint'.[2] The pilgrimage too was no longer an obligation to him, for he was early persuaded that he was too exalted to be taken to Mecca,[3] rather his own bodily frame, being the tabernacle in which the All-Highest resided, was the true Qibla, not the Ka'ba.[4]

Not only did he openly infringe the religious law, but he also completely set at naught the specifically Ṣūfī rules of conduct by which Ṣūfīs had hitherto lived. He lived on the alms of the faithful which he squandered in giving banquets in which no extravagance was spared. Holy poverty was not for him; he had got over all that in the forty years of his novitiate in which the excess of the tortures he inflicted on himself was only matched by the opposite excess of luxury in his later life. Nicholson has devoted many pages to the doings of this far from lovable eccentric in his *Studies in Islamic Mysticism*, and we will not attempt to cover again ground so little worth covering. One example must suffice. The Shaykh had received a gift of a thousand dīnārs and, as was his custom, resolved to spend the lot on one gigantic party at which candles were to be lighted at midday. This extravagance met with the disapproval of the local superintendent of police who remonstrated with the Shaykh. The Shaykh, however, retaliated by miraculously causing the candles to burn off his moustache as he tried to blow them out: 'Every candle that God lights', the Shaykh intoned, 'will burn the moustache of anyone who [dares to] blow upon it'; for Abū Sa'īd was, of course, merely the physical frame through which God manifested his power.[5]

[1] Ibid., p. 110. [2] Ibid., p. 263. [3] Ibid., p. 149. [4] Ibid., p. 247. [5] Ibid., p. 112.

The technical term for this kind of behaviour is *ibāḥat*, the 'holding permissible' of what is forbidden by the religious law. Ghazālī time and again attacks these latitudinarians savagely. 'They claim', he says, 'that they have reached such a state of intimacy with God that they are absolved from the duty of prayer and that the drinking of wine, sins of disobedience, and the living off state property become lawful to them. There is no doubt that all such persons should be killed even though there may be a difference of opinion about their eternal punishment in hell. The killing of one such person is more meritorious than the slaughter of a hundred infidels, for the harm they cause in religion is greater; they open a door to licence which cannot be closed.'[1] Yet it is Ghazālī himself who quotes Abū Sa'īd along with Abū Yazīd and Ḥallāj as having uttered words that described the ultimate truth.[2] Assuming that Abū Sa'īd's biography is not a tissue of lies from beginning to end, he must have made himself notorious as one who defied the common law of Islam. For Ghazālī, however, who quotes him with approval, he cannot have been an *ibāḥatī*; and it seems that he would only consider those persons to belong to that category who were rejected by the Ṣūfīs themselves. In Ghazālī's day Abū Sa'īd's reputation as a saint was already established; and his excesses were therefore not to be questioned.

On the legitimacy of the use of song and dance as an aid to ecstasy the opinions of the earlier Ṣūfīs had been sharply divided, and one of Qushayrī's principal criticisms of Abū Sa'īd had been for his open encouragement of this practice.[3] Abū Sa'īd's party, however, triumphed, and after him the ritual song and dance took on an ever-increasing importance, and by Ghazālī's time was firmly established. Another practice had, however, crept into Ṣūfism which was far more questionable, and that was the contemplation of, and Platonic friendship with, beautiful young men. Already in the third century of the Hijra the practice was widespread, and 'few were the Ṣūfīs who were free from it'.[4] This the

[1] *Fayṣal al-Tafriqa bayn al-Islām wa'l-Zandaqa*, in Ṣabrī, p. 94: cf. *KS.*, pp. 30–31.
[2] See above, p. 165.
[3] Ibn Munawwar, *Asrār al-Tawḥīd*, p. 85.
[4] Sulamī, *Ṭabaqāt al-Ṣūfiyya*, p. 232.

more sober-minded regarded as the 'plague of the Ṣūfīs',[1] pleasing to Satan, and a sure road to disaster.[2] Abū Sa'īd, however, encouraged the practice, claiming that Platonic love was totally incompatible with lust, and, to prove his point, he arranged a practical demonstration for Qushayrī's benefit in which his son was sent to test the chastity of a dervish who entertained for him a profound Platonic attachment.[3] By Sanā'ī's time the practice of the Platonic contemplation of physical beauty had led to the abuses that any sane person could have foreseen, and the poet has some biting things to say about it and some very nasty anecdotes to tell.[4] Ghazālī, ready as ever to excuse and defend the practices of 'accredited' Ṣūfīs while condemning the excesses committed in their name, says that to contemplate the beauty of a boy is like 'gazing at a ruddy apple or blossom'.[5] 'The consolation [one derives from the chaste contemplation of beardless youths] may be of the same kind as one gets from [looking at] water, or green pastures, or blossom, or a beautiful picture, and there can be no harm in this.'[6] If it goes beyond this, it is to be condemned.

From the point of view of the kind of Ṣūfism that Junayd and Qushayrī represented Ghazālī himself would have been regarded as an *ibāḥatī* of a very dangerous kind: and it is a matter of regret for those who, like Junayd, thought it unlikely that man can ever or under any circumstances realize himself as God and who prefer not to confuse ecstasy as such with the loving dialogue between God and the soul which the earlier Ṣūfīs claimed to have experienced—it is a matter of regret that Ghazālī should have put the whole weight of his authority in the scale of the monistic brand of Ṣūfism that had invaded the movement in the person of Abū Yazīd; and it is a matter of surprise that a man who, when all is said and done, boasted of an intelligence well above the ordinary, should have shown himself so credulously naive in his approach to the very questionable practices of the accredited Ṣūfīs. After Ghazālī, with but few exceptions, the mystical stream—in Persia at least where little effort was made at systematization—got lost in

[1] Ibid., p. 190. [2] Ibid., p. 396. [3] Ibn Munawwar, *Asrār al-Tawḥīd*, pp. 90–91.
[4] Sanā'ī, *Ḥadīqat al-Ḥaqīqa*, pp. 662, 668. [5] *KS.*, p. 380. [6] Ibid., p. 554.

the sands of religious syncretism in which monism, pantheism, and theism were inextricably mingled; yet this doctrinal confusion, so maddening to the intellect, produced a poetic flowering that has seldom been equalled.

Yet voices of protest were not confined to the rigidly orthodox who had detested the movement from the beginning. The older type of mysticism, based on the love of God, continued to flourish in the Suhrawardī order of dervishes alongside the theoretical monism of Ibn al-ʻArabī and the theologically indifferentist Maulavī dervishes of Jalāl al-Dīn Rūmī. Suhrawardī of Aleppo too, though put to death for heresy, had categorically denied the possibility of the soul ever becoming God.[1] Najm al-Dīn Rāzī, writing in the thirteenth century, was sufficiently well acquainted with other religions to know that mystical experience was by no means confined to Islam, and since he believed Islam to be the true religion, he was faced with the problem of distinguishing between types of mysticism. If Islam alone is the true religion, he thought, there must be something distinctive in Islamic mysticism which raises it above the experiences of mystics of other religions. He admits that Christian monks, philosophers, Brahmans, and Hindus in general can attain to some knowledge of the unseen by bodily *askesis* and 'purification of the heart'—this either when fully awake or in a trance state between sleep and waking. In this state they pass beyond their animal nature and are delivered from the imagination, and the soul stands self-revealed; 'lights, revelations, and visions of the unseen appear, but in many cases there is no [sense of] drawing near to God or of finding favour with him. On the contrary [these experiences] make them fall into all kinds of excesses and separate them from God (*ḥijāb-i īshān gardad*), so that they fall into unbelief and error and experience what the Qur'ān calls *instindrāj* in the verse, "We shall come stealthily upon them from whence they do not know"[2].'[3] The experience which is typical of Islam, however,

[1] See Henry Corbin, *Oeuvres philosophiques et mystiques de Shihabaddin Yahya Sohrawardi*, 1, Tehran/Paris, 1952, p. 228.

[2] Qur'ān, 7.181: 68.44.

[3] Najm al-Dīn Rāzī, *Mirṣād al-ʻIbād min al-Mabdaʼ ilā'l-Maʻād*, ed. H. H. Niʻmatallāhī, Tehran, 1312 A.H. (solar), p. 162.

is primarily moral, for it reveals the distinction between virtue and vice, the imagination is not overcome, and the mystic sees the condition of his own soul with its advances and backslidings, its soundness and rottenness: it brings him near to God and increases his faith. The essential difference between the two types of experience, Najm al-Dīn says, is that Brahmans, ascetics, Hindus, and philosophers always retain a sense of duality and 'never experience visions of the lights of the attributes of oneness'. Here, unfortunately, Najm al-Dīn is quite wrong, for whatever criticism one may make of Brahmanical mysticism, it is certainly not that it pays insufficient attention to oneness, for even those sects which have a pluralistic philosophy conceive of liberation as the attainment of *an* indifferentiable unity, even though that may not be absolute metaphysical unity. He is, however, nearer the mark when he says that they 'do not come forth from their own being'; but can one be certain that the same is not true of his superior Muslim mystic whose 'humanity is destroyed in the revelation of the light of the attributes of oneness and who enjoys the manifestation of the world of lordship' where 'the tongue which speaks the absolute mystery, does right to say, "I am the Truth".'

Yet Najm al-Dīn Rāzī does see, though not with the authoritative clarity of Junayd, that there is one mysticism of the soul and another of God. It is fatally easy to confuse the two because, after all, man is made in the image of God and is his viceroy on earth,[1] and this, he explains a few pages later, accounts for such sayings as Ḥallāj's 'I am the Truth'; man is the 'Truth' as God's representative, but not as God himself. 'It sometimes happens', he says, 'that the essence of the soul which is God's viceroy is revealed [to itself] and, since it is God's viceroy, proceeds to make the claim, "I am the Truth"; and it sometimes happens that all creatures fall down in obeisance before the viceregal throne of the soul, and it makes the mistake of thinking that perhaps it is God. . . . The lower soul (*nafs*), to satisfy its thirst, drinks in this delusion, for it is not every traveller [on the Ṣūfī path] who can distinguish between truth and error, but only those on whom God looks with favour and who

[1] Qur'ān, 2.28.

are preserved from the bondage of the lower soul and the guile of God.'[1]

The *makr* or 'guile' of God we have met with before both in Junayd[2] and Qushayrī;[3] it is the snare precisely that God sets for the spiritual pride of the monist who thinks that because his soul, at its deepest level, is *an* undifferentiated monad, it must therefore be identical with Allah who is *the* absolutely One. This mistake is all the more easily made in that the soul does have a glory of its own which quite transcends all everyday experience. 'The soul too,' writes Najm al-Dīn, 'has a glory of its own, and in this matter travellers [on the path] fall into many an error. Sometimes when the soul reveals itself, the traveller takes it for an experience (*zawq*) of the revealed glory of God. Many a traveller has been deceived at this stage and thought that he has attained to the revealed glory of God.'[4] This is one of the reasons, Najm al-Dīn says, why it is essential to have a qualified spiritual director.

Najm al-Dīn then proceeds to write pages on the varieties of mystical experience and he is, quite naturally, not always consistent. The similes he employs, however, are worth considering. He likens a man to a tree and the love of God to fire, and 'so long as a branch of the tree that is man obtrudes its human qualities, the sincere lover will grasp the axe of "There is no god" with the hand of sincerity and strike at the base of the branch and cast it on to the fire of "but God". Then does the fire . . . seize upon it, and in the proportion that it robs it of its being as wood, it transforms it into the being of fire, so that the whole tree which is man and all the branches of his humanity are delivered over to be devoured by that fire, and the fire blazes in every part of the being of the tree until the being of the whole tree becomes fire. Hitherto it had been a tree, but now it becomes nothing but pure fire.'[5] The soul, then, when seized upon by the divine fire, is slowly transmuted into the fire itself, but although Najm al-Dīn then quotes a verse the purport of which is that God bids the soul leave nothing of itself in existence, it may be inferred that the simile intends to con-

[1] Rāzī, *Mirṣād al-'Ibād*, p. 177. [2] See above, p. 150. [3] See above, p. 119.
[4] *Mirṣād al-'Ibād*, p. 175. [5] Ibid., p. 188.

vey that the divine fire which devours the tree is itself peculiar to that particular tree. In fact we read a little further on that 'fire is a blessing to the wood since it brings out its hidden scent', and the scent of each kind of wood differs as the personalities of different men differ:

> When both [kinds of wood] are cast upon the fire together,
> The case of the willow is not the same as that of sandalwood.

For it is only the fire that brings out the fragrance of sandalwood above all other timbers.[1] The 'Living flame of love', then, not only transforms the soul into itself, it also brings out the essence of the soul from its material hulk: the fire is of God, but the fragrance of the soul. The soul is deified, it is true, but its own deification is like the deification of no other created thing; and there is as rich a variety in the divine eternal life as there is in this world: and God, though in a sense he is 'all in all', is also 'all things to all men'.

> Love came and entered my veins and skin like my very blood
> Till it emptied me [of self] and filled me with the Beloved.
> The Beloved seized upon all the parts of my being:
> For me a name of me remains, all the rest is he.[2]

Thus, four centuries after Junayd, Najm al-Dīn Rāzī once again exposes what he considers to be the error of the monists, and he did this in defence of orthodoxy.

Quite different is the case of Ibn Ṭufayl. A native of Andalusia who flourished in the twelfth century, Ibn Ṭufayl was in religion a sceptic, and the concluding portion of his sole surviving work, a mystical allegory called *Ḥayy ibn Yaqẓān*, 'Living son of Wakeful', is a mild but sympathetic critique of the main beliefs of Islam and, indeed, of all institutional religion based on revelation. The dogmas of Islam, he maintains, are merely symbols of the truth that Ḥayy ibn Yaqẓān, who represents himself, had experienced,[3]

[1] Ibid., p. 189.

[2] Ibid., p. 190.

[3] Ibn Ṭufayl, *Ḥayy ibn Yaqẓān*, ed. A. Ḥakīm, Beyrouth, 1954, p. 75: for translation see Simon Ockley (revised by A. S. Fulton), *The History of Hayy ibn Yaqzan*, London, 1929, p. 166. I reproduce Ockley's translation wherever possible.

for Ibn Ṭufayl claims to be writing 'from some little experience' (*al-dhawq al-yasīr*) of contemplation.[1]

In the *Ḥayy ibn Yaqẓān* his thesis is that man can attain to the vision of God entirely on his own and without the aid of any specifically religious framework. The hero Ḥayy grows up on an island of which he is the sole human inhabitant. He is found by a gazelle who suckles him and whom he comes to regard as his mother. Ḥayy, then, in the course of one short life, lives through the whole history of human civilization: he has to learn how to clothe himself and how to defend himself against animals stronger than himself. At the age of seven his foster-mother, the gazelle, dies, and Ḥayy is faced with the mystery of life and death, for he sees all too clearly that the dead carcase bears no relation to the creature who had suckled him and whom he had grown to love. Therefore, he concluded, the essence of his foster-mother, the gazelle, cannot reside in matter. Ḥayy thus finds himself in the position of the writers of the early Upaniṣads: he asks himself, 'What is the *ātman*? What is it that constitutes the self of a given being?' And his reasoning is not unlike theirs. He observes fire and how it changes everything into itself, and, on dissecting the body of the gazelle, he discovers that in the animal's heart too there remains a hot vapour. This, he concludes, is what must keep it alive. Brahman, then, is breath, for it is this hot vapour that preserves the life of the multiple organism that is the body and without which alone it cannot live. This, in turn, brings him up against the problem of unity and multiplicity, the many and the One. He saw that an animal body was infinitely manifold in structure, but was nevertheless a single whole animated by one spirit. So too he came to regard the unity in diversity which constituted species: horses, he saw, were all one in their 'horseness', though individually distinct. Or, in truly Hindu fashion, he would consider the unity of substance in water, which is essentially the same though it may be contained in a variety of vessels. Further observation led him to conclude that it was form in the Aristotelian sense, not matter, that made things what they are; but this form was forever

[1] Ibid., p. 10 (text). Not in the translation.

changing, and since inert matter could not be the cause of change, what then could it be?

Despairing of finding the answer on earth he turned his attention to the heavens, and seeing that there all was regular circular motion, he concluded, rather illogically, that the whole universe was one vast living organism which must be impelled by a First Mover. Further consideration leads him to the conclusion that this Being who is First Cause, Prime Mover, and Master Craftsman, is also Pure Existence, giving existence to everything that exists: it is Being, Perfection, Plenitude, Beauty, Glory, Power, and Knowledge.[1] Having convinced himself by reason that such a being existed, Ḥayy longed to know him by experience; and this longing he could only interpret as a longing for something he had already seen but had subsequently forgotten. But how was the experience to be gained?

The surest way that suggested itself to him was the study of his own immaterial essence by which he had reached the certainty that there was an Absolute Being. The pursuit of this study led him by imperceptible stages to the empirical conclusion that his soul was 'not to be apprehended by any of the senses or by the imagination, nor to be known by the means of any other instrument but itself alone; it attained the knowledge of itself by itself, and was at once the knower, the act of knowing, and the thing known, the faculty and the object. Neither was there any difference between any of these, because diversity and separation are the properties and adjuncts of bodies; but body was no way concerned here.'[2] This ontological unity that he experienced in himself, he says, resembled the necessarily self-existent Being,[3] and just as, by intensive introspection, he had become a unified monad in which the distinction between subject and object was obliterated, so, he concluded, must the necessarily self-existent Being be devoid of all multiplicity in its essence. He therefore tried to transcend himself and to pass beyond all sensation of himself and all

[1] *Ḥayy ibn Yaqẓān*, p. 48 (text): p. 108 (translation).
[2] Ibid., p. 56 (text): pp. 124–5 (translation).
[3] Ibid., p. 57 (text): p. 126 (translation).

things but God. Then 'all disappeared and vanished "like scattered dust"[1] and amongst them his own essence disappeared too, and there remained nothing but this One, true, perpetually self-existent Being'.[2]

On emerging from the ecstasy he reflected on the experience and 'began to think that his own essence did not at all differ from the essence of that true Being, but that they were both one and the same thing, and that the thing that he had taken before for his own essence, distinct from the essence of the true One, was in reality nothing at all, and that nothing existed but the essence of this true One'.[3] He had reached this stage which, for Ghazālī, was the 'reality of realities', beyond which, he thought, it was impossible to go: he had realized himself as the necessarily self-existent Being. This, however, Ibn Ṭufayl dismisses as a 'misgrounded conceit' (*shubha*) and he too, like Najm al-Dīn Rāzī and Martin Buber, stresses that this delusion can scarcely fail to arise, so overwhelming does its authority appear to be. 'This misgrounded conceit of his', he says, 'had like to have firmly rooted itself in his mind unless God had pursued him with his mercy and directed him by his gracious guidance; and then he perceived that it arose from the relics of that obscurity which is natural to body and the dregs of sensible objects. Because that much and little, unity and multiplicity, concentration and diffusion are all of them attributes of body. But we cannot say of these separate essences which know the essence of this true One, that they are many or one, because they are immaterial. . . . But the explication of things in this place is very strait and difficult; because if you go about to express what belongs to these separate essences, by way of multitude, or in the plural, according to our present way of speaking, this insinuates a notion of multiplicity, whereas they are far from being many; and if you speak of them by way of separation, or in the singular, this insinuates a notion of identity, and this is impossible.'[4]

[1] Qur'ān, 56.6.
[2] *Ḥayy ibn Yaqẓān*, p. 64 (text): pp. 139–40 (translation).
[3] Ibid., p. 65 (text); p. 142 (translation).
[4] Ibid., p. 66 (text): pp. 143–4 (translation).

Ibn Ṭufayl's point is that when you are discussing mystical experience, you must use terminology which applies primarily to material things, and this distorts the experience. What, however, primarily interests us here is that Ibn Ṭufayl, like Najm al-Dīn Rāzī and Rāmānuja, distinguishes clearly between the mystical experience of the self in which the soul experiences its own extra-temporal ground, and an experience of God as Absolute Being which the soul readily imagines is an identity of essence. These he regards as being quite distinct. In the experience of the self there can be no preliminary stage of passionate longing because you are only looking for your self, but what he describes as the experience of Absolute Being is only possible once a longing for God has been roused. Najm al-Dīn Rāzī had seen that it is fatally easy to mistake the self-revelation of the self or soul for the self-revelation of God. Ibn Ṭufayl is less easily deceived, for he only sees the danger of a 'misgrounded conceit' when full contact has actually been made with God: *then* the mystic can hardly help thinking he *is* God in identity. This 'misgrounded conceit', which Ghazālī conceived to be the 'reality of realities', he can only dismiss when God 'directs him by his gracious guidance'. True, 'the explication of [these] things is strait and difficult', and Ibn Ṭufayl can only say that the true *unio mystica* cannot be correctly described in terms either of unity or of multiplicity. Perhaps he is trying to express what Junayd expressed so much better, that in the mystical union the soul is annihilated as to its purely human qualities and recreated into God's life in a way that is uniquely appropriate to it.

Let us now recapitulate very briefly the substance of these lectures. Hindu mysticism originates in the Upaniṣads where no clear distinction is drawn between the human soul which is regarded as being eternal by nature, and God: hence in the Vedānta self-realization is necessarily interpreted as meaning that the soul realizes itself as the Absolute. The same experience is interpreted by the Sāṁkhya-Yoga as meaning no more than that the soul enjoys its own individual eternity. The *Śvetāśvatara* Upaniṣad and the Gītā then assert that there is a personal God who is higher than the impersonal Absolute, and the Gītā adds that this God is a God of love who is most easily approached in humble devotion. Rāmānuja then draws a quite clear distinction between God and Brahman or the Absolute which he defines simply as the extra-temporal and extra-spatial mode of existence in which the soul has its being. This mode of existence it has in common with God: but to realize oneself as eternal is not to realize oneself as God, it is only the essential first stage in which the soul leaves behind all its links with matter and mind, and frees itself for its encounter with God. The phase of liberation can be achieved without any feeling of love; the second phase is wholly dependent on it. So far India.

Islam starts with a conception of God as wholly distinct from his creation; but Ṣūfism teaches that God can be experienced by those who wait upon his call with a loving heart, and this will lead to a union with him in which the soul still retains some trace of individuality. This, the mysticism of Muḥāsibī and Dhū'l-Nūn, receives a violent shock when Vedāntin ideas are introduced from India *via* Abū Yazīd of Bisṭām. Mistaking the mystical experience of the undifferentiable oneness of the self for identity with God, Abū Yazīd changes the whole course of Islamic mysticism. Junayd of Baghdad, however, takes up the challenge and shows that identification of the self with God is simply what he calls 'the first isolation' of the soul itself: it is a trap that God sets for the spiritually proud. The isolation is then shattered by God, if he will, and the soul then enters into an I/Thou relationship with its creator in which God overwhelms it and appropriates it to himself, and the soul lovingly submits, accepting all the suffering that this submission brings in its wake. The soul's union with God is a unique relationship of each individual soul with God in which suffering is turned to joy. Nor is the monist tide which Abū Yazīd had unleashed opposed by Junayd alone. Both Najm al-Dīn Rāzī, defending Islamic orthodoxy, and Ibn Ṭufayl, defending sanity, expose the monist's pretention to be God as the 'misgrounded conceit' it so manifestly is.

APPENDIX A

Some Crucial Passages from Rāmānuja's Commentary on the Bhagavad-Gītā

I

The Nature of the Soul

(*a*) BG. 2.12

'Never was there a time when I was not, nor thou, nor these lords of men; nor will there ever be a time hereafter when all of us will not be.'

Commentary: 'Never was there a time when I', the Lord of all, 'was not'. This means that in time without beginning which precedes the present 'never was I not': that is, I [always] was. And thou too, never was there a time when thou wast not, nor yet [all] these souls (*kṣetrajña-*) which are subject to my dominion: they [too always] were. 'Nor will there ever be a time hereafter', in the future, 'when' I and you, 'all of us, will not be'; that is, we will [always] be. Just as there can be no doubt that I, the Lord of all and Highest Soul, am eternal, so too are you to understand that you, souls indwelling bodies, are also eternal. This passage proves that there is an essential difference between God, the Lord of all, on the one hand, and human souls on the other, and that the latter differ among themselves, for God himself says so. . . .

(*b*) BG. 2.17

'Know that that [Brahman] by which the universe is pervaded is indestructible and that no one can bring about its destruction, for it is imperishable.'

Commentary: 'Know that' the category of the soul (*ātmatattva-*) 'is indestructible'. The category of the soul is what is intelligent (*cetana-*), and 'the universe' [of matter] which falls under the category of what is non-intelligent and distinct from the category of the soul which is intelligent is 'pervaded' by it. Nothing that is distinct from the soul can cause its destruction since it, [what is distinct from the soul] is pervaded by it and is more gross that it, whereas the soul cannot be destroyed because it pervades [all else] and is infinitely subtle. . . .

(*c*) BG. 2.18

'These bodies which belong to a (or the) eternal embodied soul are declared to have an end, but the soul is indestructible and incommensurable.'

Commentary: 'These bodies have an end,' i.e. are by nature doomed to destruction. [Material objects] like an earthenware vessel whose nature is to increase [or diminish] demonstrably come to an end. . . . But 'the soul is indestructible' because it is incommensurable; for the soul cannot be grasped by measurement (or logical proof—*prameyatayā*) because itself is what measures [and proves]. . . . The soul cannot be understood as an aggregate of many [parts], for everywhere it is apprehended as being other than the body, being that which measures and of one form. It is that which says in the body, 'I know this'. No different mode of existence is to be apprehended in the measuring [and knowing soul] corresponding to difference of place which distinguishes one body from another. Hence, since [all souls] are of the same form and, of their nature, neither increase [nor decrease], and since it is they who measure [or know] and pervade [all material things], they must be eternal. . . .

(*d*) BG. 2.20

'At no time is it born or dies; it has [never] come to be nor will it come to be hereafter. Unborn, abiding, eternal, ancient, it is not slain when the body is slain.'

Commentary: 'It is not born nor does it die.' The words are [significantly] in the present tense. Birth and death, the common experience of all who dwell in a body, can never touch the soul. 'It has never come to be nor will it come to be hereafter.' This does not mean that the soul did come to be at the beginning of a cosmic era and will not exist at the end of it. The birth at the beginning of a cosmic era attributed by Scripture to Prajāpati and all other [contingent beings] and their death at the end of it, refer to the body only and do not affect the soul. Hence the soul which informs all bodies is 'unborn', and therefore 'abiding and eternal'. It is unaffected by the constant and mysterious transformations that characterize matter. Thus it is 'ancient', i.e. eternally pre-existent (*purātana-*), yet it is ever new, and to be perceived as something always uniquely fresh. So, 'though the body is slain the soul is not slain'.

(*e*) BG. 2.25

'The soul is called unmanifest, unthinkable, changeless. Hence if thou knowest it, thou canst not grieve [at the destruction of the body].'

Commentary: 'The soul is unmanifest'—is not made manifest [i.e. cannot be demonstrated] by the kind of proofs that are applicable to finite objects. It follows, then, that it is different in kind from all finite objects; and since this is so, it is 'unthinkable'—it cannot be thought of as being associated with this or that essence (*svabhāva-*). Hence it must be 'changeless', i.e. incapable of modification.

(*f*) BG. 2.30

'For all eternity the soul embodied in the body of anyone at all is invulnerable: therefore thou shouldst not grieve for any contingent being.'

Commentary: Though 'the body' belonging to a god or any other contingent being be slain, 'the embodied soul' must be deemed 'invulnerable for all eternity'. Therefore contingent beings ranging from the gods to immovable objects, though [contingent in that they are] possessed of different forms, are alike (*samāna-*) and eternal *per se* (*svarūpataḥ*) and in their essence, as we have demonstrated above. Differentiation and transitoriness are attributes of the body; hence 'thou shouldst not grieve for any contingent being' whatever.

(*g*) BG. 12.3–4

'But those who reverence the imperishable, undefinable, unmanifest, omnipresent, unthinkable, perpetually unchangeable, unmoving, constant, who restrain the company of the senses, whose consciousness is always unruffled (*sama-buddhi-*), and who take pleasure in the well-being of all creatures, they too attain to me.'

Commentary: 'But those who reverence the imperishable', etc. The 'imperishable' is the essence (*svarūpa-*) of the individual soul. It is 'undefinable' because, being other than the body, it cannot be defined by such words as 'god', ['man'] etc.; hence it is not perceptible to the eye and other organs of sense. It is 'omnipresent and unthinkable' because, though present everywhere in the bodies of gods, [men] etc., it is different in kind from them and cannot be thought of in any specific form. Hence it is 'perpetually unchangeable' because common to all [ensouled creatures] but essentially unconnected with specific forms that distinguish one class of being from another or one individual from another. It is 'unmoving' because it is not subject to modification and does not depart or fall away from its own individual form. Hence it is 'constant', i.e. eternal.

'Who restrain the company of the senses', that is, who perfectly restrain the company of the senses consisting of seeing and so on from all their natural occupations.

'Whose consciousness is always unruffled' means that their consciousness of souls which everywhere indwell the bodies of gods and other contingent beings in all their different forms, remains the same in that they recognize that the soul has but one form—the form of [supra-sensuous] knowledge.

Hence 'they take pleasure in the well-being of all creatures', that is, they cease to take pleasure in the discomfiture of any creature. Such *Schadenefreude* is due to the soul's relating the differing forms of gods etc. [which other souls indwell] to its own ego.

[To sum up]: Even 'those who reverence the imperishable attain to me': this means, they come to possess [their own] soul which shares with me a common form as being unaffected by the vicissitudes of earthly life (*asaṁsārin-*). . . . The difference between the 'perpetually unchangeable' defined by the word 'imperishable' and the Highest Brahman [= God] will be discussed in 15.16 [where it is said]: 'There are these two persons in the world, the perishable and the imperishable. The perishable is all contingent beings, the perpetually unchangeable is the imperishable. The Highest Person is other [than these] and is also called the Highest Self.'

(*h*) BG. 13.16

'[Brahman] is undivided in contingent beings, but seems to be divided. It must be known as what sustains contingent beings.'

Commentary: Soul-stuff abides in all contingent beings from gods and men downwards and is 'undivided' in that souls have one form as being intelligent subjects. Ignorant people, judging by the different forms of gods [men], etc., think 'I am a god', 'I am a man'; so it seems to be divided. When we say 'I am a god' or 'I am a man', it is to be understood with reference to a species, but when we say 'He who *knows* this' (as we have remarked before), it is to be understood as referring to something of a different category from the body, because we are speaking of an intelligent subject. . . . What sustains contingent beings (the earth, etc.) which can be classified as being possessed of bodily form 'must be known' as being of a different category from all beings that need to be sustained.

(*i*) BG. 6.29–30 (cf. 4.35)

'He whose mind is integrated by Yoga, who sees the same in all things, sees the soul as abiding in all things and all things in the soul. [But] for the man who sees me everywhere and sees all things in me, I will never be lost nor will he be lost to me.'

Commentary: The sameness [seen] in one's soul and that of other contingent beings consists in the one form they share—intellect (*jñāna-*)—for they are all essentially separate from matter. Only in so far as they are connected with matter [in their unliberated state] are they different. Hence 'he whose mind is integrated by Yoga sees the same in all things.' 'In all things or everywhere' means in all souls in so far as they are unconnected with matter, and 'the same' refers to the sameness of their form which is intellect. Thus 'he sees his own soul as abiding in all things and all things in his soul'. This means that he sees that his own soul has a form that is common to [the souls of] all contingent beings and *vice versâ*. Or, in other words, when one soul is directly experienced (*dṛṣṭe*), all soul-stuff is thereby experienced because all soul-stuff is the same [as being eternal]. This is what the phrase 'seeing the same in all things' means.

Then, after he has attained to the stage of fruition [of his own soul] he comes to realize his own likeness (*sādharmya-*) to me: 'stainless he attains to supreme likeness' (*Muṇḍaka* Up., 3.1.3). This likeness to me spoken of [in the Upaniṣad] he [now] sees in all soul-stuff that has shaken itself free from good and evil and remains fixed in its own essence. The words 'He who sees me everywhere' viz. in [all] soul-stuff, 'and sees all things' viz. soul-stuff 'in me' means that, because souls resemble each other [in being eternal], by experiencing one soul one experiences others as being similar to it. To such a man who experiences the essence of his own soul 'I will never be lost', i.e. I will never pass beyond his vision because we share a common nature. Nor will he pass out of my ken though it is myself that I experience, for he sees that his own soul is similar (*sama-*) to me because in fact it is so.

II

God and the Soul

(*a*) BG. 10.3

'He who knows me as the unborn, beginningless Great Lord of the world, is among mortals undeluded and liberated from all ills.'

Commentary: The word 'unborn' shows that the Lord is different in kind from non-intelligent matter that is liable to change and from intelligent beings which, being involved in the world process, are contaminated by matter. Birth is the union of an intelligent being involved in the world process with unconscious matter due to deeds committed in former lives.

The word 'beginningless' shows that the Lord is different in kind from the liberated soul which, though unborn, nonetheless has a beginning, for the 'unborn' condition of the liberated soul has a beginning. That is to say, since it was involved in evil in former lives, it still has a propensity towards evil. Hence the word 'beginningless' applied to the Lord means the opposite to this because he has no such propensity.

Thus 'he among mortals who is undeluded knows' that I am in essence the opposite of what can be involved in evil and incapable of it; he knows me as 'the Great Lord of the world'. . . . 'Undeluded' means one who is free from the delusion that I am one [or identical] with anything and so *not* different in kind from all else; and the 'undeluded' man is thus 'liberated from all ills' which might prevent him from falling down in worship of me. . . .

God, therefore, is the Great Lord of the world. Being the very opposite of all that is imperfect or evil (*heya-*) and the unique source of indefectible, perfect, and incommensurable good (*kalyāṇa-*), and having omnipotence (*niyamana-*) as his unique and personal nature, he is different in kind both from non-intelligent matter which is ruled by the laws of cause and effect, and from intelligent [soul-stuff] whether in a state of bondage or liberation, from all in fact which is subject to his rule. So whoever is free of the delusion that God is not wholly different in kind from all else and knows me as such, is released from all ills.

(*b*) BG. 15.17

'But the Supreme Person is another, known also as the Supreme Soul. He, the imperishable Lord it is who has entered the three worlds and sustains them.'

Commentary: 'But the Supreme Person is other' than what has been described as the perishable and the imperishable, other than souls (*puruṣas*) both bound and liberated. Because he is in a different category [from all else] he is 'known also as the Supreme Soul'. Simply by being described in all Scripture as the 'Supreme Soul', the Supreme Person must be understood to be in a different category from all souls (*puruṣas*) whether bound or liberated. For 'it is he who has entered the three worlds and sustains them. . . .' The three worlds are proved by scriptural authority to be (i) non-intelligent matter, (ii) the intelligent [soul] involved in matter, and (iii) the liberated [soul]. He who enters these three worlds and sustains them with his very essence (*ātmatā-*) must be in a different category from what is pervaded and sustained.

That he is in a different category from the three worlds above-mentioned, however, also follows from the fact that he is 'the imperishable Lord'. For he who is of imperishable (*avyaya-*) nature, must be in a different category from both non-intelligent matter which is perishable, from the intelligent [soul] which is bound to conform to matter because it is bound up with it, and from the liberated [soul] which was formerly involved in it because such involvement in unconscious matter is natural (*yogya-*) to it. To sum up: [God is] the Lord of these three worlds and in a different category from all that is subject to his dominion.

(*c*) BG. 10.20

'I am the soul dwelling in the heart of all contingent beings: I am their beginning, middle, and end.'

Commentary: 'I dwell in the heart of all contingent beings' who form my body as their soul (*ātmatayā*); and the soul in a body is in every sense its support, ruler, and master, as subsequent verses will show. . . . Thus as the soul of all contingent beings 'I am their beginning, middle, and end', viz. the cause of their origination, their continued existence, and their demise.

(*d*) BG. 11.40 (cf. 7.7)

'Homage to thee from before, and homage to thee from behind. Homage to thee from all sides, O thou All. Infinite is thy power, measureless thy might. All dost thou encompass, therefore art thou all.'

Commentary: 'Infinite is thy power, measureless thy might. All dost thou encompass' as being the soul [of all] (*ātmatayā*), 'therefore art thou all'. Since thou dost encompass all non-intelligent and intelligent entities as their soul and since all intelligent and non-intelligent entities form thy body and are modes of thy being, so do all modes of being meet in thee. Thou art indeed the [one true] subject of predication to which all predicates refer.

III

Self-realization and the Love of God

(*a*) BG. 6.47

'But of all Yogins I consider that one the most integrated who worships me with faith, his inmost soul lost in me.'

Commentary: . . . The Yogin mentioned [who worships me with faith his inmost soul lost in me] is more integrated than all others. In their [common] inferiority as compared to this Yogin there is nothing to choose between ascetics and all the other types of Yogin: they are like a lot of mustard seeds set beside Mount Meru. Certainly some mustard seeds may be better than others, some worse, but in comparison to Mount Meru they can only be collectively defined as low.

'His inmost soul lost in me.' By 'inmost soul' is meant the mind which is the receptacle of all external and internal impressions. Such a Yogin's mind, then, from the excess of love he bears me, is lost in me because I am different in essence from all else. Out of the excess of his love for me, he cannot continue to exist without me.

'He worships me with faith': so exceedingly great is his love for me that he hastens to take hold of me, unable as he is to bear so much as a moment's separation from me.

To me the originating, sustaining, and re-absorption of the world . . . is but a game. I am wholly untouched by evil and am the depository of indefectible and perfect wisdom, strength, lordship, might, power, and light, and all fair qualities.

My divine form is the depository of all radiance, loveliness, fragrance, delicacy, beauty, and youth—desirable, congruous, one in form, unthinkable, divine, marvellous, eternal, indefectible, perfect. My essence and nature are not to be limited by word or thought. I am an ocean of boundless compassion, moral excellence, tenderness, generosity, and sovereignty, the refuge of the whole world without distinction of persons. I, the one ocean of tenderness to all who resort to me, take away the sorrows of my devotees. [By my incarnation] I can be seen by the eyes of all men, for without putting aside my [divine] nature, I came down to dwell in the house of Vasudeva, to give light to the whole world with my indefectible and perfect glory and to fill out all things with my own loveliness. . . .

(*b*) *Introduction to* BG. 7 (cf. *Introduction to* BG. 3)

In the first six chapters the teaching concerning the nature of the individual soul was expounded as well as the discipline to be practised by the aspirant. This was [merely] an ancillary [discipline] leading up to the worship of God; and this in turn is but a means to attaining to God [himself] who is the ultimate goal, the Supreme Brahman, the indefectible and unique cause of the entire universe, the omniscient, all-Being, whose will is the real, the omnipotent, glorious Nārāyana. . . .

(*c*) BG. 12.11–12

'But if, resorting to my *yoga*, thou canst not do this, then abandon the fruit of all actions and control thyself. For better is knowledge than practice, and contemplation than knowledge. Abandoning the fruits of actions is better than contemplation. From abandonment comes peace forthwith.'

Commentary: 'If, resorting to my *yoga*, thou canst not do this': if thou canst not perform actions for my sake, which is merely part of the discipline of devotion, even when thou hast embraced this discipline which entails understanding of my attributes and shows itself in an exclusive love of me, then embrace the *yoga* of the unmanifest which leads to the understanding of the essence of the soul; for this [too] may give rise to the highest devotion. . . . By means of this you may 'abandon the fruits of all actions'. For once a man has eliminated all the evil in him, he will become aware, through my love, that I alone am the [true] goal [of his striving]. . . . Thus he will first perform actions without thought of their fruits, and this will be equivalent to worshipping me; then he will attain self-realization which will lead to the removal of all the obstructions [to true knowledge] caused by ignorance and to the individual soul's witnessing itself as being essentially a part of me. Once this has happened, loving devotion to me will arise of its own accord.

So far as the soul's good is concerned, understanding of the nature of the imperishable [soul] resulting in the immediate apperception of it (*aparokṣa-jñānam*) 'is better than the practice' of meditation, if the latter is arid and devoid of exceeding great love; and 'contemplation' of the soul as a means of self-realization is better than an immediate apperception of the soul, if this is incomplete. 'The performance of actions combined with the abandonment of their fruits' as a means to such contemplation is better than contemplation if the latter is imperfect. Actions performed without reference to their fruits, however, will immediately produce peace of mind because all evil will have been put away. Peace of mind leads to contemplation of the soul, contemplation to apperception, apperception to immediate realization, immediate realization to the highest devotion. So the man who is incapable of practising devotion should cultivate his soul. But the best course for the man of unquiet mind who would cultivate his soul is to engage in actions without regard to their fruits: let him forget about self-realization (*ātma-jñāna-*) if he would reach his goal.

(*d*) BG. 7.18

Commentary: Just as [my devotee] who approaches me as his ultimate goal cannot maintain himself in existence without me, so too I cannot maintain myself without him. Thus he is my very soul.

(*e*) BG. 8.14

Commentary: 'He who constantly' (i.e. all the time) 'and always' (i.e. from the moment he first exerted himself [on my behalf]) 'bears me in mind with no thought for anything else', that is to say, he whose recollection of me is so deeply suffused with love that he cannot maintain himself in existence without this overwhelming love of me and recollection of me—'he can easily attain to me, for he is a Yogin who is ever integrated (*nitya-yukta-*)', i.e. one who desires perpetual union[1] [with me]; for I [myself] can indeed be won, not merely my mode of existence which includes such things as sovereignty.

Because I can be easily won and because I cannot bear separation from my devotee, I actually choose him; that is, it is I who bring his worship to its [true] fruition which is to attain to me, since that is what worship [of itself] tends towards; it is I who remove the obstacles that stand in his way and give him an unbounded love for myself.

(*f*) BG. 9.2

Commentary: [The devotee], though he has come to possess me, is not himself destroyed, and though I give myself to one who worships me in this wise, it seems to me that I have done nothing for him.

(*g*) BG. 18.65

Commentary: Whoever loves me beyond measure, him will I love beyond measure [in return]. Unable to endure separation from him, I cause him to possess me. This is my true promise: you will come to me.

[1] This must be what Rāmānuja means by *nitya-yoga-* as the *tadviyogam* ('separation from him') of the following paragraph shows.

APPENDIX B

For the convenience of readers we reproduce here two texts from which lavish quotation was made in the course of our lectures. The first is the so-called 'ascension' (*mi'rāj*) of Abū Yazīd. The texts of Sahlajī and 'Aṭṭār are translated in parallel columns so that the reader can see at a glance how the latter interpreted the former. 'Aṭṭār's version of the 'ascension', moreover, contains much material that is not in Sahlajī, and where necessary I have added the earlier sources for it in parallel columns.

The second text is a translation of the part of Junayd's *Kitāb al-Fanā* published by Abdel Kader in the *Islamic Quarterly*, i, 79–83. Dr. S. M. Stern has kindly checked the translation through with me.

I

The *Mi'rāj* of Abū Yazīd

[Al-Sahlajī], *Kitāb Manāqib Sayyidi-nā Abī Yazīd al-Bisṭāmī*, ed. A. Badawī, Cairo, 1949, pp. 138–41.	Farīd al-Dīn 'Aṭṭār, *Tadhkiratu'l-Awliyā*, ed. R. A. Nicholson, London/Leyden, 1905, i, 172–6.
1. I looked upon my Lord with the eye of certainty,	I looked upon God (*ḥaqq*) with the eye of certainty
2. after that he had turned me away from all that was not he,	after he had brought me to the stage of independence of all creatures,
3. and had illumined me with his light;	and had illumined me with his light;
4. and he showed me marvels from his secret being (*sirr*),	and he manifested to me the marvels of [his] mysteries (*asrār*),
5. and he showed me his 'He-ness'.	and revealed to me the grandeur of his 'He-ness'.
6. And through his He-ness I looked on mine 'I-ness',	From God I looked at myself,
7. and it vanished away—	and pondered on the mysteries and attributes of my self.
8. my light in his light,	Beside the light of God my light was darkness;
9.	beside the greatness of God my greatness became sheer vileness;

10.	my honour in his honour,	beside the honour of God my honour became sheer conceit (*pandār*).
11.	my power in his power.	
12.		There all was purity, here all defilement.
13.		When I looked again,
14.	And I saw mine I-ness in his He-ness,	I saw my being (*būd*) by his light;
15.	my great qualities (*a'ẓām*) in his greatness, my exaltation in his exaltation.	I understood that my own honour derived from his greatness and honour,
16.		[and] all that I did, I was [only] able to do through his power.
17.		Whatever the eye of my mortal frame perceived, it perceived through (*az*) him.
18.	And I looked upon him with the eye of truth (*ḥaqq*);	I looked [upon him] with the eye of equity and truth (*ḥaqīqat*).
19.		All my own worship [of him] was from God (*ḥaqq*), not from me,
20.		and I had thought that it was I who worshipped him.
21.	and I said to him:	I said:
22.	'Who is this?'	'O Lord God, what is this?'
23.	And he said:	He said:
24.	'This is not I, nor other than I.	'All that am I, and none other than I.'
25.	There is no god but me.'	
26.		That is to say, 'It is you who perform actions, but it is I who give you the power and enable you to do so.
27.		Until my grace (*tawfīq*) comes into operation, nothing can come of your obedient service (*ṭā'at*).'
28.		Then my vision, because it saw him [only], closed its eyes to me;
29.	And he transmuted me from mine I-ness into his He-ness,	and he accustomed [my] vision to the heart of the matter (*aṣl-i kār*) and to his own He-ness.
30.	and caused me to cease from my selfhood (*hūwiyya*) in his He-ness.	He annihilated me from my own existence and made me eternal (*bāqī*) with his eternity,
31.		and made me honourable.

32.	And he showed me his He-ness alone,	He showed me his own selfhood unhampered by my own existence.
33.		Necessarily the Truth (*ḥaqq*, God) increased the truth (*ḥaqīqat*) in me.
34.	and I looked upon him through his He-ness.	
35.	And when I looked on God through God,	From God (*ḥaqq*) I looked on God,
36.	I saw God by God;	and I saw God in truth (*ḥaqīqat*);
37.	and I remained in God through God for a time,	and there did I abide
38.	having neither breath,	and rest.
39.	nor tongue,	I made full the ear of endeavour,
40.	nor ear,	and the tongue of need I withdrew into the mouth of unfulfilled desire.
41.	nor yet knowledge,	I abandoned acquired knowledge,
42.		and made away with the trouble caused by the lower soul which commands [to evil].
43.		For a time I remained bereft of faculties (*bī-ālat*),
44.		and with the hand of Divine Grace (*tawfīq*) I swept the rubbish from the road of first principles;
45.	till God planted wisdom (*'ilm*) in me from his wisdom,	and God had compassion on me and gave me eternal wisdom (*'ilm*),
46.	and [gave me] a tongue from his loving-kindness,	and put a tongue from his loving-kindness in my mouth,
47.	and an eye from his light.	and created an eye for me from his light [so that] I saw all created things through God.
48.	And I looked upon him by his light,	When I communed in prayer with God with the tongue of his loving-kindness,
49.	and had wisdom from his wisdom,	and acquired wisdom from the wisdom of God,
50.	and communed in prayer with him with the tongue of his loving-kindness,	and looked upon him by his light,
51.	and said:	
52.	'What have I to do with thee?'	
53.	And he said;	he said:

54.	'I am thine through thee;	
55.	there is no God but thee.'	'O thou All, without the All and with the All, without means (*ālat*) and with means.'
56.	I said:	I said:
57.	'Do not beguile me with myself:	'O Lord God, I will not be beguiled with this,
58.	I will not be content with myself apart from thee and without thee,	nor would I be independent of thee in mine own being.
59.	that I may only be content with thee apart from thee and without me.'	That thou shouldst be mine without me is better than that I should belong to myself without thee,
60.		and that I should speak to thee through thee is better than that I should speak to myself without thee.'
61.	And he bestowed himself upon me without myself [being there];	
62.	and I communed with him in prayer without myself [being there];	
63.	and I said;	
64.	'What hast thou for me from thyself, O my desire?'	
65.	And he said:	He said:
66.	'Thy debt to me is [to obey] my commands and prohibitions.'	'Now give ear to the religious law and do not transgress my commands and prohibitions,
67.	And I said:	
68.	'What have I from thy commands and prohibitions?'	
69.	He said:	
70.	'My praise of thee is in my commands and prohibitions.	
71.	I thank thee for what thou hast kept of my commandments,	so that thy striving may gain thanks from me.'
72.	and I love thee for what thou hast eschewed of my prohibitions.'	
73.	And I said:	I said:
74.		'By the religion I hold and the certainty my heart possesses,

75.	'If thou thankest, bestow the thanks for it upon thyself;	if thou thankest, it is better that thou shouldst thank thyself rather than a slave;
76.	and if thou blamest, thou art in no wise one to be blamed,	and if thou blamest, thou art free from fault.'
77.	O my desire, my hope [of deliverance] from my suffering,	
78.	and the cure of my misery.	
79.	Thou dost command,	
80.	and thou art the commanded.	
81.	There is no god but thee.'	
82.	Then was he silent toward me,	
83.	and I knew that his silence meant that he was well pleased.	
84.	Then he said:	He said to me:
85.	'Who taught thee?'	'From whom didst thou learn?'
86.	I said:	I said:
87.	'He who asks knows better than he who is asked.	'He who asks knows better than he who is asked,
88.		for he is both the desired and he who desires,
89.	Thou art the answerer and the answered,	both the answered and the answerer.'
90.	thou art the questioner and the questioned.	
91.	There is no god but thee.'	
92.	So did God's testimony against me by himself conclude.	After he had seen the purity of my inmost soul (*sirr*),
93.	And I was well pleased with him through him,	
94.	and he was well pleased with me through himself.	then did my heart hear a cry from the good pleasure of God,
95.		and he signed upon me his satisfaction.
96.	For through him am I,	
97.	and he is he.	
98.	There is no God but he.	
99.	Then he illumined me with the light of essence (*dhāt*);	And he enlightened me,
100.		and caused me to pass away from the darkness of the lower soul and the defilements of the flesh (*bashariyyat*);

101.		and I knew that it was through him that I lived.
102.	and I looked upon him with the eye of [divine] bounty.	And of his bounteous grace I spread the wide carpet of joy in my heart.
103.	And he said:	He said:
104.	'Ask what thou wilt of my bounty	'Ask whatever thou wilt.'
105.	that I may give it thee.'	
106.	I said:	I said:
107.		'I ask for thee, for
108.	'Thou art more bounteous than thy bounty,	thou art more bounteous than bounty;
109.	thou art more generous than thy generosity;	and greater than generosity;
110.	[looking forth] from thee I find satisfaction in thee;	and [looking forth] from thee I have found satisfaction in thee.
111.	and at last I have attained to thee.	Since thou art mine,
112.		I have rolled up the royal decree of [divine] bounty and generosity.
113.		Do not keep me away from thee,
114.	Offer me not what is other than thee,	and offer me not what is other than thee.'
115.	and repel me not with what is other than thee.	
116.	Beguile me not with thy grace and generosity, nor with thy bounty;	
117.	for bounty proceeds from thee for ever,	
118.	and to thee does it return.	
119.	Thou makest [all things] return [to thee], and to thee is the return;	
120.	thou art the desirer and thou the desired.	
121.	From thee is the desired one [the mystic] cut off, and through thee is petition cut off from thee.'	
122.	And he made no answer to me for a time.	For a time he made no answer to me, [Then he placed a crown of generosity on my head, (= 175)]
123.	Then he answered me, and said:	and said to me:

124.	'Truth hast thou spoken,	'Truth dost thou speak,
125.		and truth (*ḥaqīqat*) dost thou seek, for
126.	and Truth hast thou heard,	thou hast seen Truth,
127.	and Truth hast thou seen,	and heard Truth.'
128.	and Truth hast thou affirmed.'	
129.	I said:	I said:
130.	'Yea, thou art the Truth,	
131.	and by the Truth is Truth seen;	'If I have seen, it is through thee that I have seen,
132.	thou art the Truth,	
133.	and by the Truth is Truth affirmed;	
134.	thou art the Truth,	
135.	and to Truth doth Truth return,	
136.	and by Truth is Truth heard:	and if I have heard, it is through thee that I have heard.
137.	thou art the hearer and thou the giver of hearing;	First didst thou hear, only then did I hear.'
138.	thou art the Truth and thou the speaker of Truth.	
139.	There is no god but thee.'	
140.	And he said:	
141.	'What art thou but the Truth? (*Or* Thou art nothing but the Truth).	
142.	By the Truth hast thou spoken.'	
143.	And I said:	And I spoke much praise of him.
144.	'Nay, thou art the Truth;	
145.	and thy word is Truth,	
146.	and through thee is Truth Truth.	
147.	Thou art thou:	
148.	there is no god but thee.'	
149.	And he said to me:	
150.	'What art thou?'	
151.	I said to him:	
152.	'What art thou?'	
153.	He said:	
154.	'I am the Truth.'	
155.	And I said:	
156.	'I am through thee.'	
157.	He said:	
158.	'If thou art through me,	

159.	then I am thou, and thou art I.'	
160.	So I said:	
161.	'Do not beguile me with thyself apart from thyself.	
162.	Nay, thou art thou:	
163.	There is no god but thee.'	
164.	And when I had attained to the Truth	
165.	and dwelt with the Truth in (*bi-*) Truth,	
166.	he furnished me with wings of glory and majesty.	Therefore did he give me wings of majesty,
167.	And I flew with my wings,	so that I flew forth
168.	but did not reach the end of his glory and majesty.	in the wide places of his glory,
169.		and saw the marvels of his creation.
170.	And I called on him to succour me against himself,	When he understood my weakness,
171.	for I had no power to bear with him except [it came] through him.	and recognized my need,
172.	And he looked upon me with the eye of munificence,	
173.	and strengthened me with his strength.	he strengthened me with his strength,
174.	He adorned me	and adorned me with his bounty,
175.	and crowned me with the crown of his generosity.	and placed a crown of generosity on my head,
176.	And he isolated me by means of his own isolation,	
177.	and unified me through his own unity,	and opened the door of the palace of union to me.
178.	and invested me with his own attributes which none can share with him.	
179.	Then he said to me:	
180.	'Make thyself one with my oneness,	
181.	and isolate thyself in (*bi-*) my isolation,	
182.	and lift up thy head in the crown of my generosity.	

183. Glory in my glory,
184. and exult in my exultation;
185. and go forth with my attributes to my creatures,
186. that I may see my own selfhood (*hūwiyya*) in thy selfhood.
187. Whoso sees thee sees me,
188. and whoso seeks thee seeks me,
189. O thou, my light in my earth,
190. and my ornament in my heaven.'[1]
191. And I said:
192. 'Thou art my sight in my eye,
193. and my knowledge in my ignorance.
194. Be thyself thine own light that thou mayst be seen by thyself.
195. There is no God but thee.'
196. And he answered me with the tongue of good pleasure, and said:
197. 'How well thou knowest, O my servant.'
198. I said:
199. 'Thou art the knower, and thou the known;
200. thou art the isolator and thou the [absolutely] single.
201. Be thou isolated in (*bi-*) thine own isolation
202. and unified in (*bi-*) thine own unity.
203. Busy me not with thyself away from thee.'
204. So did God's testimony against me in (*fī*) his isolation and by his unity in his unity conclude.
205. And I dwelt with him in his isolation without myself being isolated,

[1] §§ 167–90 seem to be a loose paraphrase of what appears to be the original *mi'rāj* text given by Sarrāj (Nicholson, pp. 384, 382, *see* below §§ 351–60 and 310–28).

206.	so that I dwelt with him through him.	
207.		When he perceived that
208.	My attributes were annihilated in his,	my attributes were finished off (*bar-sīd*) in his,
209.	my name fell away in his,	
210.	and my 'first' and 'last' fell from off me into his.	
211.	And I looked upon him through his essence (*dhāt*),	
212.	which none who would qualify it may see,	
213.	and to which none who 'know' can attain,	
214.	and which workers of deeds understand not.	
215.	And he looked upon me with the eye of essence,	
216.	after my name had fallen away [from me],—	
217.	and my attributes, my first and my last, and my distinctive marks.	
218.	And he called me by his [own] name,	he gave me a name from his own presence,
219.	and surnamed me with his He-ness,	and honoured me with his own self-hood;
220.	and communed with me in (*bi-*) his oneness.	and oneness (*yak-tā'ī*) became manifest.
221.		Duality was done away with.
222.	He said:	And he said:
223.	'O I.'	'What thy good pleasure is, that is even ours,
224.		and what our good pleasure is, that is thine.
225.		Thy speech admits of no defilement,
226.		and none can seize upon thine I-ness in thee.'
227.	And I said:	
228.	'O thou.'	
229.	And he said to me:	
230.	'O thou.'	

231. So God's testimony against me by himself concluded.	
232. He did not name me by any of his names but that I named him thereby,	
233. nor did he attribute to me any of his attributes but that I attributed it to him.	
234. And all things were cut away from me through him,	Then he make me experience the wound of his jealousy,
235. and for a while I remained without soul or body like one who is dead.	
236. Then did he revive me with his life,[1]	and again revived me.
237. after he had caused me to die.	I issued from the furnace of his testing, pure.
238. And he said:	Then he said:
239. 'Whose is the kingdom to-day?'	'Whose is the kingdom?'
240. And when he had revived me,	
241. I said:	I said:
242. 'God's, the One, the overwhelming.'	'Thine.'
243. And he said:	
244. 'Whose is the name?'	
245. I said: 'God's the One, the overwhelming.'	
246. And he said:	He said:
247. 'Whose is the command to-day?'	'Whose is the command?'
248. And I said:	I said:
249. 'God's, the One, the overwhelming.'	'Thine.'
250. And he said:	He said:
251. 'Whose is the choice?'	'Whose is the choice?'
252. I said:	I said:
253. 'The Lord's, the All-Compeller.'	'Thine'.
254. And he said: 'I have made thee to live with my life,	
255. made thee to reign over my kingdom,	
256. named thee with my name,	

[1] Reading *ḥayyāti-hi* for *ḥayyātī* in accordance with § 254.

257. given thee to rule with my rule,
258. caused thee to understand my choice,
259. and conformed thee to the names of Divinity (*rubūbiyya*) and attributes of eternity.'
260. I said: 'I do not understand what thou wantest.
261. I belonged to myself, yet thou wast not satisfied;
262. and I belonged to thee through thee, and [still] thou wast not satisfied.'
263. And he said: 'Belong neither to thyself nor to myself.
264. Verily I was thine when yet thou wast not:
265. so be mine [as] when thou wast not.
266. And belong to thyself even as thou wast,
267. and be mine even as thou wast.'
268. And I said: 'How shall this be to me except through thee?'
269. And he looked upon me for a moment with the eye of power,
270. and annihilated me by his Being,
271. and became manifest in me in his essence;
272. and I existed through him:
273. and the prayer of communion ceased.
274. Then the Word became one,
275. and the All through the All became one.
276. And he said to me: 'O thou.'
277. And I said to him: 'O I.'
278. And he said to me: 'Thou art the alone (*fard*).'
279. I said: 'I am the alone.'
280. He said to me: 'Thou art thou.'
281. I said: 'I am I.

282. But if I were I as an ego, I would not have said "I",
283. but since I never was an ego, then be thou thou, yea, thou.'
284. He said: 'I am I.'
285. My speaking of him as "I" is like my speaking of him as "he"—denoting unity.
286. And my attributes became the attributes of Lordship,
287. and my tongue a tongue proclaiming the divine unity,
288. and my attributes—He—that is: 'he is he, there is no god but he,—
289. and what was was what[1] it was by his Being,
290. and what is is what it is by his Being—
291. my attributes were the attributes of Lordship,
292. and my traces the traces of eternity,
293. and my tongue a tongue proclaiming the divine unity.

['Aṭṭār omits §§ 254–93 of which §§ 294–309 which now follow would appear to be a very free paraphrase.]

294. Since these words were the same as he had heard at the beginning of creation, he wished to demonstrate to me that if his mercy had not preceded [his wrath], creation would never have had any rest,

295. and were it not for his love, his power would have wreaked ruin on all things.

296. He looked on me with the eye of overwhelming power through the intermediary of his all-compulsion, so that no one saw any trace of me.

297. Then, in my drunkenness, I cast myself upon every water-course, and in

[1] Reading *mā* for *mim-mā*.

every crucible I melted my body in the fire of [the divine] jealousy.

298. I spurred on the steed of quest in the broad desert, but I saw no prey more worthy than destitution, nor did I find anything better than total helplessness (*'ujz*). No lamp did I see more bright than silence, nor did I hear any word better than wordlessness.

299. I took up my dwelling in the palace of silence, and put on the shirt of long-suffering till matters came to a head.

300. He saw that my outward and inward man were void of the disease of humanity (*bashariyyat*, the flesh), opened a gash in my darkling breast, and gave me a tongue to celebrate [his] divine separateness and unity.

301. Therefore I now have a tongue of eternal grace, a heart of divine (*rabbānī*) light, an eye of godlike operation.

302. By his succour do I speak, by his power do I grasp.

303. Since by him I live, never shall I die.

304. When I have reached this stage, my gestures are eternal, and my expressions everlasting;

305. my tongue is a tongue proclaiming unity, and my soul a soul [witnessing] separateness.

306. I speak not out of myself, that I might so discourse, nor do I myself speak, that I might mention [anything].

307. It is he who moves my tongue whithersoever he will,

308. and I therein am but an interpreter, speaking in truth.

309. He it is, not I.

	(Sarrāj, *Kitāb al-Luma'*, ed. Nicholson, p. 382)	(Sahlajī, p. 116)
310.	Once he raised me up,	Once I was raised up,
311.	and placed me before him,	until I stood before him;
312.	and said to me:	and he said to me:
313.	'O Abū Yazīd,	'O Abū Yazīd,
314.	verily my creatures long to see thee.'	verily my creatures desire to see thee.'
315.	And I said:	Abū Yazīd said:
316.		'O my beloved,
317.		but I do not long to see *them*;
318.		but if thou desirest this of me,
319.		then I cannot oppose thee.
320.	'Adorn me with thy unity,	So adorn me with thy unity,
321.	and clothe me in thine I-ness,	
322.	and raise me up to thy oneness,	
323.	so that when thy creatures see me,	so that when thy creatures see me,
324.	they may say:	they may say:
325.		
326.	"We have seen thee,	"We have seen thee,
327.	and thou art that,"	and thou art that,"
328.	yet I will not be there at all.'	yet I will not be there at all.'
329.		And so did he do.
330.		
331.		He set me up,
332.		and adorned me, and raised me up.[1]
333.		Then he said:
334.		'Go forth to my creatures.'
335.		And I took one step away from him towards [his] creatures,
336.		and at the second step
337.		I fainted.
338.		And he cried aloud:
339.		'Restore my beloved,
340.		for surely he cannot endure without me.'
341.		

[1] Cf. §§ 320, 322.

('Aṭṭār, contd.)

310. Now that the Lord had magnified me,
311.
312. he said to me:
313.
314. 'Creatures desire to see thee.'
315. I said:
316.
317. 'I do not desire to see them.
318. If thou desirest to bring me forth before [thy] creatures,
319. I will not oppose thee.
320. Adorn me with thy unity,
321.
322.
323. so that when thy creatures see me,
324.
325. and look upon thy handiwork,
326. they will have seen the Creator,
327.
328. yet I will not be there at all.'
329. He granted me my desire,
330. and placed a crown of bounty upon my head,[1]
331. and caused me to pass beyond my human condition.
332.
333. Then he said:
334. 'Go forth before my creatures.'
335. I put forth one step from his presence;
336. At the second step
337. I fell headlong.
338. I heard a cry:
339. 'Bring back my beloved,
340. for he cannot exist without me,
341. and knows no path except to me.

[1] Cf. §§ 122, 175.

	Sarrāj, op. cit., p. 384	Sahlajī, p. 116
342.	[Abū Yazīd] said:	Abū Yazīd said:
343.	'As soon as I reached his unity,	'When I reached his unity—
344.		and that was the first glimpse of union—
345.		I set out on a journey of the understanding (*bi'l-fahm*) which lasted ten years,
346.		
347.		
348.		
349.		
350.		until my understanding was exhausted.
351.	I became a bird	Then I became a bird
352.	whose body was of oneness,	whose body was of oneness,
353.	and whose wings were of everlastingness,	and whose wings were of everlastingness,
354.	and I went on flying in an atmosphere of relativity (*kayfiyya*) for ten years,	and I went on flying in an atmosphere of relativity for ten years—
355.	until I entered an atmosphere a billion times as large;	flying eight billion times the distance between God's throne and the earth—
356.	and I went on flying,	and I went on
357.	until I reached the broad plain of eternity.	until I skirted everlastingness.'
358.	In it I saw the tree of oneness (*aḥadiyya*).'	He said: 'Then I overlooked union (*tawḥīd*)
359.	Then he described the soil [in which it grew], its root and branch, its shoots and fruits.	
360.	Then he said:	
361.	'I looked and knew that all this was deceit (*khud'a*).'	in which creation had vanished from the mystic, and the mystic had vanished from creation.'[1]
362.		

[1] From another saying recorded by Sarrāj (Nicholson, p. 387): 'I overlooked the plain of not-being, and I went on flying in it for ten years until I fared from not-being in not-being through not-being. Then I overlooked negation (*taḍyī'*) which is the broad plain of union. And I went on flying through not-being in negation until I was completely lost [negated] in negation [loss]. . . . Then I overlooked union in which creation had vanished from the mystic and the mystic had vanished from creation.'

	Hujwīrī, *Kashf al-Maḥjūb*, ed. Zhukovsky, Teheran reprint, A.H. 1336, p. 306	'Aṭṭār, contd.
342.	[Abū Yazīd] says:	And he [Abū Yazīd] said:
343.		'When I reached unity—
344.		and that was the first glimpse I had of union—
345.		for years I ran in that valley with the feet of understanding (*afhām*),
346.	My inmost soul (*sirr*) was rapt into the heavens,	
347.	and it did not look upon anything;	
348.	heaven and hell were displayed to it, but it paid attention to nothing;	
349.	and it was drawn up beyond [all] contingent beings and all that veiled him from its sight.[1]	
350.		
351.	I became a bird,	until I became a bird
352.		whose body[2] was of oneness,
353.		and whose wings were of everlastingness.
354.	and flew continuously in an atmosphere of essence (*hūwiyya*),	I flew continuously in an atmosphere of relativity (*chigūnagī*).
355.		
356.		
357.	until I overlooked the broad plain	
358.	of oneness (*aḥadiyyat*) and in it I saw the tree of eternity without beginning.	
359.		
360.		
361.		When I had vanished from [the sight of] created things,
362.		I said: "I have reached the Creator."

[1] *See* §§ 380–2.

[2] Reading *jism* for *chashm* in accordance with the parallel texts.

363.		Then I raised my head from the valley of Lordship,
364.		and quaffed a cup the thirst for which could never, never be quenched.[1]
365.		Then for thirty thousand years I flew in the atmosphere of his unity,
366.		and for another thirty thousand years I flew in deity (*ilāhiyyat*),
367.		and for another thirty thousand years [I flew] in isolation.
368.	When I looked,	When these ninety thousand years were completed, I saw Abū Yazīd.
369.	all that was I.	Whatever I saw, all that was I.
370.		Then did I traverse four thousand deserts,
371.		and reached the end.
372.		When I looked, I saw that I had [only] reached the starting-off point (*bidāyat-i daraja*) of the prophets.
373.		Then I went on for a while in that infinity,
374.		so that I said:
375.		"Nobody has ever reached a point higher than this,
376.		and it is not possible that there is any stage more lofty than this."
377.		And when I looked closer, I saw that my head was laid at the feet of one of the prophets.
378.		Then I realized that the journey's end of the saints is [only] the starting-point of the prophets.
379.		To the final stage of the prophets there is no end.
	(Sahlajī, p. 86)	
380.	He raised up my soul and I pierced the spiritual world (*malakūt*).	Then my soul passed beyond all the spiritual world,

[1] From a saying recorded by Sahlajī, p. 89: 'Travel in the broad plain of union until you reach the house of isolation. Then fly in the broad plain of isolation until you come to the valley of everlastingness. And if you thirst, you will be given a cup in memory of which your thirst will nevermore be quenched thereafter.'

381.		and heaven and hell were displayed to it, but it paid attention to nothing (cf. §§ 346–8).
382.		Whatever was brought before it, it could not abide.
383.	No soul of a prophet did I pass but that I greeted it and gave it my peace	No soul of a prophet did it encounter but that it greeted it.
384.	except the soul of Muhammad.	When it reached the soul of Muṣṭafā [Muhammad],
385.	And lo! around his soul	it saw there a hundred thousand seas of fire without end
386.	were a thousand veils of light	and a thousand veils of light.
387.		Had I [so much] as dipped my foot into the first sea,
388.	which all but burst into flame[1] at the first flash [I saw].	I would have been burnt
389.		and would have given myself over to destruction.
390.		Consequently I became so distraught with awe and bewilderment that there was nothing left of me (*hīch na-mān-dam*).
391.		However much I longed to see [but] the tent-peg of the tent of Muhammad, the Messenger of God, I dared not.
392.		Although I had reached God (*ḥaqq*), I had not the courage to approach Muhammad.'
393.		This means that anyone can reach God in accordance with his capacities,
394.		for God is with all things;
395.		but Muhammad precedes them in a special sacred enclosure.
396.		Hence until you have crossed the valley of 'There is no god but God',
397.		you cannot attain to the valley of 'Muhammad is the Messenger of God'.
398.		Yet truly both valleys are one,
399.		as I said in a previous anecdote about [Abū Yazīd's] disciple, Abū Turāb:

[1] Reading *taḥtariqa* for *takhtariqa*.

400.		he saw God, but had not the strength to see Abū Yazīd.
	(Hujwīrī, p. 306)	
401.	I said:	Then Abū Yazīd said:
402.	'O Lord God,	'O my God, all that I have ever seen has all been I.
403.	There is no way for me to thee so long as this "I" persists,	There is no way for me to thee so long as this "I" persists,
404.	and I find no escape from this my selfhood.	and I find no escape from this my selfhood.
405.	What shall I do?'	What shall I do?'
406.	The command came:	The command came:
407.	'O Abū Yazīd, if thou wouldst be delivered from thine own selfhood (*to-ī*), thou must follow in the footsteps of our friend [Muhammad].	'If thou wouldst be delivered from thine own selfhood, thou must follow in the footsteps of our friend, Muhammad, the Arab.
408.	Wipe thine eye with the dust of his feet as with a collyrium,	Wipe thine eye with the dust of his feet as with a collyrium,
409.	and never cease to follow in his footsteps.'	and never cease to follow in his footsteps.'

II

Abū't Qāsim al-Junayd, *Kitāb al-Fanā*, *Islamic Quarterly*, I, 79–82

Praise be to God who severs all attachments of those who are attached only to himself and bestows realities on those who cleave to him and put their trust in him, enriching them and granting them his love. He confirms the mystics (*'ārifīn*) in his party and grants them degrees in his gifts to them: he shows them the power he manifests out of himself and bestows on them of his bounty from himself so that [evil] suggestions do not affect them or bring them under their sway. Nor are those qualities to be found in them which, by their provenance [? from the Devil], might lead them to fail, for they are predisposed (*intiṣāb*) towards the realities of union [which they achieve] by passing through (*nifādh*) isolation in accordance with his call. The preconditions of finding high favour with him are at hand; hidden things will be manifested to them and the Beloved will draw near.

Then I heard [Junayd] say: 'He bestowed himself on me; then was I hidden from myself by myself, for I am indeed my own worst enemy. Woe to me because of myself. He beguiled and deluded me through my own self away from him. My presence was the cause of my absence [from him]; and my delight in contemplation was the perfection of my striving. But now my powers are annihilated, so anguished is my innermost soul (*sirr*). I find no savour in existence nor sweetness in the majestic vision, nor do I experience bliss *quâ* bliss, nor torment *quâ* torment; and [all mystical] savour has flown away from me. No words can any longer describe me; no description comes to mind and no motive urges [me] on. In his revelation of himself the matter stands as it always stood in the beginning.'

I said: 'What is it [then] that has voiced these words through you—"no description comes to mind and no motive urges [me] on"?'

He said: 'I spoke when I was no longer in ecstasy (*bi-ghaybatī 'an ḥālī*). Then an overpowering vision, plain and manifest, was revealed to me. He annihilated me in creating me [anew], even as he created me in the beginning when I was yet no thing. I could not prefer [anything] to him [? *or* have any effect on him] since he is beyond effect; nor could I predicate anything about him for to him alone does predication belong. Did he not obliterate all trace of me by his own attribute? and obliterated as I was, all knowledge failed me, so near was he. He is the originator and he it is who brings us back [to himself].'

I said: 'What do you mean when you say, "He annihilated me in creating me [anew] even as he created me in the beginning when I was yet no thing"?'

He said: 'Do you not know that God has said, "[Recall], when thy Lord took from the children of Adam, from their loins, their posterity, and made them testify as to themselves: 'Am I not your Lord?' and they said, 'Yea, we testify'." Here God tells you that he addressed them when they did not [yet] exist except in so far as he "existed" them; for he was [eternally] "existing" [his] creation in a manner that was different from his "existing" individual souls (*anfus*), in a manner that he alone knows, a manner that none but he can find out. He was "existing" them, encompassing them, witnessing them in the beginning when they were no thing apart from their eternal being, [in which] state they were from all pre-eternity;—and this is the divine (*rabbānī*) existence and divine (*ilāhī*) awareness which is proper to him alone. Therefore did we say that when he "existed" man, causing his will to flow over him as he wished, [endowing him] with his most exalted attribute in which none can share, this [form of] existence was without doubt the most perfect and the most efficacious—the best, most victorious, most truly triumphant, overpowering and overwhelming to the object of revelation—so that all trace of the creature is obliterated and his [creaturely] existence passes away; for no human quality or existence can stand up to him, as we have said before, [for this form of existence] proceeds from God and his overwhelming power (*qahr*). However this is only metaphorically applied to souls. Bliss [in this context] is not the kind of bliss we normally understand by that word; and generosity as applied to God is not what we usually mean by "generosity"; for God neither feels nor is felt, nor does he change in essence. No one knows the nature of the graces he bestows on his creatures, for this is a reality (*ma'nā*) that is exclusively divine (*rabbānī*) known only to him and deriving from his power alone. This is why we said that God annihilates the object of revelation; and when he overwhelms, he is perfect in his overwhelming and supremely worthy of predominance and omnipotence.'

I said: 'But what do such people experience if, as you say, their name, existence, and knowledge have been wiped out?'

He said: 'Their experience consists in God being in them (*bi-him*) and in his revelation to them in word and transcendent power: it does not result from their own striving or from any perception or imagination [they may have] after he has subdued them, for these he obliterates and destroys. He does not lay hold of them nor is he related to them. So how could they describe or experience something they have never been confronted with that they might endure it, and with which they have no relationship that they might know it? What I mean by this is actually illustrated by a tradition; for has it not been handed down [to us] concerning the Prophet, that he said: "God has said: 'When my servant draws ever nearer to me by performing works of supererogation, then do I begin to love him; and once I have started to love him, I become his ear with which he hears and his eye with which he sees.'" The tradition is actually longer than this, but this will suffice for the purposes of my argument in this context. Now, once God has become the ear by which he hears and the eye by which he sees, how can such a conception be formulated in a way that corresponds to his nature (*kayfiyya*), or how can it be defined in a way that can be understood? Should anyone claim to be able to do so, his claim would be false: for this is something we cannot understand, [as we could something] that is subject to extension and which can be understood and known. This tradition can only mean that God strengthens him, aids him, guides him, and shows him what he wills, as he will, to enable him to reach his appointed goal in conforming him to the Truth [God]. This is God's action in him; and these are graces bestowed by God on him, deriving from God alone rather than from [the mystic] who experiences them; for they do not in any way proceed from him [the worshipper] nor are they by his agency. Rather they simply happen to him from [a source that is] other than himself, for these graces are more suitably and appropriately to be attributed to what is other than themselves. So it is legitimate that they [should be described] as a hidden attribute, but they are not to be attributed to him [the worshipper directly], as we have said before.'

I said: 'But how can "presence be the cause of absence, and the delight in contemplation be the perfection of striving?" For everyone here knows that enjoyment and experience demand the presence [of an enjoyer and experiencer], they do not [arise by] striving and absenting oneself.'

He said: 'That is "knowing" in the generally accepted sense of the word and a mode of experience as usually described. But the élite and those highly privileged among them who have become estranged [from themselves] by the strangeness of their spirituality [are different; for] with them their presence *is* absence, and their delight in contemplation *is* effort; for all trace and idea they may experience in themselves or which *quâ* themselves they may witness, has been obliterated from them—they themselves being obliterated in what overwhelms and obliterates them and does away with their attributes. Now God indwells them (*qāma bi-him*), though he is far away from them (*qāma ʿan-hum*) in so far as they *have*, and although his utter perfection indwells them he confirms claims against them (?). They experience bliss in him in a manner unseen as the most delightful [form of] existence though it is not a mode of existence [at all as commonly understood], because it is God appropriating [them] and divine omnipotence (*qahr*) overwhelming [them].

'And when the soul loses this unseen bliss which the lower soul (*nufūs*) cannot perceive and in which the senses cannot participate, they grow used to their annihilation from themselves and find their eternal mode of existence which this annihilation impedes. But when God makes the souls [again] present to their egos (*anniyya*), he causes them to find [again] their specific nature, and so they are separated from the commerce they had with him and he with them. So they grieve for themselves and grow used to their [merely human] nature, for God deprives them of this first fulfilment and most perfect grace, and they return to discursive thought and ratiocination. Grief settles upon them and the pang of loss abides with them, present as they are to themselves and their contingent existence (*kā'in wujūdi-hā*). So they yearn for sensual desire and return to a condition of need. For how should their banishment not fret them after they had been absent from themselves or their yearning after they had been filled?

'At this point the mystics' lower souls ascend to green pastures, pleasing prospects, and verdant gardens—all else is torture to them, including that first experience they long for in which hidden things enveloped them and which the Beloved appropriated [to them]. Alas, alas for them.

'Now, when God refers to "attribute", he refers to something which cannot be shared. He means thereby the appropriation of a [given soul] to that [attribute]. One who has been so appropriated[1] to an attribute or who bears it constantly in mind or who has been pre-elected therefore, should not—since this is the mode of his election—have present before him either objective manifestations (*bawādī ʿalay-hi*) or purely personal motives. This attribute of his is preserved after the annihilation [of the purely human attributes] in all its reality, and though he vanish before God's presence in him, power [enters him] from [God] who overcomes him, indwells him, and overwhelms him. Then when he is brought into God's presence and called to witness, his mere presence

[1] Reading *musta'tharan li-hā* for *mustataran*.

[there] guarantees the fact of his individual appropriation [to God] (*isti'thār*), and all traces [of him] are obliterated in his witnessing; and so he finds no way to obtain a remedy over against the pure existence with which God [now] overwhelms him. And so [God] is seen in his most exalted attribute and most fair names. It is only at this point that the law of suffering comes into operation for those who are adapted to it. They lend themselves to the attractive power of God, persist, and refuse to be beguiled, and that which had obliterated them in omnipotence itself—an exalted station and a noble relationship—continues with them.'

I said: 'What you tell me is indeed amazing. But how is it that those people worthy of this exalted relationship should also be subject to suffering? How can this be, I should like to know?'

He said: 'Now understand this. After they have [first] sought him by doing (*fī*) what he wills and [then] repudiated him, they will then seek the field of suffering for his sake, so that he may [once again] overwhelm them to the discomfiture of their [renascent human] attributes; for delight in things is [once again] present with them. God thus puts a veil between him and them so that they give way to their ego (*anniyya*), busy themselves with the senses, and delight in the contemplation (*ru'ya*) of themselves, dwelling in pride, enjoying the fruits of their meditation, overcome by omnipotence. But how should you understand this? For nobody understands it or knows what it means except the initiated: no one else can endure it. Or can you understand why they should [first] seek God, [then] repel him, and [then] try to approach him by means of what is a mere manifestation from him; and by using [what are certainly] realities as means, they [really] seek aid against him? For God had caused them to exist in his "existing" of them and had confirmed in and on them his most hidden secrets which connect [them] with him. All trace [of their human personality] is obliterated and all objectives erased, so that relationships [between God and man] succeed each other, [the worshipper's] rank becomes ever more exalted, for he has lost all sense preception and his lower soul is annihilated.

'Then he makes the annihilation that is within these souls' annihilation present to them, and shows them the existence that is within their existence. However, what he makes present to them [proceeds] from themselves, and what he shows them [proceeds] from their "selves" (*anfus*), [and so it] is an almost imperceptible obstacle (*sitr*) to them and a well-nigh transparent curtain. It makes them feel the pang of loss and the intensity of the effort [they have made], for they are separated (*istitār*) from what is not susceptible to cause and are in the presence of what is so susceptible and can be associated with effects(?). So they seek him where he had sought them, that is, in what he knew concerning their "selves", for they now dwell in power and have attained to the reality of high favour [with Him]. He dwells in them and occupies them, and, thanks to him, all that ever was or was not in the order of contingency (*ṣifa*) wells up from him within them, though the pang of suffering may increase.'

I said: 'Then describe to me the different modes of this suffering which they experience in so strange a manner and which [appear to] bring them near [to God].'

He said: 'Well, they become satisfied with what has already appeared to them, lose all sense of destitution, and abandon all sense of judgement. They preen themselves on the victory [they think they have obtained] by their own efforts and power and overweening pride. But [in truth] they had been looking on things with what [in them] was theirs, without passing upwards to what is God's, and so they induce distinction and separation because they see and experience with their two eyes, whereas God overwhelms with his two commands. And when God's manifestations appear to them, [God] causes them to take refuge from him in their own [attributes] so that they exult and glory in their isolation. At this state they go forth without any repining towards him, preferring [to him] that in which their joy is isolated, playing the wanton with him, so sure are they of his forbearance. They do not see that return will be demanded of them and that an account will be exacted from them. When this happens, it is God's guile that encompasses them in a manner they do not understand.'

I said: 'What you say is beyond my reason and increases my confusion. Please try to speak a little more intelligibly.'

He said: 'Well, once the mystics who accept suffering (*ahl al-balā*) encounter God's *fait accompli* (*ḥādith*) within them and the exercise of his authority over them, their inmost essences (*asrār*) are thrown off their balance and their souls are distraught for life eternal. Their habitual haunts offer them no refuge nor can their acquired habits (*amākin*) hide them [from God]. Desperately do they yearn for him who causes them to suffer, and bitterly do they wail at the loss of him who is far away. Their [sense of] loss distresses them, and their [sense of] finding [God] humbles them as they yearn and ache for him, longing for him in their ecstasy. Their yearning he requites with a raging thirst which ever increases and grows in their bowels, while they strive desperately to know themselves and are lavish in losing themselves. He gives them a thirst for him and all manner of mourning and grief. He raises for them all manner of signs (?) causing them to savour the taste of denudation (*faqr*) and renewing for them the prospect of enduring [yet more] striving; yet even in the aftermath of their troubles they incline [towards him], longing to be chastised with grief, seeking to be made whole, clinging to any trace of the Beloved as he reveals himself [to them], viewing what is remote with the eye of propinquity. So are they completely concealed [from themselves], for they have lost the veil [that hid God from them] and they are no longer divided from him. Affliction [is removed] from them and they are no longer punished. And how should any veil divide them from him? for they are his captives, imprisoned[1] before him, and even as they are afflicted, they find favour with him in that they are destroyed in what is manifested to them. They no longer aim at looking after themselves, content with God's love and their dependence on him and their nearness to him. In the swiftness of their awakening they behold the myriad glances [that proceed] from him so that the very destruction [of their human individuality] is [itself] drowned in the tide that flows over them in eternal being and violent suffering, until their very suffering is turned to joy and their abiding in it brings them delight in God, for they see that he is near to ward off their suffering and to draw its sting. Then the soul no longer turns away from the burden of suffering out of faint-heartedness, nor is it grieved by it nor chafed. These are the [real] heroes of mystical experience because God has revealed his secrets to them, and they have taken up their abode in his omnipotence (*qahr*), awaiting his command, that God [himself] may fulfil a deed performed.

[1] Reading *muḥtabasa* for *muḥtasaba*.

INDEX

Abbreviations: A=Arabic. P=Persian. S=Sanskrit.

abad (A. 'post-eternity'), 7
Abdel Kader, 146, 198
Absolute, 45, 47, 64, 78, 95, 99, 111, 112, 113, 114, 115, 130, 172, 185, 187, 188; being the, 36, 74, 113. *See also* Brahman
Abū 'Alī al-Sindī, 93, 95, 100, 102
Abū Nu'aym al-Isfahānī, 103
Abū Sa'īd ibn Abī'l-Khayr, 8, 20, 104, 105, 118, 119, 120, 137, 148, 155, 165, 166, **176–8**, 179; 'all is He', 120, 168; flouts the religious law, 104, 146
Abū Turāb, 217
Abū Yazīd al-Bisṭāmī, 8, **93–134**, 136, 137, 145, 152, 154, 155, 157, 165, 166, 176, 178, 179, 188, 212, 214–6, 218; claims superiority to Prophet, 108, 120, 128; expelled from Bisṭām, 116; 'Glory be to me', 98, 117, 121, 168; his last words, 117; 'I am He', 14, 20, 93, 98, 107, 109, 113, 114; *mi'rāj* ('ascension') of, 116, 122, **124–34**, 140, **198–218**; neglects religious duties, 104, 107–8, 109, 120; on love, 106
Adam, 139, 163, 174, 219
advaita (S. 'non-dualism'), 8, 10
ahaṁkāra (S. 'ego'), 14, 32, 127
Ahura Mazdāh, 22
akṣara (S. 'imperishable'), 39, 46, 53; development of the idea, **47–8**; equated with 'knowledge', 53
'ālam (A. 'cosmos'), 160
'ālam-i amr (P. 'world of the Word'), 16, 26, 37, 158, 159
'ālam-i khalq (P. 'world of creation'), 16, 37, 158, 159
Aleppo, 180
All, the, 27, 39, 42, 65, 132, 140, 175, 195, 201, 209; being the, 8, 19, 32, 33, 44, 84, 85, 105, 119, 125, 126, 127, 133, 175, 216; merging into, 86; proceeds from the One, 31
Allah, 107, 112, 114, 117, 156, 172, 173, 182. *See also* God (Muslim)
amr (A. 'word'), 155, 156, 157, 159, 171, 174
Andalusia, 183
angels, 142, 148, 158, 169, 171
'aql al-kullī (A.'Universal Intelligence' q.v.), 155–6
Arberry, Professor A. J., 93, 128, 160; his definition of mysticism, 5, 11
archetype of the self, 87–8, 89
Aristotle, 67, 90
Arjuna, 59, 66, 68, 71, 74, 76
ātmabodha (S. 'self-realization' q.v.), 71
ātma-darśana (S. 'vision of the soul'), 81
ātman (S. 'self' q.v.), 29, 49, 51, 62, 65, 68, 87, 88, 95, 99, 135, 143, 148, 151, 184; as arrow, 50; as body, 24, 29; as the All and the Lord, 40; as the One, 33, and the Lord (*Iśā* Up.), 45; as universal soul, 32, 45; category of (*ātmatattva* q.v.), 88, 134; chooses, 50, 53; deliverance from, 127; different meanings of, 45, **57–8**; in all